Introduction to the Law of Kazakhstan

Introduction to International Law

Introduction to Belgian Law (2001)
Introduction to Brazilian Law (2011)
Introduction to French Law (2008)
Introduction to German Law (second edition 2005)
Introduction to Greek Law (third edition 2008)
Introduction to Hungarian Law (1998)
Introduction to the Law of Israel (1995)
Introduction to the Law of Kazakhstan (2012)
Introduction to Italian Law (2002)
Introduction to Polish Law (2005)
Introduction to the Law of South Africa (2004)
Introduction to Swiss Law (third edition 2004)
Introduction to Turkish Law (sixth edition 2011)
Introduction to the Law of the United States (second edition 2002)

Introduction to the Law of Kazakhstan

Edited by

Zhenis Kembayev

Wolters Kluwer
Law & Business

Published by:
Kluwer Law International
PO Box 316
2400 AH Alphen aan den Rijn
The Netherlands
Website: www.kluwerlaw.com

Sold and distributed in North, Central and South America by:
Aspen Publishers, Inc.
7201 McKinney Circle
Frederick, MD 21704
United States of America
Email: customer.service@aspenpublishers.com

Sold and distributed in all other countries by:
Turpin Distribution Services Ltd.
Stratton Business Park
Pegasus Drive, Biggleswade
Bedfordshire SG18 8TQ
United Kingdom
Email: kluwerlaw@turpin-distribution.com

Printed on acid-free paper.

ISBN 978-90-411-3892-7

Printed and Bound by CPI Group (UK) Ltd, Croydon, CR0 4YY.

List of Contributors

Maria Baideldinova Dalpane, LL.M, PhD, Assistant Professor, KIMEP School of Law, Almaty, Kazakhstan

Gani Bitenov, MA, LL.M, Doctor of Civil Law Candidate (McGill)

John J.A. Burke, PhD, Professor, KIMEP School of Law, Almaty, Kazakhstan

Daniyar Kanafin, C.Sc., Member of the Presidium of the Almaty Attorneys' Board, Almaty, Kazakhstan

Zhenis Kembayev, LL.M, PhD, Professor, KIMEP School of Law, Almaty, Kazakhstan

Aigoul Kenjebayeva, LL.M, C.Sc., Managing Partner of Salans Law Firm, Almaty, Kazakhstan

Irina Mezhibovskaya, C.Sc., Associate Professor, Kazakh National Al-Farabi University, Almaty, Kazakhstan

Roman Nurpeissov, LL.M, JD, Assistant Professor, KIMEP School of Law, Almaty, Kazakhstan

Roman Podoprigora, D.Sc., Professor, KIMEP School of Law, Almaty, Kazakhstan

Yevgeniy Porokhov, D.Sc., Director of Institute of Finance and Tax Law, Almaty, Kazakhstan

Igor Rogov, D.Sc., Professor, Chairperson of the Constitutional Council of Republic of Kazakhstan, Astana, Kazakhstan

Maidan Suleimenov, D.Sc., Professor, Director of Research Institute of Private Law, Almaty, Kazakhstan

Sergey Udartsev, D.Sc., Professor, Kazakh Humanitarian-Juridical University, Astana, Kazakhstan

Summary of Contents

Table of Contents

List of Abbreviations

Art.	Article
BIT	Bilateral Investment Treaty
CC	Civil Code
CIS	Commonwealth of Independent States
CIT	Corporate Income Tax
CLJS	Constitution Law on the Judicial System and the Status of Judges
CPC	Civil Procedure Code
CrC	Criminal Code
CrPC	Criminal Procedure Code
CRK	Constitution of the Republic of Kazakhstan of August 30, 1995
CU	Customs Union
C.Sc.	Candidate of Science
D.Sc.	Doctor of Science
ENU	L.N. Gumilev Eurasian National University
ENT	Unitary National Test
EU	European Union
EurAsEC	Eurasian Economic Community
GSW	Goods, Services and Works
ICSID	International Centre for Settlement of Investment Disputes
JSC	Joint-Stock Company
KazGU	S.M. Kirov Kazakh State University
KazGYuA	Kazakh State Juridical Academy
KazGYuU	Kazakh Humanitarian-Juridical University
KazNU	Al-Farabi Kazakh National University
KazSSR	Kazakh Soviet Socialist Republic
KIMEP	Kazakhstan Inst. of Management, Economics and Strategic Research

KZT	Kazakhstan Tenge
LBP	Law on Business Partnerships
LC	Labor Code
LdC	Land Code
LoC	Law on Concessions
LI	Law on Investment
LIT	Law on International Treaties of the Republic of Kazakhstan
LLP	Limited Liability Partnership
LMF	Law on Marriage and Family
LNCO	Law on Non-commercial Organizations
LNLA	Law on Normative Legal Acts
LPE	Law on Private Entrepreneurship
LSEZ	Law on Special Economic Zones
LSP	Law on State Property
LSS	Law on State Service
MOG	Ministry of Oil and Gas
MCI	Monthly Calculation Index*
MINT	Ministry of Industry and New Technology
NASRK	National Academy of Sciences of the Republic of Kazakhstan
NU	Nazarbayev University
OECD	Organisation for Economic Cooperation and Development
PIT	Personal Income Tax
PSA	Product Sharing Agreement
RK	Republic of Kazakhstan
RSFSR	Russian Soviet Federative Socialist Republic
SEZ	Special Economic Zone
SUL	Law on Subsoil and Subsoil Use
TsiK	Central Executive Committee of the Congress of Soviets
UK	United Kingdom of Great Britain and Northern Ireland
UN	United Nations
UNCTAD	United Nations Conference on Trade and Development
US	United States of America
USD	United States Dollar
USSR	Union of Soviet Socialist Republics
VAT	Value Added Tax
WTO	World Trade Organization

*A monthly calculation index (MCI) is a scale used in Kazakhstan for expressing the monetary value, calculating social payments and also incrementing fines. It is set annually by the Law of RK "On Republic Budget". As of 2011, one MCI is equal to KZT 1,512 (Kazakhstan Tenge) or about USD 10. This index's amount changes periodically (usually upwards and usually in January of every year).

Foreword

The contributors of this book set out to write a review of the legal system of Kazakhstan, an independent country with enormous potential to grow in stature on the world's stage. We believe they have clearly succeeded in this effort. In the following pages, you will find a concise but complete review and analysis of many major branches of Kazakhstani law, with a critical eye towards not just the letter and spirit of the law, but also how it is enforced in everyday life.

Such a work is especially critical at this moment in time. The ninth largest country in the world in terms of territory, Kazakhstan is a truly Eurasian country constituting a bridge between Europe and Asia. It borders Russia in the north, and this boundary is the longest continuous land frontier in the world. Kazakhstan's eastern neighbor China is becoming a global superpower, while to the south Turkmenistan, Uzbekistan and Kyrgyzstan—whose titular ethnic groups all share a Turkic heritage with the Kazakhs—present both challenges for security and stability, and opportunities for increasing integration and commerce.

Once an important transit point on the Silk Road, the territory now known as Kazakhstan found itself a part of the Hun, Mongolian, Turkic, Russian and Soviet Empires at various times in its history. The independent state that now controls this essential area at the center of Eurasia still finds itself at the crossroads of social and economic, cultural and ideological relations between the East and West, and so it is unsurprising that the country is multi-confessional, with Islam and Orthodox Christianity being the two most popular religions, and essentially bilingual, with Kazakh considered the state language but Russian used "on equal grounds" in all state institutions.

Due to its pro-business legal environment and abundant natural resources—it is one of the biggest exporters of oil, gas, uranium and many other minerals in the world—it is now a major recipient of foreign direct investment, with more and more transnational corporations opening branches in the country. And Kazakhstan is becoming an increasingly important actor on the world stage, holding the chairmanship of OSCE in 2010 and often serving as the regional leader in Central Asia.

The country's legal system has also undergone an incredible rate of change in the last 20 years. From the Russian Revolution in 1917 until gaining independence on December 16, 1991 the republic was an integral part of the Soviet Union, and thus was a country with socialist ideology and a state-managed economy. However, after obtaining its independence, Kazakhstan committed itself to the principles of a democratic and rule-of-law state based on a market economy. Since that point, Kazakhstan has embarked on a path of political transformation and economic development while trying to create its own unique identity by uniting more than 100 different ethnic and religious groups. Scholars wishing to study legal systems during times of transition can find few better subjects.

This book's value resides in helping the reader to learn not only about the historical facts of Kazakhstani law but, most importantly, about the existing legal system of this Eurasian country. The readership intended for this book may range from those who know nothing about the law of Kazakhstan to those who are legal experts. A unique aspect of this book is that it is one of the first attempts to provide insight into the legal history of Kazakhstan and guide readers through the historical development of the Kazakh statehood. Furthermore, the book is invaluable to those who are interested in specific areas of the Kazakhstani legal system, such as, *inter alia*, Constitutional Law, Administrative Law, Civil Law, Family Law, Criminal Law, Criminal and Civil Procedure, etc. Each of these subjects is covered by an independent, unbiased expert in the field, who endeavored to share their thoughts on the implications of legal rules and read between the lines so as to clarify the ambiguities of the law. Together, the authors fill an indispensable need for a systematic and comprehensive account of Kazakhstani law, and do so in an eminently readable fashion.

But what truly differentiates this book from the substantial scholarship already undertaken with respect to the law and legal system of Kazakhstan is the fact that it is written and published in English. It is the perfect opportunity for English-speaking readers, be they in Kazakhstan, the Netherlands or anywhere else, to be introduced to Kazakhstan—its historical facts, cultural peculiarities and, most importantly, its law. Given that English is one of the most commonly spoken languages in the world, the book transcends cultural and geographical borders to enable audiences from very different backgrounds to plunge into the study of Kazakhstani law.

Kazakhstan now stands at a crucial moment as it attempts to complete its transition to the market system, diversify its economy and maintain ethnic harmony. This book is your guide through these complicated and fascinating transformations, full of clear writing and profound insights. Whether you are just discovering this engaging area of law or are looking for an easy way to review what you already know, We think you will find this book extremely useful and rewarding.

Terence Blackburn
Dean of KIMEP School of Law
(2010–2011)
Kiel Ireland
American Graduate student at KIMEP

Preface of the General Editors

This book is intended to provide a concise introduction to the law Kazakhstan and to highlight its distinctive features. It is the first book on Kazakh law in English and it is especially important today when Kazakhstan is increasingly gaining importance on the international arena. We hope that the book will serve the needs of law students, practitioners and scholars, who are interested in studying the legal system of Kazakhstan.

Prof. Dr. Tugrul Ansay, M.C.L., LL.M. (Columbia),
Founding dean of the Law School, Koç University
Prof. Don Wallace, Jr LL.B. (Harvard), Chairman,
International Law Institute, Washington D.C.

Preface and Acknowledgments

This book is the first-ever comprehensive overview of the legal system of Kazakhstan in English. The need for such book has become apparent in recent decades, with Kazakhstan taking an important place in the international community and playing an ever-growing role in international relations, consequently attracting increasing attention throughout the world.

The main purpose of the book is to provide an introduction to the most important areas of the law of Kazakhstan for all interested readers, be they academics, practitioners, government officials or students. While it is impossible to cover all aspects of Kazakhstani law, which is (like any other legal system in the world) extremely complex and highly dynamic, the book aspires to offer its readership a compact, coherent, systematic and reliable overview of the major legal concepts, principles and developments of the legal system of Kazakhstan.

Each chapter of the book covers a major area of law summarizing the leading doctrines and/or analyzing current and developing trends in that particular field. After initial accounts introducing the legal history of Kazakhstan, the basic features of its legal system and the Kazakhstani legal education system, the book comprises a number of specific topics of public and private law, including substantive and procedural law. In addition, each contribution provides a bibliography referring the reader to the most important publications for more detailed reading.

It is evident that the main beneficiaries of this book (like the entire series of introductory books to different legal systems) will be scholars and students of comparative law and practitioners and government officials dealing with Kazakhstan. Additionally, the book is intended to serve as a text for the students who take the Introduction to the Law of Kazakhstan course at KIMEP-University in Almaty, and will be the first volume – among many planned – to be published by the newly established KIMEP School of Law.

According to the editorial policy of the book series, each chapter was contributed by a different expert in the concerned sphere. Although such a collaborative approach unavoidably compromises uniformity of style and structure, it certainly enhances the expertise and scholarship of the book by allowing the involved professionals to express their views and visions. Consequently, the contents of the various chapters were left to the discretion of their authors, who determined the substance of, and took responsibility for, their contributions according to their own best judgment.

Many chapters were contributed by professors teaching at the KIMEP School of Law and were written in English (although some required substantial editorial work), while others were translated from Russian into English. Attempts were made to make the contributions consistent with each other at least structurally and to conform the style and the legal terminology to the American usage.[1]

This preface cannot be complete without an expression of well-deserved recognitions and acknowledgments. With deep gratitude I would like to thank all the authors for their outstanding efforts, their creative contribution and their patience with editorial interference. My special thanks go to my research assistant Kiel Ireland, an American graduate student at KIMEP, who thoroughly reviewed each chapter to ensure that the language was clear and coherent. Also, this book could not have come to fruition without the generous support of Professor Tugrul Ansay, a co-editor of the book series in which the book has been published. Moreover, I would like to thank KIMEP President Dr. Chang-Young Bang, without whom KIMEP would not exist, and my colleagues throughout my university, who have always supported me in this and other endeavors. Furthermore, I am very grateful to German Academic Exchange Service and the Alexander von Humboldt Foundation, which provided me a very gracious support throughout my academic career. Finally, I must mention my colleagues John Burke, Joseph Luke and Vladimir Tyutyurikov, who contributed their time and expertise to improving several chapters of this book.

Zhenis Kembayev
Almaty, Kazakhstan
October 2011

1. Some legal terms are provided with their translations (in Chapter 1 only in Kazakh; thereafter in Kazakh and in Russian). Translations are given in singular; the first version is Kazakh, the second Russian. If only one translation is given, that translation is identical for both Kazakh and Russian.

Chapter 1

Legal History of Kazakhstan

Zhenis Kembayev

I. EARLY STATEHOODS

Located in the heart of Eurasia, Kazakhstan has a long and remarkable heritage. Humans have inhabited its territory since the earliest Stone Age. The domestication of livestock between 9000 and 6000 BC led to the evolution of animal husbandry and the emergence of many mobile and social nomadic communities in Eurasia that, despite the huge area they occupied, developed a common identity.

A. Empires of the Sacae and the Huns

The first well-documented state in the region emerged around the first millennium BC, when the vast Eurasian steppe stretching from Hungary to Mongolia came under the control of the nomadic tribes known to the ancient Persians as the Sacae (or Saka) and to the Greek historians Herodotus and Strabo as the Scythians.

According to historical accounts, the Sacae were among the earliest people to master the art of horseback riding and were well-known for their prowess in war. Their power was sufficient to repel an invasion by the Persian king Darius I in 513 BC and Alexander the Great in 329 BC. But the Sacae were remarkable not only for their fighting ability but also for the civilization they produced. Since the nomad state needed artisanal goods and supplemental agricultural products, the Sacae developed either consensual or forced alliances with nearby sedentary people,

Zhenis Kembayev, *Introduction to the Law of Kazakhstan*, pp. 1–21.

who provided these items in exchange for animal products and military protection. Another major source of the Sacae's wealth was certainly the fact that they controlled a significant part of the Silk Road, a trade route linking China, Persia and Europe that existed as early as about 1000 BC. As a result, they were able to develop a class of wealthy aristocrats who left opulent tombs filled with numerous articles of gold and other precious materials. Archaeological evidence gathered from the contents of many burial grounds (kurgans), which are still found also in many parts of today's Kazakhstan, verify that the Sacae founded a very rich and powerful statehood. Their state was a union of allied tribes united for the purposes of regulating pastures and organizing a common defense. The Sacae sovereign was identified with the Sun God, and his authority was transmitted to his son.

However, in the period 300–200 BC, the Sacae were gradually overrun by the Huns, another alliance of united tribes of pastoral nomads. The Huns' complete command of horsemanship and speed of strategic movement brought them numerous overwhelming victories. Appearing from the Eastern end of the Eurasian steppes, they extended their domination over the territory of what is now Kazakhstan. Similar to the Sacae's state, the Hun Empire was a hereditary monarchy where the monarch was both the political and spiritual leader. However, he was not considered as a living God and acted rather as a priest having divine ancestry.

The Hun Empire was a very complex hierarchy and at the height of its power, it included a number of different sub-organizations. On the territory of modern-day Kazakhstan the two most famous sub-groups were the Usun and the Kangly. Accounts of the emergence of the Usun state, which controlled a zone stretching along the Ala-Tau Mountains and encompassing the basins of Lakes Balkhash and Issyk-Kul known as *Zhetysu* (the Land of Seven Rivers), appeared in Chinese sources around 160 BC. Historical annals offer a demographic description of the Usun state, showing that it numbered over 630,000 people. The Kangly state was located along the Syr-Darya River and was known by 125 BC as a nomadic federation of some 600,000 individuals, with 120,000 men able to bear arms. It is also documented that the Usun and the Kangly states, both of which had a hold over considerable parts of the Silk Road, introduced their own codes of law and tax administration.

During the fourth and fifth centuries AD, the Huns spread from Central Asia to the plains between the Volga and the Dniester and eventually extended their empire into what is now Germany. The Huns' advance culminated in a series of wars under Attila, the most famous of their rulers, who pushed both parts of the Roman Empire, East and West, to the verge of destruction. After Attila's death in 453, however, his empire split into many parts, which began quarreling among themselves. The power of the Huns was broken, and they gradually disintegrated as a social and political unit.

B. Turkic Empires

After the fall of the Hun Empire, the new leading element among the various steppe people in Eurasia became a nomadic confederation of Kök Turks (Blue or Celestial

Turks, previously one of the numerous tribes constituting the Hun Empire). Having defeated the Rouran (Juan-Juan), an alliance of Mongolic nomads, the leader of the Kök Turks, Bumin, proclaimed himself "Khaghan" (Emperor) of the Turkic "Khaghanate" (Empire) in 552.

Soon the Turkic Khaghanate encompassed territories from Northeastern China to the Black Sea and possessed a ramified system of government. The second-highest official was a Khaghan's relative with the title *Yabgu*, all other close male relatives held the title of *Tegin* (prince). Succession was by an avuncular system, wherein a father was succeeded not by his son, but an elder brother by a younger brother, and a younger uncle by a senior nephew. In line to the throne, *Tegins* received *Uluses* (provinces) to rule. In each *Ulus*, there were both high-ranking administrators called *Tarkhans* and inferior ones, known as *Buyuruks*.

In 603, due to the internecine wars, the *Khaghanate* splintered into two polities—Eastern and Western. Most of the area of today's Kazakhstan became a part of the Western Turkic Khaghanate, a nomadic alliance of 10 tribes (primarily decedents of the Usun and Kangly who were collectively known as *On-Ok* or "ten arrows"). In the meantime, conflicts between the world powers over control of the Silk Road resulted in a war between Eastern Turks, Persians and Avars on the one side and Western Turks, Chinese and Byzantines on the other. The war significantly weakened both the Eastern and the Western Khaghanates. After the Eastern Khaghanate submitted to China (630), the Chinese launched a war against the Western Khaghanate (640). As a result, China established control over most of the territories of today's Kazakhstan (reaching as far as Bukhara and Samarkand) by 659, while Bulgars, Magyars and Khazars separated from the Khaghanate.

Despite all the setbacks, the Zhetysu's nomadic tribes reunified and created an independent statehood in 699 which became known as the Turgesh Khaghanate and continued the traditions of the Kök Turks. The new empire was of considerable size, consisting of 20 provinces (with about 7,000 households each), but it could not claim control of the entire steppes. The rise of the Turgesh Khaghanate coincided with the emergence of other Turkic-speaking nomadic associations: the Karluk (to the north of Zhetysu), Kimak (to the north-west) and Oghuz (to the west) tribes. The Turgeshs had to establish relations with these tribes while continuing to struggle against Chinese and Arab invasions. Maintaining a powerful warrior caste, the Turgeshs managed for an extensive period of time to blunt all external threats, and even to rule over a significant part of Transoxania. But internecine feuds ultimately weakened their Empire. As a consequence, in 751 Arab and Chinese armies clashed on Turgesh territory, near the Talas River, attempting to establish control over the region.

The battle of Talas brought victory to the Arabs in large part due to the active support of the Karluks. The Karluks, who initially lived in Altai and along the Irtysh River, were in a position to actively participate in the affairs of both the Turgesh and the Eastern Turkic Khaghanates. In the 740s, when the Karluks helped the Uighurs come to power in the Eastern Khaghanate, their leader, in a rearrangement of the nomadic hierarchy, was elevated to the status of a *Yabgu* (which implied the "heaven-mandated" right to rule over a large tribal grouping).

Soon, when the Karluks tried to topple the Uighur Khaghanate and were defeated in the contest, they were compelled to migrate westward.

Supported by the Abbasid Caliphate in exchange for their loyalty, the Karluks gradually became the strongest force in the region, forcing the submission of the Turgesh and incorporating them into their confederation by 766. Thus, the Karluk leaders started to control Zhetysu (which since the Sacae times had been considered a sacred land, the possession of which was one of the major legitimating factors for the execution of power) and continued the traditions of the Turkic Empire by establishing their own Khaghanate, which dominated over significant parts of the Silk Road, and asserting their independence from both the Chinese and the Arabs (although closely cooperating with the latter).

C. Karakhanid Khanate

In the meantime, a new and formidable kind of force was spreading into Central Asia—the religious power of Islam. Bursting out of Arabia, Muslim armies had brought a huge part of the globe—from Spain to India—under a new Islamic empire in less than a hundred years from the death of the prophet Muhammad in 632. Despite stiff initial resistance from the Turkic tribes, the Arabs took Bukhara in 709 and Samarkand in 712 and gained a strong foothold in Transoxania (and thus in the southern part of present-day Kazakhstan). Although the Muslims, despite many attempts, failed to establish control over the nomadic peoples by force, Islam penetrated the steppes through the achievements of civilization. Flourishing in the "Islamic Golden Age" during the reign of the Abbasid Dynasty (750–1258), the Muslim world and its new religion became especially attractive to the ruling elites of the nomadic associations.

The relations between now-Islamic Transoxania and the nomads intensified under the Samanids, who ruled an empire encompassing the settled areas of Central Asia and Greater Iran starting from 819. Unsurprisingly, historical sources begin to mention sizable groupings of Karluk (and also Oghuz) tribesmen who had gone over to Islam and constituted an important part of the Muslims' Armed Forces. These people gave birth to the new dynasty of Karakhanids and established thereby the Karluk-Karakhanid Khaghanate in 840 following a bipartite system of rule typical of the Turk imperial tradition. Giving Islam the status of an official state religion in 940, the Karakhanid Dynasty significantly facilitated its spread throughout all of Central Asia and what is now Western China. With the disintegration of the Samanid dynasty, the Karakhanids took over their territories in Transoxania and established their own independent statehood in 999, which became known as the Karakhanid Khanate (the word "*khaghanate*" transformed into "*khanate*" with the "gh" sound becoming silent in the dialects of many Turkic tribes).

In the eleventh century, the Karakhanids fractured due to constant internal warfare and were forced to accept the suzerainty of new steppe kingdoms (first, the Seljuk Empire, which was founded by the Oghuz and, at the height of its power, controlled a vast area stretching from the Hindu Kush to Eastern Anatolia; and subsequently the Karakitay Khanate). As a part of the nomadic empires, the Karakhanids enjoyed a highly autonomous status until 1211 when they were devastated by the Karakitay confederation (led by the Naiman tribe) in retaliation for not rendering assistance against the advancing Mongol army of Genghis Khan. The following year the Karakhanid Dynasty was extinguished, but its political and legal legacy, which combined nomadic Turkic culture with Islamic sedentary institutions, was certainly one of the major factors that predetermined the subsequent development of the statehood in Kazakhstan and in the entire Central Asia.

D. Karakitay Khanate

Another important transformation of steppe life occurred when nomad people began to supplement their ancient tribal organization by borrowing Chinese administrative experience for the management of state affairs. The political weakness of China caused by the collapse of the Tang Dynasty in 907 allowed various nomadic confederations to regularly overrun Chinese territories while continuing to control ancestral steppe lands.

This kind of interaction resulted in the emergence of such hybrid states as the Tangut, Juchen and (most importantly for Kazakhstan) Karakitay Empires, whose rulers began to set up a centralized bureaucratic system and to divide their army into tens, hundreds and thousands, putting appointed officers in charge of each unit. As a result, the fragility previously inherent in steppe confederations based on blood brotherhood could now be removed. From then on, the extinction of nomadic states could not result from internal disruption, but only from conquest at the hands of another even more bureaucratically organized force.

By 1140 most of Central Asia had fallen under the domination of the Karakitay Khanate, a nomadic empire of a new, advanced type that was created by a Mongolic dynasty but that mostly consisted of Turkic-speaking tribes (a model that would later also be followed by the Mongol Empire). Due to their superior organization, the Karakitays could subdue the Karluks, Uighurs, Naimans and Karakhanids but were overthrown by Genghis Khan, who achieved a much higher degree of centralization and whose state and armies were led by men appointed on the basis of their demonstrated efficiency, regardless of hereditary rank.

E. Mongol Empire

A series of tribal wars in the Eastern part of the Eurasian steppes led to the unification of Mongol and Turkic tribes under the leadership of Genghis Khan ("Universal Ruler" in Turkic) and the creation of the Mongol (or, to be more precise, Mongol-Turkic) Empire in 1206. The first target of the united nomadic tribes became China, and by 1215 the entire area north of the Huang-He River was in the hands of Mongols. Then Genghis Khan turned his attention westward, subdued the Karakitay Khanate in 1218 and brought under his control the whole of Central Asia by 1221. By the time of his death in 1227, the great conqueror controlled most of the Eurasian steppe as well as significant parts of the Chinese, Indian and Middle Eastern civilizations. His substantial contributions to the efficiency of the Mongol state and legal structure enabled his successors to create the largest empire in world history, extending from the Pacific to the Mediterranean.

Just as the Mongols incorporated the knowledge and technologies of the conquered civilized societies into their traditional nomadic military strategy, they recruited a sedentary class of scribes, record keepers and tax collectors into their state apparatus. In addition, they introduced a very advanced communications system, called the *yam* (post-horse station), which supplied food, horses and services across the vast empire. The *yam* system enabled non-stop delivery of information and also encouraged travel and trade across Eurasia (this period of open trade, which re-established the Silk Road and connected the East and West, became known as the *Pax Mongolica*).

In legal and judicial affairs, Genghis collected existing nomadic law in a set of laws, called *Zhasak* or *Yassa*, and supplemented it with his *Zharlyks* (imperial edicts). The Zhasak served as the official legal system for his empire and was a comprehensive code that dealt with not only prohibited behavior and punishments but also rules of procedure, jurisdictional limits and ownership rights. The major goal was to eliminate any disputes between all people within the empire. The rules included, *inter alia*, sharing food with travelers and severe punishments for the theft of livestock (especially horses), abduction of women and defection among warriors. The Zhasak was enforced strictly with very stiff punishments for violators. Many offenses were punishable by death, but the penalties also included corporal punishments and fines (thieves could be forced to pay nine times the worth of the object stolen).

The nomadic law also provided that the offspring of one's first wife must be honored above all other children and inherit everything. Also, it was stipulated that the empire is a common *Ulus* (the joint property) of the entire imperial family who constituted the ruling class. The concept of the common *Ulus* found expression in the institution of the "Kurultai" (general council), in which all the members of the imperial clan participated to elect new Khans and make important decisions.

Accordingly, Genghis Khan, before his death, divided the Empire among his four major sons from his first wife. The western and most of the northern parts of present-day Kazakhstan were included in the realm of the eldest son Jochi while the southern part became a constituent territory of the realm ruled by second son Chagadai. The third son, Ögödei, received western Mongolia and the youngest, Tolui, (also following nomadic customs) inherited the ancient Mongol homeland of Eastern Mongolia. Splitting his Empire into branches, Genghis Khan nominated Ögödei (as the son who was the most able and most acceptable to his brothers) as his successor. In the spring of 1229, the Kurultai duly elected Ögödei as the new emperor.

Ögödei greatly expanded the Mongol Empire and called himself "Khaghan" (at that time this term started to mean as much as the *Khan of Khans*). The rulers of the other three branches of the Empire received the titles of Khans. Recognizing the supremacy of the Khaghan in strategic decision-making, Khans were independent rulers within the scope of their realms and exercised administration through their officials, "Baskaks" (this term means in Turkic "the one pressing down [the seal]" and was first applied in the Karakitay Khanate). However, with Ögödei's death in 1241, the branches fell increasingly into conflict, which led to a major change in the order of succession. At the Kurultai of 1251, enlarged by the presence of powerful commanders, the great Khan chosen was not a son of the House of Ögödei but Tolui's son Möngke, who was, however, the last ruler who held the title of Khaghan.

F. Altyn Orda

According to nomadic customs, the eldest son, on reaching manhood, was given a wife and his share of the inheritance; he then moved away and set up his own camp, independent but still allied to his family. The other brothers followed in due order, but each one nearer to the "home camp" than his next older brother. The youngest, as "guardian of the hearth and fire" remained with his parents and received the residual heritage. Consequently, the most remote western portion of the Genghis Khan's empire formed the territorial endowment of Jochi.

Since the Mongol Empire claimed universal power, there were no territorial limits westward of the Jochi's realm. In 1235 the Jochi's successor, Batu, was given responsibility for the invasion of Europe. By 1241, he had conquered all of Russia and Eastern Europe, and was intending to invade Western Europe when he received news of the death of Ögödei. In order to participate in the choice of a successor, Batu turned back, saving Europe from apparent devastation. He was hostile to the would-be successors from the House of Ögödei and contributed substantially to their fall.

In 1242, he established the state of "Altyn Orda" (meaning the Golden Palace, Center or Headquarters) at the lower stretch of the Volga River. The longest lasting of the four branches of the Mongol Empire, the Altyn Orda was also the least Mongolian, being predominantly constituted by Turkic tribes and frequently also called the *Kipchak Khanate*, after the most powerful of those tribes. The territory of the Altyn Orda encompassed the territories from the Carpathian Mountains to Balkhash Lake and the Ob River. Batu Khan accepted the loss of Eastern Europe and concentrated on firming his control over Russia in alliance with Russian princes (like Alexander Nevsky), who successfully used the Altyn Orda against Teutonic and Swedish invaders. The Russian principalities retained their own rulers and internal administration, but they were tributaries of the Khan, who confirmed princely succession and exacted taxes. The Khan's authority in Russia and elsewhere was represented either by Baskaks or by local princes, many of whom were willing to work for the Altyn Orda (the most successful among them were the princes of Moscow who grew wealthy as middlemen in collecting tribute).

Initially, the Khans themselves were under the suzerainty of the Khaghan. Thus, in 1257 Möngke gave his consent to Batu's brother Berke to take the Khan's throne. But with Möngke's death, Berke refused to recognize Möngke's brother Kublai as the Khaghan, so the Mongol empire effectively disintegrated. Berke was also the first ruler to embrace Islam and replace Mongolian with Turkic (which was spoken by the overwhelming majority of population) as the official language. Under Özbeg Khan (reigned from 1312 to 1341), the Altyn Orda became a world power, overseeing a large portion of the Silk Road and maintaining intensive trade relations with Byzantium, Egypt and Genoa.

However, in the late fourteenth century permanent internecine warfare among the Orda leaders, attempts by the Russian princes to end tributary payments and, most importantly, devastating blows dealt by Timur (Tamerlane) resulted in the decline of the Altyn Orda. Fully destroying Sarai, the capital of the Altyn Orda, and deporting all its skilled craftsmen to his own capital, Timur expected in particular that Samarkand would replace Sarai as the primary city along the Silk Road. In the fifteenth century the Orda disintegrated into a number of parts, the Crimea, Kazan, Astrakhan, Nogai, Siberia and Ak Orda Khanates, which started to fight each other for dominance in the region. However, it was the principality of Moscow that came to a position of preeminence in Eurasia and entered into the political inheritance of the Altyn Orda. Having united Russian lands, the Kremlin annexed the Kazan (1552), Astrakhan (1556), Siberian (1600) and Nogai (1634) Khanates; the Crimean and the Ak Orda Khanates followed suit in the eighteenth century.

II. KAZAKH KHANATE

A. Emergence

Throughout its existence, the Altyn Orda consisted of western (Kök Orda) and Eastern (Ak Orda) wings. The Kök Orda was ruled by the line of Batu Khan and the Ak Orda by the line of another of Jochi's sons, Orda. Following the disintegration of the Altyn Orda, the Ak Orda became known additionally as the Uzbek confederation (this name referred to Özbeg Khan, an admired ruler of the Altyn Orda, and thus was obviously aimed at the re-establishment of the collapsed empire). However, this goal was not achieved, and in 1465, a significant number of confederates under the leadership of Kerey and Janibek separated from the Uzbeks and adopted the name Kazakh ("Independent" or "Free"). Thereafter the Uzbeks began to move south into Transoxania (what is now Uzbekistan), assimilating with the sedentary population and adopting their lifestyle while the Kazakhs remained in the north, continued their nomadic traditions and established their own Khanate with Janibek becoming the first Kazakh Khan.

B. Political Structure

During the late fifteenth and throughout the sixteenth centuries, the Kazakhs were able to consolidate a nomadic empire stretching from the Caspian Sea to the Altai

Mountains. The Kazakh confederation significantly expanded under Kasym Khan (ruled 1509–1518) who welcomed in his realm all Turkic-speaking nomadic tribes, both from what used to be the Altyn Orda (Jochi's realm) as well as from the southern part of today's Kazakhstan (Chagadai's realm). Reportedly, the Kazakhs were able to bring 200,000 horsemen into the field and thus were the masters of virtually the entire steppe region.

However, with Kasym's death, there was a substantial weakening of the Khan's authority, and the Khanate disintegrated into three separate groupings, called *Zhuzes* ("Hundred" in Kazakh): the *Great* (*or Senior*) *Zhuz*, the *Middle Zhuz* and *Little* (or *Junior*) *Zhuz*, encompassing the southern, northern-central and western parts, respectively, of present-day Kazakhstan.

Each Zhuz was headed by a Khan and included a number of tribes led by chieftains known as "Sultans." In turn, each tribe was divided into clans headed by a *Bi* (a judge) or a "Batyr" (a warrior) while clans were composed of "auls" (the basic Kazakh nomadic unit). An aul, which usually numbered 30–40 households, consisted of a few related families and was headed by an "Aksakal" (an elder, "White Beard" in Kazakh). Related Aksakals met to choose a Bi to represent the greater family (the clan) in negotiations with other families, to mediate internal disputes, regulate migration and allocate pastureland. Although the title of a Bi often went from father to son, the office was not hereditary and could be reassigned if the elders so chose. A significant role in the decision-making was also played by Batyrs (military commanders).

The Bis and Batyrs met to choose the Sultans from among the offspring of Orys Khan (who was the ruler of Ak Orda in 1361–1375 and descendent of Jochi's son Orda). The Sultans ruled over particular clans and governed relations between them, being the major decision makers, judges and military commanders within their territory. The Sultans (along with distinguished Bis and Batyrs) were responsible for electing the Khan (from among those who could trace their descent to Orys Khan) at a general council (called "Kurultai" or "Maslikhat") that met annually to affirm the Khan's leadership, to advise him and to receive his instructions.

As a rule, the Khan served for life and was succeeded first by his brother and then by his son. Nonetheless, in order to become Khan, an individual had to prove his own competence, and his merits had to be well-known to all Kazakhs (note that the Kurultai's meetings were usually held before a vast congregation of people). In this regard, it should be noted that nomadic traditions greatly rewarded military skills. Therefore, demonstrated martial abilities were required for selection as Khan, since the Khan had to lead a formidable force of mounted warriors in military campaigns. Furthermore, throughout his rule, the political power of the Khan was very much dependent on his military prowess. When a strong personality came to the power in one of the Zhuz, he was also able to overcome the dissociation of the three confederacies and become the pre-eminent authority and the single Khan of Kazakhs. Examples include Hak-Nazar Khan (1538–1580) and Tauekel Khan (1586–1598), who succeeded in reuniting all three Zhuzes. In doing so, they embarked upon a number of campaigns against the Shaybanid dynasty (which then ruled Transoxania) successfully re-establishing their power over the ancient Kazakh lands of what is now Southern Kazakhstan (including the town of

Turkestan, which became the capital of the Kazakh Khanate) and even expanding their control over Tashkent and Samarkand.

However, in the seventeenth century, the decentralization of the Kazakh Khanate again became prevalent. The growth in power of local rulers was reflected in the fact that the Khan's power was now limited by the Council of Bis, which in particular required the Khan to collect taxes only in times of war (deviating from the previous rule of paying an amount equal to 5% of the livestock available annually). The Khan was responsible for strategic decision-making in the fields related to preparing defensive arrangements and declaring wars, allocating pasture-lands for the clans and choosing the place and time for the confederation's migration (which also was of great military significance). Nonetheless, with respect to internal issues, the Bis and Batyrs had far more influence than the Khan, as they were responsible for the distribution of lands between the auls and the families and had direct command over warriors.

At the same time that Kazakh statehood was transforming into a kind of representative monarchy, it became threatened by a grave and imminent peril. In what is now north-west China, a powerful nomadic confederation of Dzungar (West-Mongol) tribes emerged and made attempts to conquer the Kazakh Khanate. As a result, the Kazakhs were involved in a series of sanguinary wars with the Dzungars that lasted from the early seventeenth century to the 1770s. When the three Kazakh confederations were consolidated by a strong leader like Tauke Khan (1680–1718), they could successfully repel Dzungar aggression; but when they failed to unite, the invaders could bring a reversal in the fortunes of war and penetrate deep into Kazakh territory.

C. Kazakh Customary Law of Fourteenth to Fifteenth Centuries

Sources of Law: The major source of Kazakh law of fifteenth to eighteenth centuries was the *Adat* (customary law that developed through many centuries). Although Islam has already established its presence in the Kazakh steppes, Sharia did not play any significant role in the legal system. Therefore, the Kazakh Khans repeatedly attempted to systematize Kazakh customary law, with the earliest set of rules compiled under Kasym Khan. Nevertheless, the most famous codification was written under Tauke Khan and is known as *Zheti Zhargy* (Seven Charters). The code provided rules with respect to, in particular, state and military administration, property law, law of obligations, family law, criminal law, and civil and criminal procedure. Along with customs, there were other sources of law such as *Bidin Biligi* (decisions of judges) and *Erezhe* (resolutions of judicial councils).

Property Law: In Kazakh customary law, there was no individual right to private property on land, as land was the joint property of the tribe. How to distribute land among members of the tribe was decided by tribal leaders, Bis together with Aksakals. Livestock was under joint family ownership. Other movable property could be owned by individuals.

Law of Obligations: As a rule, contracts were concluded orally. Since monetary circulation was undeveloped, the most frequent types of contracts included barter and lend agreements with livestock being the main subject matter. Kazakh society also recognized such obligations as *amanat-mal*, *zhylu* (or *kyzyl köteru*), *zhurtshylyk*, *Asar* and *konagasy*.

Under the amanat-mal obligation, wealthy people were obliged to lend a part of their livestock to their impoverished fellow tribesmen and share animal products and offspring. Zhylu (or kyzyl köteru) required all tribesmen to help those congeners who suffered from natural diseases. Should a blood relative be obliged to pay a debt, a fine or a *kalym* (bride price), his fellow tribesmen were expected to contribute with an amount commensurate with their wealth. One of the most common obligations was Asar, which meant that fellow tribesmen had to assist their relatives in building winter camps, digging wells, etc., in exchange for meals. If these obligations were not observed, the offending individuals could be brought before a Bi or Aksakal and forced to comply. Another obligation, konagasy, applied not only with respect to tribesmen but anyone who found himself in a Kazakh aul, and required the providing of meals and an overnight stay. In case of inhospitality, a traveler could go to the court and demand a significant fine (in the amount of no less than a horse and a fur coat).

Family Law: The head of the family was unquestionably the father (the husband), who could dispose of the family property but not to the detriment of the other members of the family. There was no testamentary succession. At the time of marriage, the elder sons had the right to receive their inheritance of an *Üi* (a yurt, a portable, felt-covered dwelling) and a part of the father's herd. The *Kenzhe*, the youngest son, remained in his father's Üi, which he inherited with his share of the herd. Although the bulk of the family property was distributed among sons, a substantial part of the wealth was set aside for the dowry of the daughters.

Marriages were arranged by parents, and no considerations were given to the sentiments of the prospective pair. Sometimes marriages were set in infancy and even pre-natally. One of the major principles of marriage was exogamy, prohibiting marriage between individuals with a common ancestor within seven generations. The family could be polygynous. However, in general a family could not afford to pay the *kalym* (bride-wealth, which varied from a low of 17 to a high of 77 horses) for more than one wife. Moreover, each wife had to have her separate household. Thus, only wealthy Kazakhs could have two or more wives. Even though a special privileged position was given to *Baibishe*, the first wife, each married woman could independently manage her household (obtained from the husband) and remained the owner of her dowry.

Sometimes marriages could be concluded without the payment of bride-wealth (for example, in the case of an exchange marriage involving an arranged and reciprocal exchange of spouses between two groups). Also, Kazakh law provided for the practice of levirate marriage, whereby a widow was obligated to marry her deceased husband's brother and maintain his line.

Criminal Law: Kazakh customary law differentiated between deliberate (*zhaman kylyk*) and unintended (*katelyk*) crimes. Direct intent (*zhaman oi*) significantly aggravated liability. Further, several types of accessories were delineated: performer (*kunaker*), organizer (*uiymdastyrushy*), abettor (*azgyrushi*) and accomplice (*kömekshi*).

The following types of punishment were distinguished: corporal punishment, capital punishment, buyout (kun), fine (aiyp), surrender of a criminal to the injured party and expulsion from the community. Corporal punishment could be assigned for blasphemy or for disrespect for parents. Capital punishment was applied very rarely and only for especially grave crimes. It could be replaced by a kun, should the injured party agree. The amount of a kun depended on the gravity of crime and the social status of the victim. The murder of an ordinary member of a tribe was punished by a disbursement of 1,000 sheep (or 200 horses or 100 camels). The amount of the punishment was double for the murder of a Bi or a Batyr, and sevenfold for the murder of a Sultan. The value of a woman's life was half that of a man's. Most of the crimes against a person or property were punished by an aiyp which was measured in so called *togyz* (nine pieces of different livestock (either camels, horses or sheep) depending on the gravity of the crime). For example, a thief had to return all of what was stolen and also pay three togyz. Should a criminal (and his tribesmen) not be able (or willing) to pay a kun or an aiyp, he could be delivered over to the injured party. In this case, the criminal could be forced to work off the amount of the punishment or be assigned any other punishment up to the death penalty. In the event of recidivism, a criminal could be expelled from the community and be deprived of all his rights.

Court and Legal Process: Judicial power belonged to the Bis, so by the end of the eighteenth century this term had come to mean judge. Legal proceedings were open and adversarial, and only the injured party could initiate it. The major purpose of a Bi was to reconcile the parties. Great significance was given to the swearing of oaths (*zhan beru*), which were one of the main forms of evidence. A perjurer could be expelled from the tribe, so refusal to swear an oath was considered an admission of guilt. A Bi collected up to 10% of all fines levied, and his decisions were mandatory. The defeated party could appeal the decision before the Khan. The Khan could revise or confirm the decision. In the latter case, the claimant could be accused of attempting to undermine the Bi's reputation and be given corporal punishment. Should the defeated party not observe the decision of the Bi, the injured party had the legitimate right to a "barymta" (a punitive raid which could cause significantly more damage).

III. KAZAKHSTAN UNDER THE RULE OF THE RUSSIAN EMPIRE

A. Establishment of Russian Rule

More than 150 years of Kazakh-Dzungar warfare completely devastated both sides. Meanwhile, Russia had emerged from centuries of turmoil to become a world power of growing importance. The process of incorporating the Kazakh hordes into the Russian Empire commenced in the early eighteenth century. This was generally considered by the Kazakhs to be the preferable option to submission to the Dzungars and later (from 1758, when the depleted Dzunghar Khanate was destroyed by the Qing Dynasty) to the Chinese. In 1731, the *Little Zhuz* accepted Russian protection, followed by the *Middle Zhuz* in 1740. However, Russian influence in the eighteenth century was minimal, and Kazakh rulers, especially Ablai Khan (1711–1781), who skillfully played China against Russia, were unrivalled sovereigns of the steppe.

However, after Ablai Khan's demise, Russia gradually came to dominate local affairs, suppressing Kazakh independence and imposing the Russian administrative system. Following a series of Kazakh rebellions, the most extensive of which was that of Batyr Srym in 1792–1797, the Russian authorities took even more active measures to abolish Kazakh autonomy. By 1824, they had succeeded in abolishing the Khan's power in the Little and the Middle Zhuzes. Despite repeated uprisings, notably by Ablai Khan's grandson Kenesary in 1841–1847, Russia steadily tightened its grip over Central Asia in the so-called Great Game between it and Great Britain, and eventually established control over the entire Kazakh homeland, conquering the *Great Zhuz* by 1865.

B. Law Reforms in Kazakhstan in the Nineteenth Century

In 1822 a legal document called "Regulations on Siberian Kirgiz" was promulgated (Kazakhs were termed by the Russian Imperial administration as Kirghiz or Kirghiz-Kaisak in order to distinguish them from the Cossacks). The document was drafted by Mikhail Speranskiy (one of the most prominent Russian statesman of the time) and provided a strategy aimed at the gradual incorporation of the steppe into the Russian empire by dividing the territory into administrative units, establishing local administrative institutions and appointing elites to serve in new administrative posts. The Regulations also intended to restrict nomadic migrations and promoted transferring to sedentary agriculture.

However, due to the Kazakhs' fierce resistance, the Russian empire was only able to start implementing its strategy in 1867–1868 when, according to the "Provisional Statutes," the Kazakh lands were divided between three Governor-Generalships (ruled by Governor-Generals): Orenburg, West Siberia and Turkestan (with their centers respectively in Orenburg, Omsk and Tashkent). All of these Governor-Generalships consisted of a number of oblasts headed by inferior military governors who commanded troops stationed within each territory. Each oblast was divided into "uezds" also headed by Russian officers who were assisted by Kazakh aristocrats (the Kazakh Sultans could continue to use their titles, but they were not recognized as part of the nobility of the Empire unless, through service, they were appointed to it). The uezds were divided into "volosts" (1,000–2,000 households) and the volosts into auls (100–200 families). The volosts and auls were not based on tribes but on territory. The authorities of the two lower administrative levels were ethnic Kazakhs, who were subordinated to the uezd commander. Thus, in contrast to the previous decades, the policy of appointing only native aristocratic elites as local links between Russian colonizers and the indigenous population was abandoned.

The Provisional Statutes further created three types of courts. *First*, military courts, which prosecuted the following crimes: assassinating officials; inciting opposition to the government; raiding treasury transports, as well as telegraph and post offices; and murdering a person who wanted to convert to Christianity. *Second*, imperial courts, which were governed by the general laws of the Empire and tried criminal and civil cases between members of the arriving Russian population, between Kazakhs and non-Kazakhs and among Kazakhs if both sides in a dispute agreed to turn to the court. The imperial courts could also prosecute Kazakhs who were accused of committing serious crimes such as murder, raiding trade caravans, barymta, damaging state property, etc. The imperial courts had three instances: (1) Uezd Court; (2) Oblast Administration (which contained a special legal section); and (3) the Ruling Senate (located in St. Petersburg). *Third*, people's courts (or courts of Bis), which were governed by Kazakh customary law and which remained the main institution for resolving legal cases among Kazakhs through the end of the imperial period.

The temporary Statutes of 1867–1868 were replaced by the 1886 "Turkestan" and 1891 "Steppe" Statutes (with the latter applicable in most of the Kazakh territories). These Statutes continued to bureaucratize the organization and management of regional administration. However, the most important aspect of the new legislation was the rule that all land in "excess of Kazakh needs" (i.e., more than 40 acres of land per household) was to be given over to the Public Land Fund, administered by the Ministry of State Property. Following the abolition of serfdom in Russia in 1861, the Russian government started to stimulate the movement of Russian and Ukrainian settlers into Siberia and Kazakhstan. Whereas the 1867–1868 Statutes had established the principle of state ownership of the steppe lands, the 1891 Statute provided the implementation mechanism of how this control would be exercised and asserted that the government had the power to seize lands forcibly from those who refuse to comply. As a result, the influx of settlers reached more than 140,000 people per year in the period between 1906 and 1914. This enormous migration was a substantial part of the imperial government's efforts to stem peasant unrest in Russia by creating a class of landowners. However, the seizure of Kazakh land and the restriction of traditional nomadic routes caused significant frictions between the indigenous population and the new settlers, resulting in a widespread uprising against the Russian Empire in 1916.

IV. KAZAKHSTAN DURING THE SOVIET ERA

A. Establishment of Kazakh Autonomous Soviet Socialist Republic

Russian imperial rule ended with the Russian Revolutions of 1917. In December 1917 Alash Orda, a party of Kazakh intellectuals, proclaimed the autonomy of the Kazakh people. During the Russian Civil War (1918–1921), Alash Orda leaders initially sought recognition (offering their support in exchange) from the anti-Bolshevik forces known as the Whites. When they refused, Kazakh leaders appealed to the Bolsheviks and received assurances from them that Kazakh autonomy would be maintained.

On August 20, 1920 the Bolsheviks' leader, Vladimir Lenin, signed a Decree on the establishment of the "Kirgiz Autonomous Soviet Socialist Republic" and the creation of a Congress of the Republic's Soviets as the supreme organ of the new Republic. The Congress met on October 4–12, 1920 in Orenburg (which became Kazakhstan's first capital) and established the Republic. The Congress of Soviets elected the Central Executive Committee (TsiK) as the legislative body during the interim of the sessions of the Congress. In turn, the TsiK elected its Presidium, the permanently functioning organ, and the Council of People's Commissars, the actual government, which had the authority to issue decrees carrying the force of law (these decrees were then routinely approved by the Presidium, the Tsik and the Congress at their next respective sessions). In December 1922 the Union of Soviet Socialist Republics (USSR) was founded, and the Kazakh Republic was incorporated into the USSR as a component part of the Russian Soviet Federative Socialist Republic (RSFSR).

In 1924, following the philosophy of Lenin, which stated that all people had to go through a national stage of development before they can build socialism, the Bolsheviks decided to delineate new borders in Turkestan, dividing the region among its major ethnic groups. As a result, the Kazakh Autonomy received all southern Kazakh lands but returned the Orenburg region to Russia. In February 1925, the Kazakh capital moved to Kyzyl-Orda and in April Kazakhstan was renamed the "Kazakh Autonomous Soviet Socialist Republic." In December of that same year, when the regional Communist Party conference was held, approximately 52% of its delegates were Kazakh (compared to only 11% in 1924). However, all Alash Orda members who had played significant roles during the first years of the Republic were gradually removed from their positions. By 1929, when the capital was relocated to Almaty, most of the Alash Orda leaders (who were the Kazakh national elite) were liquidated as "bourgeois nationalists."

B. Constitution of 1937 and Promotion to Union Republic

In the late 1920s, Soviet leaders instituted a rigorous program to collectivize agriculture into large state farms in order to decrease prices for agricultural products and enable the state to acquire the capital necessary for the development of heavy industry. Regarding Kazakhstan, it was decided that collectivization could only be achieved if the nomadic economy and the political authority of the old social order was destroyed simultaneously. Thus, collectivization for Kazakhstan meant the forced settlement of Kazakh nomads.

After collectivization (and thus "denomadization") was achieved (at the cost of at least 1 million people who died from famine and another million who fled from the country), on December 5, 1936 Kazakhstan was promoted to the status of a constituent republic of the Soviet Union, with the official name of the Kazakh Soviet Socialist Republic (KazSSR). On March 26, 1937 the first Constitution of Kazakhstan was adopted. Its provisions fully corresponded with, and were even largely identical to, those of the 1936 Constitution of the USSR, also known as the "Stalin Constitution." This Constitution formally made Kazakhstan a sovereign state, having equal rank with all other constituent (union) republics of the USSR and even the right of free secession from the Union.

Reiterating the respective provisions of the "Stalin Constitution," the first Constitution of the KazSSR provided that the Communist Party was "the vanguard of the working people in their struggle to strengthen and develop the socialist system and is the leading core of all organizations of the working people, both public and state" (accordingly, any opposition was effectively outlawed). The Constitution replaced the three-tier parliament (Congress of Soviets, TsiK, Presidium of TsiK) by a two-tier one: the Supreme Soviet and its Presidium. The Supreme Soviet of the KazSSR, which met twice annually, was proclaimed to be the highest state organ implementing legislative functions (its legislative acts, however, could not contradict the laws of the USSR). The Supreme Soviet elected its permanent Presidium, which had the right to issue decrees and interpret laws. The executive arm of the government was represented by the Council of People's Commissars of the KazSSR (which was fully subordinated to the analogous organ of the USSR); and the judicial branch by a three-level court system: (1) the Supreme Court, (2) Regional Courts, and (3) People's Courts. In addition, special courts (especially military tribunals) could be established as provided by the Union's legislation.

In 1944 amendments to the "Stalin Constitution" were adopted allowing each Union's republic to establish their own commissariats for foreign affairs and defense (in order to be recognized as independent states and join the United Nations). Although only Ukraine and Belorussia were admitted to the UN, Kazakhstan retained its foreign and defense commissariats which were renamed as ministries in 1946 and were practically branches of the USSR's respective ministries.

C. Development of the Legal System of Soviet Kazakhstan

In the first post-revolutionary years, as the old Russian legal system deteriorated, Kazakh customary law and traditional rural leadership were revived. However, after its consolidation, Soviet power resolutely began to do away with "vestiges of the past'' by using its relentless force, raising the ''ideological awareness'' of the population through political education and propaganda and by involving increasing numbers of supportive Kazakhs in the state machinery.

In 1920–1921 the Council of People's Commissars of the Kazakh Autonomy adopted decrees prohibiting *kun, barymta*, *kalym* and polygamy. In 1924, the courts of Bis were banned under threat of criminal punishment; in 1928, a resolution was enacted on the confiscation of property and expulsion of *Bais* (wealthy persons). Nevertheless, the hold of the traditional leadership was broken only by the collectivization and the subsequent industrialization of Kazakhstan.

These major processes, along with the massive participation of Kazakhs in World War II, large-scale deportations of ''untrustworthy'' ethnic groups (Germans, Poles, Koreans, Chechens, Ingush, Turks, Kurds, Crimean Tatars, Greeks, etc.) to Kazakhstan, and the ''Virgin Lands'' campaign (bringing Kazakh grazing land under grain cultivation) led to the transformation of Kazakhstan into one of the major economic components of the former USSR. At the same time, however, it was the only Soviet republic in which the eponymous nationality was a minority, constituting about 30% of the population. This factor also significantly contributed to the ultimate elimination of the traditional lifestyle and customary law.

After Stalin's death, the competences of the Union's republics were broadened to some extent, so they could now decide issues related to their administrative divisions and adopt their own civil, criminal, procedural and later labor legislation within the principles established by the Union's framework legislation. Thus, on July 22, 1959 the Criminal Code and the Criminal Procedure Code of the KazSSR were adopted, followed by the Civil Code and the Civil Procedure Code, both of December 28, 1963; the Code on Marriage and Family of August 6, 1969; and the Labor Code (LC) of July 21, 1972, to mention the most important enactments only.

D. Constitution of 1978 and the Soviet Perestroika

On October 7, 1977 the USSR adopted a new Constitution (the so-called Brezhnev Constitution). The rationale was provided by the Preamble, which stated that ''the aims of the dictatorship of the proletariat have been fulfilled'' and the USSR represented not only workers and peasants but ''has become the state of the whole people.'' Guilt was no longer to be imputed based on class origin. In addition, the Constitution provided more extensive treatment of basic rights, which made it easier for the Soviet leadership to maintain that the USSR had outstanding achievements in this field. Furthermore, all Union republics were guaranteed their sovereignty and the right to freely secede from the Union. However, during the time of monolithic unity of the Communist Party (from the emergence of the USSR through the end of 1980s), these provisions were purely theoretical and propagandist.

Like the other 15 republics of the USSR, the Kazakh SSR conformed its Constitution to the new federal model in 1978. As in all other Soviet republics, the Communist Party was recognized as ''the leading and guiding force of Soviet society and the nucleus of its political system." This provision fully reflected comprehensive control of all aspects of social and political life by a very powerful and hierarchically structured Party machine that was the essence of the Soviet system. Also, no significant changes were made with respect to the principles of state organization. The Supreme Soviet was still formally proclaimed to be the highest state organ but, in reality, political power belonged only to the leadership of the Communist Party and primarily to its General Secretary.

However, Gorbachev's policy of *Perestroika* ended the Communist Party's "vanguard" status. The constitutional amendments of March 1990 abolished the leading role of the Party in society and state. Hard-line elements in the Party tried to reverse the course of events and launched the August Coup in 1991. However, the coup collapsed in only two days, and almost immediately the Communist Party was formally banned. In subsequent months, the Party was stripped of its control of the government, internal-security agencies and Armed Forces. By December 1991, the Soviet Union ceased to exist.

V. LEGAL DEVELOPMENT OF INDEPENDENT KAZAKHSTAN

A. Proclamation of Independence

Kazakhstan took its first step towards independence on October 25, 1990, when the Supreme Soviet of KazSSR adopted a Declaration of State Sovereignty (which basically reaffirmed the provisions of the Constitution of 1978). However, full sovereignty and its current name "Republic of Kazakhstan" were attained by the country only on December 16, 1991, when the Constitutional Law on State Independence was adopted. On December 21, 1991 Kazakhstan, along with other states of the former USSR, signed agreements that confirmed the extinction of the USSR and established the Commonwealth of Independent States, an organization fully based on the principle of the sovereign equality of its participants and the inviolability of their borders. On March 2, 1992 Kazakhstan became a UN member.

B. First Constitution of January 28, 1993 and Reasons for Its Failure

The collapse of the USSR converted the Constitution of 1978 from a merely formal text to an important document. Despite the popular election of the first President of Kazakhstan, Nursultan Nazarbayev, on December 1, 1991, the Soviet-styled Constitution based on the ascendancy of representative councils (the Soviets) gave the legislative branch an obvious supremacy over the executive branch. This situation was obviously dissatisfactory to Nazarbayev, who proposed a draft of a new Constitution to the Supreme Soviet on June 1, 1992. After intense debate, the legislature adopted the Constitution, and it went into force on January 28, 1993.

The Constitution contained an extensive catalog of personal, political, economic and social rights. The state language was explicitly determined to be Kazakh; the Russian language was initially given status of a "language of interethnic communication" and then even elevated to the second official language. Three branches of the state power were created, each operating on the principle of strict separation; thus neither the Supreme Soviet nor the President could prematurely terminate the authorities of each other. The legislative branch was endowed with numerous important powers (to amend the Constitution, to adopt and interpret laws, to approve and control the budget, to give consent to the appointment of the Prime Minister and many other important ministers and officials, etc.) and could effectively balance and control the executive branch. The executive branch was headed by the President, who was elected every five years and for no more than two terms. The judicial branch consisted of the Supreme Court, the Supreme Arbitration Court, the Constitutional Court and local courts. All judges were freed from the direct political control that existed in the communist era and given full independence.

Along with political transformation, the newly established country was going through unprecedented market-oriented reforms (in the form of the so-called shock therapy program) and exceptional economic crisis. As the market reforms proved exceedingly difficult to implement and resulted in the bankruptcy of much of the post-Soviet economy, a bitter conflict arose between the reform-oriented executive and the communist-dominated legislature. As a result, President Nazarbayev (using his control over mass media and his popularity among people of Kazakhstan, who credited him with maintaining order in the country) started to exercise political pressure upon the "Soviet-era" Parliament forcing it into a "voluntary disbandment." Although such a step was not foreseen by the Constitution, on December 12, 1993 the Parliament terminated its authority by way of "self-dissolution."

On March 7, 1994 the Republic held its first multi-party legislative elections. Even though the President's supporters apparently emerged as the strongest force in the new legislature, in a situation of catastrophic economic decline many of the new parliamentarians became willing to establish themselves as a genuine opposition. As a result, tensions between the President and the Parliament continued to flare, achieving a peak at the end of 1994 when the legislature refused to adopt a new draft budget. That was probably the final confrontation that fueled Nazarbayev's dissatisfaction with the rigid model of separation of powers and its inability to facilitate the process of economic transformation.

The solution came from a rather unexpected place. Following a complaint brought by a frustrated parliamentary candidate who argued that she could not win in the parliamentary elections of 1994 due to a number of irregularities in her electoral district, on March 6, 1995 the Constitutional Court (which had earned a solid reputation for its commitment to establishing the rule of law) issued a ruling stipulating that the powers of the Supreme Soviet are "unconstitutional." Without any delay President Nazarbayev declared the legislature (despite the protests of the parliamentarians) to be dissolved.

C. CONSTITUTION OF KAZAKHSTAN OF AUGUST 30, 1995

The fact that the course of events leading to the dissolution of the Supreme Soviet was methodically orchestrated is evidently confirmed by the establishment of the Assembly of the Peoples of Kazakhstan, a representative body composed of all the ethnic groups of Kazakhstan and designed to perform consultative functions. Established on March 1, 1995 (a few days before the termination of the powers of the legislature), on March 24, 1995 the Assembly called for a nationwide referendum on the extension of the President's term in office, which was set to expire in 1996, through the year 2000. By conducting a referendum, Nazarbayev intended to provide himself a legitimate foundation from which to start the constitutional reform and to avoid standing for re-election in 1996 (in the middle of economic reforms that necessitated tough decisions and painful policies).

Official results of the referendum, held on April 29, 1995 indicated nearly unanimous support (more than 95% of votes in favor) for the extension of Nazarbayev's term. Meanwhile, Nazarbayev ordered the drafting of a new Constitution. The first draft of this new Constitution, which would significantly expand presidential powers, was presented to the public in early July. Among those who criticized the draft were a number of judges of the Constitutional Court who argued that the new Constitution would be detrimental to the creation of a democratic state and civil society. The leadership's response was that the second draft of the Constitution, made public at the beginning of August 1995, fully changed the conception of the constitutional judiciary and created a much weaker Constitutional Council (thus abolishing the Constitutional Court).

On August 30, 1995 more than 95% of Kazakhstan's voters approved the new Constitution in a referendum. Although some international observers monitoring the referendum expressed their doubts that the attendance of voters achieved the required quorum of 50%, in all likelihood an overwhelming majority of the people of Kazakhstan came to the referendum in order to support the policy of political stability that they associated with the personality of the President.

Having consolidated his hold on Kazakhstan's political structures, President Nazarbayev started fundamental legal reforms that allowed the country to maintain stability and to make significant progress toward developing a market economy. Though in the midst of a process of unprecedented fundamental transformation, on the one hand, and an attempt to restore national statehood, on the other hand, Kazakhstan remained united and established a modern legal system. The current objectives pursued by the country include diversifying the economy away from overdependence on natural resources and becoming one of 50 most competitive countries in the world. At the same time, however, the excessive concentration of political power in the presidency entails the weakness and fragility of the legislature, stalls efforts at democratic reforms and jeopardizes civil liberties. Consequently, Kazakhstan's progress towards true democracy and rule-of-law remains insufficient; there is still a considerable danger of the country ultimately losing its rudimentary democratic institutions and fully reverting to some form of authoritarian rule.

Selected Bibliography

J. Aitken, *Nazarbayev and the Making of Kazakhstan* (Continuum, London, 2009).

Z. Dzhunusova, "The Democratic Tradition of Kazakhstan in Historical Context", in Y. Ro'i (ed.), *Democracy and Pluralism in Muslim Eurasia* (Routledge, London, 2004).

S. Fuchs, *Очерки истории государства и права казахов в XVIII и первой половине XIX в.* [*Essays on the History of State and Law of Kazakhs in the XVIII and the first half of the XIX centuries*] (Yuridicheskaya Kniga Astana, St. Petersburg, 2008) [in Russian].

L. Gumilev, *Древние тюрки* [*Ancient Turks*] (Nauka, Moscow, 1967) [in Russian].

S. Kanter, "Constitution Making in Kazakhstan" (1993) 5 *Int'l Legal Persp.* 65.

Z. Kenzhaliev & S.O. Dauletova, *Казахское обычное право в условиях Советской власти (1917–1937)* [*Kazakh Customary Law under the Soviet Power*] (Gylym, Almaty, 1993) [in Russian].

T. Kulteleev, *Уголовное обычное право казахов* [*Customary Criminal Law of Kazakhs*] (Academy of Sciences of KazSSR, Alma-Ata, 1955) [in Russian].

R. Ludkowski (ed.), *Constitution-Making in the Region of Former Soviet Dominance* (Duke University Press, Durham, London, 1996), 443.

V. Martin, *Law and Custom in the Steppe* (Routledge, Curzon, London, New York, 2001).

M.B. Olcott, *The Kazakhs* (Hoover Institution Press, Stanford, 1995).

S. Sartayev (ed.), *История государства и права Казахской ССР* [*History of State and Law of Kazak SSR*], vol. I (Mektep, Alma-Ata, 1982), vol. II (Mektep, Alma-Ata, 1984) [in Russian].

S. Zimanov, *Политический строй Казахстана конца XVIII-первой половины XIX вв.* [*Political System of Kazakhstan in the End of the XVIII and the First Half of the XIX Centuries*] (Academy of Sciences of KazSSR, Alma-Ata, 1960) [in Russian].

S. Zimanov (ed.), *Қазақтың ата заңдары* [*Ancient Kazakh Laws*], vols. 1–10 (Žeti Žargi, Almaty, 2001–2009) [in Kazakh].

Chapter 2
Basic Features of the Legal System

Zhenis Kembayev

I. LAW OF KAZAKHSTAN IN A COMPARATIVE PERSPECTIVE

Starting from the second half of the nineteenth century, when the territory of what is now Kazakhstan was fully incorporated into the administrative and legal system of the Russian Empire, the country gradually became part of the civil law tradition, which differs significantly from the common law of the Anglo-American countries in its sources, substantive content and the operative procedures of law.

Having its roots in ancient Rome, the civil law tradition developed in the states of continental Europe and has been adopted in many regions throughout the world as a consequence of the European expansion that took place from the fifteenth through the twentieth centuries. Although the legal system of the Russian Empire has different historical roots from other countries of continental Europe, by the time Russia fully established its control over the Kazakh steppes, Russian legislation was modeled after the laws of the most advanced European countries and was based on codified acts (i.e., a systematic and comprehensive compilation of legal rules and principles developed and compiled by legal scholars and adopted by legislative bodies). Accordingly, by the time of the Russian Revolution of 1917, the civil law tradition was firmly rooted in Kazakhstan (even though it came by an indirect route and as a substantial part of oppressive colonization policies).

The law of the Russian Empire influenced very much the formation of the Soviet legal system. In fact, Soviet Law preserved many characteristics of the civil

Zhenis Kembayev, *Introduction to the Law of Kazakhstan*, pp. 23–35.

law system. The law was based on written legal codes adopted by the legislative organ with the purpose of creating a unified legal system throughout the country. Also, the role of Soviet judges differed considerably from that of their counterparts in common law systems. Like in other civil law jurisdictions, Soviet judges were state officials who administered the codes and other regulatory acts but could not establish new laws themselves. Based on these shared characteristics, some authors argued that the Soviet legal system (despite certain dissimilarities) remained in principle within the civil law tradition.[1]

At the same time, however, the Soviet legal system had significant differences from classic civil law countries. It proclaimed Marxism as its official ideology and created a state that had placed all means of production under state ownership and established total state control over all aspects of public activities. The ideology imposed by the Communist Party was hostile to the state and law (as vestiges of the past), proclaiming that they would "wither away" after a communist society was completely built. According to Marxist doctrine, the abolition of private ownership was an absolute prerequisite for a communist society. Therefore, the new regime terminated the legal system of the market economy, including property, contract, business and commercial law and assumed full control over industry and agricultural production.

Although there were limited market elements (e.g., consumers were free to choose the goods and services on which to spend their money), state-managed enterprises became the predominant form of organization of production and distribution. The flipside of the command economy was an extremely centralized political system that did not recognize any separation of power, based on the absolute dominance of the Communist Party. As a result, Soviet Law became purely an instrument for the implementation of state policy aimed to bring about an orderly transformation of the USSR to a communist society. Because of this, some scholars argue that, despite technical similarities between the Soviet legal system and the civil law systems of Western Europe, a new family of "socialist" legal systems had emerged alongside the common law and civil law systems.[2]

No matter which theory is correct, it is clear that subsequent to the disintegration of the Soviet legal system and the collapse of the Soviet Union, Kazakhstan (re-)joined the civil law family, this time as an independent state. This fact can clearly be observed by the constitutional provisions on the recognition and guarantee of private property (which enjoys the same degree of protections as the state property) and the freedom of entrepreneurial activities. Also, in contrast to the socialist times, the judiciary has been separated from the executive and the legislative branches of state power, and the courts are now composed of professional judges who must be fully independent and may not be members of political parties.

---

1. See J. Quigley, "Socialist Law and the Civil Law Tradition" (1989) 37 *American Journal of Comparative Law* 781.
2. See W. Burnham, P. Maggs & G. Danilenko, *Law and Legal System of the Russian Federation* (Juris Publishing, New York, 2009), 1-7.

At the same time, however, the Soviet legacy has left its marks on Kazakhstan's legal system. Despite large-scale privatization, the government's role in the economy is much more visible than in traditional civil law countries. The effects of the Soviet administrative style are felt at every level and in every branch of state power. In particular, they are obviously reflected in the creation of an over-centralized political system dominated by the President and the existence of a one-party Parliament. Moreover, the (Western) European concept of civil society as separate from state authorities clashes with the Kazakhstani ruling elites' view that the activities of democratic institutions should support and be fully in line with official state policies.

II. RECOGNIZED SOURCES OF LAW AND THEIR HIERARCHY

A. Generally

Like in every other country of the civil law tradition, Kazakhstan's jurisprudence attaches a great significance to the theory of sources of law. In doing so, the prevalent legal doctrine typically distinguishes between two major meanings of "sources of law." First, in their most "fundamental" sense, the sources of law are understood to be the socio-economic order of a particular society that gives birth to and shapes the distinctive political, economic and legal superstructure of a society. Second, in their "formal" meaning, the sources of law are the rules or norms created, sanctioned or recognized by the authorized state organs in a duly established manner.

Accordingly, Kazakhstan's science of law follows the theory of legal positivism, which argues that law is synonymous with positive norms, which, in turn, means that the only valid law is normative law. This approach is fully reflected in the Constitution of the Republic of Kazakhstan (CRK), which stipulates that the "functioning law" in the Republic is constituted by "the Constitution, the legislative acts, other regulatory legal acts, international treaties as well as resolutions of the Constitutional Council and the Supreme Court of the Republic" (Article 4 I CRK).

B. Types of Sources of Law and Their Hierarchy

Constitutional provisions on the sources of law are primarily elaborated by the Law of RK of March 24, 1998, No. 213-I, "On Normative Legal Acts" (LNLA). This law defines a "normative legal act" (*normativtik-qüqyqtyq akt*, *normativno-pravovoi akt*)[3] as "an official document . . . adopted by referendum or by an

---

3. Translations of terms are given in singular. Hereinafter in this book the first version is Kazakh, the second Russian. If only one translation is given, that translation is identical for both Kazakh and Russian.

authorized organ or an official that establishes, amends, terminates or suspends norms of law" (Article 1 LNLA). Furthermore, it determines the hierarchy of "normative legal acts" (or in other words regulatory acts) and provides detailed rules on how they are adopted, published, interpreted, systematized and registered.

Unlike common law, which does not ascribe special priority to certain sources of law, Kazakhstan's legal system is based on a formalistic hierarchy of sources of law, i.e., the regulatory acts. According to the LNLA, there is the following hierarchy of such acts in Kazakhstan: (1) the Constitution; (2) laws introducing amendments and additions to the Constitution; (3) constitutional laws and decrees of the President having the force of a constitutional law; (4) codes; (5) laws and decrees of the President having the force of a law; (6) resolutions of the Parliament and its chambers (Article 4 II LNLA).

The above-mentioned acts are followed by the so-called sub-law acts which are "to be adopted on the basis of and in execution of the Constitution and legislative acts of RK" (Article 1 LNLA). The sub-law acts include: (7) decrees of the President; (8) resolutions of the Government; (9) orders of ministers and other heads of central state organs; and (10) acts of local representative and executive bodies (Article 4 II LNLA). The Law provides clearly that all lower-level regulatory legal acts may not contradict superior acts (Article 4 III LNLA). Should there be any contradiction in the provisions of regulatory legal acts of different levels, the norms of the higher acts must be applied. Should there be any contradictions in the provisions of regulatory legal acts of the same level, the norms of the act that was adopted later must be applied (Article 6-I, III LNLA).

Resolutions of the Constitutional Council and the Supreme Court were not formally included in the above hierarchy of acts. However, the LNLA says that resolutions of the Constitutional Council "shall be based on the Constitution of RK and all other regulatory legal acts shall not contradict them" (Article 4 VI). A special place in the system of regulatory acts is also taken by resolutions of the Supreme Court, which are not subject to the hierarchy rules set for the regulatory acts in Kazakhstan and are defined as regulatory acts containing "explanations on the issues of how to apply legislation" in judicial practice and, as such, are mandatory to all lower courts of Republic of Kazakhstan (RK; see the resolution of the Constitutional Council of March 6, 1997, No. 3, "On the official interpretation of Art. 4 I of the Constitution . . . "). Thus, resolutions of the Supreme Court are binding legal acts but are not binding precedents as in the sense of common law. They are issued on the basis of review of the lower courts' practice on certain type of matters rather than with respect to a single case, i.e., they follow the *jurisprudence constante* rather than the *stare decisis* principle.

All regulatory acts in Kazakhstan are subject to registration with the organs of justice of RK, which keep the state registry of all regulatory acts (Article 47 I LNLA).

III. DOMESTIC SOURCES OF LAW

A. The Constitution

According to the Constitution of RK, "the Constitution shall have the highest juridical force and direct effect on the entire territory of the Republic" (Article 4 II). Under the above-mentioned resolution of March 6, 1997 the Constitutional Council ruled that the courts in Kazakhstan "when hearing judicial cases must apply the Constitution of RK as an act of direct effect in all necessary cases." Also, the Constitution states that the courts may not apply laws and other regulatory legal acts infringing on the constitutional rights and liberties of individuals, which means that the courts must evaluate the contents of applicable laws or other regulatory acts for their conformity to the Constitution. Should a court find that a legal act subject to application infringes on constitutional rights and liberties, it must suspend legal proceedings and address the Constitutional Council with a proposal to declare that law unconstitutional (Article 78 CRK).

In the hierarchy of regulatory legal acts, the fundamental law of Kazakhstan is followed by special legislative acts (laws) that introduce amendments and additions to the Constitution. According to the Constitution, laws of this kind may be adopted only by a majority of no less than three-fourths of the total number of the deputies of each chamber (Article 62 III). In the modern constitutional history of Kazakhstan (since August 30, 1995), three such laws have been adopted: the first on October 7, 1998, the second on May 21, 2007 and the third on February 2, 2011.

B. Legislative Acts

In accordance with the LNLA, there are four kinds of legislative acts in Kazakhstan: (1) constitutional laws and decrees of the President having the force of a constitutional law; (2) codes; (3) laws and decrees of the President having the force of a law; and (4) resolutions of the Parliament and its chambers.

First of all, it should be mentioned that the Constitution of RK provides for a special type of legislative act called a "constitutional law" (*konstitutsiyalyq zang, konstitutsionnyi zakon*), which is adopted on issues stipulated by the Constitution (Article 62 IV CRK). Specifically, the Constitution foresees the adoption of such laws with respect to the legal status of the President, the Parliament, the Government, the Constitutional Council, the judicial system, elections and the state symbols of Kazakhstan. A constitutional law has a hierarchical status below the Constitution but higher than ordinary laws (statutes). In line with its status, it is adopted by a majority of no less than two-thirds of the total number of the deputies of each chamber of Kazakhstan's Parliament. Should the President of RK veto a constitutional law, his rejection may be overruled only by a majority of three-fourth of the deputies in each chamber. Also, it should be noted that a constitutional law (like all other legislative acts) may also be adopted by the President in the event that the Parliament delegates its legislative powers to him (such delegation is possible for a term not exceeding one year by a majority of two-thirds of the deputies of each chamber at the initiative of the President) (Article 53 III CRK).

Constitutional laws are followed by the most commonly encountered legislative acts in Kazakhstan, "codes" (*kodeks*) and ordinary "laws" (*zang, zakon*).

A code is defined by the LNLA as a systematized legislative act regulating one of the currently 16 different categories of "the most important social relations of similar nature." Consequently, the law foresees the existence of 16 codes in the legal system of Kazakhstan. At present 15 of the following codes are already in force: (1) the Budget Code, (2) the Civil Code, (3) the Civil Procedure Code, (4) the Ecological Code, (5) the Water Code, (6) the Land Code, (7) the Forest Code, (8) the Tax Code, (9) the Customs Code, (10) the Labor Code, (11) the Criminal-Executive Code, (12) the Code on Administrative Offenses, (13) the Criminal Code, (14) the Criminal Procedure Code, and (15) the Code on the People's Health and the Health Care System. In addition, one more systematized act, the Family Code, is being discussed and prepared for adoption.

In accordance with the Constitution, an ordinary "law" is an act adopted by the Parliament that regulates important public relations and establishes fundamental principles and standards dealing with: (1) the legal capacity of individuals and legal entities, civil freedoms and rights, obligations and responsibilities of individuals and legal entities; (2) conditions of ownership and other rights of property; (3) the fundamentals of the organization and activity of state bodies and bodies of local self-administration and state, and military service; (4) taxation and the establishment and levying of duties and other obligatory payments; (5) the republican budget; (6) issues of the judicial system and legal proceedings; (7) education, health care and social provisioning; (8) the privatization of enterprises and their property; (9) environmental protection; (10) the administrative-territorial structure of the Republic; and (11) ensuring defense and security of the state (Article 61 III CRK).

Both codes and ordinary laws are adopted by the vote of the majority of the total number of deputies of the Parliament's chambers (i.e., an absolute majority). However, codes occupy a higher position in the hierarchy of sources of law than ordinary laws and decrees of the President having the force of a law (which means that the latter must be fully in line with the respective codes).[4] For this reason, the LNLA requires the Parliament to adopt codes (as well as amendments and additions to them) only following no less than two readings in each chamber (Article 25 II LNLA).

In addition, the Parliament and both of its chambers may adopt regulatory resolutions (*normativti qauly, normativnoe postanovlenie*). In doing so, the Parliament adopts resolutions within the limits of the joint competences of both of its

4. Note, however, that the respective Code may provide for exceptions and allow ordinary laws to prevail in certain areas. Thus, the Civil Code provides in particular that civil legislation applies to relations relating to the use of natural resources only in instances when these relations are not regulated by the legislation on the use of natural resources (Art. 1 III CC).

chambers. The chambers adopt such resolutions within the scope of their separate, exclusive and independent competences (furthermore, the Parliament and its chambers may, within the limits of their competences, also adopt appeals, declarations and statements that are, however, not considered to be regulatory acts).

Last but not least, it should be noted that legislative acts also include decrees of the President having the force of law. Such decrees are only adopted under the following circumstances. The Constitution entitles the President to determine the priority of consideration of drafts of laws in the Parliament and to declare the consideration of a certain draft of law to be urgent, signifying that the Parliament must consider this draft within a month from the day of its submission. If the Parliament does not meet this requirement, the President may issue a decree having the force of law which will be in effect until the Parliament adopts a new law in the course of due legislative procedure (Article 61 II CRK).

C. SUB-LAW ACTS

The LNLA defines a "sub-law act" (*zanga qosymsha akt, podzakonnyi akt*) to be "a regulatory act that is not legislative and is adopted on the basis and in pursuance of the Constitution and the legislative acts of RK" (Article 1).

The highest among sub-law acts in Kazakhstan are decrees (*zharlyk*,[5] *ukaz*) of the President. According to the Constitutional Law of RK of December 26, 1995, No. 2733, "On the President of the Republic of Kazakhstan," decrees of the President serve the following purposes: (1) implementation of the constitutional authorities of the President; (2) maintenance of the concerted functioning of all branches of state power and the responsibility of the state organs before the people of Kazakhstan; (3) legal regulation of issues that do not belong to the legislative competence of the Parliament or other state organs; and (4) resolution of strategic issues of economic and socio-political development of RK (Article 21 II). Decrees of the President must fully correspond to the Constitution and the legislative acts of the Republic (Article 45 I CRK). At the same time, it should be noted that, especially in the early days of Kazakhstan's independence, decrees of the President have been in essence "temporary laws" that are in force until the Parliament adopts a legislative act in a given area.[6]

Decrees of the President are followed in the hierarchy of acts by resolutions of the Government. These resolutions (*qauly, postanovlenie*) are adopted by a majority vote by the Government's members and are signed by the Prime

5. See the name of the acts issued by Genghis Khan (See Chapter 1 "Legal History").
6. The President may also adopt directions (*bilik, rasporyazhenie*) which are not considered to be regulatory acts and are adopted on issues of operative and individual character (e.g., appointment or dismissal of officials who do not have constitutional status). The President's directions may not contradict to the Constitution of RK, legislative acts of RK or decrees of the President.

Minister.[7] The Prime Minister may also issue directions (*ökim, rasporyazhenie*). Both the resolutions of the Government and the directions of the Prime Minister may not contradict the CRK, the legislative acts or the decrees and directions of the President (Article 69 III CRK). The Constitution also provides that the President may terminate or suspend completely or partially the effect of the acts of the Government and the Prime Minister (Article 44 III).

Ministers (heads of central executive bodies that constitute the Government) and Chairpersons of Agencies (central executive bodies which are not a part of the Government) may issue orders (*buiryq, prikaz*). The acts of other central state bodies, like resolutions of the Central Elections Commission and the Estimation Committee for Control over the Implementation of the Republican Budget, also belong to this same level of regulatory acts. Acts of ministries and other central executive bodies may be terminated or suspended completely or partially by the Government of RK.

Regulatory acts may also be issued by local representative and executive bodies within the limits of their competences. Thus, "Maslikhats" (local representative bodies) may issue decisions (*sheshim, reshenie*) and "Akimats" (local executive bodies) may adopt resolutions (*qauly, postanovlenie*) that are signed by "Akims" (heads of the local executive bodies). In addition, the Akims are also entitled to issue decisions (*sheshim, reshenie*) dealing with regular administrative matters. The acts of the Maslikhats, the Akimats and the Akims have a binding force on the territories of the respective administrative-territorial divisions. The decisions of the Maslikhats that do not correspond to the Constitution and the legislative acts of RK may be terminated by the respective Maslikhats themselves or by the court. The acts of the Akimats and the Akims may be terminated or suspended by the President, the Government, a superior Akimat or Akim, the respective Akimat or Akim themselves or by the court.

All regulatory acts of ministries and other central executive bodies as well as of local representative and executive bodies that are related to rights, freedoms and obligations of citizens, are not only subject to state registration with the organs of justice but also require this registration to enter into force (Article 38 I LNLA). Furthermore, their registration may be denied, in particular if they: (a) infringe upon the rights and freedoms of citizens; (b) contradict superior regulatory acts; (c) go beyond the limits of the competences of the organs that adopted them; (d) have received no prior consent of the higher organs if such consent was required; or (e) affect the interests of private entrepreneurs and have no expert conclusions from accredited associations of private entrepreneurs attached (Article 38 II LNLA).

Also, it should be noted that the LNLA differentiates between "main" and "derivative" regulatory acts. In doing so, the Law defines the latter as an act that is adopted simultaneously with its respective main act and serves as an integral part of that main act (in the form of an attachment). Derivative regulatory acts include

7. The Prime Minister may also issue directions (*bilikter, rasporyazheniya*) that, like the President's directions, treat routine administrative matters and may not contradict the Constitution of RK, the legislative acts or the decrees and directions of the President of RK.

regulations (*reglament*), statutes (*erezhe, polozhenie*), guidelines (*tartip, pravilo*) and instructions (*nusqau, instruktsiya*). The place of the derivative regulatory acts in the hierarchy of acts is determined by the level of the respective main act (Article 3 IV LNLA). Usually, derivative regulatory acts are adopted as sub-law acts.

IV. INFLUENCE OF INTERNATIONAL TREATIES

A. INTERNATIONAL TREATIES AS SOURCES OF LAW

According to the Law of RK of May 30, 2005, No. 54-III, "On International Treaties of the Republic of Kazakhstan" (LIT), international treaties of RK may be concluded by: (a) the President of RK (on behalf of the Republic); (b) the Government of RK; and (c) state organs that are directly subordinated to the President, as well as central executive bodies within the limits of their competences defined by the legislation of RK (Article 2 LIT).

Furthermore, this law stipulates that international treaties of RK are subject to ratification by the Parliament of RK if they require the amendment of existing legislation or the adoption of new laws, or if they are related to: (1) human rights and freedoms; (2) territorial issues, including the delimitation of the exclusive economic zone and the continental shelf; (3) principles of interstate relations; (4) disarmament, international peace and security as well as collective security; (5) participation of the Republic in international organizations if such treaties foresee the transfer of a part of the sovereign authorities of the Republic to those international organizations or establish the binding power of decisions taken by their organs with respect to the Republic; (6) state loans; and (7) rendering economic and other assistance except for the humanitarian aid. Also, the ratification is mandatory if it is stipulated by the treaty itself or foreseen in the agreement of the parties (Article 11 LIT).

Ratified international treaties have priority over the laws of the Republic and may be directly implemented except in cases when the application of an international treaty requires the promulgation of a law (Article 4 II CRK). Consequently, in the hierarchy of sources of law, ratified international treaties occupy the rank directly after the Constitution, laws introducing amendments and additions to the Constitution, resolutions of the Constitutional Council and constitutional laws and decrees of the President having the force of a constitutional law. Should an international treaty of RK (or a part of it) be recognized as contradicting to the Constitution, it (or its particular part) may not be implemented (see the resolution of the Constitutional Council of May 18, 2006, No. 2).

International treaties of RK that entered into force without ratification do not have priority over the laws of the Republic and may be implemented only if they do not contradict the legislation of RK. An exception to this rule is constituted by treaties which were concluded before the adoption of the Constitution of 1995, provided that their priority is directly foreseen by the respective laws of the Republic.

B. Movement towards the Creation of Regional Supranational Law?

The RK has been an active participant in the regional integration processes that have taken place in Eurasia since the collapse of the Soviet Union. From the very beginning, Kazakhstan has supported the creation of an economic union within the framework of the Commonwealth of Independent States (CIS). However, when efforts to maintain the single economic space inherited from the USSR failed, Kazakhstan joined those CIS countries that were willing to integrate their economies, even if only among themselves. As a result, on January 20, 1995 Kazakhstan agreed to create a Customs Union (CU) with Belarus and Russia. This alliance led to the establishment of the Eurasian Economic Community (EurAsEC) on October 10, 2000, an international organization that currently also unites Kyrgyzstan, Tajikistan and Uzbekistan (the latter, however, suspended its membership in November 2008). The Community's first few years of existence did not provide grounds for optimism about the progress of multilateral integration. However, after many years of negotiations, on October 6, 2007 Belarus, Russia and Kazakhstan decided to establish a CU by 2011. Also, it was announced that the CU would be subsequently, whenever possible, joined by all other EurAsEC Member States. On January 1, 2010 the common Customs Code came into force (one year ahead of the initial plan) and thus common external tariffs were established. Moreover, there are also plans to facilitate integration processes further and to create a single economic space by January 1, 2012.

In the course of these events, Belarus, Russia and Kazakhstan came to an agreement to establish the Commission of the Customs Union, which was created to facilitate the development of the CU and is designed to obtain "on a step-by-step basis a part of the authorities of the state organs of the Member States" (Articles 1 and 2 of the Agreement on the Commission of the Customs Union). The Commission's major responsibilities include the execution of the decisions of the Interstate Council (which is the supreme organ of the alliance, consisting of the heads of state and government of the Member States) and the monitoring of the implementation of the international treaties aimed at the establishment of the CU. The Commission is composed of the deputy heads of government of the Member States (or other government members vested with necessary authority), who work in the Commission on a permanent basis and meet at least once every month. But the most prominent feature of the Commission is certainly its ability to adopt decisions according to the principle of "weighted voting" (which is commonly used only in supranational organizations). Thus, the Commission is entitled to make binding decisions with a two-thirds majority vote; for these purposes Russia has 57 votes while Belarus and Kazakhstan have 21.5 votes each.

In October 2009, the Prime Minister of RK requested the Constitutional Council to provide clarification as to the legal nature of the decisions of the Commission. Addressing this request, the Constitutional Council first referred to the fact that the Constitution of RK does not indicate any norm "foreseeing the possibility of transferring authorities of the state organs to international organizations or their organs." At the same time, however, it emphasized that the RK is a sovereign state that may independently formulate and realize its domestic and foreign policy on the basis of its Constitution. Furthermore, the Council noted that the Parliament of RK, representing the sovereign will of the people of Kazakhstan, adopted in due procedure the Law on International Treaties of RK, which provides, *inter alia*, that Kazakhstan may ratify international treaties enabling the participation of the Republic in international organizations that feature the transfer of a part of the sovereign authorities of the Member States to those international organizations. Accordingly, Kazakhstan may be a member of even those international organizations whose organs are able to adopt mandatory decisions with respect to the RK by a majority of votes.

Since the Agreement on the Commission of the Customs Union was properly ratified by the Republic of Kazakhstan, the Constitutional Council stated that its provisions have priority over the laws of the Republic and may be directly implemented. In view of the Agreement's provision that the Commission may take binding decisions, the Council denoted that Kazakhstan "must carry out all necessary organizational and legal measures for the implementations of this provision, including the adjustment of the national legislation." Furthermore, the Constitutional Council referred to Article 4 I of the Constitution stipulating that "the functioning law in the Republic of Kazakhstan" consists of "international treaties and other commitments of the Republic." Stipulating that the execution of the decisions of the Commission "should be considered as the implementation of other commitments of the Republic," the Constitutional Council provided that the decisions of the Commission have priority over the laws of the Republic.

At the same time, the Constitutional Council resolved that the decisions of the Commission of the Customs Union (like organs of any other international organization) may not have priority over the laws of the Republic in the event that they infringe upon the constitutional rights and freedoms of individuals in Kazakhstan. Also, the Constitutional Council stipulated that the decisions of the Commission (like organs of any other international organizations) may not contradict the Constitution of RK. In particular, it was emphasized that the decisions of any international organizations may not violate the sovereignty of RK, its territorial integrity or its form of government (see the resolution of the Constitutional Council of November 5, 2009, No. 6).

It should be noted, however, that any Member State that is not willing to accept a decision adopted by the Commission may refer the matter to the Interstate Council. The Interstate Council will then decide the matter by consensus. Furthermore, any Member State may address the Interstate Council with a request to revise any decision of the Commission.

V. FINDING THE LAW

The LNLA stipulates that all legislative acts of RK and international treaties to which Kazakhstan is a party must be published. It also requires the publication of all regulatory acts related to the rights, freedoms and obligations of citizens. The publication of such acts is a necessary precondition of their application (Article 30 I).

According to the Law, the following official journals are to be published both in the Kazakh and Russian languages in Kazakhstan: (1) the Parliament's Bulletin which appears twice a month and publishes the texts of all legislative acts and ratified international treaties of the Republic; (2) Corpus of Acts of the President and the Government; and (3) Corpus of Acts of the Central Executive and Other Central State Bodies (the latter two journals are supposed to be published on a weekly basis).

In addition, the Law of RK of March 30, 1995, No. 2155, "On the National Bank of the Republic of Kazakhstan," provides that regulatory acts of the National Bank of RK are to be published in its official heralds: *"Kazakstan Ulttyk Bankinin Khabarshysy"* (in Kazakh) and *"Vestnik Načionalnogo Banka RK"* (in Russian) (Article 4 of the Law). Also, the Law on International Treaties of the RK stipulates that all international treaties of RK are to be published in the *"Bulletin of International Treaties of RK"* both in Kazakh and in Russian (Article 24 LIT).

The official publication of regulatory acts is also done by periodicals that are entitled to do so by the Government of RK on a competitive basis. Usually this right is given to daily newspapers *"Yegemen Kazakhstan," "Zang Gazeti," "Kazakhstanskaya Pravda,"* and *"Yuridicheskaya Gazeta"* (the former two published in Kazakh, latter two in Russian).

However, at present the most convenient way to do legal research on the law of Kazakhstan is to refer to the leading commercial database of the country, *"Information System Paragraph."* Of particular interest is a major component of it called "*Yurist*," which contains not only a very extensive databank of regulatory acts adopted in Kazakhstan (both effective and no longer in force) but also, *inter alia*, drafts of law considered by the Parliament of RK, judicial decisions of both the Supreme Court and local courts, international treaties of RK, model document and contract forms, and numerous commentaries. Also to be mentioned is the internet portal *Zakon*, which offers the latest news on legal developments in the country and provides free access to many important regulatory acts and judicial decisions. Also, there is a growing tendency to get access to regulatory acts or judicial decisions through the respective state organs' websites. Last but not least, much legal information can be found on the Internet in general by typing a query in Kazakh or Russian into Google or other search engines.

Selected Bibliography

E. Abaydeldinov, *Соотношение международного и национального права Республики Казахстан* [*Correlation of International Law and National Law of Republic of Kazakhstan*] (Kazak Universiteti, Almaty, 2002) [in Russian].

M. Baimakhanov, *Избранные труды по теории государства и права* [*Selected Works in Theory of State and Law*] (VŠP Adilet, Almaty, 2003) [in Russian].

M. Baimakhanov (ed.), *Функции государства в условиях современного мира: на материалах независимого Казахстана* [*Functions of State in the Modern World: Experience of Independent Kazakhstan*] (KazGYuU, Almaty, 2005) [in Russian].

Z. Kembayev, *Legal Aspects of the Regional Integration Processes in the Post-Soviet Area* (Springer Verlag, Berlin, Heidelberg, 2009).

A. Nussberger, "Supranationales Recht jenseits des Ural" (2010) 56 *Osteuropa Recht* 113–128.G. Sapargaliyev & A. Ibrayeva, *Мемлекет және құқық теориясы* [*Theory of State and Law*] (Žeti Žargi, Almaty, 1998) [in Kazakh].

S. Zimanov, *Проблемы государственно-правовой науки и юридическое образование в Казахстане* [*Problems of State-and-Law Science and Higher Juridical Education in Kazakhstan*] (Arys, Almaty, 2009) [in Russian].

Chapter 3

Legal Education and Science in Kazakhstan*

Sergey Udartsev

I. LEGAL EDUCATION IN KAZAKHSTAN

A. Historical Background

In the 1930s–1940s, Kazakhstan suffered years of forced collectivization of the indigenous Kazakh population and became a destination for forced deportation of many ethnic groups of the former USSR. Having survived this colossal tragedy, Kazakhstan experienced rapid progress in its economic and cultural development. The Kazakh steppes were home to the horrific Semipalatinsk nuclear polygon, closed after the Soviet Union's dissolution, but at the same time, also to the Cosmodrome "Baikonur," from which the first spaceship was launched from the Earth.

In 1936, Kazakhstan received the status of a union republic and from then on the country began developing its system of higher legal education and science. In 1938 the Alma-Ata State Law Institute was created as the first institute of higher legal education in Kazakhstan. During the Great Patriotic War (1941–1945) Almaty became the seat of the USSR's leading law school—the First State Legal Institute of the People's Commissariat of Justice of the USSR, which was created on the dual authority of the Alma-Ata and the evacuated Moscow State

* Translated by Joseph Luke.

Zhenis Kembayev, *Introduction to the Law of Kazakhstan*, pp. 37–51.

Law Institutes. The activity of the joint Institute gave a powerful impetus to the further development of legal education and science in Kazakhstan.

In 1955, the Alma-Ata State Law Institute was reorganized into the Law Faculty of the S.M. Kirov Kazakh State University (KazGU) which is now Al-Farabi Kazakh National University (KazNU). The Faculty of Law of KazGU in the 1980s was one of the strongest in the USSR. During that time more than 3,000 law students studied law at KazGU at the government's expense (legal education, like all education in the USSR, was free for everyone). The language of instruction was Russian, and highly qualified professors and teachers worked in the Faculty, many of whom were well known beyond Kazakhstan. Other major scientific and educational institutions included the Institute of Philosophy and Law of the Academy of Sciences of the Kazakh SSR, the Faculty of Law of Karaganda State University and the Karaganda High School of the Ministry of Internal Affairs of the USSR.

Entrance into a faculty of law was competition based. Those who had worked three or more years or who had served in the Armed Forces were given preference. Among those who gained entry without serving in the Armed Forces were 20–40 candidates for every position. Five years of education was required for the specialty of "jurisprudence"; studying at night school or through correspondence school took six years. Upon graduation every student was assigned his/her position by a special state interagency commission. Those graduates who received recommendations from the academic council of the faculty (as a rule those who had earned only the highest grades during their studying) could sit for a supplemental examination and on a competitive basis enter into a three-year graduate program (*aspirantura*) to prepare a Candidate of Science Dissertation. Only a few scholars ever defended a Doctor of Science dissertation, which was usually written 10–20 years after they had defended their candidate's dissertation.[1] It was assumed that in the intervening time they had produced a significant volume of scholarly publications, including textbooks and monographs. Academics and academic teaching work was considered prestigious—a professor's salary was commensurate with that of a minister. Professors had a high level of supplementary additional state social benefits (including their own medical and sanitary health resort service). In an environment of relatively low prices, this allowed for a high standard of living. As a result, by the 1980s a number of distinctive academic schools of thought existed in Kazakhstan in various legal fields. Kazakhstani law students excelled at all-Union contests and intellectual Olympiads achieving many individual and team victories, in contests in overall legal disciplines as well as in individual disciplines.[2]

1. Editor's note: The Candidate of Science degree was a first post-graduate scientific degree in the USSR, which was awarded for original research that constituted a solution of a scientific problem. The Doctor of Science degree was a post-doctoral degree, which was awarded for a substantial and sustained contribution to scientific knowledge.
2. For more information see S. Udartsev, "Legal System and Legal Policy in Kazakhstan: Problems Related to the Post-Soviet Period" (2005) 1 *Kazakhstan Law for Foreigners* 12–23.

B. Development of Legal Education in Kazakhstan

1. From Unlimited Liberalization to a Search for the Optimal Order

After the fall of the USSR in December 1991, Kazakhstan became an independent state. In 1992, the development of private education commenced. Permission to create private institutions of higher learning (by a simplified process for receiving a license to open them) and a general desire of the population to give children a higher education led to the creation of numerous new institutions in the first half of the 1990s.

The opening of new private institutions (or new branches of existing institutions) *en masse* has a number of explanations: (a) the liberal policies of a young state; (b) the lack of experience in private education and its regulation; (c) the necessity of decreasing the state's expenditures in the social sphere; (d) the desire of many people to open their own institutions; (e) an increase in the demand to receive higher education after the Soviet period's strict competitive system for high-school graduates ended; (f) the lobbying of bureaucrats; (g) corruption, etc.

The professorial teaching staff at KazGU became the basis for the creation of numerous new institutions and their branches, both state and private, in other cities. For example, in 2002–2003 there were 177 educational institutions in Kazakhstan, of which 127 were private. In many of them, independent of their specialty, even in agrarian and technological colleges, law faculties were created. At the start of the twenty-first century, there were more than 100 institutions, faculties and branches in Kazakhstan that trained lawyers, with about 25 in Almaty alone. Often, multiple law faculties would be created in regional centers where, earlier, no law students had been trained and no law professors existed. In 2006, 91,000 law students were educated in Kazakhstan (20,000 of them in Almaty), overwhelmingly on a fee basis. Unfortunately, the quality of education in many private and regional state institutions was low, which resulted in a significant decrease in the prestige of legal education and science.

The Ministry of Education and Science of RK had to undertake a set of measures to bring order to the system of higher education, including legal education. In 2004 a State Interim Test was introduced for students, including law students, to be taken after their second year. Bad results on this test could trigger a state inspection of the institution's corresponding program ahead of the regularly scheduled one. Furthermore, great attention is given to the modernization of educational institutions' methodology and information technology.

In 2007–2008, in accordance with the new Law of RK of July 27, 2007, No. 319-III, "On Education," aimed at raising the quality of higher education, over 30 institutions, as well as the branches of every Kazakhstani educational institution were closed; many of these had been training grounds for large numbers of lawyers. Moreover, in recent years the Ministry established more stringent control and monitoring of the current licensing standards for educational institutions.

Still, at the beginning of 2011, 148 institutions were operating (nine national, two international, 32 state, 12 military, 93 private, including 16 corporations with state participation), which together boasted over 595,000 students. On average in the world there are 232 students per 10,000 people; in Kazakhstan this index was higher at around 422.5 students.[3] Thus, Kazakhstan must focus on increasing quality rather than quantity in higher education.

Because some institutions used price "dumping" in order to attract more students, the state introduced a minimum cost of education. Thus, in accordance with the Resolution of the Government of RK of March 4, 2011, No. 232, the amount of state grants for bachelor programs and the average cost of paid education was set for the 2010–2011 academic year at KZT 342,900 (about USD 2,340) for all state institutions except for the six national universities. These six universities are especially supported by the state, so a state grant in the national universities was set at KZT 635,800. The cost of education for a master's program for the 2010–2011 academic year was set at KZT 421,000 for all institutions and KZT 643,300 for the six national universities.

2. Transfer to the Bologna System

In 2002, the experimental transition to a system using credits in master's programs began. Starting from September 1, 2004 all educational institutions and law faculties began using credits and following the Bologna principles.[4] These principles provide numerous advantages, such as mutual recognition of diplomas as well as student and academic staff mobility.

After receiving a bachelor's degree and passing the entrance examinations for foreign language and specialized subjects, a student can continue his/her education by obtaining the next degree, a master's degree. Two programs operate at the master's degree level: (a) a one-year "field-oriented" program; and (b) a two-year "academic-pedagogical" program. The bachelor's and master's degrees are considered to be "academic" and awarded by the institution itself.

Those having achieved an "academic-pedagogical" master's degree have the right to participate in a competition to receive a state grant to study in a PhD program. For the selection of the best doctoral students, starting from 2011 a doctoral degree may only be received through a state grant given on a competitive basis. According to the Law of RK of February 18, 2011, No. 407-IV, "On Science," the PhD, like the earlier Candidate of Science and Doctor of Science degrees, is an important academic degree, and thus it is conferred only under the strict control of the Ministry of Education and Science.

---

3. See Ministry of Education and Science of RK, "Strategic Plan for 2011–2015 (Annex to the Resolution of the Government of RK of 19 February 2011, No. 160)" [in Russian] <http://www.educontrol.kz/ru/strategicheskii_plan_ mon_rk_na _ 2011_2015_gody> (July 12, 2011).
4. Editor's note: The Bologna Process was initiated in 1999 with the signing of the Bologna declaration. The main aim of the effort is to establish standards that will allow university degrees to be compared across Europe (and beyond).

The state program for the development of education from 2020 on foresees the creation of the Center for the Bologna Process and Academic Mobility, which will promote the introduction and development of international educational standards in Kazakhstan. Plans are to have two Kazakhstani educational institutions to be rated among the world's best universities—one by 2015 and another by 2020. By 2015, 50% of Kazakhstan's institutions must have independent national accreditation, by 2020, 65%. In addition, 20% of institutions must have their programs accredited by 2015, with that number rising to 30% by 2020.

The development program is aimed at ensuring academic freedom as provided by the Bologna Process framework. There will be a gradual increase in the percentage of disciplines a university may choose to offer according to its own needs. Also, the elective components will be increased within educational programs: in bachelor's programs up to 70%, in master's up to 80%, and in doctorate's up to 90%–95%. By 2011, 30 Kazakhstan institutions had already signed the Magna Charta Universitatum (Bologna) and that number is growing. They are actively cooperating with European institutions, including those that have also recently accepted the Bologna Process principles.

3. Legal Education of the Population

The curriculum of all of Kazakhstan's general university-level schools and colleges includes a basic course on the principles of law.[5] In addition, students of all higher education institutions not specializing in legal education take a course on "Foundations of Kazakhstan Law." In almost every city, secondary professional learning institutions called "legal colleges" operate. These colleges provide training in the legal specialties of attorney assistant, secretary to court agencies, etc. Their graduates receive diplomas of "lawyer with secondary professional education." As a rule, many of the graduates afterwards enter faculties of law or institutions of legal education for a shortened three-year program that is available in practically every educational institution. Although increasing attention is paid to the legal education of the population, the level of legal knowledge is still not very developed.

4. Legal Educational Institutions of Kazakhstan

Presently, under the classification category of "Law," the Ministry authorizes four types of bachelor's programs: (i) general "jurisprudence" programs; (ii) "international law" programs; (iii) a special program for "law-enforcement activity"; and (iv) a special program for "customs activity."

5. Moreover, certain schools also offer additional optional legal courses. Notably, in the late 1990s the "Soros-Kazakhstan" Foundation supported the development and publication of experimental textbooks on subjects such as "Law for All," "Democracy for All," etc. The Foundation has also provided support under programs such as "Legal Reform," "Education" and "Travel Grants."

Education in all of these majors is offered at the following institutions: Al-Farabi Kazakh National University; L.N. Gumilev Eurasian National University (ENU); Kazakh Humanitarian-Juridical University; E.A. Buketov Karaganda State University; Abay Kazakh National Pedagogical University, D.A. Kunaev University, Caspian Public University (which includes the formerly independent Academy "Adilet"); among others.

Also, there are institutions that specialize in the major of "law-enforcement," such as the Academy of the Ministry of the Internal Affairs of RK, the Academy of the Committee of the Criminal Executive System of the Ministry of Justice and the Academy of the Financial Police (the latter also trains specialists in "customs"). It should be noted that a special Court Academy (which is a unit of the Academy of State Service under the President of RK) offers master's programs providing special training for individuals who wish to work for the judicial system; and the newly established Law School of the Kazakhstan Institute of Management, Economics and Strategic Research (KIMEP) runs a Master's in International Commercial Law program that is taught in English.

In regular institutions, there are three education programs, each with a different duration: (a) a general four-year program after general secondary education; (b) a three-year program for people who have already obtained a degree from a legal college (i.e., a secondary professional learning institution); (c) a two-year program for people who have already obtained a university-level degree in another field.

Anyone has the right to enter into a law faculty if he/she has documents verifying that he/she: (a) obtained a general secondary education;[6] and (b) achieved the minimum passing score on the Unitary National Test (ENT) for entering a higher institution. In "non-civilian" institutions, which train lawyers for law-enforcement agencies, there are special admission rules including, for example, testing the physical condition of the applicant.

In the 12 years since the capital city was relocated, legal education has been actively developed in Astana. The Kazakh Humanitarian-Juridical University (KazGYuU), the country's leading legal education institution, is now located there. It has a significant number of students and four research centers. It regularly organizes many international conferences, forums, seminars, round tables, Olympiads, competitions, etc. They are sponsored not only by the university itself but also by different state agencies as well as international and domestic organizations. It is a training center in the area of legal education, developing drafts for state educational standards and model syllabi for the legal disciplines. Moreover, with the goal of encouraging creative approaches to resolving legal issues and scientific competitiveness, KazGYuU has held national contests to nominate the "Professor of the Year," "Docent of the Year," "Teacher of the Year" and "Textbook of the Year" since 2005.

KazGYuU, along with the Faculty of Law of Al-Farabi KazNU and the Faculty of Law of L.N. Gumilev ENU (Astana) constitutes a triumvirate of leaders

6. Those persons whose education documents were issued abroad must have them nostrified.

among law schools of Kazakhstan. In this regard, it should also be noted that KIMEP, which is consistently at or near the top of national ratings of institutions of higher learning,[7] has started to develop its own School of Law in recent years. In 2008, it launched the new master's program (see above), with a new bachelor's program following in 2011. Taking KIMEP's tradition into account, one can expect it to soon achieve a very high level in the education of lawyers, with the active participation of foreign experts.

5. State Support of Legal Education

Much has been done to develop the legal education system: (a) state financing was increased;[8] (b) the Unitary National Test was introduced; (c) the President's "Bolashak" program, which provides grants for studying abroad for 3,000 students annually, was founded; and (d) since 2005 annual competitions have been organized by the Ministry of Education and Science, through which 200 grants have been awarded annually to the best Kazakhstani teachers (more than KZT 2 million each).

After a deep economic crisis in the 1990s, the state attempted to encourage those fields that suffered the most during that period and, in particular, now supports education in the pedagogical, technical, medical and agrarian fields; legal education enjoys much less state support. Currently, an overwhelming percentage of students in law programs study on a fee basis. The languages of instruction are Russian and Kazakh, with an ever-growing proportion of students studying in the latter. Thus, in accordance with the decision of the Ministry of Education and Science, 220 educational grants (out of 35,425 provided by the state, or 0.62%) for bachelor's in law programs were allocated for the academic year 2010–2011, with 60% provided for programs in Kazakh. The state also supports teaching in Kazakh and has encouraged a large amount of work on methodology and the preparation of textbooks. However, this activity still needs significant additional efforts.

Moreover, according to the Resolution of the Government of RK of March 4, 2011, No. 232, 80 grants were designated for "academic-pedagogical" and 100 for "field-oriented" master's degrees in law for the 2010–2011 academic year. Furthermore, additional grants were given for studying towards a master's degree in law enforcement. Thus, 30 grants were designated for the Almaty Academy of the Ministry of Internal Affairs; 20 grants for the Karaganda Academy of the Ministry of Internal Affairs; 35 for the Academy of the Financial Police; and 10

7. Since 2005 the Ministry of Education and Science composes ratings on institutions of higher learning in Kazakhstan. In the category of humanities and economics (law belongs to that group) in 2005, first place was held by the Law Academy "Adilet"; in 2006 and 2007 by KIMEP, with KazGYuU in second place; in 2008 by KazGYuU; and in 2009, 2010 again by KIMEP.
8. For example, in 2009, despite the financial crisis, more than 11,000 additional state educational grants were provided for students who have earned top marks, etc.

for the Academy of the Committee of the Criminal Executive System of the Ministry of Justice.

Until recently a significant number of both bachelor's and master's students studied abroad through the Bolashak program (mostly in Russia, the United States, Germany, the United Kingdom and China). However, in 2010 Nazarbayev University (NU) was founded in Astana. Many of NU's professors come from leading foreign universities; its language of instruction is English, and the state has accorded it a "special status." Therefore, according to the Kazakhstani government, NU provides the possibility of earning a Western-quality bachelor's degree while remaining in Kazakhstan, and so the presidential grants of the Bolashak program are now awarded only to master's and doctorate students or for certain academic projects.

6. Problems in Legal Education

Despite many achievements, the system of higher education experiences many problems associated with a weak IT base, insufficient numbers of highly qualified law teachers and inadequate learning resources (e.g., libraries). Moreover, educational institutions are still subject to government bureaucratic control regardless of their level of development. However, the recent establishment of the financially powerful Nazarbayev University, which is becoming a leader in Kazakhstani higher education and has received complete autonomy, triggered attempts to elaborate the next generation of government standards providing more academic freedom for institutions of higher learning.

The absence of an effective stimulus for attracting additional Kazakhstani and foreign investments to institutions of higher learning can also be added to the list of the legal education system's problems. Moreover, the constitutional provision on the equality of state-owned and private institutions is not consistently implemented with respect to the financing of science, public social support of teachers and providing scientific grants for academics.

Furthermore, accreditation issues must still be resolved. In one analytic report, it was observed that the educational system of Kazakhstan is dominated by "institutional licensing, attestation and accreditation. The center of attention is the institution as a total organism. This type of control, which enables the identification of the strongest institutions as a whole (in absolute terms), turns out to be less effective with respect to evaluation of each of the numerous individual majors . . . [As a result,] institutions are divided into "good" and "bad," with the presumption that in "good" institutions everything is good, which often turns out to be an error. For real quality control it is necessary . . . to check every program that an institution has."[9] To be mentioned also is the often merely formal character of the quality control.

---

9. S. Udartsev, "Национальная система оццнки качества высшего образования" ["National System of Quality Evaluation of Higher Education System"], in *Prikladnye Issledovaniya v Oblasti Obrazavatel'noy Politiki* (Soros-Kazakhstan, Almaty, 2002) [in Russian]; See also

Yet another challenge is that insufficient work is done on the continuing education of teachers. In some institutions, it is practically absent, especially in weak, private ones. In many institutions, there is relatively low pay, especially for beginning teachers. This prevents attracting talented youth to the teaching profession. One can see the statistical aging of the teaching and academic profession: presently, the percentage of Doctor of Science degree holders who are over 60 is 47.4% while the percentage of Candidates of Science degree holders who are over 40 is 70%; the average age of an academic is around 55 years old.[10]

Academic mobility is still not widespread among law institutions and is only done by individual students, as a rule, taking part in foreign exchange programs. The leadership in many institutions is not interested in organizing such projects for students and discourages the development of mobility programs, fearing the loss of students as sources of income. Even though the Association of Higher Education Institutions was created, it is not yet effectively operating. In addition, academic mobility is also restrained by the bureaucratic system of state grants. These grants are given for studying in specific institutions, and the Ministry has not yet elaborated a flexible system ensuring the mobility of grant holders.

7. Perspectives on the Development of Legal Education

Regardless of the numerous above-mentioned problems, the training of lawyers is gradually increasing in quality. More attention is devoted to teaching important practical knowledge and skills and introducing more new elective courses for student choice. In light of increasing globalization, the use of international techniques in teaching law is becoming more widespread and systematic. Gradually, inter-institutional cooperation is developing in recognition of the fact that even for well-established institutions, it is preferable to follow a certain specialization, to establish mutually beneficial cooperative links with other institutions and to prevent unfair competition.

On December 7, 2010 the President of RK issued a Decree approving "The State Program of Educational Development of the Republic of Kazakhstan for 2011–2020." Its goals are to develop human capital by making quality education more accessible and to increase the competitiveness of Kazakhstan's education system in order to achieve sustainable economic growth and social prosperity. In particular it foresees a deeper introduction of the Bologna Process principles and, in part, the development of academic freedom. Issues of legal education are also touched upon in "Conceptions of the Legal Policy of RK for the period 2010 to

M. Narikbayev & S. Udartsev, "Система образования Казахстана: проблемы, резервы развития, задачи на завтра" ["Educational System of Kazakhstan: Problems, Reserves of Development and Tasks for Tomorrow"] (2009) 8 *Zanger. Vestnik Prava RK* 9-20.

10. See Ministry of Education and Science of RK, "Strategic Plan for 2011–2015 (Annex to the Resolution of the Government of RK of 19 February 2011, No. 160)" [in Russian] <http://www.educontrol.kz/ru/strategicheskii_plan_ mon_rk_na _ 2011_2015_gody> (July 12, 2011).

2020" established by the Decree of the President of RK of August 24, 2009. In part this states:

> Society and state need a new type of lawyer, patriotically attuned and oriented to the protection of human rights and freedoms, to the interests of society and the state.... It is expedient to set down the path of consolidating the possibilities of the state for deciding the problems of educating a lawyer who can handle different issues under contemporary circumstances. Such an approach allows RK to avoid wasting state resources and increase the quality of a lawyer's education.

II. LEGAL EDUCATION IN KAZAKHSTAN

A. Historical Background

Before 1917, only one Kazakh (Zhakyp Akpayev) had ever defended his master's thesis in law (doing so at St. Petersburg University). The first major step towards the development of legal science coincided with creation of the Alma-Ata State Law Institute in 1938. Another significant impetus was given by the activity of the First State Legal Institute of the People's Commissariat of Justice of the USSR in Alma-Ata during World War II. In 1942, on the initiative of the evacuated Moscow scholars, a section for the study of the history of the state and law of Kazakhstan was organized. In 1945 a Department of Law was founded in Kazakhstan's branch of the Academy of Sciences of the USSR (in 1955, it became the Department of Philosophy and Law and in 1958 the Institute of Philosophy and Law of the Academy of Sciences of the Kazakh SSR), with a famous Kazakh scholar T.M. Kulteleyev as its first head.

The first generation of Kazakhstani law professors and scholars completed their education and initially worked in various institutions of the USSR, from which they were then sent to work in Alma-Ata (the most prominent of them included T. Kulteleyev, L. Dyukov, S. Bulatov and S. Fuchs). In 1948 in Moscow the first doctoral dissertation on the law of Kazakhstan was defended by Fuchs, who provided a profound analysis of the historical development of Kazakh legal customs.

The second generation of academic lawyers received, as a rule, their education in Kazakhstan, although Candidate and Doctor of Science dissertations were still defended in Moscow, Leningrad, Saratov and other cities. Thus, in 1961, S. Zimanov became the first ethnic Kazakh lawyer, who defended his Doctor of Science dissertation (doing so at the Institute of State and Law of the Academy of Sciences of the USSR in Moscow). In 1967 Prof. Zimanov also became the first full member of the Academy of Sciences of the KazSSR in jurisprudence (and in 2010 his complete works were published in 10 volumes).

Starting from 1970s preparation of doctoral dissertations and their defense took place more and more frequently in Alma-Ata, and eventually in Karaganda as well. Alma-Ata became one of the USSR's leading centers of legal sciences, along with Moscow, Leningrad, Kiev, Sverdlovsk, Saratov and Kharkov. Publications by Kazakhstani scholars included the legal series *Scholars' Works* and *Scientific Notes* of KazGU, the anthologies *Juridical Sciences* and *Legal Science of Kazakhstan*, the journals *Bulletin of the Academy of Sciences KazSSR* and *Proceedings of the Academy of Sciences KazSSR: Series on Social Sciences*. Also, many important monographs and textbooks were published on various legal topics, in particular on Kazakhstan's history of state and law (especially by S. Zimanov, S. Sartayev); theory of state and law (M. Baymakhanov); constitutional law (G. Sapargaliev, K. Kotov); civil law (Y. Basin, M. Suleimenov, A. Didenko); and criminal law (G. Polenov, G. Baimurzin). Many legal scholars took part in the preparation of both Union- and Republican-level legislation. Unfortunately, much of what they wanted to introduce was not possible to incorporate into the law as the final decision remained with the Communist Party apparatus. Nevertheless, the role of Kazakhstani legal scholars, especially in the less politicized branches of law such as civil, criminal, environmental, procedural and labor law, was rather large and did not come down to just the affirmation of a decision that had already been made.[11]

B. Development of Legal Science in Independent Kazakhstan

1. The Search for New Models of Cooperation between State and Science

In 1991 the Academy of Sciences of the Kazakh SSR became the National Academy of Sciences of the Republic of Kazakhstan (NASRK), which still remained the most authoritative academy (even though a number of other scholarly associations emerged such as the National Academy of Natural Sciences, the Academy of Social Sciences, the Academy of Legal Sciences, etc.).

However, when Kazakhstan took the step of integrating science and higher education in the year 2000, the Institute of State and Law of NASRK was incorporated into KazGYuU's structure as one of its departments. Subsequently, NASRK itself was reorganized into an independent association of scholars. In doing so, scientific research financing was changed from permanent state financing (implying permanent staff) to competitive grant financing (meaning the existence of provisional scholar groups). On the one hand, this move enabled the legal science to be uncoupled from ideology and be separated from the state. It also decreased the administrative interference in academic research and introduced a new progressive system of forming academic elite. On the other hand, this move resulted in a decrease in state support, weakening (hopefully temporarily) research

11. For more information see S. Tlepina, "Эволюция государственно-правовой науки в Казахстане (1930–1991 гг.)" [*Evolution of State-and-Law Science in Kazakhstan 1930–1991*] (KazGYuU, Almaty, 2005) [in Russian].

infrastructure and lowering the prestige of academics. Still, the newly adopted Law of RK of February 18, 2011, No. 407-IV, "On Science" emphasizes grants and the competitive financing of science, including the participation of foreign experts, even more.

It is evident that the activity of state organs constantly demands the further development of applied and fundamental scientific research. Accordingly, it is essential to have a system of large scientific institutes for researching national, comparative and international law. Thus, it is necessary to combine the existing small departmental research units into more effective research institutes that can develop quality intellectual work. Therefore, one can predict that more powerful state and private legal research institutes will be created in the near future to help solve applied and theoretical legal problems.

2. Development of Applied and Independent Research

Important institutional pillars of modern legal science in Kazakhstan are the Institute of State and Law of KazGYuU; the Research Institute of Private Law of KazGYuU; the Research Institute of Civil Law; and the Institute of State and Law of Al-Farabi KazNU.

In the last decades important research activities were conducted in many areas of Kazakhstani legal system. Numerous collective and individual monographic studies were published analyzing the development of the institutions of civil society and the multi-party political system; the evolution of the form of government; the strengthening of parliament's status; the interaction of Kazakhstan with the evolving systems of the world's economy and politics; the implementation of international law standards in national legislation; and the relationship of private and public law. In addition, issues such as improving the activity of courts and law-enforcement agencies; decreasing bureaucratic barriers for business development; promoting an economy of innovation; and defending intellectual property were examined. Much work continues to be done in the areas of legal regulation of human rights and freedoms; private property; subsoil use; foreign investment; and corporate social responsibility. Other areas of attention for law scholars include issues of humanizing criminal punishment, the introduction of criminal responsibility for juridical persons, the fight against corruption and organized crime, the creation of the necessary circumstances for equality of the parties in criminal proceedings, environmental issues, etc.

These scientific works facilitate gradual improvements in the effectiveness of legal regulation and public administration, the resolution of potential social conflicts, the creation of favorable circumstances for the development of an innovative economy, the promotion of the formation of a rule-of-law and democratic state and the protection of national interests in the face of globalization.

When Kazakhstan became independent, its legal publishing industry initially suffered a deep crisis. Even as late as 1995 any attempt to find Kazakhstani legal books could end in frustration as, apart from printed copies of regulatory acts and small runs of instructional aides produced by educational institutions, there was very little Kazakhstan-produced literature. Now there are specialized legal publishers, such as *Zheti Zhargy* (Almaty), which publishes works on law for academics and practicing lawyers. However, the special legal book market still requires development. Also, Kazakhstan has a number of scientific legal journals. The more important ones are: *Jurist* (which boasts an advanced web-site); *Pravo i Gosudarstvo* (Law and State) (published by KazGYuU); *Legal Reform in Kazakhstan*; Scientific Proceedings of the Law Academy *Adilet*; Bulletin of L.N. Gumilev ENU; Bulletin of Al-Farabi KazNU; *Zanger*; *Preduprezhdenie Prestupnosti* (Prevention of Criminality); Bulletin of E.A. Buketov Karaganda State University; *Femida*; etc.

Every year dozens of national and international academic conferences and "round tables" on legal issues are held. To be noted are the traditional annual "Civil Law Reading" conferences, conducted by the Research Institute of Private Law of KazGYuU and an "August Reading" on constitutional law developments (held on the eve of Kazakhstan's "Constitution Day") organized by the Constitutional Council of RK.

Since independence many academic lawyers have been in high demand and several of them have taken high-level government positions (such as Profs. Baymakhanov, Narikbayev, Shaykenov, Akuyev, Rogov and others). They have actively participated in preparing legislation as members of consultative groups, expert government councils and commissions under various government agencies. Their scientific commentaries on codes and laws have been a valued contribution to the further development of the legal system. Many academic lawyers who are involved with providing expertise on elaborating drafts of regulatory legal acts work with the following institutions: (a) the Institute of Legislation of RK (formerly under the Ministry of Justice, now an independent state institution); (b) the Institute of Scientific Evaluation and Analysis of KazGYuU; (c) the Scientific Institute of L.N. Gumilev ENU; and (d) the Institute of State and Law of Al-Farabi KazNU, which make a significant contribution to the improvement of the legislative process.[12]

3. Reforming the System of Attestation of Academic Staff

Before December 2010, the defense of doctoral and candidate dissertations were conducted before dissertation councils that existed in various faculties and institutes and were approved by the Supreme Attestation Committee under the Ministry or Education and Science. Since 1993 over 1,500 Doctoral and Candidate of Science Dissertations on legal science (in Russian and increasingly in Kazakh) were registered. The anthologies of these dissertations give a sufficient understanding of

12. Thus, from 2005 to 2011 the Institute of Scientific Evaluation and Analysis of KazGYuU produced 3,580 expert opinions on general legal matters. In 2010 the Institute of Legislation of RK gave legal opinions on 29 state programs and 43 drafts of laws. See Z. Busurmanov "Право в эпоху глобализаЦии" ["Law in the Age of Globalization"] <http://www.izrk.kz> (June 30, 2011).

the broad spectrum of academic interests and research of Kazakhstan's legal scholars.[13]

Kazakhstan has now decided to stop conferring the degrees of Candidate of Sciences and Doctor of Sciences and, consequently, now awards the degrees of Master's, PhD and discipline-based doctorates.[14] The new system of graduate-level education has certain advantages over the old one: (a) a broader educational program; (b) mandatory study abroad; (c) a foreign co-supervisor for the dissertation; and (d) requirements to publish the results of the research in leading foreign publications. However, certain weaknesses have been found, most notably that there is a lower level of quality of doctoral dissertations due to the relative lack of time given to writing the doctoral dissertation in comparison with even the candidate's dissertation, not to mention doctor's dissertation, which were completed under the earlier academic system.

A new generation of academics is being prepared. The Ministry of Education and Science annually holds national competitions for student academic work on jurisprudence. With the purpose of developing student scholarship, the leading institutions organize student conferences and publish anthologies of student research. Since 2010, Master's and PhD students have been required to publish a short summary (*avtoreferat*) of their dissertations describing their main research results before defending their thesis (this was always done with respect to Candidate and Doctor of Science Dissertations). The summaries of dissertations include abstracts in English and Kazakh or Russian and are published on the websites of the institutions where the defense takes place.

Selected Bibliography

G. Sapargaliyev, A. Mindagulov & A. Salimgerey (eds.), *Сборник тем кандидатских и докторских диссертаций за 1993–2001 гг. по юридическим наукам* [*Collection of Topics of Candidate and Doctoral Dissertations 1993–2001*] (KazGYuA, Almaty, 2001) [in Russian].

S. Udartsev, "Legal System and Legal Policy in Kazakhstan: Problems Related to the Post-Soviet Period" (2005) 1 *Kazakhstan Law for Foreigners* 12–23.

S. Tlepina, *Эволюция государственно-правовой науки в Казахстане (1930–1991 гг.)* [*Evolution of State-and-Law Science in Kazakhstan 1930–1991*] (KazGYuU, Almaty, 2005) [in Russian].

M. Narikbayev & S. Udartsev, "Система образования Казахстана: проблемы, резервы развития, задачи на завтра" ['Educational System of Kazakhstan:

13. See G. Sapargaliyev, A. Mindagulov & A. Salimgerey (eds.), Сборник тем кандидатских и докторских диссертаций за 1993–2001 гг. по юридическим наукам [*Collection of Topics of Candidate and Doctoral Dissertations 1993–2001*] (KazGYuA, Almaty, 2001) [in Russian].
14. It is important to note that Kazakhstan's legislation establishes additional salary for those who hold the academic degrees of Candidate and Doctor of Sciences. At the present time in state educational institutions the additional salary for PhD and discipline-based doctorates are of the same amount as for those who have Candidate or Doctor of Sciences degrees.

Problems, Reserves of Development and Tasks for Tomorrow'] (2009) 8 *Zanger Vestnik Prava RK* 9–20 [in Russian].

S. Udartsev, *Famous Professor Sultan S. Sartayev (in Russian, Kazakh, Kyrgyz, English, German, Turkish and Chinese)* (Däuir, Almaty, 2010).

S. Udartsev, *Учителя и коллеги* [*Teachers and Colleagues*] (Raritet, Almaty, 2011).

Chapter 4
Constitutional Law

Zhenis Kembayev

I. FUNDAMENTALS OF THE CONSTITUTIONAL STRUCTURE OF REPUBLIC OF KAZAKHSTAN

The Constitution of 1995 proclaimed the RK to be a "democratic ... [and] rule-of-law ... state whose highest values are an individual, his life, rights and freedoms" (Article 1 I).[1] In addition, however, the Constitution stipulated the following "fundamental principles of the state's activity": (a) public concord; (b) political stability; (c) economic development for the benefit of the entire nation; (d) Kazakhstani patriotism and only then (e) resolution of important issues of the state affairs by democratic methods (Article 1 II). Thus, the Constitution fully reflected President Nazarbayev's vision of Kazakhstan's development: "economy first, then politics" and "democracy is not the beginning of [Kazakhstan's] path, it is the end."

All other basic tenets of Kazakhstan's constitutional structure (which include: (a) a strong presidential form of government; (b) a centralized unitary state;[2] (c) a

1. Unless otherwise stated, all citations in this chapter refer to the Constitution of RK of August 30, 1995.
2. As a unitary state, Kazakhstan is composed of administrative-territorial units with fully unified legal regimes. It consists of 14 regions (oblasts) and two cities (Astana and Almaty) with special "republican" status. These 16 first-level administrative units are subdivided into (as calculated by the author) 168 districts (rayons). Also it should be mentioned that on December 23, 1995, Kazakhstan and Russia entered into an agreement whereby Russia would lease the city of

Zhenis Kembayev, *Introduction to the Law of Kazakhstan*, pp. 53–71.

social state; and (d) a secular state) are basically designed to serve the "fundamental principles of the state's activity" exactly in the order of priority indicated above. The major aim of this combination of a strong presidency, a centralized government and a social state is obviously to ensure public harmony and political stability in a multi-ethnic and multi-confessional country that had no tradition of democracy.

It should also be noted that even though Kazakhs and other Muslim ethnicities living in Kazakhstan have made efforts to revitalize their Islamic traditions, Kazakhstan fully committed itself to the principle of secularism and did not assign a special status to Islam. There is not a single reference to God in the Constitution, justified again by the need to maintain public harmony and avoid any confrontation between major religious groups, Muslims and Orthodox Christians. The same rationale is clearly visible in the language policy of Kazakhstan, according to which Kazakh is considered the state language but Russian is also given official status and allowed to be used on equal grounds in state institutions (Article VII).

II. LEGAL STATUS OF INDIVIDUALS

The Constitution of 1995 proclaims that the people of Kazakhstan consider themselves "a peace-loving and civil society, dedicated to the ideals of freedom, equality and concord" (the Preamble) and that the highest values of the RK are an individual, his life, rights and freedoms (Article 1 I). Consequently, it provides an extensive list of personal, political, economic, social and cultural rights and freedoms of individuals in Kazakhstan. Also, it should be noted that on December 20, 1991 (almost immediately after it acquired independence) Kazakhstan adopted a liberal law on the citizenship, which declared eligible for citizenship all people who had been permanently residing in the territory of the country at the moment the law came into effect.

For the first time in Kazakhstan's history, the Constitution of 1995 allowed the private ownership of land (though within the limits established by legislation), a step that may be considered a breakthrough on the path from a socialist society to a market-oriented economy. Furthermore, the Constitution does not contain the right to labor, the "holy" and rigorously observed right of the socialist times, providing only for the right of freedom of labor.

Also, unlike the Constitution of 1993, the current fundamental law does not include the so-called guarantee of the essential content of constitutional rights and freedoms and incorporates two significant reservation rules: (1) "obligation to desist" (Exercise of a citizen's human rights and freedoms must not violate rights and freedoms of other persons or infringe on the constitutional system and public morals) (Article 12 V); and (2) "justification to intervene" (Rights and freedoms of

---

Baykonur and the adjacent area enclosing space launch facilities for a period of 20 years. On January 9, 2004, a new agreement extended the lease to 2050.

an individual and citizen may be limited . . . to the extent necessary for protection of the constitutional system, defense of the public order, human rights and freedoms, and health and morality of the population) (Article 39 I).

Another important limitation (which is actually a unique feature of this Constitution) stipulated that "any actions capable of upsetting interethnic harmony shall be deemed unconstitutional" (Article 39 II). Though "interethnic concord" is without a doubt essential in a multi-ethnic state like Kazakhstan, the term itself is of a very vague and indistinct nature and potentially permits the government to take action against its critics in a wide-ranging variety of cases.

In addition, a significant disadvantage compared to the Constitution of 1993 was the elimination of provisions guaranteeing the judicial protection of constitutional rights and freedoms and providing for the possibility of the submission of constitutional complaints by individuals (which obviously contradicts the appreciation of human rights and freedoms in the Preamble and Article 1 of the Constitution).

III. STRONG PRESIDENCY: KAZAKHSTANI MODEL

A. GENERALLY

The Constitution of 1995 explicitly provides that Kazakhstan is a "state with a presidential form of government" (Article 2 I). However, in contrast to its American and French counterparts, Kazakhstan's presidency may be described as a super-presidential one, a fact that can easily be seen by looking at the Kazakh leader's diverse roles as: (1) the head of state representing Kazakhstan both within the country and in international relations (Article 40 I); (2) the highest official determining the primary course of domestic and foreign policy in the RK (Article 40 I); (3) the arbiter ensuring concerted functioning of all branches of state power (Article 40 III); (4) "the guarantor of rights and freedoms of individuals" and the "symbol and guarantor of the unity of the people and the state power" ensuring responsibility of the state institutions before the people (Article 40 II); and (5) the guarantor of the inviolability of the Constitution, exclusively entitled to initiate any amendments or additions to the Constitution (Article 40 II). In performing his last-mentioned task, the President may choose whether he pursues the constitutional changes through Parliament, which would have to ratify them by a three-fourths majority in both chambers, or through conducting a nationwide referendum, which can be endorsed only by the President (Articles 53 I, 62 III, 44 X). In addition, the President is guaranteed by the Constitution full immunity from prosecution for all potential criminal acts, except high treason (Article 46).[3]

3. The constitutional provisions on the legal status of the President are supplemented by the Constitutional Law of RK of December 26, 1995, No. 2733, "On the President of the Republic of Kazakhstan."

Additionally, on July 20, 2000 a Constitutional Law was adopted that bestowed on Nazarbayev the status of "the First President" assuring his full inviolability and providing him significant privileges and authority even after he retires from the presidential office (in particular, he will remain Chairperson of the Assembly of Peoples of Kazakhstan and will become a member of the Constitutional Council and of the Security Council).

As for the more recent events, on May 13, 2010 the Parliament adopted a Constitutional Law granting the title of the *Elbasy* (the leader of the nation) to the incumbent President. The new law reiterated his life-long immunity and provided additional exemptions to him. In particular, the private property of both the President and his family members, their premises, banking accounts, means of transportation and communication, archives and documents will be immune, while "damage of the President's images" and "distortion of the President's biography" will constitute a criminal offense.

Although the President refused to sign the Constitutional Law on the Leader of the Nation in an open letter to the nation (saying that its main provisions were already stated in the Constitution), Nazarbayev did not return it to the Parliament (i. e., he did not formally use his right of veto). According to the Kazakhstani legislation (Constitutional Law of RK of October 16, 1995, No. 2529, "On the Parliament and the Status of its Deputies," Article 19 II, III), since the legislative act was neither signed nor vetoed by the President, it entered into force without the President's signature one month after its submission. Thus, on the eve of his 70th birthday Nazarbayev acquired the title of *Elbasy*, a position that is clearly indicative of the high degree of centralization of political power in the hands of the President.

B. Elections and Term of Office

The President is elected by universal, equal and direct suffrage under a secret ballot by citizens of legal age. A candidate who receives more than 50% of the votes is deemed elected; if none of the candidates receives the above number of votes, a second round of elections is held between the two most successful candidates.

Originally, the Constitution provided that the President is to be elected for a five-year term, and that the same person may not be elected more than two times in a row; further it was stipulated that a person eligible for the office of the President must be a natural-born citizen who has a perfect command of the state (i.e., Kazakh) language, has lived in Kazakhstan for not less than 15 years and is not younger than 35, nor older than 65.

However, from the very beginning, it was clear that these requirements would not suit the long-term interests of Nazarbayev (who was born in 1940). The course of events was facilitated by the Russian financial crisis of August 1998 which caused inflation to increase and currencies to depreciate in many post-Soviet countries (the peak of the crisis for Kazakhstan was predicted to be the year 1999). On October 7, 1998, the Parliament, at the time fully controlled by the supporters of Nazarbayev, adopted constitutional amendments which increased the term of presidential office to seven years, raised the lower age limit for candidates to 40 years and eliminated the upper age limit. On the next day, the "Mazhilis" (lower house of Parliament) announced the next presidential election to be held in three months. Thus, the election, originally scheduled for 2000, was moved up by more than a year, enabling Nazarbayev to avoid the vagueness and uncertainty of the upcoming critical year and giving opposition candidates little time to prepare.

In the elections of January 10, 1999, which were once again criticized by international observers for failing to meet democratic standards (especially because Nazarbayev's strongest potential challenger, former Prime Minister Kazhegeldin, was refused registration as a candidate on procedural grounds), Nazarbayev was re-elected to another seven-year term, receiving the votes of almost 80% of the electorate.

Another constitutional rule stipulating that regular elections of the President must be held on the first Sunday of December became subject to intense scrutiny in 2005. Since the President's seven-year mandate was supposed to terminate only in January 2006, a number of Nazarbayev's supporters demanded that the next elections would be conducted in December 2006. In this situation the Mazhilis approached the Constitutional Council with the request to give official interpretation of the respective constitutional provisions. On August 19, 2005, the Constitutional Council issued a resolution that the elections must take place on the first Sunday of December of 2005 substantiating its decision by the fact that otherwise the President would govern the country for 11 months without proper legitimation. On December 4, 2005, Nazarbayev was re-elected for a new seven-year term in a landslide victory. The central electoral commission announced that he had won over 90% of the vote with the turnout of nearly 77%.

The obvious discrepancy as to the number of terms provided by the Constitution had been already resolved by the Constitutional Council on June 20, 2000, in a resolution stating that "taking into account . . . that the adoption of the Constitution of 1995 profoundly changed the constitutional system . . . the first term of office of the President . . . must be counted from the moment of his official entrance upon the duties, i.e., 20 January 1999."

The final point at this issue was put to rest by the most recent constitutional amendments introduced on May 21, 2007. The newest version of the Constitution provides that: "One and the same person may not be elected as the President more than two times in a row. The present limitation shall not apply to the First President of RK" (Article 42 V).

As for the most recent events, on December 23, 2010 a public initiative group was created with the aim of setting up a referendum on extending Nazarbayev's term of office until 2020 (instead of conducting presidential elections scheduled for 2012). On December 27, 2010 the group was registered by the central electoral commission, and very soon it was said to have gathered more than 5 million signatures (amounting to 55% of eligible voters, while the law requires 200,000 in order to forward a request to the President to hold a referendum). On January 6, Kazakhstan's Parliament passed a constitutional amendment in favor of a referendum to extend the rule of Nazarbayev until 2020, bypassing the 2012 election. Nazarbayev vetoed the amendment, but on January 14 the Parliament unanimously overrode the President's veto. Still on January 17, the President referred the amendments to the Constitutional Council which on January 31 declared the proposed referendum unlawful. Although the President has the right to veto a Constitutional Council's decision, he announced that he would comply with it and renounce the proposed referendum. At the same time, he proposed holding a pre-term presidential election. As a result of the elections which were held on April 3, 2011, Nazarbayev was re-elected for another seven-year term with over 95% of the votes against three nominal candidates.

C. President and the Executive

Although the Constitution creates a formally dual executive branch that includes, along with the President, the Government as a separate organ "implementing the executive power of RK" (Article 64 I), the President is the dominant figure and fully controls the executive branch.

The Government "in its entire activity" is responsible to the President and thus has a purely administrative character. The President may preside at the meetings of the Government on especially important issues and terminate or suspend the effect of the Government's actions (as well as those of local executive bodies). He may also, at any time, and at his own discretion, remove the Prime Minister (which would also denote the termination of the powers of the entire Government) or any other member of Government from office (Article 44 III). Furthermore, the Constitution defines the Government as a "corporate organ," which means that those members who do not agree with the policy pursued by the Government, as actually determined by the President, must resign or face removal from office (Article 68 I). It is also very telling that the members of the Government must take an oath not only to the people but also to the President (Article 65 III).

D. Presidential Powers in Foreign and Defense Policies

In his capacities as the head of state and the highest official, the President represents Kazakhstan in international relations and directs foreign policy. Under the current Constitution, the President conducts negotiations and signs international treaties of the Republic, signs ratification instruments and accepts credentials and letters of recall of diplomats accredited to Kazakhstan. He also appoints and recalls heads of diplomatic representative offices of RK to foreign states and international organizations (Article 44 VI, XI).

The President is the Commander-in-Chief of the Armed Forces of RK. He appoints and dismisses the high command of the Armed Forces. Also, the President commands the Republican Guard and the (even more elite) Presidential Guard, which are directly subordinate to him. In the event of a serious and immediate threat to the democratic institutions, independence, territorial integrity and political stability of the Republic and security of its citizens, the President may take special measures and declare a state of emergency after consultations with the Prime Minister and the Chairpersons of the Parliament's chambers. In the case of aggression against the Republic or immediate external threat to its security, the President may impose martial law on the entire territory of the Republic or, in particular areas, declare a partial or total mobilization and immediately inform the Parliament, which has the final say on issues of war and peace (Article 44).

E. Consultative Bodies under the President

The President is assisted in exercising his considerable powers by a very influential state body, the Administration of the President, which is directly subordinate to him.[4] The Administration includes the Head of the Administration and his deputies, the Secretary of the Security Council, the Head of the Highest Judicial Council, presidential aides and advisers, the Head of the Chancellery of the President and other staff. The primary purpose of the Administration is to provide credible and well-timed informational, analytical, legal, protocol and other support of the activities of the President.

Another consultative body which is created by the President is the Security Council.[5] The Council's membership includes the Chairperson of the Mazhilis, the Chairperson of the Senate, the Director of the Foreign Intelligence Service *Syrbar*, the Minister of Internal Affairs and the First Deputy Minister of Defense. The main functions of this organ consist of analyzing issues of national security and submitting corresponding proposals and recommendations to the President.

An important role in Kazakhstan's constitutional system is played by the Assembly of the People,[6] an institution created by the President with the major aim of "providing interethnic concord in the process of the formation of a common civil identity and competitive nation in Kazakhstan" (Article 3 of the Law on the Assembly). As the First President of the country, Nazarbayev is entitled to be the life-long Chair of the Assembly. The Assembly consists of regional assemblies and a central body. The membership of both the regional assemblies and the central body is composed of representatives of ethno-cultural and other public associations, state officials and prominent individuals. The regional assemblies are headed by regional *Akims*. The day-to-day work of the Assembly is done by its secretariat, which is a part of the Akim's cabinet, and its permanent council. The latter proposes new members of the Assembly to the Assembly's plenary session. Once

4. This body operates on the basis of the Regulations "On the Administration of the President" confirmed by the Decree of the President of RK of March 11, 2008, No. 552.
5. The Council's activities are governed by the Regulations "On the Security Council of RK" confirmed by the Decree of the President of RK of March 20, 1999, No. 88.
6. The major legal act underlying the Assembly's activities is the Law of RK of October 20, 2008, No. 70-4, "On the Assembly of the People of Kazakhstan."

approved by the Assembly's plenary session, the candidates are then confirmed by the regional Akim. The members of the central body are proposed by the regional assemblies, then approved by the central body's permanent council (the composition of which is determined by the President) and subsequently endorsed by the President. The main functions of the Assembly include the development of recommendations on preventing any conflicts between different ethnic and religious groups.

Also, the Constitution foresees the position of a State Secretary, who is appointed by the President.[7] His key responsibilities are to submit proposals to the President on issues of internal and foreign policy, to represent the interests of the President based on his instructions and to coordinate the activities of the Assembly of the People of Kazakhstan and a number of presidential advisory bodies (such as the Commission on Human Rights, Commission on the Struggle against Corruption, Commission on State Awards, Commission on Personnel Training Abroad, etc.).

F. President and the Legislature

In contrast to the Constitution of 1993, the Constitution of 1995 puts the President in a superior position vis-à-vis the legislature. In addition to his enormous powers with regard to both the formation of Parliament and the legislative process, the current Constitution even foresees the possibility to delegate legislative powers to the President for a term not exceeding one year, if approved by a two-thirds vote of each chamber of Parliament (Article 53 III). This rule reflects the experience of the early 1990s when the President, in a deep political crisis, combined both the executive and legislative power within his office on a temporary basis.

Another departure from the Constitution of 1993 is the President's right to dissolve either the entire Parliament or only its lower chamber, the Mazhilis (Article 63 I). The constitutional amendments of May 21, 2007 require the President to conduct consultations with the Chairpersons of the Parliament's chambers and the Prime Minister before taking decision on the dissolution of the Parliament. At the same time, unlike the original text of the Constitution of 1995, which stated specific reasons for the dissolution like: "expressing a vote of no confidence in the Government," "twice refusal to give consent to the appointment of the Prime Minister" and "political crisis resulting from of insurmountable differences between the Parliament's chambers or Parliament and other branches of state power," the present text is silent on concrete reasons for the dissolution of the Parliament, leaving it fully at the discretion of the President.

Theoretically, the Parliament may also remove the President from office, but only in the case of high treason and following an extremely complicated procedure requiring the following steps: the approval of the indictment by a three-fourths

7. The legal standing of the Secretary is defined by the Decree of the President of RK of August 13, 2007, No. 379, "On the Status and Authorities of the State Secretaries."

majority of the total number of deputies of each chamber, the positive conclusions of the Supreme Court and the Constitutional Council with regard to the factual and legal basis of the charges, the adoption of the decision within two months from the moment of the accusation, and should the impeachment process fail, the termination of the powers of the deputies who initiated the consideration of this issue; all of which makes the impeachment process virtually impossible (Article 47).

IV. LEGAL STATUS OF THE PARLIAMENT OF RK

A. STRUCTURE AND ELECTIONS

The Parliament of RK is the highest representative body of the Republic performing legislative functions (Article 47 I).[8] Unlike the unicameral legislature under the Constitution of 1993, the current parliament consists of two chambers: the Senate and the Mazhilis.

The Senate is composed of two deputies from each of the 14 administrative regions (oblasts) as well as from the cities of Almaty and Astana, who are elected at a joint session of the local representative bodies. In addition, the President may currently choose 15 senators "with regard to the necessity of maintaining representation of ethnic-cultural and other significant social interests in the Senate" (Article 50 III).

In contrast to the Senate, the configuration of the Mazhilis was subject to frequent changes. Originally, it was composed of 67 deputies elected in one-mandate constituencies. This rule served as the basis for the first elections to the Mazhilis conducted on December 9, 1995. The strongest political parties, which acquired 24 and 12 seats respectively, were the People's Unity Party and the Democratic Party, both strongly pro-presidential parties. The rest of the seats were filled by independent candidates who were, however, largely also supporters of Nazarbayev.

On October 7, 1998, the composition of the Mazhilis was slightly modified, with the addition of 10 deputies to be elected on the basis of the "party lists" of those political parties that received not less than 7% of votes. On February 12, 1999, after the merger of several pro-presidential parties and movements, including the People's Unity Party and the Democratic Party, a new party, *Otan* ("Fatherland" in Kazakh) was established, which immediately outlined a program fully supportive of the President. As a result of the second elections to the Mazhilis on October 10, 1999, Otan obtained 24 of 77 seats, including 4 distributed between the political parties. The other four parties that received parliamentary mandates were the Civil (11 seats), Agrarian and Communist (three seats each) and People's Republican (one seat) Parties. Thirty-five deputies did not formally represent

---

8. Along with the Constitution, the legal status of the Parliament is primarily also regulated by the Constitutional Law of RK of October 16, 1995, No. 2529, "On the Parliament of the Republic of Kazakhstan and the Status of its Deputies."

any political parties but were overwhelmingly associated with the government and big business, and supported either Otan or two other pro-presidential parties, the Civil or the Agrarian.

The third election to the lower chamber, held on September 19, 2004, resulted in Otan winning 42 seats. A bloc formed by two other pro-presidential parties (the Civil and Agrarian Parties) obtained 11 seats; "Asar," the party led by the President's daughter Dariga, won four seats; and the moderate opposition party *Ak Zhol* obtained only one seat. Although pro-presidential parties fully dominated the parliament, by the middle of 2006 the President became especially concerned with Asar's independence and decided that "the country should have fewer but stronger parties that would efficiently defend the interests of the population." On July 3, 2006 Asar declared its decision to merge with Otan. Soon thereafter it was announced that the Civil and Agrarian Parties would follow in Asar's footsteps and also merge with Otan. On December 22, 2006, at the enlarged Otan's party congress, its delegates voted to rename the party to *Nur-Otan* (*Nur*, as in the three first letters of the President's first name, means "Ray of Light" in Kazakh).

Further, the constitutional amendments of May 21, 2007 completely altered the structure of the Mazhilis, both with respect to the number of deputies and the method of their election. Currently, the lower chamber consists of 107 deputies: 98 of them are now elected on the basis of the "party lists" and nine are elected by the Assembly of the People of Kazakhstan (Article 51 I; see *supra*). The Assembly, which previously played only a consultative role, has thus acquired permanent political significance.

Soon after the Constitution was amended, a group of parliamentarians requested the Constitutional Council to provide an opinion on whether the Mazhilis could dissolve itself. On June 18, 2007 the Constitutional Council rejected such a possibility. However, on next day, a majority of the Mazhilis' deputies sent a request to the President saying that "the present Mazhilis must not block reforms" and calling for the premature dissolution of the chamber. On June 20, the President dissolved the Mazhilis and called for extraordinary elections. On July 4 at a Nur-Otan's emergency congress, Nazarbayev became the Chairman of the Party, which in the August 18 elections received more than 88% of the vote and all seats in the Mazhilis.

B. Political Parties

A political party in Kazakhstan is a voluntary association of citizens that expresses their political will, enables them to participate in the formation of representative and executive state bodies as well as bodies of local self-government and represents their interests in those bodies. A political party must satisfy certain requirements: (a) it must have regional divisions in all 14 regions of the country (as well as the cities of Astana and Almaty); and (b) it must have not less than 50,000 members in total and at least 700 members in each of the regions.

The creation and functioning of a political party is prohibited if its purpose or actions are directed towards a forcible change of the constitutional system, violation of the integrity of the Republic, undermining the security of the state, formation of unauthorized paramilitary units or inciting social, racial, national, religious, class or tribal enmity. Political parties based on professional, racial, ethnic or religious affiliation are also not permitted. Nor may a political party have structural subdivisions within organs of state power or local self-administration. Military servicemen, members of law-enforcement organs and organs of national security as well as judges may not be members of political parties, nor may they support any political party. Political parties are further prohibited from interfering in the instructional process of educational institutions.

Political parties of foreign states may not operate on the territory of Kazakhstan. Also, foreign states, foreign legal entities, foreign citizens and stateless persons as well as international organizations may not finance political parties in the Republic. The headquarters of political parties and their structural subdivisions must be located within the territory of Kazakhstan (see the Law of RK of July 15, 2002, No. 344-2, "On the Political Parties").

C. Competences of the Parliament

The competences of Kazakhstan's Parliament are differentiated into the following groups: (1) competences exercised at joint session of the chambers; (2) competences exercised in separate sessions of the chambers through consecutive consideration of issues, first in the Mazhilis and then in the Senate; (3) exclusive jurisdiction of the Senate; (4) exclusive jurisdiction of the Mazhilis; and (5) independent competences of each chamber.[9]

At a joint session of the chambers, the Parliament may, *inter alia*, exercise the following authorities: (a) introduce amendments or make additions to the Constitution by a three-fourths majority of the deputies of each chamber at the proposal of the President; (b) approve reports by the Government about the implementation of the republican budget (the disapproval of a report denotes the expression of a vote of no confidence in the Government); (c) delegate legislative powers for a term not exceeding one year to the President by a two-thirds vote of the deputies of each chamber at the initiative of the President; (d) decide issues of war and peace; and (e) approve the use of the Armed Forces of RK abroad at the proposal of the President (Article 53).

At separate sessions of the chambers through consecutive consideration of issues first in the Mazhilis and then in the Senate, the Parliament implements its major function, namely to adopt ordinary laws (by a majority of votes) and constitutional laws (by a majority of two-thirds). Following this procedure, the

9. This type of competences refers to the same authorities exercised by both chambers independently (as opposed to exclusive jurisdiction, when chambers are responsible for the separate exercising of different authorities).

Parliament in particular adopts laws with respect to approving the republican budget; establishing or terminating taxes; deciding issues of state loans or rendering economic assistance by RK; ratifying or denouncing international treaties of the RK, etc. (Article 54).

The exclusive jurisdiction of the Senate includes, *inter alia*, the election of the judges of the Supreme Court at the proposal of the President and the approval of the appointment of the Chairperson of the National Bank, the Procurator General and the Chairperson of the Committee of National Security by the President. Exclusive competences of the Mazhilis consist of giving consent to the appointment of the Prime Minister by the President, announcing regular elections of the President and expressing a vote of no-confidence in the Government (Articles 55, 56).

Finally, major independent competences comprise appointing members of the Constitutional Council (each chamber in twos), the Central Election Committee (each chamber in twos) and the Republican Budget Audit Committee (each chamber in threes). Further, each chamber may hold parliamentary hearings of the members of the Government on issues of the Government's activities (at the initiative of one-third of the deputies) (Article 57).

D. Legislative Process

According to the Constitution, the right to initiate legislation belongs to the President, the Members of Parliament and the Government (Article 61 I). Along with his own right to initiate legislation, the President may also charge the Government with presenting a legislative draft to the Mazhilis (Article 44 III).

The legislative process can only start in the Mazhilis and is divided into three major stages. First, a draft of the law must be considered and approved by a majority of votes from the total number of the deputies of the Mazhilis. Second, if the draft is approved by the Mazhilis, it is transmitted to the Senate, where it is considered for no more than 60 days and must be approved by a simple majority. If the draft is rejected by the Senate, the Mazhilis may submit it to the Senate for a second discussion and a new vote that will require a two-thirds majority; however, any draft rejected twice by the Senate may not be submitted again during that same parliamentary session. Third, if the draft is approved by the Senate, it is submitted to the President. In order to come into effect, a law must be signed by the President. If the President refuses to sign the act, the Parliament may theoretically overrule the President's veto by confirming the draft with a two-thirds majority in both chambers (Article 44 II). The Constitutional Council can also participate in the legislative process by considering whether a draft law is in compliance with the Constitution (provided the Council is appealed to by the authorized state officials).

It should be noted that both the President and the Government have significant capacities to intervene into the legislative process. The President has the right to declare a particular draft law urgent; in this case, the Parliament must consider this draft within a month from the day of its submission. Otherwise, the President may issue a decree having the force of law which will be in effect until the Parliament adopts a new law. The Prime Minister may, up to twice a year, request a vote of confidence on the occasion of the presentation of a bill sponsored by the Government. If confidence is not refused by a two-thirds majority of the deputies, the draft law is deemed adopted (Article 44 II).

The subordinate nature of the Parliament is made obvious by the provision stipulating that all drafts envisioning a reduction of state revenues or an increase in expenditures may only be submitted with the approval of the Government, except for those drafts which are initiated by the President (Article 61 VI).

V. LEGAL STATUS OF THE GOVERNMENT OF RK

The Government of RK effectuates the executive power and in its entire activity is responsible to the President (Article 64 I, II). It is a collegial organ consisting of the Prime Minister, Deputy Prime Ministers, ministers and other appointed officials. The work of the Government is organized and supervised by the Prime Minister (Article 67 I).[10]

It is explicitly stated that "the Government shall be formed by the President according to the procedure stipulated by this Constitution" (Article 65 I). The current procedure encompasses the following five stages: (1) the President must consult with the fractions of the political parties represented in the Mazhilis on a candidate for the office of the Prime Minister; (2) the President introduces the candidate for Prime Minister to the Mazhilis in order to obtain its consent; (3) with the consent of the Mazhilis, the President appoints a Prime Minister; (4) the President appoints at his own discretion foreign, defense, interior and justice ministers and may also release them from office; and (5) at the proposal of the Prime Minister (which is due within 10 days after his appointment), the President determines the structure of the Government and appoints its other members (Articles 44 III and 65 II). The members of the Government take an oath both to the people and the President.

Though it is "in its entire activity" fully responsible to the President, the Government may also be accountable to the Parliament. Following parliamentary hearings of the members of the Government (which may be initiated by one-third of the deputies of each chamber), both the Mazhilis and the Senate are entitled to adopt (by a simple majority) an appeal to the President to discharge a member of the Government from office due to his non-observance of the laws of the Republic. If the President refuses such an appeal, the deputies may raise the same issue on expiration of six months from the first appeal. In this case, the President will have to release that member of the Government from office (Article 57 VI).

Members of the Government are independent in making decisions within their competence and bear personal responsibility before the Prime Minister for the

10. In addition to the Constitution, the status of the Government is principally also regulated by the Constitutional Law of RK of December 18, 1995, No. 2688, "On the Government of the Republic of Kazakhstan."

activity of bodies subordinated to them. However, members of the Government who disagree with the policy pursued by the Government must resign or be released from office.

The major function of the Government is to carry out state policy in the economic and social fields. It is also responsible for conducting foreign and defense policy and maintaining security and public order. It presents a draft of the Republican budget to the Parliament and ensures its implementation, and it introduces drafts of laws into the Mazhilis and ensures their enforcement. The Government manages state property and administers the activity of all central and local executive bodies (with the right to terminate or suspend their acts) (Article 67).

In order to carry out its duties, the Government adopts resolutions and the Prime Minister issues directives. Both the resolutions of the Government and the directives of the Prime Minister must be in full compliance with the Constitution, legislative acts and presidential decrees and resolutions.

VI. CONSTITUTIONAL COUNCIL OF RK

The Constitutional Council is a permanent body whose primary objective is to ensure the supremacy of the Constitution throughout the territory of Kazakhstan.[11]

The Council consists of a Chairperson and six other members. The Chairperson and two members are appointed by the President while the Chairpersons of Senate and Mazhilis each appoint two members. The members are appointed for a six-year term with one-half of the Council up for renewal every three years. The ex-Presidents of the Republic have the right to be life-long members of the Constitutional Council (Article 71).

The major functions of the Constitutional Council include: (1) deciding the validity of presidential and parliamentary elections as well as nationwide referenda; (2) considering whether laws adopted by Parliament comply with the Constitution before they are signed by the President; (3) considering whether international treaties of the Republic comply with the Constitution before they are ratified; and (4) providing official interpretation of constitutional rules.

Also, the Council must provide its conclusions as to whether established constitutional procedures were observed in cases where the President is released from office prematurely due to continued incapacity to perform his duties or discharged due to a charge of high treason (Article 72).

The decisions of the Council (resolutions, opinions and messages) necessitate a majority vote by its members. None of the members may abstain or recuse themselves from the decision-making (Article 33 IV). If the votes are equally divided, the Chairperson's vote is decisive (Article 71 II). The resolutions of the Council come into effect from the day they are adopted and are binding on

11. The specific aspects of this organ's activities are governed by the Constitutional Law of RK of December 29, 1995, No. 2737, "On the Constitutional Council of the Republic of Kazakhstan."

the entire territory of the Republic (Article 74 III) as they are an integral component of Kazakhstan's law (Article 4 I). However, the Council's resolutions may be objected to, in whole or in part, by the President. In that case they will not be considered adopted unless the President's objections are overruled by two-thirds vote by the members of the Constitutional Council (Article 73 IV).

The sessions of the Constitutional Council are organized only when it is petitioned by the following major political actors: (a) the President, (b) the Chairperson of the Senate, (c) the Chairperson of the Mazhilis, (d) a group of deputies of not less than one-fifth of the total number of parliamentarians, or (e) the Prime Minister (Article 72). In addition, the Constitutional Council may also be appealed to by Kazakhstani courts in cases where they find that a law or other regulatory legal act subject to application infringes on the rights and liberties of individuals; in such cases the courts must suspend legal proceedings and address the Constitutional Council with a proposal to declare those acts unconstitutional (Article 78). The Constitutional Council must pass a resolution within one month from the day of the appeal. This period of time, at the demand of the President, may be shortened by 10 days if the issue is urgent (Article 73 III).

VII. JUDICIAL POWER IN KAZAKHSTAN

A. Principles of Administering Justice

The Constitution of 1995 introduced a unified system of courts of general jurisdiction based on territorial principle and established the following guiding rules of effectuating justice: (1) justice in Kazakhstan is exercised only by the courts (the functions of courts may not be delegated to or appropriated by any other bodies or officials); (2) judicial power is administered on behalf of RK and is intended to protect the rights, freedoms and interests of its citizens and organizations as well as to ensure the observance of the Constitution, laws, other regulatory legal acts and international treaties of RK; (3) the jurisdiction of the courts extends to all cases and disputes arising from the interpretation of the Constitution, laws, other regulatory legal acts and international treaties of RK; (4) decisions, sentences and other judgments of the courts have an obligatory force on the entire territory of RK; (5) criminal procedure is carried out with the participation of jurymen; and (6) the establishment of special or extraordinary courts under any name is not allowed (Articles 75, 76).[12]

Although the judiciary has been freed from the direct political control that existed during the Soviet era, it remains financially weak (even though certain improvements have taken shape recently). In this regard it should be noted that the Constitution requires the state to provide adequate funding and proper conditions

12. Along with Constitution, the legal status and the structure of the judicial power is also governed by the Constitutional Law of RK of December 25, 2000, No. 132-II, "On the Judicial System and the Status of Judges" (CLJS).

for the operation of courts and the activity of judges so as to ensure the possibility of complete and free exercise of justice (in particular the Constitution says that all judges must be provided with housing) (Article 80).

B. Structure of the Judiciary System

According to the Constitution, the judiciary system of Kazakhstan consists of the local courts and the Supreme Court of the Republic (Article 75 III).

The local courts exist at two levels. The lower level is represented by district and equated (town, inter-district) courts which are the courts of first instance. The upper level is constituted by regional and equated (city courts of Astana and Almaty) courts which serve as courts of appeal and cassation (Article 2 Constitutional Law on the Judicial System and the Status of Judges (CLJS)). The regional courts also keep and analyze judicial statistics, generalize court practice and provide methodological assistance to district courts as to the application of legislation (Article 12 CLJS). Upon the request of the President, specialized courts (military, financial, economic, administrative, juvenile, etc.) may also be created both at the district and the regional levels (Article 3, 3-1 CLJS).

The Supreme Court is the highest judicial body for civil, criminal and other cases in Kazakhstan. Its major functions include the following: (1) supervision over the activities of local courts; (2) cassation review of awards of local courts according to its jurisdiction; (3) repeated cassation of all other matters considered by local courts under the cassation procedure; (4) interpretation of issues of judicial practice; (5) analyzing and generalizing court practice; (6) adoption of regulatory resolutions for the clarification of court practice (Article 17 II CLJS).

The Chairpersons and judges of the local and specialized courts are appointed by the President at the recommendation of the Highest Judicial Council (which is headed by a Chairperson appointed by the President and consists of the Chairperson of the Constitutional Council, the Chairperson of the Supreme Court, the Procurator General, the Minister of Justice, deputies of the Senate, judges and other persons appointed by the President). The Chairperson and judges of the Supreme Court are elected by the Senate at the proposal of the President of RK based also on the recommendation of the Highest Judicial Council (Article 82).

C. Status of Judges

Courts consist of permanent judges who, when executing justice, must be independent and subordinate only to the Constitution and the law. Any interference in the activity of the court in the exercise of justice is prohibited and punishable by law (in particular, judges may not be held accountable for specific cases) (Article 77 of the Constitution). A judge may not be arrested, subject to detention or arraigned on an administrative or criminal charge without the consent of the President (or the consent of Senate with respect to judges of the Supreme Court) based on a conclusion of the Highest Judicial Council of RK, except if the judge is apprehended on the scene of a crime or has committed grave crimes (Article 77 II).

According to the CLJS, a judge must strictly observe the Constitution and laws of RK, be faithful to his professional oath, follow judicial ethics, resist corruption and maintain the secrecy of judicial conferences (Article 28 CLJS). Should a judge violate these requirements or commit a disciplinary offense, his powers may be terminated by a special disciplinary-qualification committee (Article 34 II CLJS). Otherwise, a judge's powers may be terminated only on the grounds of: resignation; discharge at personal request; impossibility to perform duties due to health problems; recognition as incapable; entering into force of a condemnatory judgment; termination of citizenship; appointment or election to another office; abolition of the court; conclusion of the judicial jury (special body that determines professional suitability of a judge); attainment of 65 years of age (the official age limit); or death or recognition as demised (Article 34 I CLJS).

D. Procurator's Office

The Procurator's Office (*prokuratura*) is an independent state institution that is accountable to the President. It exercises the highest supervision over the exact and uniform application of laws and other regulatory legal acts in Kazakhstan and may take measures to eliminate any violation of the law. The Constitution also stipulates that the Procurator's Office may appeal regulatory legal acts which contradict the Constitution and the laws of the Republic (Article 83 I). However, the respective legislative act that would govern the procedure of raising such an appeal is still not adopted.

Although the Procurator's Office is not part of the judiciary, there is a notable interrelation between them. In particular, the Procurator's Office represents the interests of the state in court and conducts criminal prosecutions within the limits stipulated by law. Also, it ensures the legality of preliminary investigations, inquests and inspections, and administrative and executive legal procedures.

The Procurator's Office is a unified, centralized system that is headed by the Procurator General and has almost the same structure as the judiciary system. The Procurator General is appointed to office by the President with the consent of the Senate. Regional (and equated) procurators are appointed by the Procurator General with the consent of the President for five years. District (and equated) procurators are appointed by the Procurator General for five years.[13]

13. The details with respect to the activities of the Procurator's Office are provided by the Law of RK of December 21, 1995, No. 2709, "On the Procurator's Office of the Republic of Kazakhstan."

VIII. LOCAL STATE ADMINISTRATION AND SELF-ADMINISTRATION IN KAZAKHSTAN

Local state administration in Kazakhstan is exercised by local representative and executive bodies ("Maslikhats" and "Akimats," respectively) that are responsible for the state of affairs in their respective territories (Article 85). Both Maslikhats and Akimats exist at two (regional and district) levels.[14]

Maslikhats express the will of the population of their respective administrative-territorial units. Deputies are elected by the population on the basis of universal, equal suffrage under a secret ballot for a five-year term. A deputy of a Maslikhat must be a citizen of Kazakhstan who has reached at least 20 years of age. The powers of a Maslikhat may be prematurely terminated by the President or by self-dissolution. Maslikhats are primarily responsible for approving development plans and the local budget of their respective administrative-territorial units. They can require the head of their counterpart Akimat to provide reports on the performance of the local budget. Also, a group of at least one-fifth of the total number of deputies in a Maslikhat can initiate a vote of no-confidence in their regional Akim. The no-confidence measure then goes to a general vote in the Maslikhat, and if the measure is supported by a simple majority, an appeal will be made either to the President or to the superior Akim to discharge the regional Akim from office (Article 87 V).

Akimats constitute part of a unified system of the executive bodies of Kazakhstan and ensure the implementation of the general policies of the executive branch in conjunction with the interests and development needs of their respective territories. The major competences of the Akimats include drafting and implementing the development plans and the local budget of the respective administrative-territorial units as well as the management of the state property within the limits of their authorities.

An Akimat is headed by an Akim who is a representative of the President and the Government of RK. An Akim may adopt decisions and resolutions that are binding within the territory of his administrative-territorial unit. Acts of Akims may be terminated by the President, the Government, a superior Akim or the courts. Akims of the regions (and the cities of Astana and Almaty) are appointed to office by the President with the consent of the respective regional Maslikhats. According to the Constitution, Akims of the Districts (and the lower administrative subunits) may be either appointed or elected to office in a manner determined by the President (Article 87 IV). Thus, on June 28, 2001 President Nazarbayev issued a Decree "On the Elections of Akims of Villages, Village Areas and Settlements" and on June 6, 2006 another Decree "On the Elections of Akims of the Districts and Major Towns." While the former decree is still in force, the latter (which introduced experimental rules on the elections of the heads of local executive bodies at the district level and applied to approximately 30% of the Kazakhstan's districts) was terminated by a new presidential decree on June 4, 2007. In accordance with the current rules, district

14. See the Law of RK of January 23, 2001, No. 148-II, "On the Local State Administration in the Republic of Kazakhstan."

Akims (as well as the Akims of major towns) are appointed by their respective regional Akims with the consent of their respective regional Maslikhats. The President has the right to release any Akim from office at his own discretion. Also, all regional Akims (as well as the Akims of the cities of Astana and Almaty) must resign upon the commencement of a new presidential term (Article 87 V).

The Constitution also provides that Kazakhstan will feature a form of local self-administration, which will enable the population to independently resolve issues of local significance and will be able to implement certain state functions (Article 89 I, II). However, the organization and activity of the bodies of local self-administration are to be governed by a separate law that has not yet been adopted.

Selected Bibliography

M. Baimakhanov et al. (eds.), *Конституция Республики Казахстан: научно-практический комментарий* [*Constitution of RK: Scientific-Practical Commentary*] (Raritet, Almaty, 2010) [in Russian].

K.W. Davis, "Purging the System: Recent Judicial Reforms in Kazakhstan" (2002) 8 U.C. Davis J. Int'l L. & Pol'y 255.

S. Issenova, "Reform of the Judicial System in RK: Review of the Effectiveness of OSCE Efforts," in A. Berg & A. Kreikemeyer (eds.), *Realities of Transformation* (Nomos, Baden-Baden, 2006).

M. Kachkeev, *Stellung der Richter in Kirgistan und Kasachstan* (BWV, Berlin, 2007).

Z. Kembayev, "Constitution of the Republic of Kazakhstan," in R. Wolfrum & R. Grote (eds.), *Constitutions of the Countries of the World* (Oxford University Press, New York, 2009).

Z. Kembayev, "The Rise of Presidentialism in Post-Soviet Central Asia: The Example of Kazakhstan," in R. Grote & T. Röder (eds.), *Constitutionalism in Islamic Countries: Between Upheavel and Continuity* (Oxford University Press, New York, 2011), 415–430.

A. Kotov, "The Parliamentary Process in the RK" (1999) 8 Widener J. Pub. L. 457.

A. Kotov, *Конституционализм в Казахстане* [*Constitutionalism in Kazakhstan*] (KazGYuA, Almaty, 2000) [in Russian].

O. Luchterhandt, "Die Verfassung der Republik Kasachstan von 1995" (1999) 47 JöR 614.

G. Sapargaliev, *Конституциооное право Республики Казахстан* [*Constitutional Law of RK*] (Žeti Žargi, Almaty, 2007) [in Russian].

M. Sarsembayev, "Parliamentary Reform in the RK" (2008) 13 *OSCE Yearbook* 115–124.

V. Malinovskiy, *Глава государства суверенного Казахстана* [*Head of State of Sovereign Kazakhstan*] (VŠP Adilet, Almaty, 1998) [in Russian].

C. Thiele, "Die Transformation Kasachstans von der Diktatur zur Demokratie" (2006) 52 *Osteuropa-Recht* 164.

S. Zimanov, *Конституция и Парламент Республики Казахстан* [*Constitution and the Parliament of RK*] (Žeti Žargi Almaty 1996) [in Russian].

Chapter 5
Administrative Law

Roman Podoprigora

I. INTRODUCTION

A. History, Subject Matter and Principles

Administrative Law of RK is one of the fundamental branches of the Kazakhstani legal system and is a part of its public law. It is a relatively new development since Kazakhstan's territory was long under the administration of the Russian Empire and then the USSR. Thus, all issues of government were decided by the bodies of tsarist and later Soviet state administration.

The most substantial impact for the creation and development of this branch was made throughout the Soviet period. During this time, Administrative Law was formed as a separate branch with its own subject matter and system. Certainly, Administrative Law was influenced by the Soviet legal and political system. It was a branch of law designed around the state authorities and not for individuals or their associations. Its nature was affected by strong ideological influences, administrative centralization, domination of state interests, neglect of individual rights, formal existence of laws and real force of sub-law acts. The modern Administrative Law of Kazakhstan continues to reflect the dramatic effects of its Soviet past.

For an extensive period of time, Administrative Law was considered as a branch of law exclusively focused on state administration. Taking into account that during the Soviet period the state interfered in nearly all aspects of social life, Administrative Law covered a significant number of administrative issues in both

Zhenis Kembayev, *Introduction to the Law of Kazakhstan*, pp. 73–87.

public and private life. The Soviet system did not recognize the concept of separation of powers and Administrative Law governed the activity of all state bodies. Due to the supremacy of state authorities and the full subordination of individuals and public associations to the state, Administrative Law did not govern issues related to administrative justice and administrative procedures.

After the collapse of the Soviet Union, a new system of political organization, which recognized the principle of separation of powers, was adopted in Kazakhstan. For the first time in its legal history, provisions involving the separation of powers, the priority of individual rights and the equality of state-owned and private property emerged. Administrative Law began to regulate the activities of executive bodies, attempting to ensure individual rights in public administration and control of state bodies and their liability.

Today, there is still no clear definition of the subject matter of Administrative Law. Most frequently, this branch of law is connected with the realization of executive power and other forms of state administration (e.g., local self-government). Also, Administrative Law covers internal relations within other branches of the state power (legislative and judicial) and encompasses judicial activity related to administrative offense cases.[1]

It is necessary to note the trend that the traditional view of Administrative Law as the law of state administration (or the law only for state administration) is changing. Increasingly, Administrative Law is now considered to be a branch that protects private persons in their relations with state administration and creates an effective regime of mutual relations between the state and private persons. Furthermore, the imperative method (which is based on the dictate of the state bodies over subordinated persons and was traditionally used by Administrative Law) is being increasingly supplemented by the contractual method since the state more and more employs agreements and other non-power instruments of social regulation.

In the contemporary political and legal regime, Administrative Law elaborated new fundamental principles such as: (a) the *rule-of-law principle*, implying that all state administrative activity must be in accordance with the law (there are still significant problems in this regard due to the fact that state officials often rely on bureaucratic and hierarchic orders rather than the law); (b) the *principle of lawfulness*, meaning that executive bodies and other bodies of state administration may issue their acts only in accordance with legislation; (c) the *principle of determined competence of state bodies* implying that all authorities of state bodies must be defined in legislation or in other regulatory acts (in other words, any actions not specifically authorized by law are prohibited); (d) the *principle of mutual responsibility* meaning that in the modern legal approach both individuals and state bodies are held responsible for their actions (which is quite different from the Soviet era, when state bodies were always presumed to be in the right); (e) the *principle of*

1. Thus, the courts consider various public law disputes that are partially regulated by the Administrative Law. Also, the courts (as well as quasi-judicial executive administrative bodies) have the right to impose different sanctions in accordance with Administrative Law.

judicial defense stipulating that all individuals and public associations are entitled to judicial protection of their rights and interests (this protection must be guaranteed by the state due to the inequality of participants of Administrative Law relations).

B. Sources, System and Relationship with Other Branches of Law

The main source of Administrative Law is the Constitution of RK, which establishes many provisions directly and indirectly related to state administration.[2] To sources of Administrative Law also belong: (a) legislative acts;[3] (b) decrees of the President of RK and regulatory acts of the central executive bodies (resolutions of the Government of RK, orders of Ministries, etc.); (c) regulatory resolutions of the Supreme Court of RK, which summarize judicial practices regarding different administrative law issues (and exemplify the penetration of the common law principle of *stare decisis* into the Kazakhstani legal system); (d) regulatory resolutions of the Constitutional Council of RK; and (e) international treaties ratified by RK (e.g., treaties on visa, road traffic and security issues).

The system of Administrative Law includes two parts: general and special. The general part governs issues related to the following: (a) subjects of this branch (viz. individuals, organizations, state administration bodies and state officials); (b) legal forms and methods of the state administration's actions; and (c) administrative procedures. The special part regulates the issues of state administration of various branches of the economy as well as political, social and cultural activity.

As to the relationship with other branches of law, Administrative Law is very close to the Constitutional Law, as it plays a crucial role in the implementation of many constitutional provisions. At the same time, Constitutional Law serves as a foundation for Administrative Law, since it establishes a legal framework for the activity of state bodies, stipulates the fundamental rights and duties of individuals in state administration and provides guarantees against illegal activity by the state. Moreover, a part of Administrative Law is devoted to issues of administrative offenses and liability, and in this sense it is similar to Criminal Law. Also, Administrative Law plays a significant role as the basis of other branches like Financial Law, Tax Law and Customs Law. Furthermore, it is very important with respect to the branches that combine public and private law provisions (such as Banking Law, Insurance Law and Land Law, where there are many rules with an administrative nature related to licensing, certification, state permissions and administrative

2. For example, section V of the Constitution is devoted to the Government as the central executive body. Also, the Constitution stipulates a number of constitutional rights and duties of citizens in the area of state administration.
3. Some of those acts comprise purely administrative norms (e.g., the Law of RK of November 27, 2000, No. 325-IV, "On Administrative Procedures"), while others contain administrative norms together with rules of other branches of law (e.g., the Law of RK of July 23, 1999, No. 453-I, "On State Service").

liability). Although Civil Law and Administrative Law are diametrically different from each other, they may regulate similar relations associated with property, family and the economy. The major difference is found in the method of regulation; while Civil Law uses the contractual method, Administrative Law employs the imperative method. The same applies to Labor Law (e.g., the labor activity of state servants is regulated by both Administrative Law and Labor Law; however, each uses its own method of regulation).

II. SUBJECTS OF ADMINISTRATIVE LAW

A. INDIVIDUALS AND ORGANIZATIONS

For an "individual" to participate in Administrative Law relations, the following legal characteristics must be met: first, legal capacity (which starts from birth) and, second, the dispositive legal capacity (which arises at the age of 18).[4] The central element of an individual's status under Administrative Law is constituted by his rights and duties within the domain of state administration. Many of these rights and duties are constitutional in nature and Administrative Law acts frequently as the instrument for the further realization of constitutional provisions since its norms provide their detailed elaboration.[5] However, Administrative Law may also restrict constitutional rights and freedoms.[6] It should also be noted that foreigners and persons without citizenship have a special status under Administrative Law,[7] which involves a number of administrative limitations applicable to them.[8] Administrative Law provides certain guarantees of the rights and freedoms of

4. A peculiarity of the individual legal status in Administrative Law is expressed in the ability to participate in administrative law relations at an early age (e.g., administrative enforcement can be applied to adolescents; pupils can submit complaints to the state education department).
5. For example, under the Constitution of RK citizens have constitutional rights to protection of health and free, guaranteed and extensive medical assistance as established by law (Art. 29). Further, they are also entitled: (a) to participate in the government of the state's affairs directly and through their representatives; (b) to address personally as well as to direct individual and collective appeals to state and local self-administrative bodies; (c) to elect and be elected into state and local self-administrations; and (d) to serve in a public office (Art. 33). However, citizens have the general constitutional duty to observe the Constitution and the legislation of Kazakhstan, and to respect rights and freedoms of other persons (Art. 34).
6. Thus, despite the constitutional right to the freedom of forming associations, all associations must be registered by authorized state bodies, and unregistered associations are prohibited. Another example includes the constitutional right to peacefully assemble and hold meetings, rallies, demonstrations, street processions and pickets, which is limited by the administrative duty to obtain permission from authorized state bodies.
7. The status of foreigners and persons without citizenship is primarily regulated by the Law of RK of June 19, 1995, No. 2337, "On Foreigners."
8. For instance, foreigners must register their passports with the police within 5 days upon arrival to Kazakhstan and notify the police about changes of their place of residence. They do not have the right to serve as state officials. Moreover, there is a special administrative sanction applied only to foreigners, administrative expulsion (deportation).

individuals. One of the most important of them is the right of an individual to submit complaints to superior state bodies or officials. Complaints may be submitted within three months after the violation and subsequently must be resolved by superior bodies or officials within 15 to 30 days. In the case of the absence of such bodies or officials, complaints may be submitted to the court.[9]

The concept of an "organization" is of a very general meaning and covers all collective subjects of Administrative Law. Unlike Civil Law, both legal entities and organizations without legal entity status can be subjects of Administrative Law.[10] Legal abilities of organizations arise from the moment of their registration at the Ministry of Justice of RK (or its territorial divisions). The status of organizations and the registration procedures depend on the type of organization (state-owned or private, commercial or non-commercial, etc.).[11] Furthermore, Administrative Law also governs some issues of both voluntary and compulsory liquidation of organizations (which are generally covered by Civil Law) due to the fact that certain reasons for termination of an organization are of a public nature (such as invalid registration; systematic violation of the charter provisions; activity prohibited by legislation or conducted without license).

Administrative Law establishes the rights and duties of organizations. Thus, organizations can apply to state bodies, obtain information, submit appeals and participate in public hearings organized by state authorities. Moreover, Administrative Law provides guarantees aimed to protect organizations' rights and interests. These guarantees include, *inter alia*, the existence of special bodies (such as anti-monopoly and procurator offices) and the right to submit appeals to superior bodies or to the court. Special attention is given to the protection of rights during state inspections or other state controls.[12] As for the obligations of organizations *vis-à-vis* state administration, some duties exist for all of them (e.g., they must submit reports to different state bodies such as tax and statistics agencies) while others only for specific types of organizations (e.g., public foundations have to publish reports in the mass media about their activities while banks and

9. Most unlawful (in)actions of the state bodies may be appealed in accordance with the Law of RK of January 12, 2007, No. 221-III, "On the Order of the Consideration of Appeals of Physical Persons and Legal Entities."
10. For instance, small religious groups without legal entity status are subject to registration in local executive bodies (see Law of RK of January 15, 1992, "On Freedom of Religion and Religious Associations"). Consequently, such groups do not have the rights of a legal entity but may have legal personality under Administrative Law (even if legal entities have more legal capacity).
11. Less demanding requirements are stipulated for commercial organizations (especially for small businesses) while non-commercial ones face more stringent obligations. The denial of state registration can be appealed in court. Social and religious associations are mandated to register and may not operate without registration (see Law of RK of January 15, 1992, "On Freedom of Religion and Religious Associations" and Law of RK of May 31, 1996, No. 3-1, "On Public Associations").
12. In this regard to be mentioned are the Law of RK of January 31, 2006, No. 124-III, "On Private Enterprise" and the Law of RK of January 6, 2011, No. 377-IV, "On State Control and Supervision" which contain a number of rules enabling organizations to effectively defend their legal interests.

insurance companies must make their balance sheets public). Furthermore, all organizations are obliged to fulfill various rules in the spheres related to public order and safety (such as sanitary, fire-prevention, ecological, construction, tax, etc.). In addition, it should be noted that currently there are 105 licensable types of activities, and organizations must obtain a license in order to exercise those activities.[13]

B. State Administration Bodies

The most important of the state administration bodies is the President of RK. Despite the fact that the President is not formally included in the executive branch of state power, he plays a significant role in determining the composition of executive power and many other issues related to its activities. Furthermore, the system of state administration bodies includes: (1) the bodies of executive power; and (2) the bodies that do not formally belong to the executive branch but nevertheless fulfill different administrative functions.

The bodies of executive power include: (a) the Government; (b) the executive bodies subordinated and accountable to the President (the so-called presidential bodies); (c) the ministries; (d) the central executive bodies that do not belong to the Government (the agencies); and (e) the local executive bodies. The status of the Government and the local executive bodies is dealt with in Chapter on "Constitutional Law," which exemplifies the close relationship between the branches of Constitutional and Administrative Law. Thus, this current section will provide a description of the presidential bodies, the ministries and the agencies.

Presidential bodies are executive bodies which are not subordinate to the Government but directly report to the President. These bodies include the Committee of National Security, the National Bank, the State Service Agency, the Financial Police Agency and the Foreign Intelligence Service *Syrbar*. The President decides all issues regarding such state bodies. He may create and terminate the Presidential bodies (except for the National Bank and the Committee of National Security, the existence of which is stipulated by the Constitution); define their structure; appoint their heads (with the Chairpersons of the National Bank and the Committee of National Security requiring the approval of the Senate) and dismiss them. However, the President does not have the right to terminate their acts (orders, resolutions). Only the respective body itself and the court have such authority.

13. The types of license and procedures of licensing are described in the Law of RK of January 11, 2007, No. 214-III, "On Licensing." Moreover, authorized state bodies may prohibit or limit certain types of activity; impose certification requirements for production and services; influence the internal structure of organizations; set pricing policies; and establish other permissive and prohibitive tools that prove a significant degree of state intervention in business and other organization activities.

A ministry is the most traditional organizational unit in the system of state administration. The number of ministries is subject to constant change.[14] In principle, the ministries are created and terminated by the President. However, the existence of certain ministries is mentioned in the Constitution (the Ministry of Foreign Affairs, the Ministry of Internal Affairs, the Ministry of Defense and the Ministry of Justice). The ministers of these four ministries are appointed by the President at his own discretion. All other ministers are also appointed by the President but at the proposal of the Prime Minister. The President may release all ministers from their offices at his own discretion. The ministries are subordinate not only to President but also to the Government. The heads of the ministries are members of the Government, and the Government approves each ministry's regulations. A ministry may issue orders which may be terminated by the ministry itself, the Government or the court.

The status of an agency is very similar to that of a ministry. The only important difference is that the chairpersons of agencies are not members of the Government.[15] The other central state administration bodies that do not belong to the Government include: (a) the departments (*mekeme*, *vedomstvo*); (b) the cabinet divisions (*apparat*); (c) the advisory-consultative bodies; and (d) special state commissions.

The departments are large structural divisions of the ministries or presidential bodies with their own legal status. As a rule, these departments implement control and supervision functions in the framework of the respective ministry or the presidential body. Examples of such departments include the Tax Committee of the Ministry of Finance, the Road Police Committee of the Ministry of Internal Affairs, the State Sanitary-Epidemiological Committee of the Ministry of Health and the Border Troops Department of the National Security Committee. As a whole, there are about 70 departments in the state administration structure. They are created and terminated either by the Government or the President (depending upon the respective department). Heads of the departments are appointed by the Minister or the President. Their acts are issued in the form of orders which can be terminated by the department itself, the respective Ministry or the court.

The cabinet divisions are bodies that support the activity of the executive and other bodies (e.g., the Chancellery of the Prime Minister or the cabinet of an "Akim"). They also fulfill certain administrative functions (e.g., the Chancellery of the Prime Minister may inspect state bodies).

---

14. As of May 2011, in Kazakhstan there are the following 18 ministries: Ministry of Foreign Affairs, Ministry of Internal Affairs, Ministry of Defense, Ministry of Justice, Ministry of Finance, Ministry of Oil and Gas, Ministry of Economic Development and Trade, Ministry of Industry and New Technologies, Ministry of Agriculture, Ministry of Transport and Communications, Ministry of Information, Ministry of Labor and Social Protection, Ministry of Emergency Situation, Ministry of Health, Ministry of Education and Science, Ministry of Culture, Ministry of Environment Protection and Ministry of Tourism and Sport.
15. As of May 2011, in Kazakhstan there are the following seven agencies: the Agency of Statistics, the Land Agency, the Anti-Monopoly Agency, the Agency on the Regulation of Natural Monopolies, the Construction Agency and the National Space Agency.

The advisory-consultative bodies such as the Security Council, the Council on Legal Policy and the Council on Religious Affairs may exist under both the President and the Government. Despite their advisory status, these bodies can also carry out administrative competences related to issuing obligatory instructions to different state bodies or inquiring for information.

Special state commissions (permanent or temporary, with or without participation of civil society representatives) deal with certain administrative functions such as the protection of minors' rights and army conscription (e.g., the Commission on the Protection of Minors' Rights contributes to the control of education and living conditions of minors, while the Army Conscription Commission decides issues regarding draft deferment).

C. State Officials

Under the Law of RK of July 23, 1999, No. 453-I, "On State Service" (LSS), a state official is a citizen of RK who occupies a position in a state body (legislative, executive or judicial) that is financed by the republican- or local-level state budgets or the National Bank and who performs duties for the implementation of state tasks and functions.[16] Issues regarding state service are dealt with by a special body in the system of state administration, the State Service Agency.

In order to be accepted to state service a person must: (a) have Kazakhstani citizenship; (b) have reached 18 years of age; (c) have the proper education, the required level of professionalism and must comply with the respective qualification requirements (Article 13 LSS). Under the legislation, there are two types of state officials: political and administrative. The political officials are those who realize political aims and tasks and who are: (a) either appointed by the President or elected by the Parliament's chambers (e.g., members of the Government, members of the Constitutional Council, judges of the Supreme Court, heads of the regional executive bodies, etc.); (b) heads of the central executive bodies such as the heads of the departments; and (c) official representatives of the President or the Government. All other officials are administrative. They are divided into 5 categories (A, B, C, D and E). Each category specifies a level in the state hierarchy (for instance, the category "A" indicates an official of the Presidential Administration) and is subdivided into a certain number of ranks showing the level of the position within that category.

Almost all state officials are appointed (and only a few are elected). Before appointment, all candidates must undergo a selection process consisting of three stages: (a) consideration of the documents; (b) testing; and (c) personal interview. Political servants, former deputies and judges are exempt from

16. It should be mentioned that there are certain groups of state officials whose service is also regulated by additional acts (such as military, police and national security officers). People who work in state organizations (e.g., medical or educational institutions) are not recognized as state officials.

such processes. The following persons cannot be admitted to state service: (a) incapable persons; (b) persons who have no right to occupy a state position by court decision; (c) persons who have medical problems; and (d) persons who have an offense (in particular, corruption) on their record. After admission to state service, administrative officials may undergo a test period of up to three months. In addition, every three years, administrative officials must go through a performance evaluation in order to check their abilities to carry out state functions properly.

Holding a state position is subject to a number of limitations. State officials are denied the following rights: (a) to be a deputy of any legislative body; (b) to conduct any other paid activity except for pedagogical, scientific or creative activity; (c) to be engaged in the activity of commercial organizations unless such participation is performed due to his official duties; (d) to represent interests of third persons in any state bodies; (e) to misuse official information, finances or property in activities not related to official office; (f) to participate in actions hindering the proper functioning of state bodies such as strikes; and (g) to use the service of third parties in connection with their official activity (Article 10 LSS). Other limitations include an obligation to transfer all corporate shares and other corporate property to a trust manager within a month after entering office (however, they may receive income from such property). Furthermore, state officials cannot occupy positions subordinate to their close relatives (parents, spouses, brothers, sisters and children). They can be members of political parties but are prohibited from creating political-party-based groups in their state bodies.

In the case of a violation of such rules, state officials are subject to either disciplinary or administrative liability. The former is imposed in cases of small disciplinary violations connected with service discipline; the sanctions include reproof, reprimand, severe reprimand, notification of incomplete service correspondence and dismissal. The latter is connected with violations that result in damage to public safety or the interests of other persons; in this case, the sanctions are either a re-proof or a fine.

There are various grounds for the termination of state service. In cases related to administrative officials, these grounds include: (a) dismissal from office by own initiative; (b) termination of contract; (c) reaching the pension age (58 for women and 63 for men); (d) giving false information regarding incomes and property; (e) non-observance of duties and limitations established by the law; (f) neglecting the transfer of designated property to a trust manager; (g) termination of citizenship; (h) perpetration of various offenses; (i) occupation of position without due selection process; and (j) negative results of performance evaluation (Article 27 LSS). Political officials can be dismissed on some of the above-mentioned grounds (such as non-observance of duties and limitations established by the law); but their office may also be terminated in case of resignation, decision of a superior body (or official) or termination of the respective state body.

III. LEGAL FORMS OF STATE ADMINISTRATION ACTIONS

Administrative Law establishes a framework that provides legal forms for activities of state administration. These forms are divided into two groups: (a) legal; and (b) non-legal. The difference is expressed through consequences. The legal forms result in legal consequences, and the non-legal do not directly involve legal consequences and have subsidiary significance covering such actions as office work, archiving, information provision and organizational work (e.g., meetings, inspection, instructions). Administrative Law pays more attention to legal forms, which mainly include (a) issuing acts (regulatory and individual) and (b) concluding administrative contracts.

A. Acts of State Administration Bodies

State administration bodies may issue regulatory legal acts which are one source of law in the Kazakhstani legal system.[17] State administration bodies issuing acts may also interpret their content. Most regulatory acts of state administration bodies (except resolutions of the Government) must be registered if they are related to individual freedoms, rights and duties. The body responsible for such registration is the Ministry of Justice, which supervises the compliance of submitted acts with the laws and other superior regulatory acts. The acts may be repealed by the body itself, a superior body or the court; also, they may be recognized in full or in part as unconstitutional by the Constitutional Council (see the Law of RK of March 24, 1998, No. 213-I, "On Normative Legal Acts").

Individual acts issued by state administration bodies are stipulated by the Law of RK of November 27, 2000, No. 107-II, "On Administrative Procedures." Only five articles of this Law are devoted to those acts (mostly connected with the requirements for drafting an act and providing rules under which individual acts may be terminated or modified by the body itself, a superior body or the court), which leaves significant space for the discretion of state authorities.

B. Administrative Contracts

This is a relatively new area of Administrative Law because traditionally all contracts were considered to fall under the domain of Private Law. Even today, many scholars, especially specialists in Civil Law, do not recognize contracts under the framework of Public Law.

At the same time, administrative contracts can be encountered more and more often in administrative practice (e.g., contracts involving state and military officials; agreements between different state bodies resolving certain

17. See section III "Domestic Sources of Law" in Chapter 2 "Basic Features of the Legal System."

public problems; and cooperation agreements between state bodies and non-government organizations). These contracts differ from Private Law contracts in the following aspects: they (a) aim at resolving state administration problems (with no goal of generating profit); (b) are usually of an organizational nature; (c) are preceded by acts of state administration bodies; and (d) are not always protected by court.

IV. LEGAL METHODS OF STATE ADMINISTRATION ACTIONS

A. Administrative Enforcement

Along with the aforementioned forms, Administrative Law deals with the methods of state administration actions that provide tools and instruments for state administration in its relations with individuals and organizations. Generally, there are two universal methods of management activity: (a) persuasion and (b) enforcement. Administrative Law focuses on the latter.

"Administrative enforcement" implies the application of special measures by state administration bodies, courts and some other (mainly state) organizations as stipulated in the legislation. Such enforcement arises in cases of administrative (or other) offenses as well as in cases of the implementation of certain state functions.

Administrative enforcement can be exercised in or outside of court. In addition, there are many other bodies entitled to apply administrative enforcement such as police, tax, customs, environmental and sanitary bodies. Unlike other forms of legal coercion, administrative enforcement can be implemented with respect to both individuals and organizations.

Different laws mention various administrative enforcement measures. What is common among all of them is the principle of legality, meaning: (a) only authorized state bodies are entitled to apply enforcement measures; (b) state bodies can apply only those measures stipulated by the laws; and (c) application of all measures must be in accordance with established legal procedures.

There are three groups of administrative enforcement measures. *The first group* outlines the measures for the prevention of legal violations and public endangerment. Such measures include inspections, examinations, quarantines and restrictions on the transport of people or vehicles. *The second group* specifies the measures used to suppress illegal actions or inactions (e.g., administrative detention, temporary termination of the activity of organizations, etc.). *The third group* covers measures of liability whose aim is the punishment of offenses (described below).

Administrative Law also deals with enforcement measures applied in the framework of administrative regimes, understood as a set of rules regulating certain issues or situations requiring special state attention. Usually, such rules are connected with additional limitations, restrictions and registrations for individuals and organizations. Administrative Law distinguishes ordinary regimes (such as passport, customs, ecological, frontier) and extraordinary regimes (such as state of emergency and martial law).[18]

B. Administrative Liability

Until the present, Administrative Law has been identified by many lawyers as only related to administrative liability issues. Certainly, administrative liability issues do occupy an important position in the system of Administrative Law, since this branch of law traditionally dealt mostly with the regulation of state police activity. Administrative punishment was a very popular instrument in the hands of the state in order to influence the behavior of individuals and their associations.

Administrative liability is one of the classic kinds of liability existing in the Kazakhstani legal system (along with disciplinary, civil and criminal liability). This type of liability is expressed by imposing special "administrative" sanctions by different state bodies for administrative offenses committed by individuals and legal entities.[19]

According to the Kazakhstani legal approach, which reflects Kazakhstan's Soviet background, administrative liability is the liability of individuals or organizations before the state (which is different from another approach that defines administrative liability as the liability of the state before individuals or organizations). Another vestige of Soviet law is the existence of a special regulatory act that provides a detailed regulation of administrative liability issues (i.e., Code of RK of January 30, 2001 "On Administrative Offenses"). This Code contains a description of about 1,000 offenses in various spheres of public life (such as sanitary, ecological, transportation, anti-monopoly, tax, customs, fire, etc.). These offenses, which are considered administrative, differ from criminal offenses in that they have no such degree of public endangerment or serious consequences.

The Code stipulates the following types of administrative sanctions: (a) warning; (b) administrative fine; (c) requisition or confiscation of property that was a tool or object of the administrative offense; (d) revocation of special rights such as a driver's license or the right to keep and bear arms; (f) revocation or suspension of a license or a special permission to engage in a certain activity; (g) suspension or prohibition of the activities of individual businesses or legal entities; (h) compulsory demolition of unauthorized buildings; (i) administrative arrest; and (j) administrative deportation of foreign citizens or persons without citizenship (Article 45).

---

18. Some regimes are specially described in separate laws such as the Law of RK of February 8, 2003, No. 387-II, "On State of Emergency" and the Law of RK of March 5, 2003, No. 391-II, "On Martial Law."

19. Recently, discussion has begun regarding the nature of the administrative liability and its affiliation with Administrative Law. There are opinions that no such liability should exist or such liability should be incorporated in criminal liability rather than being dealt with by Administrative Law.

Responsible individuals who have reached the age of 16 can be subject to administrative liability. Legal entities and in certain cases (such as tax offenses), their branches and representative offices are also subject to administrative liability. Administrative sanctions can be imposed either by courts or numerous administrative agencies including tax, customs, road police, ecological and transportation (however, individuals have the right to demand a judicial court consideration of the sanctions).

Since February 2002, there are the so-called specialized administrative courts in Kazakhstan whose purpose is to consider: (a) administrative offenses; or (b) complaints of individuals and legal entities regarding resolutions adopted by administrative agencies in the process of imposing administrative sanctions. At the same time, however, there are still no administrative courts (or similar bodies) that would deal with disputes between state bodies and citizens or their associations.

V. ADMINISTRATIVE PROCEDURE

The modern Kazakhstani legal system does not differentiate between Administrative Law and Administrative Procedure (as with respect to Civil Law and Civil Procedure; or Criminal Law and Criminal Procedure). Thus, the different procedural issues that arise in state administration are currently incorporated into Administrative Law, and there is intense debate about what subject matter Administrative Procedure should cover: (a) those related to disputes between the state, and individuals and their associations; (b) those connected with administrative sanctions; (c) those connected to positive administrative procedures; or (d) a combination of the first three.[20]

A. Positive Administrative Procedures

The Law of RK of November 27, 2000, No. 325-IV "On Administrative Procedures" stipulates four types of positive administrative procedures: (a) adoption and realization of decisions by state bodies and officials while implementing their functions; (b) internal organization procedures of state bodies; (c) consideration of citizens' appeals to state bodies and protection of their rights and interests; and (d) basic procedures of decision-making in the economic field.

The Law also provides the principles for the establishment of administrative procedures which are: (a) legality; (b) equality; (c) priority of citizens' rights and

20. This part of Administrative Law is underdeveloped due to various issues including legal culture and legal traditions. There is no comprehensive regulatory act which covers administrative procedures despite the existence of the Law of RK of November 27, 2000, No. 325-IV, "On Administrative Procedures" (this law has only 25 articles which obviously cannot cover all procedures).

freedoms; (d) prohibition of bureaucratic inflexibility (*burokratism*); (e) obligation of all citizens and organizations to follow administrative procedures; (f) mutual responsibility and balance of interests of individuals, society and the state; (g) public participation; (h) proscription of corruption; (i) observance of prohibitions and limitations established for state officials; (j) separation of competences and concerted activity of all state bodies and state officials, etc. However, the Law is only a framework without the detailed elaboration of rules that is necessary in any set of procedural regulations.

It should be mentioned that due to the political decision to use corporate management methods in the relations between the state and individuals, new approaches in the execution of state functions have been developed in recent years. Many functions of state bodies were moved into the regime of government service, which is aimed at satisfying the needs of individuals and legal entities upon their petitioning. Administrative Law governs the execution of government services and provides a number of regulatory acts that stipulate the standards and procedures of such services.

A challenge for modern Administrative Law is the establishment of electronic government. More and more services of state bodies are offered electronically and individuals and organizations use these electronic resources more frequently. Moreover, the state intends to further develop this medium of communication. However, despite numerous possibilities in this area, conservative administrative practice and technological problems pose serious obstacles for such development. One of the roles of modern Administrative Law is to facilitate this new regime of relations between the state and individuals in order to ameliorate many problems specific to state administration such as corruption, bureaucratic inflexibility and inefficiency.

B. Administrative Procedure as Applied to Judicial Proceedings

Administrative Procedure is still regulated by the norms of the Civil Procedure Code of RK of July 13, 1999. This fact can be explained by the legacy of the Soviet system, wherein disputes arising between the state and citizens were rare. It was traditionally thought that Soviet state bodies could not adopt decisions or take actions conflicting with the rights and freedoms of citizens. The notion that the state was never at fault and did not make mistakes dominated the political and the legal culture. Thus, there was no need to develop a system of administrative justice.

Under the current Constitution, everyone is entitled to a judicial defense of their rights and freedoms (Article 13 II CRK). This also includes protection from illegal actions of state bodies by the courts. Thus, in accordance with the Civil Procedure Code, any regulatory acts, as well as decisions or (in)actions of state bodies or officials, may be appealed by citizens and legal entities who believe that these acts, decisions or (in)actions violate or impede their rights, freedoms or interests or impose an illegal duty or sanction. The period for filing appeals to the court is three months from the moment when the petitioning citizens or legal entities have become aware of the violation of their rights, freedoms or interests. In doing so, preliminary appeal to a superior state body is not obligatory.

It should also be mentioned that at present discussions are going on to adopt an Administrative Procedure Code (in order to avoid situations where the same procedures are based on different codes such as the Code on Administrative Offenses and the Civil Procedure Code) and to create special administrative courts whose purpose will be to consider public law disputes.

In conclusion, it should be mentioned that modern Administrative Law of RK can be characterized as a branch of law with many discrepancies. It still has the imprints of Soviet Administrative Law characterized by the uncontested domination of state interests. Administrative Law is still frequently considered an oppressive tool in the hands of the state. After the collapse of the Soviet system, the reform of Administrative Law did not enjoy the same amount of state support as Private Law development. Moreover, it lacks attention among scholars, and this presents an obstacle for the creation of an effective public administration system.

At the same time, in the 20 years since the collapse of the Soviet Union the modern political and legal system has influenced many spheres of Administrative Law. It now more actively protects individual and private organization rights, freedoms and interests from illegal state intervention. Thus, contemporary Kazakhstani Administrative Law has significant potential to develop further and to serve its genuine purpose: to protect individuals' rights in relation to state administration, to make sure that the relationship between individuals and the state does not contradict their mutual interests and to benefit both state administration and individuals.

Selected Bibliography

R. Podoprigora *Административное право* [*Administrative Law*] (Nalogovyi Expert, Almaty, 2010) [in Russian].

R. Podoprigora, "Problems and Perspectives of the Development of Administrative Law in Kazakhstan" (2009) 12 *Jurist* 26–28 [in Russian].

A. Taranov (ed.), *Административное право Республики Казахстан* [*Administrative Law of the Republic of Kazakhstan*] General Part (Žeti Žargi, Almaty, 1996); Special Part (Žeti Žargi, Almaty, 1998) [in Russian].

V. Uvarov, *Государственная служба и управление* [*State Service and Administration*] (KazGYuU, Petropavlovsk, 2004) [in Russian].

Chapter 6
Law of Persons

Maidan Suleimenov & Zhenis Kembayev

As it is universally applied, under Kazakhstani law the term "person" implies someone or something that is recognized by law as the subject of rights and duties, i.e., someone or something that has legal personality. What is known as Law of Persons in common law systems (i.e., the law governing the legal status of persons under private law) is primarily encompassed by the General Part of the Civil Code (CC) of RK[1] and in particular by Chapter I "General Provisions" (Articles 1-11 CC) and Chapter II "Subjects of Civil Rights" (Articles 12–144 CC).

The Civil Code distinguishes and provides rules with respect to two major types of persons (or subjects of civil rights): (a) natural persons; and (b) legal entities (organizations) (Article 1 CC). Although the state (including its administrative-territorial entities) may also participate in civil law relations, it may do so only on the principle of equality with other participants of these relations (Articles 2, 111 I, 112 I CC).

1. The Civil Code of RK consists of two parts: General (adopted on December 27, 1994) and Special (adopted on July 1, 1999). It is within Civil Law tradition and was mostly influenced by the Russian Civil Code. See Chapter 2 "Basic Features of the Legal System."

Zhenis Kembayev, *Introduction to the Law of Kazakhstan*, pp. 89–108.

I. NATURAL PERSONS

A. Generally

Natural persons (*zheke tülga, fizicheskoe litso*) are defined by the Civil Code of RK to be "citizens of the Republic of Kazakhstan, foreign citizens as well as stateless persons" (Article 12 CC). According to the Constitution of RK, foreign citizens and stateless persons enjoy the same rights and freedoms and bear the same responsibilities established for the citizens of RK unless otherwise stipulated by the Constitution, laws and international treaties (Article 12 IV). The Civil Code fully reflects this constitutional provision and stipulates that all natural persons (who are also traditionally termed "citizens" in the Civil Code[2]) have equal rights and obligations unless provided otherwise by legislative acts (Article 3 VII).[3]

Natural persons (like as other subjects of civil law relations) must possess certain characteristics (the so-called means of individualization) that enable them to be differentiated among other participants in civil law relations. These characteristics include: (1) name; (2) place of residence; (3) legal address; and (4) acts of civil status.

A "name," as recognized in law, is given to a natural person at birth (Article 15 III CC). It includes a person's surname, his forename and also, at his wish, his patronymic; its major purpose is to identify a person and distinguish him from others. The Civil Code specifically provides that a natural person acquires and effectuates his rights and obligations under his own name (Article 15 I CC). After achievement of the age of 16 any person may change his surname, forename and/or patronymic upon applying to the bodies of civil registration at the place of his residence (Article 194 I of the Law of RK of December 17, 1998, No. 321-I, "On Marriage and Family" (LMF)). Also, the legislation may allow, in certain cases, the acquisition of rights and obligations by natural persons on an anonymous basis as well as the use of a fictitious name (pseudonym). The right to a name is considered to be a "personal non-property right," and it cannot be transferred or alienated to other persons. A citizen may demand the prohibition of the use of his name when this has been done without his consent. The acquisition of rights and obligations under the name of another person is prohibited. Also, any citizen may demand compensation for the harm caused to him as a result of the unlawful use of his name (Article 15 VII-IX CC).

The "place of residence" is the population settlement where a citizen permanently or primarily lives. The place of residence of persons who have not attained 14 years of age or citizens under trusteeship is deemed to be the place of residence

2. The general term "citizens" as applied in the Civil Code implies all natural persons.
3. The Civil Code of RK does not establish any restrictions of rights of foreign citizens and stateless persons. However, certain limitations are established by related legislative acts. For example, foreign citizens and stateless persons may not privately own land designated for agricultural production or forest cultivation (Art. 23 IV of the Land Code of RK of June 20, 2003, No. 442-II [LdC]). They may only lease such land on a competitive basis for a period of up to 10 years (Art. 48 II LdC).

of their parents, adoptive parents or trustees (Article 16 II CC). *The legal address* of a natural person is deemed to be the place of his registration. Another means of individualization of a natural person is *acts of civil status*, which are official documents enabling identification of each person and individualizing his rights and obligations (Article 1 XII LMF). Such documents are issued with respect to such circumstances as: birth, death, marriage, divorce, adoption, establishment of paternity or change of name (surname, patronymic name) (Article 163 LMF).

A natural person, as a subject of civil law relations, possesses legal personality (*qüqyq ielenu qabileti, pravosubektnost'*), which includes two different components: legal capacity and dispositive legal capacity. Legal capacity is the capacity of a citizen to have civil rights and bear obligations while dispositive legal capacity is defined to be the capacity of a citizen by his own actions to acquire and effectuate civil rights, to create civil obligations for himself and to perform those obligations.

B. Legal Capacity of Natural Persons

Legal capacity (*qüqyqtyq qabileti, pravosposobnot'*) is recognized in equal measure for all natural persons. It arises at the moment of birth and is terminated by death (Article 13 CC).

The Civil Code provides specific provisions as to what constitutes the basic content of legal capacity and stipulates that any citizen is entitled to have the following rights: (1) to have property by right of ownership, including foreign currency, both within the limits of the RK and beyond its boundaries; (2) to inherit and bequeath property; (3) to move freely about the territory of the Republic and select the place of residence; (4) to freely leave the limits of the Republic and return to its territory; (5) to engage in any activity not prohibited by legislative acts; (6) to create legal entities independently or with other citizens and legal entities; (7) to conclude any transactions not prohibited by legislative acts and participate in obligations; (8) to have the right to intellectual property in inventions, works of science, literature, art and any other results of intellectual activity; (9) to demand compensation for material and moral harm; and (10) to have other property and personal rights (Article 14 CC).

Obviously, the above list of legal authorities (which basically constitutes the "general" legal capacity of natural persons) is not complete, which means that natural persons may possess other rights defined either by legislative acts or by contract (i.e., they may have "special" legal capacity). In this regard, in particular to be noted are those natural persons who are engaged in entrepreneurial activity without the formation of a legal entity (individual entrepreneurs) and are given a number of additional rights (discussed *infra*).

C. Dispositive Legal Capacity of Natural Persons

Dispositive legal capacity (*äreket qabileti, deesposobnost'*) of natural persons arises in full with the ensuing of majority, that is, upon attaining 18 years of age. To be noted also is that a citizen may acquire dispositive legal capacity in full from the time of entering into marriage (Article 17 CC), which is possible according to Kazakhstani Family Law under exceptional circumstances starting from the age of 16 (discussed *infra* in Chapter 9 "Family and Inheritance Law").

It is common to differentiate two components within dispositive legal capacity of a natural person: (1) the ability to conclude transactions and other lawful actions (*mämile zhurguzu qabileti, sdelkosposobnost'*) and (2) the ability to bear contractual and non-contractual liability (*zhauapkershilik alu qabileti, deliktosposobnost'*).

Dispositive Legal Capacity of Minors: Until the age of 18, natural persons possess incomplete or partial dispositive legal capacity, the amount of which depends on the attainment of certain ages. According to the Civil Code of RK, there are two groups of minors: (1) up to 14 years of age; and (2) from 14 to 18.

For minors who have not attained 14 years of age, transactions are concluded in their names by their parents, adoptive parents or trustees (*qamqorshy, opekun*). Minors under 14 only have the right to autonomously conclude petty domestic transactions corresponding to their age, which are performed when they are concluded (Article 23 CC).

Minors in age from 14 to 18 years may conclude transactions generally only with the consent of parents, adoptive parents or guardians (*qorghanshy, popechitel'*) (in so doing, the form of such consent must correspond to the form that has been established by legislation for a transaction concluded by a minor). Still, they may autonomously dispose of their earnings, stipend and other revenues and of intellectual property created by them, and also conclude petty domestic transactions. Additionally, they may make deposits in banks and autonomously dispose of them. Furthermore, they autonomously bear responsibility for transactions committed by them and for any harm caused by their actions. However, when there are sufficient grounds, a trusteeship and guardianship agency may limit or deprive a minor of the right to autonomously dispose of his earnings or any other income (Articles 22 and 23 CC).

On January 12, 2007 the above general rules with respect to minors in age up to 18 years were supplemented by rules stipulating that minors who have attained 16 years of age may acquire full dispositive legal capacity if they work under a labor contract or are engaged in entrepreneurial activity (which is possible with the consent of their parents, adoptive parents or guardians). It is possible for a minor who has obtained 16 years of age to acquire dispositive legal capacity (defined as "emancipation" by the Civil Code) upon the decision of a trusteeship and guardianship agency in the event that the emancipation is done with the consent of their parents, adoptive parents or guardians. Should the minor's parents, adoptive parents or trustees refuse to consent, the emancipation may be done by judicial decision. Emancipated minors may acquire civil rights and autonomously bear obligations except only for those that require age qualification as established by the legislation of RK. Parents, adoptive parents or guardians may not be held responsible for obligations of emancipated minors (Article 22-1 CC).

Deprivation and Limitation of Dispositive Legal Capacity: No one may be deprived of or limited in dispositive legal capacity other than in instances provided by the legislation of RK; the proper process, as stipulated in the relevant legislation, must also be followed (Article 18 CC). According to the Civil Code of RK, there are two such instances as follows:

First, a citizen who, as a consequence of his abuse of alcohol or narcotics, places his family in a grave material position may be limited in dispositive legal capacity by the courts. An application for the limitation of a citizen's dispositive legal capacity may be submitted to the court by his family members, close relatives (parents, children, brothers and sisters), a procurator or trusteeship and guardianship agency (Article 302 I of the Civil Procedure Code (CPC)). If the court limits a citizen in his dispositive legal capacity, a guardianship is established over him. As a result, he will be able to independently conclude only petty domestic transactions; concluding any other transactions and receiving earnings, pension benefits or any other revenues and disposing of these revenues requires the consent of the guardian. If the citizen ends his abuse of alcohol or narcotics, the court may vacate the limitation of his dispositive legal capacity and remove the guardianship established over him.

Second, a citizen who, as a consequence of mental illness or feeble-mindedness, cannot understand the significance of his actions or direct them may be recognized by the court to lack dispositive legal capacity (or, in other words, to be incapable), in connection with which a trusteeship is established over him (Article 26 CC). An application for the recognition of a citizen as incapable may be submitted to the court by the same persons as with respect to the limitation of dispositive legal capacity, as well as by a psychiatric medical institution (Article 302 II CPC). Should the court recognize a citizen as incapable, all transactions in his name are to be concluded by his trustee. In the event of the recuperation of or significant improvement in the health of the citizen, a court may return him, his dispositive legal capacity, after which the trusteeship is removed (Article 26 CC).

Declaration of a Person to be Missing or Deceased: A citizen may be deemed by a court to be missing if, for one year, there is no information at his place of residence concerning him (Article 28 CC). On the basis of the decision of a court, trusteeship may be established over the property of a person deemed to be missing. Maintenance is to be issued from this property to persons whom the missing person was obliged to maintain, and indebtedness must be repaid for taxes and other obligations of the missing person. If the person has been missing for less than one year, a trusteeship and guardianship agency may still appoint a trustee to protect and manage the property upon the application of interested persons. In the event of the appearance or discovery of the missing person, the court's decision concerning the establishment of a trusteeship over his property must be vacated.

Should there be no information about a citizen at his place of residence in the course of three years, he may be declared by a court to be deceased. If a citizen was missing under threatening circumstances or giving grounds to suppose he perished from an accident, he may be declared by a court to be deceased upon the expiry of six months. Special rules apply with respect to military servicemen or other persons who are missing in connection with military actions. Those persons may be declared to be deceased upon the expiration of two years from the date of the military action's end (Article 31 CC).

In the event of the appearance or discovery of the whereabouts of a person declared to be deceased, the respective decision will be vacated by the court. Irrespective of the time of his appearance, this person may demand from any other persons the return of property preserved that passed to them without compensation. If the property of this person was alienated by his legal successor to third parties who, at the moment of the appearance of the person, had not paid the purchase price in full, the right to demand the unpaid amount will pass to the person who has appeared.

Persons to whom property of a citizen declared to be deceased has passed are obliged to return this property to him or to compensate the value thereof if it is proved that, at the moment of acquisition of the property, they knew that the citizen declared deceased was alive. The alienator of property who knew at the moment of alienation that the person declared to be deceased was alive must bear jointly and severally with the acquirer the duty to return or compensate the value of the property. If the property of a person declared to be deceased has passed by right of inheritance to the state and was sold, then after the vacating of the court' decision, he must be repaid the amount derived from the sale of the property (Article 32 CC).

An application for the declaration of a person either to be missing or to be deceased may be submitted to the court by his family members, a procurator, public associations, a trusteeship and guardianship agency or other interested persons (Article 296 II CPC).

D. Individual Entrepreneurs

The Constitution of RK guarantees everyone to have the right to freedom of entrepreneurial activity and free use of his property for any legal entrepreneurial activity (Article 26 IV). Following this constitutional provision, the Civil Code provides specifically that natural persons may engage in entrepreneurial activity without the formation of a legal entity (Article 19 CC).

The Civil Code also stipulates that the rights of such natural persons, who are called "individual entrepreneurs," will be defended and supported by the state. In particular, their rights (like the rights of legal entities engaging in entrepreneurial activity) are defended by: (1) the possibility of the effectuation of entrepreneurial activity without receiving any authorizations whatsoever except for types of activity that require licenses; (2) a maximally simple registration procedure, without prior arrangement, of all types of entrepreneurship in all spheres of the economy in one registration agency; (3) the limitation by legislative acts of verifications of entrepreneurial activity being effectuated by state agencies; (4) the compulsory termination of entrepreneurial activity only by the decision of a court rendered on grounds provided for by a legislative act; (5) the establishment by legislative acts of a list of types of work, goods and services that have been prohibited for private entrepreneurship or prohibited or limited for export or import; and (6) the imposition of liability upon state agencies, officials and other persons and organizations, as established by legislation, for illegally obstructing the activity of entrepreneurs (Article 10 II CC).

At present, mandatory state registration is required only for those individual entrepreneurs who: (1) hire a labor force on permanent basis; and/or (2) receive annual income from private entrepreneurship that exceeds the tax-free amount established by the legislation of RK.[4] The registration is done in the local tax organ at the place of his residence without preliminary permission. A certificate of the state registration must be provided within three working days upon the submission of all required documents and is issued for an unlimited period of time.

As was already mentioned, individual entrepreneurs possess special legal capacity, which is in particular expressed in the following rights: (a) to conduct any kinds of private entrepreneurship unless otherwise established by the legislation of RK; (b) to hire a labor force in accordance with the legislation of RK; (c) to establish branches and representative offices; (d) to independently set prices for produced goods (work, services) except for cases provided for by the legislation of RK; (e) to conduct foreign economic activity within their legal capacity; (f) to establish associations; (g) to participate in work of expert councils through their certified associations; (h) to petition law-enforcement and judicial bodies for the purpose of protecting their rights and legal interests; and (i) to propose to state bodies methods to eliminate causes of non-performance or improper performance of regulatory legal acts adopted to support private entrepreneurship (Article 8 I of the Law of RK of January 31, 2006, No. 124-III, "On Private Entrepreneurship" (LPE)). However, the duties of the individual entrepreneurs include (along with general requirement to observe the legislation of RK as well as rights and interests of other persons) such responsibilities as: (a) to assure compliance of output products (work, services) with the requirements of the legislation of RK; (b) to obtain licenses for conducting business subject to licensing in accordance with the legislation of RK; and (c) to maintain compulsory insurance of civil liability in accordance with the legislation of RK (Article 8 II LPE).

According to the LPE, individual entrepreneurs are differentiated into those who conduct their activity on separate and joint bases. While separate entrepreneurship is carried out by one person independently on the basis of his own property, joint entrepreneurship is conducted by a group of persons (e.g., spouses or a family) on the basis of property that belongs to them under common ownership rights.

Furthermore, the Law distinguishes small-, mid- and large-scale businesses. Individual entrepreneurs may represent either small- or mid-scale businesses. Small-scale entrepreneurs are those who employ less than 50 people and whose

4. Those individual entrepreneurs who do not use the labor of employees and receive either income taxable at the source of payment or property income are not required to register.

assets' value does not exceed 60,000 monthly calculation indexes (MCIs).[5] Mid-scale entrepreneurs are those who employ between 50 and 250 people and whose assets' value does not exceed 325,000 MCIs. Large-scale businesses employ more than 250 employees and possess assets worth more than 325,000 MCIs, and may only be legal entities.

In particular small-scale entrepreneurs may receive a number of benefits and privileges related to state programs supporting private entrepreneurship (financial assistance, concessional lending, creation and maintenance of business incubators, etc.) However, certain individual entrepreneurs may not be recognized as "small-scale businesses" and thus be supported by the state, especially those whose activity is related to: (1) the production and/or wholesale of excisable products; (2) the storage of grain; (3) narcotic or psychotropic substances; (4) gambling, show business or running lotteries; (5) radioactive materials; (6) the extraction, refining and sale of oil, oil products, gas and electrical and heat energy; (7) auditing, banking, insurance (except for the activities of an individual insurance agent); and (8) professional activity on the equity markets (Article 6 LPE).

State programs supporting private entrepreneurship may be at the republican- or regional-level or sectoral (industry-specific). They are approved by the President of RK and are mandatory for all state bodies. The Government of RK must annually submit a report to the President on the results of the implementation of state programs supporting private entrepreneurship (Article 20 LPE).

A natural person's liability for his obligations is extended to all of his property, except for property against which execution may not be levied in accordance with legislative acts (Article 20 CC).[6] In the case of the consistent inability of an individual entrepreneur to satisfy the demands of his creditor; to pay compensation to persons working under a labor contract; or to make tax, social, pension or other obligatory payments to the state, an individual entrepreneur may be deemed to be bankrupt by a court. Bankruptcy may be effectuated either voluntarily (on the basis of an application to that effect by an individual entrepreneur to a court) or compulsorily (on the basis of an application by a creditor or in cases provided for by legislation).[7] As a result of the bankruptcy, the registration of the citizen as an individual entrepreneur loses its force. Generally, bankruptcy procedures follow the same rules as with respect to legal entities (see *infra*). However, there are also certain specific regulations. Thus, the claims of the creditors are satisfied only after the court and bankruptcy manager expenses are covered. After completing the settlement of accounts with creditors, the individual entrepreneur deemed to be bankrupt is relieved from the performance of his residual obligations connected with his entrepreneurial activity, except for demands relating to causing harm to life or health and other demands of a personal character (Article 21 CC).

5. See the "List of Abbreviations" (*supra*) for an explanation of the concept of MCI.
6. A list of the property of natural persons against which execution may not be levied is established by the Civil Procedure Code of RK.
7. Such as invalid registration, repeated or severe violation of the legislation of RK or declaration of an individual entrepreneur to be missing or to be deceased (Art. 28 IV LPE).

II. LEGAL ENTITIES

A. Concept and Types of Legal Entities

According to the Civil Code, a legal entity (*zangdy tülga, yuridicheskoe litso*) is an organization that: (a) has specific separate property by right of ownership, economic management or operative management; (b) must fulfill its obligations or face the seizure of its property; (c) may, in its name, acquire and effectuate property and personal non-property rights and duties; (d) may be a plaintiff or defendant in court; (e) must have an autonomous balance sheet or financial records and a seal with its own name (Article 33 CC).

This definition establishes four distinct characteristics of a legal entity. *First*, it has a distinct organizational structure that allows it to operate as a separate person. *Second*, it has separate property owned independently from its members. *Third*, liability for its obligations is covered by its independent property. *Fourth*, it has individual legal capacity to participate in civil law transactions (substantive legal capacity) and capacity to sue and be sued in its own name (procedural legal capacity).

Legal entities are differentiated into two major types: commercial and non-commercial. A commercial legal entity is defined as "an organization pursuing profit as the basic purpose of its activity" while a non-commercial legal entity is an "organization not having profit as its basic purpose and not distributing profit as dividends to its participants" (Article 34 I CC). Thus, there are two features distinguishing a commercial organization from a non-commercial one: (a) the deriving of profit as the main purpose of the activity; and (b) the distribution of profit. Even though a non-commercial organization may also pursue entrepreneurial activity if so provided by its charter (Article 34 III CC), it may not pursue profit as its main objective. Although it may earn income, its activity's main purposes must be different (and usually are of cultural, educational, political or social nature). Furthermore, in contrast to a commercial legal entity, a non-commercial one does not distribute the net profit between the participants.

These two major types of legal entities are subdivided into various categories specifically determined by the Civil Code. Thus, a commercial legal entity may be created solely in the form of a state enterprise, business partnership, joint-stock company or production co-operative (Article 34 II CC); no other kinds of commercial organizations may be created. A different approach is taken with respect to non-commercial legal entities which may be created in the form of an institution, public association, joint-stock company, consumer co-operative, public foundation, religious association or any other form provided for by legislative acts (Article 34 III CC). Accordingly, the Civil Code contains a possibility for the establishment of new kinds of non-commercial legal entities on the basis of legislative acts. Thus, the Law of RK of January 16, 2001, No. 142-II, "On Non-commercial Organizations" (LNCO) introduced new kinds of noncommercial legal entities such as notary chambers, associations of attorneys, commerce and industry chambers, chambers of auditors, cooperatives of apartment owners and other non-commercial organizations.

B. Legal Capacity of a Legal Entity

The legal capacity of a legal entity arises at the moment of its creation and terminates at the moment of the completion of its liquidation (Article 35 II CC).

Commercial and non-commercial legal entities have different amounts of legal capacity. The former have general legal capacity, implying that they may engage in any kinds of activities, except for those expressly prohibited for either all legal entities or only specific kinds of them (prohibitions may be contained either in legislative acts or in the constitutive documents of legal entities); while the latter possess special legal capacity, i.e., they may exercise only those activities that are provided for by their constitutive documents. Thus, commercial legal entities may have any civil rights and bear any duties that are necessary for the exercise of their activities, even if they are not explicitly indicated in their constitutive documents. The only exception is state enterprises, which are commercial organizations that have special legal capacity (in fact, they may not alienate property, lease property for a long term, establish branches and subsidiaries, etc. without consent of an authorized state body).

Furthermore, it should be noted that the legal capacity of a legal entity that operates in a field requiring a license arises from the moment of receipt of that license and terminates at the moment of its withdrawal, the expiration of the period of the license or the license's invalidation resulting from procedures established by legislative acts (Article 35 II CC). The extensive list of fields requiring licensing, as well as the procedure for issuing the licenses, is determined by the Law of RK of January 11, 2007, No. 214-III, "On Licensing."

C. Establishment of a Legal Entity

A legal entity may be founded by natural persons, legal entities and the state. Certain legal entities may be created only by natural persons (e.g., general partnerships, Article 58 III CC); others, only by legal entities (e.g., associations of legal entities, Article 110 CC); while some can only be formed by the state (e.g., state enterprises, Article 102 CC). Some legal entities may require two or more founders (e.g., a kommandit partnership, Article 72 CC) while others can be created only by one person (e.g., a limited liability partnership, Article 58 II CC), who thus becomes the sole founder of a legal entity.

Depending on the nature of the founder's right to the property of the legal entity, legal entities may be divided into: "established" and "self-established" (which is comparable to the division between institutions and corporations in common law systems). The former includes legal entities whose property remains owned by a founder; in this case, he retains his independent legal personality and may manage a legal entity by means of external management (e.g., by issuing administrative orders) (Article 36 CC). When a "self-established" legal entity is created, its founders become its participants and may manage the legal entity's activities only by means of internal management (e.g., by decisions of a general meeting or a board of directors, etc.).[8]

A legal entity operates on the basis of a charter and a constitutive agreement, unless otherwise provided by legislation. Thus, business partnerships, joint-stock companies, production cooperatives, public foundations and consumer cooperatives are created on the basis of a charter and a constitutive agreement. However, if a legal entity is founded by one person, it requires only a charter and a written decision on the establishment of the legal entity (the so-called decision of a solitary founder) (Article 41 I CC). Due to their legal nature, state enterprises and institutions are created only on the basis of a charter; the same applies also to public and religious associations (Article 21 LNCO). It should also be mentioned that in the case of a limited liability partnership, its charter is the only document that defines the legal status of the partnership while the role of its constitutive agreement is merely to confirm the charter (Article 17 of the Law of RK of April 22, 1998, No. 220-I, "On Partnerships with Limited and Additional Liability"). In addition, a legal entity that is considered a small-, mid- or large-scale business (see *supra*) can operate on the basis of a model statute whose content is determined by the Government of RK (Article 41 I CC). Thus, model statutes for business partnerships, joint-stock companies and production cooperatives were approved by the Resolution of the Government of RK of September 16, 2008, No. 852.

Legal entities are subject to state registration and are considered to be created only from the moment of their registration. Generally, the state registration of legal entities (as well as the record registration of their branches and representative offices) is conducted by regional bodies of the Ministry of Justice of RK. This Ministry exercises control over compliance with the requirements of the Law of RK of April 17, 1995, No. 2198, "On State Registration of Legal Entities" and maintains the unified state register of legal entities as well as their branches and representative offices. It should also be noted that the participants of the Regional Financial Center of Almaty are registered by a special state body regulating the activity of this Center. The refusal of the registering state body to register a legal entity, or the impeding of the registration process by the registering state body, may be appealed to a court (Article 42 V CC).

D. Name and Location of a Legal Entity

A legal entity must have its own name, enabling it to be distinguished from other legal entities. The constitutive documents must include the entity's name, as well

8. See Y. Bassin, *Юридические лиЦа по гражданскому законодательству Республики Казахстан* [*Legal Entities according to the Civil Legislation of the Republic of Kazakhstan*] (VŠP Adilet Almaty, Almaty, 2000) 26.

as indicate its organization and legal form; it may include additional information provided for by legislation. The name of a legal entity may not be contrary to the requirements of legislation or to the norms of social morality. It may not designate organizational or legal forms not accepted in Kazakhstan (even if they are accepted abroad) or coincide with names of other persons (if they are not its participants or if no authorization of these persons or their heirs was received). The name of a commercial legal entity is called its "firm name" and must be registered when registering the legal entity. A legal entity has the exclusive right of use of its firm name. A person unlawfully using another's firm name will, at the demand of the possessor of the right to the firm name, be obliged to terminate the use of such name and to compensate any losses caused (Article 38 CC).

The location of a legal entity is the location of its permanently operating organ. It must be specified in its constitutive documents with a full postal address (Article 39 CC). The practical significance of the location of a legal entity consists in the designation of the place where official and business correspondence can be sent. Third parties may send correspondence to a given legal entity to the address entered in the state register; if its legal address does not coincide with its actual address, the legal entity is still formally considered to have "received" the correspondence. Furthermore, the location of a legal entity is the decisive factor for the choice of a registering body or court, the place of performance of an obligation (Article 281 CC), the choice of applicable law (Article 1113 CC), etc.

E. Recognition of Foreign Legal Entities

According to the Civil Code "foreign natural and juridical persons, and also stateless persons, shall have the right to acquire the same rights and shall be obliged to fulfill the same duties as have been provided for by civil legislation for citizens and juridical persons of RK unless provided otherwise by legislative acts" (Article 3 VII CC).[9] Thus, the RK effectively established the national regime for foreign legal entities.[10]

There are three main legal forms for foreign legal entities to exercise their activities in Kazakhstan: (1) by concluding contracts; (2) through the establishment of their branches and representative offices; and (3) through the establishment of

9. A more beneficial legal regime had been provided by the Law of RK of 1994 "On Foreign Investments" for those foreign legal entities that invested in Kazakhstan, allowing them to choose between the national and the most-favored-nation regimes. However, this Law was superseded by the Law of RK of January 8, 2003 "On Investments," which did not contain this option anymore. Nevertheless, Kazakhstan is a party to the Energy Charter Treaty, which foresees the option of either the national or the most-favored-nations regimes for foreign legal entities operating in the energy sector (Art. 10).
10. There are only a few exemptions from this regime. For example, foreign legal entities may not acquire agricultural land for their private ownership; such land may, however, be leased up to 49 years (Art. 23 IV LdC).

legal entities on the territory of Kazakhstan.[11] Foreign legal entities enjoy free access to the territory of Kazakhstan with no special permits or approvals. The only requirement is that they pay their taxes at the source of payment or through a permanent establishment (Articles 188–200 of the Tax Code of RK of December 10, 2008).

Also, it should be mentioned that the issue of registration of representative offices of foreign organizations (which are not legal entities) was raised quite often in 1990s. The legislation of RK does not foresee such a possibility; meanwhile, in many foreign countries such organizations (e.g., partnerships) are not uncommon and participate as full-fledged subjects in civil law relations despite the fact that they are not legal entities. To resolve this problem, the Special Part of the Civil Code contains a provision stipulating that "the civil legal capacity of foreign organizations that are not legal entities according to foreign law shall be determined in accordance with law of the country where the organization is established. The rules of this Code, which regulates the activities of commercial legal entities, shall apply to the activities of such organizations if the law of the RK is applicable, unless it otherwise ensues from the legislation of RK or the essence of an obligation" (Article 1101 III CC).

F. Liquidation of a Legal Entity

There is no legislative definition of liquidation in Kazakhstan. According to the academic literature, the liquidation of a legal entity is defined as the system of legal measures aimed at the termination of its activities,[12] or as the termination of its legal capacity by the means of excluding it from the state register of legal entities.[13]

Liquidation may be either voluntary or involuntary. The first option is foreseen in the provision stating that a legal entity may be liquidated on any grounds by decision of the owner of its property or the organ of the legal entity authorized to do so by its constitutive documents (Article 49 I CC). The involuntary liquidation of a legal entity is conducted on the basis of a judicial decision. A court may issue the respective decision in instances of: (1) bankruptcy; (2) the deeming of the registration of a legal person to be invalid in connection with violations of legislation during the creation of the legal entity that are of an ineradicable character (including failure to submit a corporate income tax declaration, the absence of a legal entity in the place of its location or its actual address or a lack of the necessary participants without whom a legal person cannot operate during one year); (3) the

11. See M. Suleymenov & Y. Basin (eds.), *Гражданское право* [*Civil Law*], vol. 3 (KazGYuU, Almaty, 2004), 430.
12. See K. Iliyasova & M. Balken, "Liquidation and Reorganization of a Legal Entity", in M. Suleymenov (ed.), *Субъекты гражданского права* [*Subjects of Civil Law*] (KazGYuU, Almaty, 2004), 208.
13. See R. Mametova, "Establishment and Termination of a Legal Entity", in M. Suleymenov & Y. Basin (eds.), *Гражданское право* [*Civil Law*], vol. 1 (KazGYuA, Almaty, 2000), 124.

systematic performance of an activity that is contrary to the charter purposes of the legal entity; (4) the performance of an activity without proper authorization (or the necessary license) or an activity prohibited by legislative acts or an activity that involved repeated or flagrant violations of legislation; and (5) in other instances provided for by legislative acts (Article 49 II CC).

The owner of the property of a legal entity or the managing organ of a legal entity (i.e., the person or body that ordered the liquidation of the entity) must immediately declare the liquidation in writing to the respective organ of justice (which maintains the state register of legal entities) and to the respective tax body at the place of registration. Either the owner or the managing organ must appoint a "liquidation commission" and establish the procedure and dates for the liquidation in accordance with the Civil Code. From the moment of its appointment, the liquidation commission will exercise powers relating to the management of property and affairs of the legal entity and may act in court in the name of the legal entity being liquidated (Article 50 II CC).

One of the most important grounds for the liquidation of legal entities is bankruptcy, which is defined as the court-recognized insolvency of a debtor (Article 52 CC). The legislation on bankruptcy involves two similar concepts, insolvency and incapacity; nevertheless, each of them has an independent procedural meaning. Insolvency means the inability of a debtor, established by court, to satisfy the claims of creditors with regard to monetary obligations. Insolvency serves as the basis for a creditor to petition the court to recognize the debtor to be bankrupt, and a debtor is considered to be insolvent if he does not perform his obligations within three months from the date when performance is due. Also, it should be noted that when determining insolvency, not only those obligations whose performance is already due, but also all other obligations "accepted and/or being performed" must be taken into account (Articles 1, 3 VII, 4 I of the Law of RK of January 21, 1997 "On Bankruptcy"). Thus, insolvency may at least incline a debtor to start the process of voluntary bankruptcy and at most serve as the basis for the court to recognize a debtor to be bankrupt. It should also be mentioned that there is a longstanding controversy in the scientific community with respect to the definition and delimitation of such related concepts as insolvency and incapacity. In our view, incapacity is a more stable form of insolvency.

When a legal entity is being liquidated, the demands of its creditors must be satisfied in the following priority: (1) demands relating to the recovery of alimony and compensation for harm caused to life or health; (2) demands relating to the payment of labor; (3) demands secured by a pledge of property of the legal entity being liquidated; (4) demands relating to tax indebtedness and other obligatory payments to the state budget; and (5) demands of all other creditors. The demands of each priority are satisfied after the full satisfaction of demands of the preceding priority. In the event the property of a legal entity being liquidated is insufficient, it must be distributed among the creditors of the respective priority in proportion to the amounts of demands subject to satisfaction (Article 51 CC).

G. Commercial Legal Entities

Business Partnerships: A business partnership is a commercial organization with a charter fund divided into participatory shares (or contributions) of the founders (or participants) (Article 58 I CC). Along with the Civil Code, the legal status of all business partnerships is also determined by the Law of RK of May 2, 1995, No. 2255, "On Business Partnerships" (LBP). There are four kinds of business partnerships: (1) general partnerships; (2) kommandit partnerships; (3) limited liability partnerships (LLPs); and (4) additional liability partnerships.

A "general partnership" is a business partnership whose participants bear, in the event of an insufficiency of property of the general partnership, joint and several liability for its obligations with all of the property belonging to them (Article 10 LBP). The participants of a general partnership may only be natural persons. A natural person may be a participant in only one general partnership. Another rule is that a general partnership must have not less than two participants (Article 3 LBP).

A "kommandit partnership" is a business partnership that includes, along with one or more participants bearing additional liability for the obligations of the partnership with all of their property (general partners), also one or more participants whose responsibility is limited by the amount of their contribution to the property of the general partnership (contributors) and who do not participate in the performance of entrepreneurial activity by the partnership (Article 26 of LBP). General partners in a kommandit partnership may be only natural persons, and a natural person may be a participant in only one kommandit partnership.

The activities of both limited liability partnerships and additional liability partnerships are regulated (in addition to the Civil Code and the LBP) by the Law of RK of April 22, 1998, No. 220-I, "On Partnerships with Limited and Additional Liability" (hereinafter Law on LLP). A "limited liability partnership" is a business partnership that has the following characteristics: (1) it may be founded by one or several persons; (2) it has a charter fund that is divided into participatory shares in amounts determined by the constitutive documents; and (3) its participants are not be liable for its obligations and bear the risk of losses connected with its activity only within the limits of the contributions made by them (Article 2 Law on LLP). The maximum number of participants of an LLP initially was 100 persons. However, in 2003, this limitation was abolished in connection with the termination of closed Joint-Stock Companies in Kazakhstan and the unimpeded reorganization of most of them into LLPs regardless of the amount of participants. The minimal value of the charter fund of an LLP is currently 100 MCIs. An *additional responsibility partnership* is a business partnership whose participants are liable for its obligations with their contributions to the charter fund, and in the event these amounts are not sufficient, additionally with property belonging to them in the amount of a multiple of their contributions (Article 3 I of the Law on LLP).

Joint-Stock Company: The activities of a Joint-Stock Company (JSC) are regulated by the Civil Code (Articles 85–93 CC) and the Law of RK of May 13, 2003, No. 415-II, "On Joint-Stock Companies."

A JSC is defined as a legal entity that issues shares for the purposes of raising funds for the performance of its activities (Article 85 CC). JSCs are generally commercial legal entities. However, in certain cases provided for by the legislation of RK, JSCs may also be non-commercial organizations (Article 3 II of the Law on Joint-Stock Companies). At present, examples include the Central Securities Depository (established by the Law of RK of July 2, 2003, No. 461-II, "On the Securities Market"), the Insurance Payments Guarantee Fund (established by the Law of RK of June 3, 2003, No. 423, "On the Insurance Payments Guarantee Fund"), the State Social Insurance Fund (established by Law of RK of April 25, 2003, No. 405-II, "On Compulsory Social Insurance"). At present the minimal amount of the charter fund of a JSC must be 50,000 MCIs (or about USD 500,000).

Joint-Stock Companies and Limited Liability Partnerships with Participation of the State: Legal framework for the activities of JSCs and LLPs with the participation of the state is provided by the Law of RK of March 1, 2011, No. 413-IV, "On State Property" (LSP). This law distinguishes two kinds of such legal entities: (1) JSCs and LLPs with the participation of the Republic of Kazakhstan; and (2) JSCs and LLPs with the participation of an administrative-territorial unit of RK (either a region or a district). In addition, depending on the amount and proportion of the state's property, such legal entities may be subdivided into two groups: (1) state-controlled JSCs and LLPs where the state holds a controlling stake of shares or a controlling interest in the authorized capital; and (2) JSCs and LLPs where the state does not have a dominant portion of shares or capital (Article 171 LSP).

Among JSCs and LLPs with state participation, of particular interest are national companies, national holdings and national managing holdings, which are all state-controlled JSCs. A "national company" may be created either by the Government of RK, regional-level executive bodies, cities with special "republican" status. A controlling stake of its shares may belong either to the state or to a national holding. Its major purpose is to perform activities in the core fields of the national economy or to promote the development of the regional economies. A "national holding" may be created only by the Government of RK. Generally, the Government is also its only shareholder; however, there may be also other shareholders if so stipulated by the laws of RK. The major purpose of a national holding is to the manage shares (or participation investments) of national companies as well as JSCs and LLPs with state participation. A "National Managing Holding" may be created only by the Government of RK, which is also its solitary shareholder. Its major purpose is to manage the shares of national development institutions, national companies and other legal entities (Article 1 LSP).

National holdings and national companies occupy an increasingly important place in Kazakhstan's economy. Most of the national companies, created virtually in all sectors of the economy (KazMunayGaz, KazAtomProm, KazTransGaz,

KazTemirZholy, etc.), are included in the National Managing Holding "National Welfare Fund Samruk-Kazyna." Thus, at present Samruk-Kazyna represents a powerful structure that comprises more than 500 subsidiaries and affiliates. Therefore, Kazakhstan can now be described as a country with corporate form of economic management.

Production Cooperatives: The legal status of production cooperatives is regulated by the Civil Code of RK (Articles 96–101) and the Law of RK of October 5, 1995, No. 2486, "On Production Cooperatives." This kind of legal entity is defined as a voluntary association of natural persons that is created for the purpose of the joint entrepreneurial activity of its members and is based on the combining of the property contributions (or shares) of its members and the members' personal labor (Article 96 I CC).

There must be at least two members in a production co-operative, and there is no upper limit with respect to membership. Unlike some other CIS countries, Kazakhstani legislation requires the participation of the cooperative's members in the form of personal labor.

State Enterprises: The activity of state enterprises is regulated by the Civil Code (Articles 198–208) and the LSP (Chapter 11 "Implementation of Property Rights by the State with Respect to State Legal Entities").[14] State enterprises are differentiated into those based on the right of: (1) economic management; and (2) operational management. Both of them are commercial legal entities and are endowed with property by the state. However, there are also significant differences. The former may possess, use and dispose of its property within the limits established by legislative acts. Furthermore, it bears a separate liability for its obligations; the Civil Code emphasizes that the state may not be made liable for the obligations of a state enterprise (Article 103 II CC). The latter (a state enterprise based on the right of operational management, also called a treasury enterprise) is required to possess, use and dispose of its property within the limits established by legislative acts *and* in accordance with the purpose of its property and strategic directions given by the state (Article 1 LSP). In addition, the legislation distinguishes between republican-level legal entities and municipal legal entities. A republican-level legal entity is created by the Government of RK or the National Bank of RK while a municipal one is formed by local executive bodies (Article 133 LSP). It should also be mentioned that Kazakhstani legislation contains specific provisions allowing the creation of supervisory boards within state enterprises based on the right of economic management (Articles 148–152 LSP). The creation of state enterprises is limited to certain sectors. Thus, they can be created only for certain kinds of activities, provided for by the LSP, separately for enterprises based on the right of economic management and for treasury enterprises (Article 134 LSP).

14. It should be noted that the Law on State Property has introduced the concept of "state legal entities," which comprises both state enterprises and state institutions (Art. 1 LSP).

H. Non-commercial Legal Entities

Institutions are organizations "created and financed by a person in order to perform management, social, cultural or other functions of noncommercial nature" (Article 105 I CC). Institutions may be both private and state-owned. They exercise their property rights on the basis of the right of operational management.

Also it should be noted that the Civil Code was supplemented on December 16, 1998 by additional provisions that introduced special kinds of institutions, such as state institutions. At present, the activities of state institutions are regulated by the LSP (Articles 159–165). State institutions are created by the state in accordance with the Constitution and the laws of RK and regulatory acts of the President of RK, the Government of RK and the region-level "Akims." They are maintained exclusively at the expense of the state budget or the budget of the National Bank of RK, unless additional sources of funding are determined by legislative acts.

Public Associations are "political parties, trade unions and other associations of citizens created on a voluntary basis for the purpose of the achievement of common purposes by them that are not contrary to legislation" (Article 106 I CC). They are established and operate in order to realize and protect the political, economic, social and cultural rights and freedoms of individuals; to promote the personal development of citizens, their professional interests and scientific, technical and artistic creativity; to protect the health of the population and the environment; to participate in charitable activities; to perform cultural, educational, physical and recreational activities; to protect monuments of history and culture; to promote patriotic and humanistic education; to expand and strengthen international cooperation; and to perform any other activities not prohibited by the legislation of RK. The activities of public associations are regulated also by other legislative acts (e.g., the Law of RK of July 15, 2002, No. 344-2, "On Political Parties" and the Law of RK of April 9, 1993, No. 2107-XII, "On Trade Unions").

Public Foundations are "noncommercial organizations not having membership, founded by citizens and/or legal entities on the basis of voluntary property contributions and pursuing social, charitable, cultural, educational and other socially-useful purposes" (Article 107 I CC). Along with the Civil Code, the activities of public foundations are also governed by the LCNO. This Law lists the following kinds of public foundations: (a) private; (b) corporate; (c) public; and (d) state foundations. A private foundation is established by a natural person (or a group of natural persons who are members of one family) from his (or their) own resources; it may also be established by the notarized will of a natural person. A corporate foundation is established by a legal entity or several legal entities (commercial and/or non-commercial) at their expense. A public foundation is established by natural persons who are not members of one family, and/or by public associations. A state foundation is created by the decision of state bodies that have the right to possess, use and dispose of state property in the procedure established by legislation. This type of foundation carries out the goals of the foundation at the expense of the state budget, and its property is formed at the expense of the state budget of RK in accordance with an order established by legislation as well as from other sources that are consistent with the objectives of the foundation's activity.

With respect to the last kind of public foundations, it should be noted that their existence raises serious questions. The means of the state budget should not be engaged in charitable activities. The establishment of state foundations creates a possibility of abuse of the state means by the respective state bodies. Thus, their existence is as unacceptable as the existence of public-private foundations (which provide unlimited possibilities for abuse).

Consumer Cooperatives are voluntary associations of natural persons "on the basis of membership for the purpose of satisfying material and other requirements of participants effectuated by means of combining their property (or share) contributions" (Article 108 I CC). The legal status of a consumer co-operative is defined by the Civil Code, the LNCO and the Law of RK of May 8, 2001, No. 197-II, "On Consumer Cooperative."

Religious Associations are voluntary associations of natural persons "who have combined in the procedure established by legislative acts on the basis of a community of their interests in order to satisfy their spiritual requirements" (Article 109 CC). The legal status of a religious association is determined by the Civil Code and the Law of RK of January 15, 1992, No. 1128-XII, "On Freedom of Religion and Religious Associations."

Associations of Individual Entrepreneurs and Legal Entities may be created by individual entrepreneurs and legal entities for the purposes of coordinating their entrepreneurial activity and/or representing and defending their common interests. Associations' members retain their autonomy. An association is not liable for the obligations of its members. Its members bear subsidiary liability for its obligations in the amount and in the procedure provided for by the constitutive documents of the association (Article 110 CC).

Other Forms of Non-commercial Legal Entities (not specifically mentioned in the Civil Code) include notary chambers (whose legal status is determined by the Law of RK of July 14, 1997 "On Notary"); associations of attorneys (Law of RK of December 5, 1997 "On Advocacy"); commerce and industry chambers (Law of RK of May 3, 2005, No. 47-III, "On Commerce and Industry Chambers"); and chambers of auditors (Law of RK of November 20, 1998 "On Audit Activity").

It should also be mentioned that there are also non-commercial agricultural partnerships (regulated by the Law of RK of December 25, 2000, No. 133-II, "On Agricultural Partnerships and their Associations"), which provide their services at cost. In addition, Kazakhstani legislation provides for three "specialized" consumer cooperatives: cooperatives of apartment owners and homebuilding cooperatives (both regulated by the Law of RK of April 16, 1997, No. 94-I, "On Housing Relations") as well as rural consumer cooperatives (the Law of RK of July 21, 1999, No. 450-I, "On Rural Consumer Cooperation in the Republic of Kazakhstan").

Selected Bibliography

Y. Basin, *Избранные труды по гражданскому праву* [*Selected Works in Civil Law*] (VŠP Adilet, Almaty, 2003) [in Russian].*

A. Didenko, *Гражданское право* [*Civil Law*] (Nur Press, Almaty, 2006) [in Russian].*

A. Didenko (ed.), *Гражданское законодательство Республики Казахстан* [*Civil Legislation of RK*], vols. 1–36 (VŠP Adilet Raritet, Almaty, 1998–2010) [in Russian].*

Y. Basin, *Юридические лица по законодательству Республики Казахстан* [*Legal Entities according to the Legislation of RK*] (VŠP Adilet, Almaty, 2000) [in Russian].

I. Greshnikov, *Субъекты права: Юридическое лицо в праве и законодательстве* [*Subjects of Law: Legal Entities in Law and Legislation*] (LEM, Almaty, 2004) [in Russian].

S. Klimkin, *Хозяйственные товарищества по законодательству Республики Казахстан* [*Business Partnerships according to the Legislation of RK*] (Žeti Žargi, Almaty, 2001) [in Russian].

M. Suleimenov (ed.), *Субъекты гражданского права* [*Subjects of Civil Law*] (KazGYuU, Almaty, 2004) [in Russian].

M. Suleymenov, *Избранные труды по гражданскому праву* [*Selected Works in Civil Law*] (Statut, Moscow, 2006) [in Russian].

M. Suleymenov & Y. Basin (eds.), *Комментарий к гражданскому кодексу Республики Казахстан* [*Commentary of the Civil Code of RK*] *General Part* (Žeti Žargi, Almaty, 1998); *Special Part* (Žeti Žargi, Almaty, 2000) [in Russian].*

M. Suleymenov & Y. Basin (eds.), *Гражданское право* [*Civil Law*], vol. 1 (KazGYuA, Almaty, 2000); vol. 2 (KazGYuU, Almaty, 2002); vol. 3 (KazGYuU, Almaty, 2004) [in Russian].*

* The marked works also apply to Chapter 7 "Property Law," Chapter 8 "Law of Obligations," Chapter 9 "Family and Inheritance Law" and Chapter 11 "International Private Law."

Chapter 7
Property Law

Aigoul Kenjebayeva

I. CONSTITUTIONAL PROVISIONS

The Constitution of RK recognizes the existence of both state-owned and private property and provides equal protection of the property rights of both the state and private owners (Article 6-I). It stipulates that no person may be deprived of property except by court order. However, property rights come with obligations, and the use of property must serve the public good; thus, in extraordinary cases specifically stipulated by law property may be expropriated for public use by payment of adequate compensation (Article 26 II).

Citizens of RK may privately own any legally obtained property (Article 26 I). Moreover, everyone has the right to use property for the purpose of entrepreneurial activity. However, it is also stipulated that "monopolistic activity shall be regulated and limited by law" (Article 26 IV); thus, ownership of property may be subject to anti-trust law. Furthermore, the Constitution provides that land, subsoil, waters, flora, fauna and other natural resources are owned by the state; however, within limits established by law, land may be privately owned (Article 6 III). In addition, it should be noted that foreigners and stateless persons in RK enjoy the rights and freedoms as well as bear the responsibilities established for citizens of

Zhenis Kembayev, *Introduction to the Law of Kazakhstan*, pp. 109–125.

RK unless otherwise stipulated by the Constitution, laws and international treaties (Article 12 IV).[1]

II. PROPERTY RIGHTS UNDER THE CIVIL CODE OF RK

The constitutional provisions are specified in the General Part of the Civil Code and legislative acts of RK. Thus, the Civil Code provides that inviolability of property is one of the major principles of civil legislation (Article 2 I CC). Furthermore, it stipulates that the following items may be subject to property rights: chattel; currency, including foreign currency; securities; services; intellectual property (copyrights, patents, trade names, trademarks and trade secrets); and other property (Article 115 II CC), and provides rules with respect to right of ownership and non-owner's rights; common property; acquisition and termination of property; and protection of property rights.

A. Right of Ownership

The right of ownership is defined as the right of a person at his discretion to possess, use and dispose of property belonging to him (Article 188 I CC). The right to possess is self-explanatory. The right to use is the legal ability to benefit from useful features of the property and to gain from it. Gains may be in the form of profit, accrual, crops or offspring. The right to dispose of property is the power to determine the so-called legal fate of the property, i.e., the power to decide what to do with a given property (Article 188 II CC). A question may arise whether it is necessary to differentiate between the right to use and the right to possess; but it should be taken into account that property may be possessed and used by a non-owner for the benefit of the owner, who may then be said to be using the property for his own benefit without possessing it.

The owner may at his discretion perform any actions with respect to property belonging to him. The right of ownership is absolute and in perpetuity and may be terminated only for the reasons enumerated in the Civil Code. However, ownership rights are also accompanied by a number of major obligations. Thus, the exercise of ownership rights must not encroach on the protected interests of others or of the state (Article 188 IV CC). A property owner has an obligation to take measures to prevent any harm to the environment or the health of others that may result from exercising his ownership rights. The owner bears the burden of maintaining his property, unless legislative acts or private agreements provide otherwise; the owner cannot unilaterally impose that burden on third parties. Third parties legally

1. Thus, Property Law contains a number of restrictions on foreign persons. For example, they may not own land designated for agriculture (see LdC of RK of June 20, 2003 [Art. 23 IV]); and, if temporarily present in Kazakhstan, may not own residential dwellings (see Law of RK of June 19, 1995, No. 2337, "On the Legal Status of Foreigners" [Art. 9 II]).

possessing the owner's property are entitled to compensation by the owner for its maintenance, unless otherwise agreed upon (Article 189 CC). Risk of loss is acquired at the same time as ownership rights, unless legislative acts or private agreements provide otherwise. In cases of delayed transfers of possession, the party responsible for the delay bears the risk of loss (Article 190 CC).

The Civil Code also provides rules with respect to private and state-owned property. Private ownership is defined as property owned by natural persons, non-state legal entities or their associations (Article 191 I CC). Both natural persons and legal entities may own any property not explicitly excluded by legislative acts; the quantity and value of property in private ownership may not be limited.[2] With respect to state ownership, the Civil Code reiterates the constitutional provision that land, its subsoil, water, flora and fauna, and other natural resources are exclusively state property and also provides that the peculiarities of the effectuation of the right of ownership of land and other natural resources are determined not only by the Civil Code but also by land, subsoil use and other legislation (Article 193 CC).

B. Non-Owner's Rights

Non-owners may have (a) the right of economic management of property; (b) the right of operative management of property; (c) the right to use land; and (d) easement.

The right of economic management (*sharuashylyq zhurgizu qüqygy*, *pravo khozyaistvennogo vedeniya*) is a set of rights confined to state enterprises to possess, use and dispose of state property within the limits established by the Civil Code and other legislative acts (Article 196 CC). It is not absolute ownership but a derivative right from state ownership. Hence, the state may determine the aims of the enterprise's activity; reorganize and liquidate it; exercise control over the use and the preservation of the property belonging to the enterprise; and receive part of the profit obtained by the enterprise. A state enterprise may autonomously dispose of movable property allocated to it. However, a state enterprise may not perform the following types of entrepreneurial activity without the consent of the state: (1) sell or transfer to other persons, exchange, lease out on a long-term lease (more than three years) or grant for temporary use without compensation buildings, installations, equipment and other basic funds of the enterprise; (2) create branches and subsidiary enterprises, found jointly enterprises with private entrepreneurs and joint production entities or invest production and monetary capital in them;

2. However, the property rights of a legal entity vary according to the form of business organization. If the legal entity is an economic partnership or co-operative, the founders have contractual rights to the property assigned to the entity. If the entity is an economic or operative management enterprise (see *infra*), the founders retain ownership of the property assigned to the entity. In the case of public or religious associations and public foundations, the founders retain no rights to the property assigned to the entity (Art. 36 CC).

(3) grant loans; or (4) issue suretyship or a guarantee with regard to obligations of third parties.

The right of operative management (*oralymdy basqaru qüqygy, pravo operativnogo upravleniya*) is a set of rights confined to an institution or a treasury enterprise to possess, use and dispose of state property within the limits established by legislative acts and the purposes of the activity of the institution or treasury enterprise, strategic directions given by the owner (the state) and purpose of the property (Article 202 CC). Operative management rights are also derivative of ownership rights and thus of limited nature as opposed to the property owner's absolute rights. The state may determine the purposes and content of the activity of the institution or treasury enterprise and their legal fate. It also effectuates control over the effectiveness of the use and preservation by the institution or treasury enterprise of property transferred by the owner.

The right to land use is a person's right to possess and use a piece of state-owned land, either in perpetuity (continuous land use) or within a certain term (term land use) (Article 29 I LdC). The land user may possess and use the land, but he cannot dispose of the land. The land use right is derivative from the state ownership of the land. It may be vested in state and private entities, including foreign persons (Article 30 LdC); however, foreign persons may lease land for up to 10 years only (Article 37 V LdC), and not in perpetuity (Article 34 II LdC). Land use rights are alienable subject to certain restrictions; for instance, forests, land used for recreational purposes or land used for defense purposes cannot be leased (Article 33 II LdC). A land use right arises in one of three ways: grant by the state; alienation from one land user to another; or receipt of the right through natural succession—either by inheritance or reorganization of a legal entity (Article 31 LdC). The right to use land is alienated on the basis of a civil transaction, such as a contract, bequest or lease (Article 33 LdC). Private land users, except those involved in farming and producing agricultural goods, may alienate the right freely (Article 37 III LdC). State land users are limited in their ability to alienate the right. They may not alienate their right to use land or to use it as collateral except when alienating realty located on the piece of land. The rights of state land users cannot be used to satisfy creditors' claims in bankruptcy proceedings (Article 39 LdC). Landowners and non-state land users may be deprived of their land rights for public use through judicial proceedings (Articles 84–88 LdC). Land users and owners may lose their right to use land as a result of non-designated use or use resulting in violations of the law (Articles 92–93 LdC). Additionally, landowners may lose their ownership as a result of a judicially mandated criminal sanction (Article 95 LdC).

Easement is a limited right to use another's land for a certain purpose. Easements arise from regulatory legal acts, agreements with landowners or land users, acts by the local government's executive branch, court decisions and in other instances (Article 67 II LdC). Easements that do not arise directly from a regulatory act must be registered with the state according to the procedure for registering real property rights and transactions (Article 75 III LdC). The most common examples of easements are: (1) an individual right to be present on land open to public access;

(2) an individual right of way through unmarked privately owned or used land if traversing such land does not harm or harass the landowner or land user (Article 68 LdC); (3) a right of way through another's land if passage through one's own land is impossible, extremely difficult or unreasonably expensive; and (4) the laying and operating of necessary power or communication lines, water or heat supply, irrigation, and other needs of the land, which cannot be achieved without an easement (Article 69 II LdC). Easements stemming from regulatory legal acts of local executive authorities are referred to as public servitudes and may be granted to facilitate the needs of the state and local population.[3]

The majority of easements exist on the basis of private agreements or acts of a local government's executive branch. If a regulatory legal act provides that a certain easement may be created on the basis of a contract between the holder of the prospective dominant estate, and the owner or user of the prospective subordinate estate, but the latter refuses to enter in such a contract (or offers unreasonable contractual terms), then the holder of the prospective dominant estate may file his complaint with the court (Article 67 III LdC). Easements run with the land and may only be alienated with the right for which the easement was established (Article 73 II LdC). An easement is extinguished upon the waiver of the owner or user of the dominant estate, failure to use the easement for three years, expiration of the easement's term of duration, upon the parties' consent on the basis of a court decision or other grounds provided for in the law. A public servitude is extinguished pursuant to the local executive authority's decision if the public need for which the servitude was established no longer exists. The owner or user of a subordinate estate may petition the court to extinguish the easement in cases where the holder of the dominant estate is using the easement improperly or if, in fact, no grounds for the easement exist (Article 74 LdC).

C. Common Property

When property belongs to two or more persons, they hold it under common ownership (Article 209 I CC). Property may be in common ownership with each owner's share defined (shared ownership) or with undivided shares (joint ownership) (Article 209 II CC).[4] Common ownership occurs when two or more persons receive property that may not be divided without changing the land's designation

3. Public servitudes may be granted for the following purposes: providing a right of way through the land to implement objects of public use such as cemeteries, religious sites, etc.; using the land for purposes of fixing communal, engineering, electric and other power lines and networks and transport infrastructure facilities; ensuring the water supply; moving cattle through the land; hunting, fishing and picking berries, fruits, vegetables and herbs; accessing the shoreline; using the land to hold certain cultural and social events pursuant to the state authority's decision; and other instances related to public and state interests (Art. 69 IV LdC).
4. Only individuals may own jointly. However, individuals and legal entities may have shared ownership.

(indivisible items), or may not be divided by virtue of law.[5] An agreement between the co-owners of common property or, in case of lack of agreement, a judicial decision may establish shared ownership of the common property. The shares are deemed to be equal when the co-owners' share sizes are not otherwise established by an agreement among co-owners and cannot be established on the basis of legislative acts (Article 210-I CC).[6]

A co-owner who, at his own expense, makes inseverable improvements to shared property in compliance with procedures for shared property use has the right to a proportionate increase of his share. Severable improvements of shared property become the property of the co-owner who made them, unless otherwise agreed (Article 211 CC). The disposition of shared property requires the unanimous agreement of its co-owners. The priority acquisition rights of the remaining co-owners determine how shares of shared property may be alienated. Income from using shared property becomes part of the common property and is distributed among the co-owners in proportion to their shares unless otherwise agreed. Shared property co-owners are proportionately liable for taxes, levies and any other payments and for maintenance and preservation costs, subject to an agreement to the contrary between the co-owners (Article 215 CC).

A co-owner of shared property may request partition of his share of the shared property.[7] If co-owners of shared property fail to agree on the methods and conditions of dividing the shared property, a co-owner of the shared property may claim partition of his share in kind.[8] If partition in kind is not allowed due to a legislative act or is impossible without unreasonable damage to the property, the partitioning co-owner may be paid by the other co-owners for the value of his share. Payment of compensation to a shared property co-owner by the other co-owners, instead of partitioning his share in kind, requires the consent of the departing co-owner. If the value of the share is *de minimus* and cannot realistically be partitioned, and if the co-owner has no substantial interest in the use of common assets, the court may compel the other co-owners to pay compensation to the co-owner without his consent. Upon receipt of compensation, the co-owner loses the right to his share (Article 218 CC).

The main distinction between shared ownership and joint ownership is that only certain kinds of property may be held in joint ownership: spousal property, farm property and privatized housing (Article 219 I CC). Joint co-owners collectively own and use the property unless agreed otherwise.[9] Whenever any joint co-owner enters into a transaction to dispose of property, consent of all the co-owners

5. The default rule is shared ownership. Joint ownership is established only in cases specified by the law.
6. This provision offers a default rule of equal shares that may be modified by agreement or law.
7. Appropriation may occur upon agreement of the co-owners or, if there is a lack of agreement, through judicial proceedings.
8. A co-owner may not claim partial partition of his share. Division and partition are relative – partition by one or several co-owners may lead to complete division of the common property.
9. Unlike shared co-owners, joint co-owners may not demand appropriation of their share of the joint property or payment of compensation.

is presumed as this consent is mandatory. Any joint co-owner may enter into such a transaction unless agreed otherwise (Article 220 CC). If the party acquiring the property knew or should have known that the disposing co-owner did not have the consent of the others, any of the remaining co-owners can invalidate the sale through an ultra vires claim. Transactions requiring notarization or state registration require notarized consent of the other joint co-owners. Upon division or partition of a share of joint property, shares are deemed to be equal unless otherwise specified by legislative acts or the co-owners' agreement. The basis and procedure for the division of joint property and the partition of a share out of it are the same as those for shared property (Article 221 II, III CC). The creditor of a co-owner in a shared or joint property may demand partition of the debtor's share of the common property to satisfy his claim in cases where other assets of the debtor are insufficient to satisfy the obligation (Article 222 I CC).

Generally, property acquired by spouses during marriage is joint property.[10] Pre-marital assets and assets received by an individual spouse during the marriage as gifts or as inheritance are separate property. Personal use articles except for jewelry and other luxuries, even if acquired during the marriage with joint funds, are a spouse's separate property.[11] A spouse's separate property may be converted into joint property if, during the marriage, investments were made at the expense of joint property that significantly increased the value of the separate property (as determined by the court). A claim against a spouse's obligations is limited to that spouse's separate assets and his share of the joint assets that would be due to him should the joint property be divided (Article 223 CC).[12]

Property of a "farmer holding" belongs to its members in joint ownership; however, property of a farmer holding organized as a general partnership pursuant to an agreement on joint activity is property of the members in shared ownership. Property of a farmer holding based on sole proprietorship is private property of the holding (Article 224 I CC). If a farmer holding dissolves common property, the property is divided in accordance with the rules for division of property in shared or joint ownership (see *supra*). Capital assets in the property of a farmer holding are not divided. Instead, a person exiting the farmer holding receives monetary compensation proportionate to his share of the common property (Article 225 II CC). Members of a farmer holding may form a business partnership or a productive co-operative on the basis of the farm's property. Such a reorganized farmer holding is a legal entity with its own property received as investment and other contributions by the members of the farm, or acquired as a result of its activities (Article 226 I CC).

10. Under Family Law of RK, only duly registered marriages give rise to spousal rights and obligations. Hence, property gained during cohabitation may be separate or shared property of the cohabitants but not spousal joint property.
11. This applies only to articles that are personal use articles by nature; it does not apply to articles that merely happened to be in personal use of one of the spouses.
12. If the obligation was incurred for the benefit of joint property, the court may sanction the imposition of the claim against the joint property.

D. Acquisition of Property Rights

For the most part, ownership in an object may be acquired in one of five ways: (1) creation of property—the creator owns his creation unless otherwise specified by law or by agreement;[13] (2) alienation of owned property by the owner;[14] (3) acquisition of ownerless or abandoned property;[15] (4) accumulation of share-units in a consumer-cooperative (Article 235 CC);[16] and (5) adverse possession (Article 240 CC).

In cases of newly created real (or improved) property, ownership arises when the real property object is completed, accepted (if acceptance is required by law or by agreement) and properly registered. Prior to completion and registration of real property, ownership applies to the building materials and other property from which the real property will be constructed (Article 236 CC). For tangible property created by the reprocessing of materials, the newly created tangible property belongs to the owner of the materials from which the property was built, unless agreed otherwise (Article 237 I CC). However, if the costs of reprocessing greatly exceed that of the materials, the newly created tangible property belongs to the person who reprocessed the materials, if such person acted in good faith (Article 237 II CC).

A person acquiring property through a contract gains ownership upon the transfer of possession. Transfer of possession is effectuated by handing the object to the buyer or submitting it to a transport carrier or the postal service for shipment to the buyer. If the buyer possesses the object at the conclusion of the agreement alienating the property, transfer of possession is deemed to take place at the moment the agreement is concluded. The transfer of documents of title (such as a waybill or a bill of lading) concerning the property is equivalent to transferring possession (Article 239 II CC). The acquiring person gains ownership of the property only upon registration or notarial certification or both if the transaction requires registration and certification (Article 238 II CC).

A natural person or a legal entity who is not the owner but who honestly, openly, and continuously possesses real property as his own for 15 years, or any other asset for not less than five years, acquires ownership of these assets by adverse possession (aka "squatting").[17] In cases of real property requiring state

13. Ownership in newly created objects may be contracted away. Also, in case of newly created real estate, state registration is necessary to create ownership.
14. Compulsory alienation is allowed only in cases listed in the Civil Code.
15. In cases and in the manner provided by the Civil Code, a person may acquire ownership of ownerless property, property whose owner is unknown, abandoned property or property whose owner lost ownership for other reasons,
16. Members of a consumer co-operative and other persons having the right to accumulate share-units, who fully paid their unit-share contribution for the apartment, dacha, garage or other premises granted to those persons by the co-operative for their use, acquires ownership of the indicated assets.
17. Permission by the original owner negates claim of adverse possession. Hence, adverse possession cannot be claimed against realty possessed pursuant to an agreement or grant.

registration, the person obtaining this property through adverse possession becomes the owner from the moment of registration. An adverse possessor has a right to protect his possession against third parties not having the lawful right to possess the real property. An adverse possessor may count the time period of his predecessor in right to satisfy the 15-year duration. The period of adverse possession may not start before the end of the statute of limitation period for *ejectment* or *replevin* claims (Article 240 CC).

Ownership may also be established by conversion of objects that are commonly available for collection or extraction into one's own property (e.g., fishing or hunting) (Article 241 CC), by conversion of abandoned property into one's own property (Article 243 CC),[18] by finding lost property (Article 245 CC),[19] by discovering a treasure trove (Article 247 CC)[20] and by acquisition of property confiscated from the owner (Article 248 CC).

E. Cessation of Property Rights

The right of ownership ceases after alienation by the owner of his property, relinquishment by the owner of his ownership rights, destruction of property or loss of ownership rights in any other cases specified by legislative act (Article 249 I CC). A person may relinquish ownership by announcement or by committing other actions definitely proving his rejection of possession, use and disposal of the property without intention to retain any other property rights. Relinquishment of ownership does not cause cessation of the owner's rights and obligations until another acquires ownership (Article 250 CC). Compulsory deprivation of ownership is permitted only in enumerated cases: (1) the imposition of a claim against property based on the owner's liability; (2) the compulsory alienation of property that the person may not own pursuant to the law; (3) requisition; (4) confiscation; (5) the alienation of real estate in connection with the seizure of a land plot; (6) the purchase of improvidently maintained cultural and historical valuables; and

18. A person in ownership, possession or use of land on which abandoned metal scrap, damaged goods or abandoned property whose value is apparently lower than 20 MCIs is located may turn those items into his ownership by beginning to use them or by performing any other acts that witness the conversion of an item into ownership, such as tagging or marking. Any other abandoned property recognized by the court as ownerless becomes property of the person who petitioned the court for such determination. Abandonment requires intent of the prior owner to relinquish property rights.
19. A person finding lost property must file the finding with the competent authorities such as law enforcement agencies or bodies of local government. If the property remains unclaimed for more than six months, the person gains ownership of the property.
20. A treasure trove whose owner cannot be identified becomes the property, in equal shares, of the owner of the land or the realty where the treasure trove was hidden and discovered and of the finder of the treasure trove, unless they agree otherwise. When a person finds a treasure trove by conducting excavations or searching for valuables without permission of the owner or the user of the land or the realty where the treasure trove was hidden, the treasure trove becomes property of that owner.

(7) other cases as listed in the Civil Code. Compulsory deprivation of ownership is subject to compensation except in cases of confiscation and imposition of claims against property (Article 249 CC).

F. Protection of Property Rights

The owner has the following rights protecting his property rights: (1) the right to claim recognition of his ownership (Article 259 CC); (2) the right to seek return of his property from unlawful possession by another (*replevin*) (Article 260 CC); (3) the limited right to claim property from a *bona fide* buyer (Article 261 CC); and (4) the right to demand elimination of other violations of his property rights not related to deprivation of possession (Article 264 CC). Non-owners exercising their rights of economic management, operative management or continuous land use have the same aforementioned protective rights as owners of the property (Article 265 CC).

As noted above, the owner has only a limited right to claim property from a *bona fide* buyer. If a buyer purchases property from a person without the right to alienate and the buyer did not know or should not have known about it, gave value and acted in good faith, he is a *bona fide* buyer. The owner may reclaim the property from a *bona fide* buyer only if the property was lost by the owner or lawful possessor, or was stolen from one or the other or departed from possession against their will (Article 261 I CC). Property that was acquired without compensation from a person without the right to alienate may be reclaimed by the owner in all cases (Article 261 II CC). Money and securities in bearer form cannot be reclaimed from a *bona fide* purchaser (Article 262 CC).

III. LAND AND REAL PROPERTY

Real property is comprised of land, buildings, installations, perennial plantings and other property that is firmly connected with the land; that is, objects whose movement without incommensurate damage to the purpose thereof is impossible.[21] Due to their value, aircraft, sea and river ships and spacecraft are deemed to be real property and are subject to state registration (Article 117 CC). All rights pertaining to real property, their restriction, emergence, transfer and cessation are subject to state registration.[22] The right of ownership, the right of economic management, the right of operative management, the right to use the land for a period of more than a year, pledge of real estate, real estate leases, the right to management under

21. A finer analytical distinction is that property is classified as real property, property deemed to be real property and tangible property. For all practical purposes, property deemed to be real property is real property.
22. The state registration requirement applies both to real property and to property deemed to be real property.

concession and encumbrance of real property come into being at the moment of state registration.[23] The registering agency must present registration and registered rights information upon request. The refusal of the state to register any of the above may be challenged in court (Article 118 CC).

The right of private ownership must be registered with the state (Article 43 I LdC). The right of private ownership of land is limited in that only certain kinds of land may be so owned. Kazakhstani citizens (individuals) may own land designated for private farming, gardening, forestry, industrial or non-industrial housing construction or dacha construction. Kazakhstani companies may privately own land designated for industrial and non-industrial (including residential) construction, production of agricultural goods and forestry. Foreign citizens and companies (non-governmental) as well as stateless individuals may own land designated for the above purposes, except for production of agricultural goods and forestry (Article 23 LdC). There is no private ownership of land designated for national defense, nature reserves, forest and water stock, public roads or railroads and territories of public use (except for lands occupied by private constructions and facilities) (Article 26 II LdC). Ownership of land with structures is linked to the ownership of the realty on that land. Acquisition of structures results in acquisition of the portion of land occupied by the structures. In acquiring realty, the owner has use rights of the underlying land plot or portion of it (Article 52 LdC).

Kazakhstani law also provides for the concept of both permanent and temporary land use (which is the right of persons to possess and use land owned by the state). The right of permanent land use may not belong to foreign persons, but there is no such restriction with respect to temporary land use (Articles 34, 35 LdC).

Special attention must be paid to condominiums and privatized housing, which are real property in common ownership. A condominium is a hybrid form of ownership whereby certain parts of the real estate (dwellings) are in the individual separate ownership of natural persons or legal entities, and certain other parts of real estate (common areas, the land on which the condominiums are built) are in shared ownership with all the individual owners (Article 12 LdC). The share of each owner in the common property is indivisible from his separate ownership of that part of the real estate belonging to him. The size of the parts of real estate that are in individual (separate) ownership determines each owner's share in the common property and the share of costs in its maintenance (Article 209 VI CC). When the tenant acquires privatized housing, the property passes into common ownership of the tenant and his family members who are permanently residing with him at the moment of privatization (Article 227 CC).[24]

23. Real property is registered by Ministry of Justice of RK or by its agencies. Property deemed to be real property is registered by other competent authorities. The right is created at the moment of proper registration.
24. Privatized housing is a form of common property endemic to the territories of the former USSR, where all housing used to be state property. It is housing whose ownership was transferred to the tenant and permanently co-residing members of his family pursuant to privatization laws. The peculiarities of the right of joint ownership in a privatized dwelling are determined by the Law of RK of April 16, 1997, No. 94-I, "On Housing Relations."

IV. SUBSOIL[25]

Land, subsoil and natural resources are exclusively state owned (Article 6 III CRK). Since the state cannot alienate ownership of these resources, only a certain set of rights are given to a person or an entity wishing to exploit these resources. Non-owner's rights of these resources are the right to use land, the right to use subsoil, and the right to use natural resources.

The right to use subsoil is purpose-specific and is regulated by the Law of RK of June 24, 2010, No. 291-IV, "On Subsoil and Subsoil Use (SUL) (with amendments as of July 5, 2011). It may only be granted for governmental study of subsoil, exploration, extraction, combined exploration and extraction or construction of underground facilities unrelated to exploration or extraction (Article 28 I SUL). It may be continuous or limited in duration, alienable or non-alienable, subject to compensation or free (Article 28 II SUL). The production of commonly occurring minerals for the subsurface user's own needs is conducted on the basis of permanent subsurface use rights, granted free of charge, on land plots held by the subsurface user according to private ownership or land use rights. All other subsoil use rights are limited in duration and are subject to compensation (Article 28 III SUL). The right is gained through a state grant, by alienation of the previous right-holder or by succession in right (Article 34 SUL).

In most cases, the right is granted by concluding a contract for subsoil use (Article 35 I SUL). A subsoil use contract regulates the relationship between the subsoil user and the state. A subsoil use contract is concluded with the state acting through the proper state authority after final approval of the drafts, working program and appraisals required for concluding a contract (Article 68 I SUL). A subsoil use contract comes into force only after its mandatory registration (Article 68 III SUL). With certain exceptions, contracts for exploration, extraction or combined exploration and extraction require competitive bidding (Article 35 II SUL). Other contracts may be concluded on the basis of direct negotiations (Article 35 II SUL).

Alienation of the right to subsoil use generally requires permission of the proper state authority (Article 36 II SUL). Alienation of the rights of exploration and extraction of common metals requires only the permission of the local state executive body (Article 36 II SUL). With a few exceptions, subsoil use rights cannot be alienated within two years of the conclusion of a subsoil-use contract (Article 37 X SUL).

Acquiring subsoil use rights through succession depends on whether the holder of the right is an individual or a legal entity. For individuals, transfer of the subsoil use rights to the successor(s) in right upon death of the predecessor is regulated by the Civil Code and does not require permission (Article 39 SUL). For legal entities, transfer upon reorganization of the entity requires permission of the proper authority or the local state executive body (Article 38 SUL). A person acquiring subsoil use rights also gains the right to use land within the territory

25. Editor's note: For more information see also Chapter 15 "Investment and Energy Law."

specified by the contract for subsoil use (Article 68 V SUL). The right to use land is supplementary and ceases with the termination of the subsoil use right (Article 40 III SUL).

Subsoil use rights may cease to exist in four ways: (a) expiration of the subsoil use contract; (b) expiration or revocation of the special permit for the construction of underground facilities for the stockpiling of radioactive or toxic waste or waste waters; (c) upon a government resolution prohibiting subsoil use in a certain region for reasons of national security, public health or environmental safety; or (d) upon liquidation of the legal entity holding the right to use the subsoil (Article 14; Article 40 II SUL).

At all times the state retains ownership of the subsoil and mineral resources located within it (Article 10 I SUL). Extracted mineral resources (minerals) become the subsoil user's property, unless the subsoil use contract or legislation provide otherwise (Article 10 II SUL). The subsoil user also owns "technogenic mineral formation" (Article 10 III SUL).[26] However, extraction of minerals from "technogenic mineral formations" still requires the existence of a subsoil use contract with the proper authority sanctioning extraction of a particular mineral. Processing of minerals after extraction does not qualify as subsoil use. It requires a separate license and is regulated by a separate body of law (Article 45 SUL).

Subsoil users enjoy a limited legal stability regime, whereby subsequent changes in legislation detrimental to results of the subsoil user's business activity under the contract for subsoil use do not apply to the subsoil use contract (Article 30 SUL). This protection does not cover legislative changes pertaining to national security, national defense, environmental safety, public health, taxation or customs (Article 30 SUL).

V. INTELLECTUAL PROPERTY

Under Kazakhstani law, an intellectual property right is "an exclusive right of a citizen or legal entity recognized as the result of intellectual creative activity, the means of individualization of the legal entity or of a product of a natural person or legal entity or the work or services fulfilled by them (firm name, trademark, service mark, and others)" (Article 125 I CC). They are not ownership rights, but rather exclusive use rights, and are distinguished from property rights to the material object carrying intellectual property (Article 968 CC).

The law protects products of intellectual creative activity and means of individualization of economic actors, goods, works and services (Article 961 I CC). Products of intellectual creative activity include scientific, literary and artistic works, performances, sound recordings and broadcasts of broadcasting organizations, inventions, utility models, industrial designs, artificially selected crops,

26. "Technogenic mineral formation" means accumulations of mineral formations, masses of rocks, liquids and mixtures containing useful components that are waste products of mining and enrichment, metallurgical and other types of production.

topologies of integrated circuits and confidential information including trade secrets. Means of individualization include company names, trademarks and indications of origin (Article 961 III CC). In neither case is the list exhaustive; other similar subject matter may be protected.

Intellectual property rights arise either at the moment of creation or upon the granting of legal protection by the competent authority (Article 962 CC). The law distinguishes between economic and non-economic (moral) rights to intellectual property (Article 963 I CC). Generally, economic rights are alienable and moral rights are not (Article 965 CC), but the latter can be transferred through succession (Article 977 I CC). Economic rights to intellectual property may be transferred to another person by means of a licensing agreement (Article 966 CC). Economic rights are valid for a certain period of time; moral rights exist in perpetuity (Article 969 CC).

Kazakhstani copyright law mainly follows the Berne Convention, to which Kazakhstan is a contracting party. Scientific, literary and artistic works are copyrightable (Article 971 I CC). Ideas, concepts, principles, methods, systems, processes, discoveries, facts and works of folk art are not copyrightable (Article 971 IV CC). While official documents, state emblems and signs are also not copyrightable, drafts of official documents and state emblems and signs may receive copyright protection (Article 975 CC). Copyright protection requires originality and fixation, which does not have to be permanent (public performance suffices). Copyright includes the following exclusive economic rights: reproduction, distribution, public display and creation of derivative works (Article 978 CC). In addition to economic rights, authors have moral rights, which include attribution of authorship, integrity of work, use of own name or a pseudonym and retraction (reversal of prior publication) (Article 977 CC). Exclusive rights of copyright should be distinguished from authorship—the former are alienable economic rights, whereas the latter is a non-alienable moral right. Copyright is valid for the life of the author plus 70 years or, for anonymous works or works published under a pseudonym, 70 years from the moment of publication (Article 982 CC).

A patent is a temporary grant of exclusive rights to use (Article 992 CC) inventions, utility models and industrial designs. To be patentable, an invention must be novel, non-obvious and useful; a utility model must be novel and useful; and an industrial design must be novel and useful (Article 991 II CC). To receive patent protection, the author must file an application for a patent with the patent authority. Patent rights are freely alienable, in whole or in part (Article 993 CC). The patent's validity dates to the moment of filing an application for a patent with the competent patent authority. However, patent rights may be protected only after the patent is actually issued (Article 999 II CC). Invention patents are valid for 20 years; utility model patent for five years, with a possible extension for up to three years; and industrial design patents for 10 years, with possible extension for up to five years (Article 999 I CC). For inventions, a special kind of patent (a preliminary patent) also exists, which is valid for three years with a possible extension for up to two years (Article 991 I CC). Generally, to receive patent protection in Kazakhstan the subject matter of the patent must be registered in RK. However, under international treaties in some cases foreign patents may receive protection in RK (Article 998 II CC). Remedies for patent infringement are injunction, compensatory damages and recovery of revenue obtained through patent infringement (Article 1003 CC).

A legal entity has the exclusive right to use its own name on official forms, printed publications, advertisements, billboards, brochures, invoices, goods, packaging and in other cases needed for the individualization of a legal entity. Trade names must be distinctive (Article 1020 CC). The exclusive right to use a trade name in RK covers only the trade name registered in Kazakhstan to distinguish the legal entity (Article 1022 CC). Exclusive rights to use a trade name are non-alienable except when the legal entity reorganizes or the enterprise as a whole is alienated (Article 1023 CC).

A trademark, with or without registration, is a verbal, graphic, three-dimensional or any other symbol that differentiates goods and services of one entity from similar goods and services of others (Article 1024 I CC). Trademark owners have an exclusive right to use and to dispose off the trademark. Trademark protection requires registration of the trademark, except in cases covered by international treaties (Article 1025 I CC). The date of an application's receipt by the patent authority establishes trademark priority. Trademark protection is valid for 10 years and may be extended during the last years of the term of protection for another 10 years an unlimited number of times (Article 1027 II CC). Continuous non-use of a trademark for five years without good reason may lead to the registration's annulment upon request by an interested party (Article 1028 CC). The owner of the trademark may license its use to another (Article 1030 CC). The licensing agreement must be in writing and registered with the patent authority. Failure to comply with these requirements invalidates the agreement (Article 1031 CC). The remedies for trademark infringement are injunction, compensatory damages and removal of the depicted trademark from the infringing goods and their packaging or, if removal is impossible, destruction of goods (Article 1032 CC).

Kazakhstan is a contracting party to a number of international treaties relating to intellectual property rights.[27] As the international treaties impose only minimum standards of protection, Kazakhstani law in some cases offers greater protection. For example, in addition to moral rights protected by the Berne Convention, Kazakhstani copyright law protects the author's right to use a pseudonym and his right to retract (reverse previous disclosure of) a work (Law of RK of

27. At present Kazakhstan is a party to the Berne Convention for the Protection of Literary and Artistic Works; Budapest Treaty on the International Recognition of the Deposit of Microorganisms for the Purposes of Patent Procedure; Madrid Agreement Concerning the International Registration of Marks (and the Protocol relating to it); Nairobi Treaty on the Protection of the Olympic Symbol; Nice Agreement Concerning the International Classification of Goods and Services for the Purposes of the Registration of Marks; Paris Convention for the Protection of Industrial Property; Patent Cooperation Treaty; Phonograms Convention; Strasbourg Agreement Concerning the International Patent Classification; Trademark Law Treaty; WIPO Convention; WIPO Copyright Treaty; and the WIPO Performances and Phonograms Treaty.

June 10, 1996, No. 6-1, "On Copyright and Related Rights" Article 10 I). In terms of remedies, the Law on Copyright has a list of remedies for copyright violations, including recognition of rights, restitution, injunction, compensatory damages (with lost earnings), recovery of revenue obtained through infringement and statutory damages (Article 49 I).

VI. STATE PROPERTY

According to the Civil Code, state ownership may be in the form of republic-level and municipal ownership. Republic-level ownership consists of the republic treasury and property allocated to republic-level legal entities while municipal ownership is composed of the local treasury and property allocated to municipal legal entities (Article 192 CC).

A very important amendment to the Civil Code was made on August 7, 2007, which introduced the concept of "strategic assets." These assets are defined as "the property which has a socio-economical significance for the sustainable development of Kazakhstani society, the possessing and/or using and/or disposing of which shall influence the national security of RK" (Article 193-1 CC). In particular they include: main railroad networks; main petroleum pipelines; oil refineries; national electric power networks; major power stations; main telecommunication lines; national postal network; highways; international airports and marine harbors; atomic energy, outer space and water facilities; etc. Strategic assets may be encumbered by rights of third persons or transferred to private ownership only on the basis of decision of the Government of RK in accordance with legislative acts. Also, it is stipulated that in the case of the willingness of a private person to alienate strategic assets (like in the event of his bankruptcy) the state has priority rights for acquiring strategic assets at the market price determined in accordance with the Law of RK of November 30, 2000, No. 109-II, "On Assessment Activity."

Along with the Civil Code, state ownership of property is currently regulated by the Law of RK of March 1, 2011, No. 413-IV, "On State Property," which provides detailed rules with respect to the competences of the state bodies managing the state property and the legal status of state legal entities. This Law also governs such issues as recording, monitoring and exercising control over the state property use; acquisition and termination of property rights by the state; requisitioning, nationalization and compulsory alienation of real estate property in connection with the seizure of a land plot; and privatization.

Selected Bibliography

Y. Basin, "К вопросу о понятии права собственности" ["On the Issue of the Concept of Ownership Right"], in A. Didenko (ed.), *Гражданское законодательство РК* [*Civil Legislation of RK*], vol. 17 (Yurist, Almaty, 2003) [in Russian].

J.J.A. Burke & R. Nurpeissov, "Property Law of the Republic of Kazakhstan," in D. Thomas (ed.), *Thompson On Real Property* (Lexis Nexis, New York, 2010).

T. Kaudyrov, *Гражданско-правовая охрана объектов промышленной собственности в РК* [*Civil Law Protection of Industrial Property*] (Žeti Žargi, Almaty, 2001).

M. Suleimenov (ed.), *Вещные права в Республике Казахстан* [*Rights in Rem in Republic of Kazakhstan*] (Žeti Žargi, Almaty, 1999) [in Russian].

M. Suleimenov (ed.), *Объекты гражданских прав* [*Objects of Civil Rights*] (KazGYuU, Almaty, 2004) [in Russian].

M. Suleimenov & F. Karagoussov, "The Legal Basis for the Securities Market in the Republic of Kazakhstan" (1998) 24 *Review of Central and East European Law* 451.

Chapter 8
Law of Obligations

Zhenis Kembayev & John J.A. Burke

The Law of Obligations within the legal system of Kazakhstan encompasses three disciplines: (1) contractual obligations (Contract Law), (2) non-contractual obligations (Tort Law), and (3) unjust enrichment (Quasi-Contract Law).

The primary source of the Law of Obligations is the Civil Code of RK, both the General Part and Special Part. According to the Civil Code, an obligation represents a legal duty between the obligor (called the debtor) and the obligee (called the creditor) whether based on contract, tort, or quasi-contract. An obligor is a person obliged to perform a specified action to the obligee. An obligee is the person to whom the benefit of the obligor's performance flows and the person having the legal right to demand performance from the obligor (Article 268 CC).[1]

In a comparative context, the law of contract within the legal system of RK contains not only general principles applicable to all contracts but also provides specific rules based upon transaction types. Likewise, the law of tort is predicated upon the existence of injury, not the existence of a duty of care found, for example, in British and American jurisprudence. Although differences exist between the Law of Obligations within the RK and equivalent law in other jurisdictions, nevertheless the Kazakhstani Law of Obligations contains numerous principles common to any legal regime governing contractual and non-contractual obligations.

1. The terms "obligor" and "obligee" are equivalent to the terms "promisor" and "promissee" found in common law systems. Obligations of the obligor cover actions to transfer property, to perform work, to pay money, to refrain from doing a certain act, etc.

Zhenis Kembayev, *Introduction to the Law of Kazakhstan*, pp. 127–159.

I. CONTRACT LAW

A. INTRODUCTION

Contract Law may be divided into two parts: general and special. The rules of the general part of Contract Law are contained in section I (in particular Chapter 4 "Transactions") and section III (called "Law of Obligations") of the General Part of the Civil Code. Those sections provide fundamental principles and specific rules governing all types of contracts (in particular related to the conditions of the formation, modification and dissolution of contracts; the performance of obligations; performance guarantees; the responsibility for improper performance or non-performance of obligations; and the termination of obligations). The special part of Contract Law is covered by section IV (called "Individual Types of Obligations") of the Special Part of the Civil Code. It includes 505 articles providing numerous and detailed rules that govern 21 specific types of contracts (such as purchase-and-sale contracts, barter, rent, lease, carriage and transport, credit extension, bailment, and independent work, etc.).[2]

Like most legal systems, both civil and common, the relationship between the general and the special provisions of Contract Law in the RK is governed by the principle of *lex specialis derogat generali*, i.e., in the event of a conflict between the general and the special parts, priority is given to the provisions of the Special Part of the Civil Code. Equally consistent with modern contract codes Kazakhstani Contract Law governs contract relations of individuals and legal entities according to the principle of freedom of contract. This principle (along with equality of the participants of Civil Law relations, the inviolability of ownership, the prohibition of interference in private matters, the free effectuation of civil rights and judicial remedies is considered one of the basic values underlying the entire system of Civil Law. The Civil Code proclaims that both natural persons and legal entities "shall acquire and effectuate their civil rights by their own will and in their own interest" and "shall be free in establishing their rights and duties on the basis of contracts and in determining any conditions of a contract not contrary to legislation" (Article 2 CC).

The fundamental legal principle of "freedom of contract" is supplemented by provisions that the parties may conclude a contract that is either provided for or is not provided for by legislation. Coercion to conclude a contract is forbidden except for instances when the duty to conclude a contract is provided for by an obligation embodied in legislation.[3]

2. Noteworthy is the fact that the provisions of Contract Law apply not only to civil law contracts, but also to contracts within other branches of the law, such as administrative law contracts under Administrative Law, employment contracts under Labor Law, marriage contracts under Family Law, etc.
3. For example, in the case of a public contract, see footnote 8 *infra*.

B. Concept and Types of Contract

Under the Civil Code of RK, the term "contract" (*shart, dogovor*) is a component part of the term "transaction" (*mämile, sdelka*), which is a broader concept covering both unilateral and non-unilateral (i.e., bi- and multilateral) actions of natural persons and legal entities directed towards the establishment, change, or termination of civil rights and duties (Articles 147, 148 I CC). In contrast to unilateral transactions (e.g., issuance of a power of attorney or testament) the conclusion of a contract requires the expression of the concordant will of either two (bilateral transaction) or three or more parties (multilateral transaction) (Article 147 III CC). Notably, the Civil Code contains a specific definition of a contract as an agreement between two or more persons by which an obligation is created, modified or extinguished (Article 378 I CC).

In contrast to common law systems and certain civil law systems, the Civil Code differentiates the following types of contracts: (a) *unilateral* (duties vested in one party) and *mutual* (each party is at the same time a creditor and a debtor); (b) *bilateral* and *multilateral* (depending on the number of parties involved); (c) *oral* and *written* (in contrast to the latter, the former is not committed to in writing and/or is not signed by the parties); (d) *simple written* and *notarially certified* (written contracts are divided into two groups: simple written (not requiring notarial certification) and notarially certified); (e) *consensual* and *real* (the former become effective when consent has been reached between the parties as to all essential terms of the contract, while the latter is valid when certain property is delivered to, or a certain action, is taken by one of the parties);[4] (f) *gratuitous* (not requiring consideration) and *onerous* (requiring consideration);[5] (g) *unitype* (containing merely one type of obligation) and *mixed* (containing elements of two or more types of different obligations);[6] (h) *principal* and *preliminary* (the latter is one which precedes and provides the terms of a principal contract);[7] (i) *free* (or voluntary, i.e., a contract which the parties are free to enter into at any time and determine its terms) and *compulsory* (or involuntary, i.e., a contract whereby one of

4. The majority of contracts are consensual; however, there are also a number of real ones (e.g., contracts of gift, keeping, loan and carriage of goods).
5. Under a gratuitous contract, one party is obliged to grant something to the other party without receiving payment from him or other counter-giving (e.g., contracts of gift and free use of property). Onerous contracts, which constitute the overwhelming majority of all contracts, are those where each party must receive payment or other counter-giving for the performance of his duties (Art. 384 CC).
6. Under a mixed contract, the legislation on contracts whose elements are contained in a mixed contract applies in respective parts unless it follows otherwise from the agreement of the parties or the essence of the mixed contract (Art. 381 CC).
7. Under a preliminary contract, parties are obliged to sign a principal contract. It must be concluded in the form established for the principal contract, and if the form of the principal contract has not been established, then in writing. When a principal contract is signed, it extinguishes the preliminary contract. The Civil Code also explicitly differentiates between a preliminary contract and "a protocol of intent"; the latter, unless it is expressly stipulated, is not a Civil Law contract and the failure to perform it does not entail legal consequences (Art. 390 VII CC).

the parties is required by law to conclude a contract with the other interested party);[8] (k) *jointly negotiated* (i.e., a contract the terms of which were negotiated by the initial parties) and *adhesion* (i.e., a contract with predetermined terms offered on a ''take it or leave it'' basis); and (l) *in favor of the contracting parties* and *in favor of a third party* (in contrast to the former, the latter creates rights for a non-contracting party).[9]

C. Formation of Contract

The Civil Code stipulates the procedure for formation of a contract. It requires the following four major conditions: (a) an offer; (b) acceptance; (c) conformation with the requisite form stipulated by law (i.e., written or oral, notarized or not); and (d) agreement on all the essential conditions of the specific contract.[10]

First, an offer is a proposal (in writing or in oral form) made by an offeror to another person inviting the addressee to enter into a contract with him. An offer must be definite in terms, embody the essential conditions of the proposed contract, explicitly express the intention of the offeror to conclude a contract with the person who accepts the invitation, and must be addressed to a particular person (Article 395 I CC). An offer binds the person (offeror) who has sent it from the moment of receipt of the offer by the addressee (offeree). If notice of revocation of an offer is received earlier than, or simultaneously with, the offer itself, the offer is considered to have not been received, and the revocation is effective. An offer received by the addressee generally may not be revoked within the period established for its acceptance unless otherwise stipulated in the offer itself.[11] Kazakhstani law also distinguishes between a particularized offer (i.e., one addressed to a specific person) and a public offer (i.e., one addressed to members of the general public). A public offer is one addressed to an indeterminate number of persons but contains the essential conditions of the proposed contract and, more importantly, explicitly

8. The most prominent example of a compulsory contract is a public contract, which is defined as a contract concluded by a commercial organization with respect to its duties that must be effectuated for everyone who has recourse to the duties (retail trade, carriage by common-use transport, communications services, electric power supply, medical services, hotel servicing, etc.). In doing so, this organization may not prefer one person to another with respect to the conclusion of a public contract except for the instances provided by legislation (Art. 387 CC).
9. An important implication of such contract is that once the third party beneficiary expresses an interest in exercising the rights conferred on him under the contract, the contracting parties may not unilaterally terminate the contract.
10. However, in reality the process of forming a contract goes through three steps, i.e., an offer is sent by the offeror to the offeree; the offeree considers the terms of the offer and sends a response to the offeror; and the offeror receives the acceptance sent to him by the offeree. Unless the parties otherwise agree or unless a law otherwise provides, a contract is deemed to be concluded at the time the offeror receives the response to his offer from the offeree.
11. However, the offeror may stipulate in the offer itself that it may be withdrawn at any time. Also, an offer is to be distinguished from a mere invitation to make an offer (e.g., an advertisement is not an offer but merely an invitation to make an offer).

expresses the intention of the offeror to enter into a contract with any person who accepts the conditions specified in the proposal (Article 395 V CC).

Second, acceptance is a reply from the addressee of an offer in which he expresses acceptance of an offer and an intention to enter into a contract with the offeror on the terms and conditions stipulated in the offer. An acceptance must be full and unconditional.[12] It may be oral or in writing depending on the nature of the contract itself. However, silence (or non-action) may not be considered as an acceptance unless otherwise stipulated by a legislative act, a custom of business, or a course of dealing between the parties. However, if a person who has received an offer performs an action related to the fulfillment of the conditions of the contract within the period established to accept the offer (e.g., he ships off goods, provides services, completes work, makes a payment, etc.), then that action is considered an acceptance unless provided otherwise by legislation or as specified in the offer. To be valid, an acceptance must be received by the offeror within the time limit stipulated in the offer or, absent such a time limit, within a reasonable time from the date the offer was made. If notice of revocation of an acceptance is received by the offeror earlier than or simultaneously with the acceptance itself, the acceptance is considered to have not been received (Article 396 V CC).

The contract itself generally stipulates the place where the contract was concluded (i.e., signed or *lex loci contractus*). If the contract fails to do so, a contract is considered concluded at the place of residence (or location) of the offeror. In addition, a contract generally is considered concluded at the moment the offeror receives the acceptance from the offeree. However, if the law requires that the contract be registered with a state agency, the contract is considered concluded at the time of registration. If the contract calls for the transfer of property, it is considered concluded at the moment the property is transferred.

Third, a contract must be concluded in full conformance with the requisite form stipulated by law or contract. The general rule is that, unless otherwise required by law or contract, a contract may be concluded in oral form (Article 151 II CC). However, the Civil Code specifically stipulates that the following contracts must be concluded in writing: (a) effectuated in the process of entrepreneurial activity (except for transactions performed when they are concluded, unless otherwise specially provided for by legislation the customs of business); and (b) concluded for an amount higher than 100 calculation indexes (except for transactions performed when they are concluded) (Article 152 I CC) (similar, with qualification, to the Statute of Frauds requirement for the sale of goods contained in UCC s. 2-201). Additionally, a written contract may be required in other instances provided for by legislation. In the absence of legal requirements, the parties may agree to conclude their contract in writing. Finally, in certain instances established by legislative acts or the agreement of the parties a contract must be notarized (Article 154 I CC) and in others (in accordance with legislative acts) must be

12. Acceptance of an offer on terms that are different from those contained in the offer is neither total nor unconditional. As such, a modified acceptance is not regarded as an acceptance, but rather constitutes a counter offer.

registered with a state agency (Article 155 I CC). Thus, for example, any contract of purchase-and-sale of real property must be in writing, notarized and, registered with the proper state agency.

Fourth, a contract is effective only if the parties agree on all essential terms of the contract. The goal of this requirement is to make contracts sufficiently definite and therefore enforceable. It also is based on the concept that there is a close relationship between certainty of terms and external manifestation of the will of the parties. According to the Civil Code, the essential terms of a contract are those that relate to the subject matter of the contract, as well as those that are recognized as essential and indispensable for contracts of the given type by legislation (Article 393 I CC). Thus, the meaning of "essential conditions of a contract" varies from one contract to another.[13] For example, in a purchase-and-sale contract the only essential condition is subject matter (the terms of a contract of sale are considered complete if the contract indicates the goods and determines their quantity) (Article 407 III CC), while a leasing contract must contain *inter alia* the following essential terms: the terms and deadline for the transfer of property to the lease holder, the amount and periodicity of payments and the duration of the contract (Article 567 CC).

Thus, it may be concluded that the formation of a contract under Kazakhstani law has a number of differences from the common law system of contract. It does not require the exchange of promises nor consideration. Furthermore, an offer is irrevocable prior to the expiration of the time limit established for its acceptance, unless otherwise provided by law or by the terms of the offer itself. In addition, an offer is not assignable from the offeree to a third party; it also is neither inheritable nor transferable by any other method. Finally, an acceptance must be total and unconditional; any modifications to its terms transform it into a counter offer.[14]

D. Interpretation of Contracts

The Civil Code requires the courts to apply, in sequential order of priority, the following two methods of interpretation. *First*, the court must take into account the literal meaning of the terms contained in the contract. If the terms are vague or

13. Kazakhstani Contract Law does not adopt the view that a contract is concluded and effective based upon the common terms of the offer and acceptance despite the fact that each party may have introduced additional and different terms. Under this view, the different terms are ineffective.
14. In spite of differences, Kazakhstani Contract Law overlaps in many respects with common law of contracts and the Vienna Convention on the International Sales of Goods of 1980 (CISG). For example, a contract for the sale of goods may be made in any manner to show agreement, including offer and acceptance (See Sec.2-204 UCC). Likewise, an offer by a merchant to buy or sell goods in a signed record that by its terms gives assurance that it will be held open is not revocable, for lack of consideration, during the time stated (See Sec. 2-205 UCC).Virtually identical concepts hold true for lease agreements (see Art. 2A UCC). Furthermore, the Kazakhstani law as to formation of the contract essentially follows the CISG (Arts. 14–24).

unclear, the literal meaning is determined by comparison of the relevant term with other terms of the contract and the meaning of the contract as a whole (Article 392 I CC). *Second*, if the first method fails, the court proceeds to the second step, i.e., attempt to discern the "true common will" (i.e., real common intent) of the parties by taking into account the goals and purposes of the contract. In doing so, all relevant circumstances, including negotiations and correspondence relating to the contract, prior practice of the parties, and their subsequent behavior, as well as commercial customs, may be taken into account (Article 392 II CC). The Civil Code gives priority to the literal meaning of the text of a contract over the general common intent of the contract's parties. Thus, Kazakhstani principles of contractual interpretation follow principles found in canons of construction in common law and civil law systems.

E. Performance of Contracts

The performance of a contract is the accomplishment of an action (or non-action) by an obligor (a debtor) as demanded by an obligee (a creditor). The following three main principles of contract performance are: (a) the principle of due performance; (b) the principle of real performance (or performance in kind); and (c) the principle of disallowance of unilateral refusal to perform obligation.

The principle of due performance implies that a contract must be performed in accordance with its conditions and the requirements of legislation, and in the absence of such conditions and requirements, in accordance with the customs of business turnover or other usually presented requirements (Article 272 CC). The principle of performance in kind means the accomplishment of exactly those actions (or non-actions) as provided by the contract. In this regard, the payment of a penalty and compensation of losses generally does not relieve the debtor from performing the obligation in the event of the "improper performance" of an obligation (Article 354 I CC). In the event of "failure to perform," the payment of a penalty and compensation of losses generally relieves the debtor from the performance of the obligation in kind. However, there is an exception to this rule related to a so-called individually-specified thing that may be taken away from the debtor and transferred to the creditor (Article 355 CC).[15] With respect to the third principle, "a unilateral refusal to perform an obligation or a unilateral change of its conditions shall not be permitted except for instances provided for by legislation or by a contract" (Article 273 CC).

The principle of due performance (which foresees the due accomplishment of contractual conditions with respect to the subject matter and parties of a contract as

---

15. It should also be noted that the refusal of a creditor to accept a performance that, as a consequence of delay, no longer interests him, and the payment of a monetary amount established as release-money, shall relieve the debtor from performance of the obligation in kind (Art. 354 III CC).

well as the methods, place, and time of its performance) requires more detailed consideration.

The subject matter of a contract is constituted by rights recognized under Civil Law, i.e., property (such as things, money, securities, work, services, trademarks, results of intellectual activity, etc.) and personal non-property benefits and rights (such as health, dignity, business reputation, right to name, copyright, etc.). In many instances, the legislation establishes special requirements with respect to the subject matter of a contract. Thus, monetary obligations on the territory of RK must be expressed in Kazakhstani national currency—Tenge (Article 127 CC). The use of foreign currency is permitted in certain instances, but such use must comply with the relevant legislative acts of RK (see Law of RK of June 13, 2005, No. 57-III, "On Currency Regulation and Currency Control").

Contractual obligations must be performed for the proper creditor. In particular, it is provided that the debtor may, when performing his obligations, demand evidence that performance is accepted by the creditor or by a person empowered by the creditor, and that the creditor bears the risk of the consequences of the failure to answer such a demand (Article 275 CC). The performance of an obligation may be entrusted in whole or in part to a third party if this substitution is provided by legislation or the contract, and if the third party is connected with one of the parties to the contract (Article 276 I CC). In this case, the creditor may not refuse to accept the performance. In addition, a third party, subject to the danger of losing his right to the property of the debtor as a consequence of a creditor's action against the property, may, at his own expense, satisfy the demand of the creditor without the consent of the debtor. In this event, the rights of the creditor regarding the obligation shall pass to the third person.

There are four rules concerning the methods of performing contractual obligations. *First*, a creditor generally has the right to not accept the performance in parts of an obligation. *Second*, mutual duties must be performed by the parties simultaneously; the failure to perform or to improperly perform the obligation by one party relieves the other party from both the performance of his duty and the satisfaction of counter demands. *Third*, a debtor who is obliged to perform one of two or several actions has the right to choose which action to perform. *Fourth*, in order to execute his obligations, a debtor may place money or securities on deposit with a notarial office or (in the cases established by legislation) a court[16] if the contract cannot be performed by the debtor as a consequence of: (1) the absence of the creditor or a person empowered by him to accept the performance at the place where the contract must be performed; (2) the lack of dispositive legal capacity of the creditor and the absence of his representative; (3) the evident lack of specificity as to who the creditor is with regard to the obligation, particularly in connection with a dispute between the creditor and other persons; or (4) avoidance by the

16. The placing of money or securities on deposit with a notarial office or court is considered to be performance of the contract. The notarial office or court with whom the deposit has been made must notify the creditor thereof.

creditor of accepting performance or other delay on his part (Articles 274, 284, 285, 291 CC).

If the place of a contract's performance has not been determined by legislation or by the conditions of the obligation, or is not manifest from the essence of the obligation or customs of business, performance must be made: (1) with regard to an obligation to transfer immovable property: at the location of the property; (2) with regard to an obligation to transfer a good or other property with the use of carriage: at the place where the property is handed over to the first carrier for delivery to the creditor; (3) with regard to other obligations of an entrepreneur to transfer a good or other property: at the place of manufacture or storage of the property, if this place was known to the creditor at the moment of the establishment of the obligation; (4) with regard to a monetary obligation: at the place of residence (or location) of the creditor at the moment of the establishment of the obligation; (5) with regard to all other obligations: at the place of residence (or location) of the debtor (Article 281 CC).

If a contract (explicitly or implicitly) provides for the date (or time period) of its performance, the contract is subject to performance on that day (or at any moment within the time period).When a contract does not provide for the date (or the time period) of its performance, it must be performed within a reasonable period of time after the establishment of the obligation. An obligation not performed within a reasonable period of time (and likewise an obligation whose period of performance has been determined at the moment of the creditor's demand) must be accomplished within a seven-day period from the day the creditor presents a demand concerning the performance (unless otherwise provided by the legislation, the contract, the customs of business, or the essence of the obligation) (Article 277 CC).

F. Substitution of Parties in a Contract

The Civil Code contains rules with respect to the following situations in which the substitution of parties in a contractual obligation may occur: (a) change of creditor; and (b) change of debtor. This substitution of parties in a contractual obligation is formalized by an agreement, which must be concluded in the same form as the original contract and which defines the rights or duties to be transferred (Article 346 CC).[17]

The transfer of the rights of the creditor to another person (change of creditor) may take place in the form of either *universal* succession (i.e., the succession encompassing all of the creditor's property, e.g., by the way of inheritance or reorganization of a legal entity) or *singular* succession (i.e., the transfer of a specific right).

17. Thus, an assignment of a demand based on a transaction in written (simple or notarial) form is effective only if concluded on identical formal requirements; an assignment relating to a transaction requiring state registration must be registered according to the procedure established for the registration of the transaction; and an assignment regarding a transfer of an "order security" (*ordernnaya tsyennaya bumaga*) is concluded only when the security is endorsed (i.e., signed).

The primary method of singular succession is the assignment of rights (*tsessiya*). The assignment is done by an agreement between the initial creditor (assignor) and the new one (assignee) on the transfer of rights of the former to the latter with respect to a specific contractual obligation. The following are important general rules with respect to such agreement: (a) the rights of the initial creditor pass to the new creditor in the amount and on the conditions that existed at the moment of transfer of the right (in particular, the new creditor obtains the rights securing the performance of the obligation and also other rights connected with the demand, including the right to unpaid interest) (Article 341 CC); (b) the consent of the debtor for the transfer of the rights of the creditor to another person is not required; however, if the debtor was not informed in writing about the transfer of the rights of the creditor to another person, the new creditor bears the risk of the unfavorable consequences caused by this to him (the performance of the obligation to the initial creditor shall be deemed to be performance to a proper creditor) (Article 339 II, III CC); (c) the creditor who has assigned a demand to another person must transfer to him the documents certifying the right of demand and to communicate information having significance for the effectuation of the demand (Article 342 II CC); (d) If the creditor of a specific obligation's identity has a material significance to the corresponding debtor, that obligation cannot be transferred to a new creditor (Article 345 II CC); (e) the assignment of a demand by the creditor to another person is permitted insofar as this is not contrary to legislation or a contract (Article 345 I CC); and (f) the initial creditor who has now assigned a demand is liable to the new creditor for the invalidity of the demand transferred to him, but is not liable for the debtor's failure to perform this demand, except when the initial creditor assumed a suretyship for the debtor to the new creditor (Article 347 CC).

Singular succession may also arise in the following cases: (a) the transfer of rights by the decision of a court in instances where such a transfer is permissible by law;(b) the transfer of claims to a surety or to a third-party mortgagor who has performed the obligations of the debtor in a principal obligation; and (c) the subrogation of rights to an insurance company under an insurance contract (Article 344 CC). At the same time, it should be noted that the transfer of rights inextricably connected with the person of the creditor, in particular demands concerning alimony and compensation of harm caused to life or health, is not permitted (Article 340 CC).

A change of debtor may take place in the form of a universal succession or a transfer of debt. With respect to the latter, it is stipulated that the new debtor has the right to advance against the demand of the creditor, the rights and defenses the initial debtor could have raised against the creditor. However, the transfer of debt is permitted only with the consent of the creditor.

G. Securing Performance of Contracts

The Civil Code of RK provides the following means of securing the performance of contracts: (a) penalties (*aiyp töleu, neustoika*); (b) pledges (*kepil, zalog*); (c) suretyships (*kepil bolushylyq, poruchitelstvo*); (d) guarantees (*kepildik, garantiya*);

(e) deposits (*kepilpül, zadatok*); (f) the withholding of something (*üstap kalu, uderzhanie*); and (g) margins (*kepildi zharna, garantiinyi vznos*). Participants of civil law relations may adopt other performance-securing means that are provided for by legislation (Article 292 I CC). All means of securing the performance of contracts are established on the basis of additional agreements that must be concluded in writing regardless of the form of the principal contract. The independence of those agreements from the respective principal contracts is also reflected in the provision that the invalidity of an agreement to secure an obligation does not entail the invalidity of the principal contract while the invalidity of the principal contract does entail the invalidity of the obligation securing it (Article 292 II, III CC).

A "penalty" (or fine, forfeit) is a monetary amount determined by a law or contract, that the debtor is obliged to pay to the creditor if he fails to perform or performs improperly the contract's obligation, in particular in the event of a delay of performance. With regard to a demand concerning payment of a penalty, the creditor is not required to prove that losses were caused to him. Along with contractual penalties, there are also legal penalties (determined by legislation) regardless of whether the duty to pay has been provided for by an agreement of the parties.[18] The amount of a legal penalty may be increased by agreement of the parties if this is not prohibited by legislation. At the same time, if a penalty is clearly excessive in comparison to the losses of the creditor, a court may reduce it (Articles 293–298 CC). The analogue in other jurisdictions is a liquidated damages clause that need not be found in a contract distinct from the main contract.

A "pledge" is a means of securing the performance of an obligation by virtue of the creditor (pledgeholder) having the right, in the event of the failure of the debtor to perform the obligation secured by the pledge, to receive satisfaction from the value of the pledged property preferentially before other creditors of the person to whom this property (pledgor) belongs, with exceptions established by legislative acts.[19] A pledge may arise by virtue of a contract or on the basis of legislative acts.[20] There are two types of pledges: *first*, a mortgage (including a security interest in immovable and movable property), under which the pledged property remains in the possession and use of the pledgor or a third person; and *second*, a pawn, under which the pledged property is generally transferred by the pledgor to the possession of the pledgeholder. Whoever possesses the pledged property bears the duty to preserve the pledged property and to insure it. Furthermore, pledges of property subject to state registration must be registered at the state body effectuating the registration of

18. For example, this type of penalty is provided for unlawful use of another's monetary assets (Art. 353 CC); for failure to perform or the improper performance of a carriage contract by railway (Art. 77 of Law of RK "On Railway Transport").
19. Thus, a pledge of enterprises, buildings, installations, apartments, rights to land plots and other immovable property (mortgage) is regulated by Law of RK "On the Mortgage of Immoveable Property." In this regard, the general rules on pledge contained in the Civil Code apply when other rules have not been established by the above Law.
20. For example, Law of RK "On Merchant Shipping" establishes a special type of pledge of a sea vessel.

that property. A pledge terminates: (1) with the termination of the obligation secured by the pledge; (2) in the event of improper maintenance of the pledged property upon the demand of the pledgor; (3) in the event of the destruction of the pledged property, unless the pledgor did not restore or substitute it within a reasonable period; or (4) in the event of the sale of pledged property at public sale or when such a public sale has proved impossible (Articles 299–328 CC).[21]

"Suretyships" and "guarantees" both involve the sharing of an obligation between a debtor and another party. Under a suretyship, the other party is called a surety. Should the debtor be unable to fulfill his obligation to the creditor, the surety is liable jointly and severally with the debtor (i.e., the creditor can divide the obligation between the debtor and the surety as he likes). Under a guarantee, the other party is called a guarantor. The guarantor is considered a "subsidiary" of the debtor and is responsible for the portion of the obligation that the debtor is unable to fulfill.[22] Both suretyships and guarantees terminate: (1) with the termination of the obligation secured by it, as well as in the event of a change of this obligation entailing an increase of responsibility or other unfavorable consequences for the surety or guarantor without the consent of the surety/guarantor; (2) with the transfer to another person of the debt relating to the obligation secured by the suretyship or guarantee unless the surety or guarantor has given consent to the creditor to be liable for the new debtor; (3) upon the expiration of the period of time for the performance of the obligation secured by the surety or guarantee, if the creditor has refused to accept a proper performance offered by the debtor or by the surety or guarantor; or (4) upon the expiration of the period of time of the surety or guarantee specified in the contract of suretyship or guarantee (Articles 329–336 CC).

A "deposit" is a monetary amount issued by one of the contracting parties on account of a contract of payment due from him to the other party as security for the conclusion and performance of the contract. The consequences of terminating or failing to perform an obligation under a contract secured by a deposit are the following: (1) in the event of the termination of the obligation before the commencement of the performance thereof by agreement of the parties, or as a consequence of the impossibility, through no one's fault, of the performance, the deposit must be returned; or (2) if the party that provided the deposit is responsible for a failure to perform the obligation, the deposit remains with the other party; but if the party that received the deposit is responsible, it is obliged to pay the other party twice the amount of the deposit. In addition, the party responsible for the failure to perform the obligation is obliged to compensate the other party for losses, taking into account the amount of the deposit unless otherwise stipulated in the contract.

"Withholding" is another means of securing the performance of a contract. It applies in the event of the failure of a debtor to perform an obligation relating to the

21. The concept of pledge is similar to the creation, enforcement and transfer of security rights. See UCC Art. 9 (Secured Transactions).
22. For example, if the debtor owes the creditor USD 1,000 but can only pay USD 700, the guarantor is responsible for the remaining USD 300.

payment for a particular item; it also includes the compensation of the creditor (who possesses the item) of all expenses and losses connected with the debtor's failure to perform. The creditor may withhold the item as long as the respective obligation is not performed, unless the rights to the concerned item were acquired by a third party before the item came into the possession of the creditor (Article 338-1, 338-2 CC).

Finally, the concept of *margin* is an absolutely new development in Kazakhstani legislation, having been introduced to Civil Code only in March 2011. It is defined as a sum of money which is transferred by its payer to its recipient for securing the performance of the payer's obligations related to his trading activities. In the event of non-performance of the obligation, covered by margin due to the fault of the payer, the margin remains with the other party. In the event of non-performance of the obligation through the recipient's fault, or the termination of the obligation by agreement of the parties, or the impossibility of performance, the margin must be returned to the payer (Article 338-3, 338-4 CC).

H. Liability for Violation of Contracts

The violation of a contract by a debtor may result in his liability at the demand of the creditor. There are two major forms of such liability: (a) compensation of losses and (b) payment of a penalty. However, Kazakhstani law does not address explicitly consequential damages.

A debtor who has violated a contractual obligation must compensate the creditor for losses caused by the violation (Article 350 I CC). "Losses" are understood to be expenses that have been incurred or must be incurred by the person whose rights were violated, i.e., loss or damage of his property (*real damage*), or revenues not received that this person would have received under ordinary conditions if his rights had not been violated (*lost advantage/lost profits*) (Article 9 IV CC). When the debtor voluntarily satisfies the creditor's demand, losses are determined according to prices that existed at the place of the obligation's performance on the date of such satisfaction. If the demand is not voluntarily satisfied, losses are determined according to prices that existed on the day of presenting the suit or of the actual payment. In addition, when determining the amount of lost advantage/profit, the preparations made and the measures undertaken by the creditor to receive compensation for that lost advantage must also be taken into account.

In contrast to compensation of losses (real damages or lost advantage), which is a general form of liability applied in any cases of contract violation, a penalty is a particular form of liability applied only in cases provided by legislation or by agreement of parties. Importantly, the amount of a penalty usually does not depend on the extent of the damage; thus the recovery of a penalty does not require the determination of the amount of damage and necessitates only the proving of the fact that the contract was violated. Accordingly, compensation of losses and penalties are different forms of liability. However, they may be applied simultaneously with respect to the violation of a particular contract. In this regard, legislation and agreements provide the following alternatives: (a) the recovery of only a penalty, but not of losses; (b) the recovery of losses in full above the penalty; or (c) the recovery of either a penalty or losses at the choice of the creditor. However, the general rule is that if a penalty has been established for the violation of a contract, only losses that exceed the penalty are compensated (Article 351 I CC). Moreover, in instances where limited responsibility was established for the failure to perform or improper performance, the losses subject to compensation instead of or in addition to the penalty may be recovered only up to the limits established by the limitation.

The creditor also may demand any action of a debtor to be deemed invalid if that action was performed for the purpose of evading responsibility for the violation of the obligation. In addition, an agreement of the parties concerning relieving the debtor from compensation for losses caused by a violation of the obligation that is accepted before the violation of the obligation will not be recognized as valid (Article 350 II, V CC).

Furthermore, Contract Law provides rules with respect to contracts with multiple parties, i.e., involving several creditors or several debtors. In this regard, the following types of civil liability are differentiated: (a) participatory (*ulestik, dolevaya*) liability; (b) joint and several (*yntymaqty, solidarnaya*) liability; and (c) subsidiary (*zhärdem berushilik, subsidiarnaya*) liability.

Unless it follows otherwise from the conditions of a contract or the legislation, in multi-party contracts, each of the debtors is obliged to perform the obligation in equal participatory shares (and thus bear equal participatory liability).

Joint and several liability means that the creditor, at his discretion, may proceed against all of the debtors jointly or against individual debtors separately. To this effect, the Civil Code provides that the duties of several debtors under an obligation connected with entrepreneurial activity, and likewise the demands of several creditors in that obligation, shall be joint, and several unless provided otherwise, by legislation or by the conditions of the obligation (Article 287 II CC).

A subsidiary liability is one in which the creditor must first proceed against the primary debtor in an effort to recover a debt owed. Only if, after this first recourse to the primary debtor fails, then the creditor may proceed against the secondary (subsidiary) debtor to recover the full or remaining portion of the debt. In this regard, the Civil Code stipulates that a creditor may not demand satisfaction of his demand against the principal debtor from a person bearing subsidiary responsibility if this demand can be satisfied by the principal debtor (Article 357 II).

The imposition of damages for breach of contract requires the existence of the following four conditions: (a) unlawful conduct on the part of the offending party; (b) harm suffered by the creditor; (c) causal connection between the unlawful conduct and the occurrence of harm; and (d) fault of the offending party.

Unlawful conduct is constituted by a party's non-performance or improper performance. Non-performance usually implies failure or neglect to perform while improper performance means performance containing certain errors (e.g., not on time, with defects related to goods or work or violations of other contractual conditions).

Harm suffered as a result of a breach of a contractual obligation may be either material or moral. However, Contract Law (in contrast to Tort Law) permits recovery only for material loss.[23] Kazakhstani Law defines moral harm as "mental or physical suffering experienced by a citizen as a result of the unlawful violation, derogation or deprivation of his personal non-property rights and benefits" (see Resolution of the Supreme Court of RK of June 21, 2001, No. 3, "On Application of the Legislation on Compensation of Moral Harm by Courts). Thus, the grounds for moral harm are the infliction of physical pain or mental anguish, both of which are formally absent in the case of breach of contract (however, under Tort Law, recovery may be sought both for material loss and for moral injury).

Next, a causal connection must exist between the unlawful conduct and the occurrence of harm. The absence of such a connection excludes the possibility of imposing civil liability. However, the establishment of a causal connection is in itself insufficient to determine the issue of liability, which must be independently determined.

Thus, another general rule for an obligor to be liable for breach of contract is that his conduct must be accompanied by fault (taking one of three forms, i.e., intent, ordinary negligence or gross negligence).[24] In this regard, it is stipulated that a debtor is liable for "the failure to perform and/or improperly perform an obligation when there is fault" and further that "the debtor shall be deemed to be not at fault if it is proved that he has taken all measures for proper performance of the obligation" (Article 359 I CC). Thus, Contract Law is based on the principle of presumption of fault of the debtor, which means that the burden of showing lack of fault falls upon him.

More strict rules are provided with respect to persons engaged in entrepreneurial activity (merchants). These persons bear liability unless it is proved that proper performance was impossible as a consequence of insuperable force, that is, extraordinary and inevitable circumstances, (such as natural phenomena, military actions, etc.) (Article 359 II CC). Parties may not refer to such circumstances as the absence in the market of the goods, work, or services necessary for the performance of the contractual obligations.

It should also be noted that there are situations in which the law may impose fault (and thus liability for the breach of contract) on a third party (i.e., vicarious liability). Thus, an employer is liable for the actions of his employees relating to the performance of the employer's obligation (Article 362 CC). Moreover, a debtor is liable in instances when the (non-)actions of third persons with regard to their obligations to the debtor served as a cause of the violation of the obligation. In particular, if a principal debtor delegates a duty to a third party, the principal debtor

23. With respect to the moral harm caused by a violation of a contract, the Civil Code stipulates that it must be compensated in excess of losses suffered (Art. 352 CC).
24. The form of fault plays a role only in the determination of the amount of damages. It should also be noted that in Civil Law there is no distinction between direct and indirect intent, which is very important in Criminal Law. See Chapter 13 "Criminal Law," *infra*.

is liable to the creditor for the breach of the delegated duty by the third party (Article 363 CC). Thus, it may be concluded that lack of fault on the side of a debtor and force majeure are bases for releasing an obligor from civil liability for breach of contract. Also, it is stipulated that a debtor is not obliged to pay interest with regard to his monetary obligation in the event of the delay in the performance of an obligation by a creditor (Article 366 CC).

The Civil Code also provides three grounds to reduce the amount of damages owed by the party in breach of the contract: (a) if the failure to perform or improper performance of an obligation has occurred through the fault of both parties; (b) if the creditor has intentionally or through negligence facilitated the increase of the amount of losses caused by the failure to perform or improper performance; or (c) if the creditor has not taken reasonable measures to reduce them (Article 364 CC).

I. Grounds for Voiding Contracts

The Civil Code stipulates that, in the event of a violation of the requirements with respect to the form, content and participants of a transaction, as well as the freedom of the expression of will, the transaction may be deemed invalid at the demand of the interested persons, the proper state agency, or a procurator (Article 157 I CC). Consequently, a contract may be invalidated in the event of a violation of the requirements for (a) the form; (b) content; (c) participants of a contract; and (d) the freedom of the expression of will.

Violation of the Requirements for the Contract's Form: The failure to comply with the notarial form and the requirements concerning state registration of a contract entails the invalidity of the contract (Articles 154 I, 155 I CC). The same applies to the requirement of a foreign economic contract to be in simple written form (Article 153 III CC). The failure to comply with the simple written form requirement of a contract results in its invalidity in instances expressly specified in legislative acts or in the agreement of parties (Article 153 II CC); otherwise, such a failure does not entail its invalidity, but deprives the parties of the right, in the event of a dispute, to confirm the conclusion, content or performance thereof by witness testimony (Article 153 I CC).

Violation of the Requirements for the Contract's Contents: A contract whose content does not correspond to the requirements of legislation or that is concluded for a purpose knowingly contrary to the fundamental principles of legal order or morality is invalid (Article 158 I CC). Also, the Civil Code specifically invalidates those contracts that are (a) concluded without receiving the necessary license or, the renewal of the license after the end of the period of the license's validity, or (b) engaging in unfair competition or violation of the standards of business ethics (Article 159 CC).

At the same time, a person who has knowingly concluded a transaction that violates the requirements of legislation (or the charter of a legal entity) may not demand the invalidation of the contract if such demand is caused by mercenary motives or the intention to evade responsibility (Article 158 II CC).[25] Also, if one of the contracts' participants has concluded it with the intention of evading performance of the obligation or responsibility to a third person or the state, and the other participant knew or should have known about this intention, the interested person (or the state) may demand the invalidation of contract (e.g., in the case of false bankruptcy).

Violation of the Requirements for the Contract's Participants: Contracts concluded by minors who have not attained 14 years of age, except for petty domestic transactions corresponding to their age, are invalid (Article 159 III CC). In contrast, contracts concluded by minors who have attained 14 years of age are considered valid unless they are invalidated by the court at the suit of the parents (or adoptive parents) or guardian (Article 159 IV CC).

Furthermore, a contract is invalid if it is concluded by a person deemed to lack dispositive legal capacity, as a consequence of mental illness or feeble-mindedness; if a contract is concluded by a person with limited dispositive legal capacity, it may be invalidated by the court at the demand of the guardian of that person (Article 159 V, VI CC).[26]

In addition, the Civil Code provides that a contract may be invalidated by the court if it is concluded by a citizen who has full dispositive legal capacity, but at the moment of concluding this contract, was in a state in which he could not understand the significance of his actions or guide them. This invalidation is possible only upon the suit of this citizen; other interested persons may apply to the court only after the death of the citizen, provided it was impossible to bring the suit by him personally while he was still living (Article 159 VII CC).

Violation of the Requirements for the Freedom of the Expression of Will: Contracts may also be invalidated on the basis of the violation of the freedom of the expression of will or if the will expressed does not correspond to the individual's real internal will. Grounds for invalidity of contracts include delusion, fraud, coercion, threats, bad-faith collusion between the agent of one party with the other party, and unconscionability.

A contract concluded as a consequence of mistake having material significance may be deemed by a court to be invalid upon the suit of the party who acted under the influence of the delusion. Mistake is of material significance if it is related to the nature and identity of the transaction or to certain qualities of the transaction's subject that, when discovered, significantly reduce the possibility of using the subject for the transaction's purpose (e.g., while concluding a purchase-and-sale contract, both a buyer and a seller wrongly assume the subject of the contract is a unique valuable thing). Mistake relating to motives may serve as grounds for the invalidity of the transaction only when such a motive is incorporated into the content of the transaction as either a precedent or subsequent

25. This provision roughly corresponds to the common law *unclean hands doctrine*.
26. Contracts concluded by minors under 14 years of age or persons who lack dispositive legal capacity may be deemed valid by decision of a court, at the demand of their parents, adoptive parents or trustees, if they were concluded to the advantage of the said persons.

condition (e.g., in the event of collapse of prices, a buyer may not invalidate a purchase-and-sale contract of a real estate arguing that it was bought for resale). Furthermore, it is stipulated that if the mistake was a consequence of gross negligence of the participant of a contract or is encompassed by his entrepreneurial risk, the court may reject the suit to invalidate the contract (Article 159 VIII CC).

In contrast to mistake, which implies the innocent misunderstanding by one or both parties of the facts, law or consequences of the contract, "fraud" is intentional conduct (action or non-action) of one party aimed at misrepresenting the facts or consequences of the contract to the other party. "Coercion" also is intentional conduct (to make somebody do something against his will). Coercion may be both physical and psychological, and usually is an action, rather than a non-action. *Threats* are quite similar to psychological coercion; however, unlike the latter, threats do not involve any current action, but involve threatening future consequences (sometimes even of a legal character). In many cases fraud, coercion and threats take the form of criminal conduct.[27] Another basis for invalidating a contract is bad-faith collusion between an agent of one party (the victim) with the other party, concluded on terms that are unfavorable to the aggrieved party. Contracts concluded under the influence of fraud, coercion, threats or bad-faith collusion may be invalidated by a court upon the suit of the victim.

Finally, contracts may be invalidated on the basis of unconscionability. In this regard, "a contract that a person was forced to conclude as a result of the confluence of grave consequences on conditions extremely disadvantageous for himself, which the other party took advantage of (overly onerous transactions), may be deemed by a court to be invalid upon the suit of the victim" (Article 159 IX CC). Thus, unconscionability implies the presence of the following three major elements: (a) conditions of the contract are extremely disadvantageous to the aggrieved party; (b) the aggrieved party concludes the contract as a result of the confluence of grave consequences; and (c) the other party is aware of such conditions and consequences and is willing to use them for his enrichment.

Consequences of Invalidity of Contracts: Depending on the grounds upon which a contract is voided and the conduct of each of the parties in the contract, the Civil Code contemplates the following three sets of legal consequences: (a) bilateral restitution; (b) no restitution; and (c) unilateral restitution. *First*, when a transaction is deemed to be invalid, each of the parties is obliged to return to the other party everything received under the transaction or, if it is impossible to return in kind, to compensate the loss in money (a bilateral restitution). *Second*, if the transaction is directed towards the achievement of a criminal purpose, then, if both parties had intent, everything received by them under the transaction or intended for receipt is subject to confiscation by court decision (no restitution). *Third*, if there is intent to achieve a criminal purpose on the part of only one party, everything received by that party under the transaction is returned to the other party, and

27. Thus, the Criminal Code of RK contains crimes titled "Threatening" (Art. 112 CrC); "Fraud" (Art. 177 CrC); and "Coercion to the Commission of a Transaction or to a Refusal to Commit It" (Art. 226 CrC).

the consideration received by the innocent party, or due to the innocent party under the transaction, is subject to confiscation (unilateral restitution) (Article 157 III, IV, V CC).

J. Amendment and Termination of Contracts

Any contract may be amended or terminated by the agreement of the parties and the requirements for either modification or termination of a contract are not different from those required to create a contract. In fact, agreements on the modification or on the termination of contracts must satisfy the same formal requirements as the basic contract itself (Article 402 I CC).

In addition, the Civil Code lists 10 specific grounds for the termination of a contractual obligation: (1) proper performance; (2) granting of release-money; (3) set-off; (4) novation; (5) remission of debt; (6) merger of debtor and creditor into one person; (7) impossibility of performance; (8) supervening act of state agency; (9) death of a natural person; and (10) liquidation of a legal entity (Article 367 CC). All these grounds are differentiated into: (a) those that emerge on the basis of the parties' wills and (b) those that emerge independently from the parties' wills.

The first five grounds for the termination of a contractual obligation are connected with the will of parties and are realized on the basis of their agreements. *Proper performance* is performance done by the proper person, for the proper person, at the proper place, in the proper manner, with the proper object (of the proper quality and the proper quantity) and at the proper time. Granting of *release-money* (*otstupnoe*) is analogous to "substituted performance" in common law and implies the purchase of a release from a contractual obligation (in the form of the payment of money, the transfer of property, the performance of a service, etc.). *Set-off* means the termination of an obligation by a counter-claim made by a debtor against a creditor. However, the Civil Code provides that the set-off is not permitted if the limiting period of the counter-claim has expired or if the counter-claim is related to compensation of harm caused to life or health, the recovery of alimony or maintenance for life. *Novation* is the substitution by mutual agreement of the initial obligation for another between the same persons providing either for another subject matter of the contract or means of its performance. Finally, an obligation may be terminated by the release of the debtor from his contractual duties by the creditor (remission of debt). The remission of debt may not violate the rights of other persons with respect to the property of the creditor.

Also, there are the following grounds for the termination of a contractual obligation which emerge regardless of the parties' wills. *Merger of debtor and creditor into one person* takes place, for example, in the event of the reorganization of a legal person or when a lessor purchases something he was renting. An obligation may be terminated by "impossibility of performance" if it was caused by a circumstance for which the debtor is not liable. In this event each party, having (partially) performed the obligation, may demand the return of that performed. However, if the impossibility of performance by a debtor of his obligation was caused by unlawful actions of the creditor, the latter may not demand the return of that which has already been performed by it under the obligation. The performance of an obligation may become impossible also as a result of the publication of a *supervening act of state agency*. The parties who have incurred losses as a result of the act may demand compensation. Should the act be deemed invalid by a superior state body, the contractual obligation is to be restored unless an agreement of the parties stipulates otherwise or the performance has lost interest for the creditor. A contractual obligation is also terminated by *the death of either the debtor or the creditor* if performance cannot be made without their personal participation, or the obligation is otherwise inextricably connected with their personalities. In the event of *the liquidation of a legal entity* (whether a debtor or a creditor), its obligations are also terminated except for instances when the performance of its obligations is placed on another legal entity by legislation. The reorganization of state agencies does not entail the termination of their obligations; their performance will generally be entrusted to the agency at whose disposition the assets of the respective budget will be.

Note that a contract may be changed or dissolved by court upon the demand of one of the parties in the event of a "material violation" of the contract (i.e., a violation of a contract by the other party, which entails for the other party such damage that it is deprived in significant degree of that which it had the right to count on when concluding the contract) (Article 401 II CC). Furthermore, a contract may be changed or dissolved upon the application of one party in the following instances: (a) the other party is deemed bankrupt in the procedure established by the legislation; (b) the change or repeal of an act of a state agency on the grounds of which the contract was concluded; and (c) in other instances provided for by legislation or the contract (Article 404 CC). In the event of a unilateral change or dissolution of the contract, the party must warn the other party thereof by not later than one month.

II. TORT LAW

A. INTRODUCTION

Tort obligations in modern Kazakhstani legal science are defined as delictual obligations (deriving from the Latin word *delictum*, which means a violation of the law).[28] It follows that, similar to common law, the infliction of damage is a

28. Accordingly, Tort Law is generally referred to as Delict Law (*deliktnoe pravo*). Under Roman Law, the very same as in Kazakh Customary Law, torts were of a common origin with crimes, but subsequently have substantially diverged from the latter. Thus, Roman Law differentiated between a public offense (*delictum publicum*, i.e., a crime) and a private wrong (*delictum privatum*, i.e., a civilly actionable wrong). Both contiguity and the difference of torts and crimes are fully reflected also in contemporary Kazakhstani legal system. Thus, many crimes under the Criminal Code of RK are also actionable torts (such as assault, insult, defamation); however, it may not be conversely.

necessary but insufficient condition for the commission of a tort in Kazakhstan. It is common ground that a tort is a civil wrong (as opposed to a criminal wrong) and provides a remedy to the injured party. It also is common ground that the primary distinction between a contractual and non-contractual obligation is that the latter imposes mandatory obligations based generally upon social policy whereas the former is the result of voluntary agreement. However, unlike the common law, the Tort Law of RK uses the event of damage as the starting point to determine fault and to compensate the victim. Furthermore, the Tort Law of RK is not indexed according to the traditional common law paradigm: intentional torts, negligence, and strict liability, though these concepts are laced throughout the Kazakhstani Law of Obligation.

The Law of Torts is contained in section III (called "Law of Obligations") of the General Part of the Civil Code and section 47 of the Special Part of the Civil Code (Obligations Arising Due to Infliction of Damage). This section has 37 Articles and consists of the following four divisions: (1) General Provisions; (2) Compensation of Damage Inflicted on the Life and Health of a Natural Person; (3) Compensation for Damage Caused Due to Defects in Goods, Works and Services (Product Liability); and (4) Compensation for Moral Damage. Equally important are the following regulatory acts: Resolution of the Supreme Court of RK of July 9, 1999, No. 7, "On Practice of Application of the Legislation on Compensation of Harm Caused by Illegal Actions of State Bodies in Criminal Procedure"; Resolution of the Supreme Court of RK of July 9, 1999, No. 9, "On Some Issues of Application of the Legislation on Compensation of Harm Inflicted on Health of Citizens"; Resolution of the Supreme Court of RK of December 22, 2000, No. 16, "On Practice of Application of the Legislation on Protection of Environment"; and Resolution of the Supreme Court of RK of June 21, 2001, No. 3, "On Application of the Legislation on Compensation of Moral Harm by Courts." Kazakhstani law governing non-contractual obligations follows the main lines of Tort Law found in most legal regimes by recognizing the primary categories of non-contractual obligations.

However, the classification of torts found in the main divisions of the Civil Code Special Part reflects the profound differences between the Tort Law of RK and the common law. A cursory review of the Civil Code Special Part reveals that Tort Law is not an analogue of common law due to an absence of demarcation of classic torts, such as trespass to land, nuisance, battery, false imprisonment and invasion of privacy, to cite a few examples. Only if Tort Law is read and interpreted in its broadest sense would it cover these classic torts of the common law. Even then, the Civil Code lacks the architecture of rules that have developed to ascertain the commission of tort in these domains and the setting of appropriate compensation. In addition, Kazakhstani Tort Law is distinct in certain approaches, such as burden of proof, determination of fault and the commission of torts by the state.

Consistent with most legal systems, a tort implies that a person (a victim) has suffered a loss or harm as the direct result of the conduct of another person (the tortfeasor). The main purpose of Tort Law is to shift the loss sustained by the victim to the tortfeasor. However, the conduct of a person that results in loss or damage does not inexorably lead to liability. Liability is predicated upon the circumstances of each case. Conduct may be fault based or non-fault based. It may be lawful or unlawful. In any event, liability for infliction of damage requires that the conduct of the tortfeasor has caused the infliction of harm upon the victim. Thus, Tort Law determines when an event resulting in harm to property, person or non-material values is actionable under law. This proposition is broad enough to cover the torts found in the common law paradigm, except that neither the General nor the Special Part of the Civil Code contains explicit and specific rules for each tort.

In addition, and consistent with most legal systems, the function of Tort Law is threefold: (1) compensatory; (2) punitive; and (3) preventive. The compensatory function restores the status of the victim to where it was before the losses were caused by the tortfeasor. Losses are quantified in monetary terms, regardless of whether or not the losses are tangible or intangible, pecuniary or non-pecuniary. The punitive function punishes the tortfeasor by requiring the payment of compensation to the victim. Finally, the preventive function deters the commission of civil law wrongs in the future both by the tortfeasor (through application of punitive measures) and by potential third parties (through public dissemination about the legal consequences of causing injury or harm to others).

B. Parties to a Tort Obligation

The parties involved in non-contractual obligations are primarily the tortfeasor and victim. Both parties may be any subject of Civil Law (a natural person, a legal entity or the state). A victim of a tort may demand compensation for any harm caused to him. If the tortfeasor does not voluntarily satisfy the demand, a victim may file a claim in court to recover the payment of compensation.

A natural person may be recognized as a tortfeasor, if the natural person has the ability to bear contractual and non-contractual liability (*zhauapkershilik alu qabileti, deliktosposobnost'*). Such ability is given to those natural persons who have full or partial dispositive legal capacity; i.e., minors under 14 and incapable persons may not be tortfeasors. Liability for the tort committed by a minor is borne by his legal representatives (parents, adoptive parents or trustees) unless the latter prove that the harm did not arise because of their fault (Article 925 I CC). With respect to torts committed by minors between the ages of 14 and 18 years, their legal representatives bear only subsidiary liability (unless they prove that the harm did not arise through their fault) (Article 926 CC). In this instance, the victim has recourse against legal representatives only if the minor lacks revenue or other property sufficient to compensate harm, and the victim establishes that harm is related to fault conduct of the minor's representatives.[29] When a person deemed to

29. Also, a court may place liability on a parent deprived of parental rights for harm caused by his minor children during three years after the deprivation of parental rights if the behavior of the child which entailed the causing of the harm was a consequence of the improper effectuation of parental duties (Art. 927 CC).

lack dispositive legal capacity causes harm to a victim, his trustee or the organization obliged to effectuate supervision over that person is responsible to provide compensation (unless the legal guardians of the incapacitated individual prove that the harm did not arise through their fault) (Article 927 CC).[30]

A legal entity may be recognized as a tortfeasor. The actions of employees when performing labor (or employment, official) duties are considered the actions of the legal entity (vicarious liability). In this regard, the Civil Code provides that a legal entity must compensate harm caused by its employees (Article 921 I CC). A legal entity that has compensated harm caused by its employee when performing his official or other labor duties has the right of recourse (regression) against this employee in the amount of the compensation paid (Article 933 I CC). In the event of reorganization of a legal entity responsible for harm caused to the life or health of a natural person, the legal successor assumes the duty to pay compensation to the victim. (Article 945 I CC).

The state may be recognized as a tortfeasor. The Civil Code provides that harm caused to a natural person or a legal entity as a result of the issuance of an act of a state agency failing to correspond to a law or other regulatory act is subject to compensation at the expense of the state treasury of RK (Article 922 II CC). The Civil Code also stipulates that the state is liable in tort if a victim suffers both material and moral harm caused as a result of an illegal conviction; illegal imposition of criminal responsibility; illegal detention or confinement under guard; illegal imposition of an undertaking not to leave (e.g., the territory of RK) or of an administrative sanction in the form of arrest; or illegal confinement to a medical (psychiatric) institution. In each case, the state must compensate of the victim (Articles 923 I, 951 III CC) (see also section IV on "Strict Tort Liability"). In the event of compensation by the state due to harm caused by an official of agencies of inquiry or preliminary investigation, procurator's office or a court, the state has the right of regression (or recourse) against this official if his fault has been established by the judgment of a court that has entered into legal force (Article 933 III CC).

C. Concept and Elements of Tort

The Civil Code of RK does not contain a legal definition of what is a tort. However, as previously stated, torts are wrongful acts (or omissions to act) that result in injury to property or non-material values[31] of natural persons and/or legal entities, and for which the injured party is entitled to compensation (Article 917 I CC). This

30. The Civil Code provides also that if the harm was caused by a person who could not understand the significance of his actions or direct them as a consequence of his mental disturbance, the duty to compensate the harm may be placed by a court on a spouse, parents or children who have reached majority, who knew about the mental disturbance of the harm-causer but did not raise the question of deeming him to lack dispositive legal capacity (Art. 930 III CC).
31. Personal non-material benefits and rights are life, health, dignity of the individual, honor, good name, business reputation, inviolability of private life, personal and family secrecy, right to

definition gives ground to differentiate the following four elements of a tort: (1) unlawful conduct (action or non-action) of the tortfeasor; (2) infliction of harm;(3) causation between the conduct of the tortfeasor and the harm suffered by the victim; and (4) fault of the tortfeasor. It is the unitary character of the elements of a tort in Kazakhstani law that principally differentiates the Kazakhstani approach to non-contractual obligations as opposed to the paradigmatic scheme previously referenced.

Unlawful conduct of the tortfeasor is the first element required to establish the commission of a tort. This requirement implies that the tortfeasor breached a rule-of-law (and the general duty imposed by law on all persons, i.e., the duty not to cause injury to others). This rule is consistent with the "duty of care" imposed upon persons found in most legal regimes, the breach of which is a necessary predicate of the tort of "negligence." However, the Civil Code does not provide criteria to determine an "unlawful act," contrary to the common law where judicial decisions fill in the interstices created by Codes.

Lawful conduct generally does not result in tort liability. Thus, harm inflicted by reason of "necessary defense" is not compensable if the action did not exceed that which was reasonable and necessary under the circumstances (Article 919 CC). However, in exceptional situations (explicitly provided by legislation), lawful conduct may lead to tort liability (Article 917 III CC). A person may be liable to a victim when harm is caused to that victim in a state of extreme necessity. For example, when a tortfeasor attempts to eliminate a danger that the tortfeasor itself has caused, and that danger is threatening the safety of the tortfeasor and third parties, the tortfeasor may be liable in tort for harm caused to a victim, even though action in a state of extreme necessity is lawful conduct (Article 920 CC).[32] Nevertheless, dependent upon circumstances, a court may allocate loss based upon comparative negligence between the tortfeasor and third party, and in limited cases, exempt the tortfeasor from liability partially or wholly. Unlawful conduct is actionable only in situations where the law specifically requires action on the part of the tortfeasor (e.g., the duty of a physician to ensure the safety of patients).

"Infliction of harm" is the second element required to establish the commission of a tort. The Civil Code provides that a person, who has caused harm to the person or property of a natural person or to the property of a legal entity, must pay compensation in full (Article 917 I CC). Harm may be material or moral (emotional) (Article 951 CC). Material harm is compensated either in kind (repair a given thing or provide a new one) or in monetary form, both actual losses and lost advantage/profit. The Civil Code also provides that a person whose non-material values have been violated has the right to compensation for moral harm

name, right to authorship, right to inviolability of work, and other non-material benefits and rights (Art. 115 III CC).

32. Taking into account the circumstances under which such harm was caused, the court may place the duty of compensating it: (a) to a third person in whose interests the harm-causer acted; (b) to both this third party and the harm-causer in proportion; or (c) to relieve both this third party and the harm-causer fully or partially from compensation of the harm.

(emotional suffering as a result of the injury) (Article 141 I CC), and that moral harm caused by a violation of an obligation must be compensated in excess of material losses (Article 352 CC). "Moral harm" as emotional suffering finds its corresponding analogue in common law where recovery for emotional distress alone is specifically recognized in tort.

Harm generally must be compensated in full. However, under certain circumstances, the amount of compensation may be decreased or increased. The amount of compensation may (or must) be decreased by a court if: (a) the gross negligence of the victim resulted in an increased degree of harm; and (b) the liability of the tortfeasor emerges regardless of fault (Article 935 II, V CC). The Civil Code also provides that a court, at the request of the tortfeasor, may reduce the amount of compensation if his property status (ability to pay) has decreased due to disability or reaching the age of retirement in comparison to his ability to pay at the time of the tort (except for instances when the harm was caused by actions committed intentionally) (Article 942 CC). The Civil Code also provides specifically that a victim who has partially lost labor capacity may require from tortfeasor a respective increase of the amount of his compensation if the labor capacity of the victim has decreased in connection with the causing of impairment of health in comparison with the victim's labor capacity at the time of the commission of tort (Article 942 I CC). Harm to the victim resulting from the latter's deliberate conduct is non-compensable (Article 935 I CC).

"Causation" is the third element required to establish the commission of a tort. Causation must be direct and immediate to qualify as the proximate cause of the injury. The tortfeasor's conduct must be the necessary antecedent to the victim's injury. If the victim's injury would have occurred without the tortfeasor's conduct, or the tortfeasor's conduct is too remote to establish proximate causation, the conduct of the tortfeasor cannot be deemed the proximate cause of the harm.[33]

Fault of a person is the fourth element required to establish the commission of a tort. Fault is generally a prerequisite for liability. Tort Law is based on the principle of presumption of fault of the tortfeasor. No such presumption exists at common law for fault-based torts; rather the victim has the burden to prove that the tortfeasor committed an intentional act (intentional torts) or breached a duty of care owed to the victim (negligence). In this regard, the tortfeasor bears the burden to prove that his conduct lacked fault (and thus unlawfulness) while the victim bears the burden to prove only that he suffered harm, and that there is a causal connection between the harm suffered and the unlawful conduct of the tortfeasor.[34] However, along with fault-based tort liability (the general rule), Kazakhstani Tort Law also recognizes no-fault (or strict) tort liability (discussed *infra*).

---

33. Note that neither the General nor the Special Parts of the Civil Code of RK contain a definition of the terms "cause" or causation.
34. In this regard, it should be noted that full dispositive legal capacity for natural persons to bear tort (and contractual) liability (*deliktosposobnost'*) commences at the age of 18 years (see Chapter 6 "Law of Natural Persons" *supra*) while the legal capacity of legal entities arises at the time when the legal entity is registered with the proper governmental authorities.

While a tortfeasor is liable only for torts based upon fault, there are exceptions to this rule. The exceptions are related to the liability of the tort of minors and persons lacking dispositive legal capacity. In these instances, the Civil Code may provide for the imposition of vicarious tort liability (discussed *supra*). In addition, it is provided that a person, who has caused harm in such a state that he could not understand the significance of his actions or control them, is not liable for the harm caused by him (Article 930 I CC).[35] But if the tortfeasor is responsible for creating a situation that has caused his inability to understand the significance of his actions or direct them, for example by the use of alcoholic beverages, narcotics, or other means, the tortfeasor is not to be relieved from liability.

D. Strict Tort Liability

Kazakhstani Tort Law recognizes liability without fault or strict liability in tort. *First*, legal entities and natural persons engaged in hazardous activity that affect persons (transportation, industrial enterprises, construction, etc.) may be held strictly liable in tort. Such persons are obliged to compensate the harm caused by the hazardous activity unless the tortfeasor proves that the harm resulted from a consequence of insuperable force or the act of the victim. The duty of compensation of harm is placed on the legal entity or a natural person who possesses the source of hazardous activity by right of ownership, right of economic or operative management, or other legal basis (right of lease, power of attorney for the right to operate means of transport, etc.). Harm caused as a result of the interaction of more than one source of hazardous activity (e.g., collisions of means of transport) to third persons is compensated by the tortfeasors jointly and severally (Article 931 CC).[36]

Second, strict liability in tort is recognized with respect to harm caused to life, health, or property of a natural person or the property of a legal entity as a consequence of design, prescription, or other defects of a good, work, or service, and also as a consequence of unreliable or insufficient information or warnings concerning the good (or work, service). In this case, the harm is subject to compensation by the seller or manufacturer of the good or by the person who fulfilled the work or rendered the service regardless of fault (Article 947 CC). However, these rules are applied only in the instances of the acquisition of the good (or

35. But in cases where harm is caused to the life or health of the victim, the court may, taking into account the property status of the victim and the harm-causer, and also other circumstances, place the duty with regard to compensation of harm fully or partially on the harm-causer (Art. 930 I CC).

36. Should the harm be caused to the possessors of these sources, it must be compensated on general grounds. The following rules apply: (a) harm caused through the fault of one party must be compensated by that party in full; (b) harm caused through the fault of two or more parties must be compensated in proportion to the degree of fault of each of them. In case of impossibility to establish the degree of the fault of each of the parties, the liability must be distributed equally among them. If neither party has fault in the infliction of damage, each of the parties bears a risk of losses incurred by them (Art. 931 II CC).

fulfillment of work, rendering of service) for purposes of personal consumption (and not for use in entrepreneurial activity).

Third, the Civil Code provides that compensation of moral harm must be effectuated regardless of the fault of the tortfeasor when: (1) the harm is caused to the life or health of a citizen by a source of increased danger; (2) the harm is caused to a citizen as a result of his illegal conviction; illegal bringing to criminal responsibility; illegal detention or confinement under guard; illegal imposition of undertaking not to leave or of an administrative sanction in the form of arrest; illegal placement to a medical (psychiatric) institution; or (3) the harm was caused by the dissemination of information that constitutes a defamatory act (Article 951 III CC).

Fourth, the Civil Code provides that harm caused to a citizen as a result of his illegal conviction; illegal bringing to criminal responsibility; illegal detention or confinement under guard; illegal imposition of undertaking not to leave or of an administrative sanction in the form of arrest; or illegal placement to a medical (psychiatric) institution must be compensated by RK in full regardless of fault of the officials of the agencies of inquiry or preliminary investigation, procurator's office or court (Article 923 I CC).

E. Compensation of Damage Inflicted on the Life and Health of a Natural Person

A natural person has a right to compensation of harm caused to his life or health when performing contractual obligations as well as labor (service) and military duties.

This compensation must include: (1) earnings (or revenue) lost by the victim which he had or could be determined to have; and (2) additional expenses incurred caused by the impairment of health, including expenses for: (a) treatment; (b) additional nourishment; (c) acquisition of medicines;(d) prosthetics;(e) outside care; (f) sanatorium-resort treatment; (g) the acquisition of special means of transport; and (h) training for another profession, if it is established that the victim needs these types of assistance and care and does not have the right to receive them free of charge (Article 937 I CC).

The amount of earnings (or revenue) lost by a victim is subject to compensation determined by percentages of average monthly earnings (or revenue) before the mutilation or other impairment of health (and thus the loss of his capacity to labor). Lost earnings (or revenue) include all types of payment for labor, under labor and civil law contracts both at the principal place of work and at secondary jobs levied with income lax. Compensation is set-off by benefits paid for the period of temporary lack of labor capacity or pregnancy and birth leave. Revenues from entrepreneurial activity, and also author's royalty, are included in lost earnings, the revenues from entrepreneurial activity being included on the basis of tax inspectorate data. All types of earnings (or revenue) shall be taken into account in the amounts credited before the withholding of taxes. If stable changes improving his financial status (e.g., increase of earnings in the post held, transfer to higher-paid work, completing higher education, etc.) occurred in the earnings (or revenue) of the victim before the mutilation or other impairment of health was caused to him, when determining his average monthly earnings (or revenue) only the earnings (or revenue) which he received or should have received after the respective changes are taken into account.

Compensation of harm caused by a reduction of labor capacity or the death of a victim is made by monthly payments. When there are justifiable reasons, the court, taking into account the ability to pay of the tortfeasor, may at the demand of the victim, award him compensation as a single payment, but in an amount that does not exceed compensation required over a three-year period (Article 944 I CC).

Compensation of Harm in Event of Impairment of Health of Person Who Has Not Attained Majority: In the event of mutilation or other impairment of health of a minor who has not attained 14 years (youth) and does not have earnings (or revenue), the tortfeasor must compensate the expenses caused by the impairment of health. When the minor reaches the age of 14, and also in the event of the causing of harm to a minor ranging in age from 14 to 18 years who lacks earnings (or revenue), the tortfeasor must compensate the victim not only for expenses caused by the impairment of health but also for harm connected with the loss of or reduction of his labor capacity, proceeding from 10 times MCI established by law. If at the time of the impairment to his health a minor had earnings, the harm must be compensated by proceeding from the amount of the earnings, but not lower than 10 times MCI. Should a minor commence labor activity, he may demand an increase of the amount of compensation of harm based upon earnings received by him, but not less than the amount of remuneration established for the post occupied by him or the earnings of a worker of the same qualifications at his place of work.

Compensation of Harm to Persons Who Have Incurred Damage as Result of Death of Breadwinner: In the event of the death of a victim (who is the primary or sole source of household income), the right to compensation belongs to: (1) persons lacking dispositive labor capacity dependent on the deceased or had on the day of his death the right to receive maintenance from him; (2) a child of the deceased born after his death; (3) a parent, spouse or other member of the family, regardless of labor capacity, who did not work and cared for the children, grandchildren, brothers and sisters who had not attained 14 years and who were dependent on the deceased; and (4) persons who were dependent upon the deceased at the time of death and who subsequently are deemed to lack labor capacity within five years after his death. A parent, spouse or other members of the family who does not work and cares for children, grandchildren, brothers and sisters of the deceased and later are deemed to lack labor capacity during the period of effectuating care retain the right to compensation of harm after the period of care has terminated. Compensation is paid to a minor until the age of 18 years; to a student older than 18—until completion of his study, but not more than up to 23 years of age; to women older than 55 and men older than 60 years—for life; to disabled persons—for the period of disability; to a parent, spouse or other members of the family engaged in caring for children, grandchildren, brothers and sisters dependent on the deceased—until the dependent attains 14 years of age.[37]

Subsequent Change of Amount of Compensation of Harm: A victim who has partially lost labor capacity may at any time require from the tortfeasor an increase in the amount of compensation if the victim's labor capacity has decreased compared to the capacity that existed prior to the time the tort occurred, and damages for compensation were awarded. The amount of compensation is subject to indexation in the event of an increase in the cost of living (Article 943 CC). By contrast, a tortfeasor may demand a respective reduction in the amount of compensation if the labor capacity of the victim has increased compared to the capacity that existed prior to the time the tort occurred, and damages for compensation were awarded. A tortfeasor also may demand a reduction in the amount of compensation for harm if his property status (ability to pay) in connection with disability or attainment of pension age has declined compared with the status the tortfeasor had at the time the court entered the award of compensation for harm (except for instances when the harm was caused by actions committed intentionally) (Article 942 CC).

F. Compensation for Product Liability

Kazakhstani law recognizes the tort of product liability. This liability stems from a person, usually a manufacturer, of introducing into the stream of commerce a product that contained a defect prior to its introduction to the market place. It also extends to the failure to provide adequate information and warnings about the ordinary use of the product. If a person (natural or juridical) suffers harm to life, health or property, as a consequence of defects in design, prescription, manufacture of goods or provision of service, or failure to provide reliable or sufficient information concerning the good, work, or service, the seller, manufacturer or provider is strictly liable in tort.[38] In such cases, the liability of the seller (the manufacturer or the executor) arises regardless of whether the victim was in privity of contract. In the case of consumers who are natural persons, the right to sue is predicated upon the fact that the defective product harmed a victim, regardless of whether or not the victim was the purchaser of the goods.

However, to a limited extent, when goods (or fulfillment of work, rendering of service) purchased (acquired) for a commercial purpose (for use in entrepreneurial activity), fault is a requirement for liability (Article 947 CC). The Civil Code stipulates that the seller or manufacturer of a good or executor of work or service may be relieved from liability if it is proved that the harm arose as a consequence of

---

37. By contrast, the common law recovery in damages is principally based on quantifying the value of the life of the deceased, often using the expert testimony of an economist, payment of other expenses (e.g., medical and funeral), plus punitive damages, if any.
38. Kazakhstani law governing "product liability" goes further than similar law in the US and European Union (EU) by providing a remedy for commercial users of products and for providing strict liability for defective information.

insuperable force or a violation by the consumer of the established rules for the use of the good or the results of the work, service or their keeping (Article 950 CC).

The Civil Code provides that the victim may recover compensation from either the seller or manufacturer. In addition, the victim may sue both the seller and the manufacturer. Should only the seller be named in the complaint, the seller may file a counter-claim against the manufacturer as a co-defendant in the lawsuit. Further, harm caused as a consequence of defects of work or service is subject to compensation by the person who fulfilled the work or rendered the service (executor). The law also requires the seller (the manufacturer or the executor) to bring to the attention of the consumer any and all relevant information regarding the good (or work, service), including information on how to use the product. The failure to deliver complete or reliable information concerning the good (or work, service) is subject to compensation by the seller (the manufacturer or the executor) (Article 948 III CC).

The Civil Code establishes periods for compensation of harm caused as a result of defects of good, work or service. Thus, harm caused as a consequence of defects of a good, work, or service shall be compensated if the harm arose during the established periods for the fitness of a good (or work, service), and if the period of fitness is not established, within 10 years from the date of production of the good (or work, service). Beyond these limits, harm is subject to compensation if: (a) the period of fitness is not established in violation of the requirements of law; (b) the person to whom the good was sold (the work was fulfilled, or the service was rendered) was not warned about necessary actions upon the expiry of the period of fitness and possible consequences in the event of the failure to fulfill those actions (Article 949 CC).

Both a natural person and a legal entity may be a victim of a tort based on product liability. The type of harm required is generally material harm, i.e., harm to the life, health or property of a natural person or the property of a legal entity. However, if the victim is a consumer who is using the defective product for a non-commercial purpose, he also may recover compensation for moral harm suffered as a result of a defect in the product, provided the seller is at fault (the manufacturer or the executor). The right to seek recovery for moral harm in products liability cases is granted to consumer under the Law of RK of May 4, 2010, No. 274-IV, "On the Protection of the Rights of Consumers" (Article 21 of the Law).

G. Compensation for Moral Damage

The Civil Code defines moral damage as "the violation, derogation or deprivation of personal non-property benefits and rights of natural persons and legal entities, including moral or physical sufferings (humiliation, irritation, depression, anger, shame, despair, physical pain, detriment, state of discomfort, etc.) experienced (endured, suffered) by the victim as a result of violation of law committed against him" (Article 951 I CC). Moral harm caused by actions (or failures to act) that violate the property rights of a natural person is not subject to compensation, except for cases provided for by law (Article 951 IV CC).

As a rule, the tortfeasor, who has committed a fault-based tort, must compensate the victim for moral damage. However, moral damage is subject to compensation regardless of the fault of the tortfeasor if: (a) it is inflicted on the life and health of a natural person by a source of increased danger; (b) it is caused to a natural person as a result of his illegal conviction; illegal bringing to criminal responsibility; illegal detention or confinement under guard; illegal imposition of undertaking not to leave or of an administrative sanction in the form of arrest; or illegal confinement to a medical (psychiatric) institution; (c) it is inflicted by disseminating information that constitutes a defamatory act; and (d) in other cases provided for by law.

Compensation of moral harm is paid in the form of currency (Article 952 I CC) regardless of the type of harm subject to compensation (Article 952 III CC). When determining the amount of compensation, the court considers both subjective and objective criteria to determine the extent of moral and physical suffering of the victim.

III. UNJUST ENRICHMENT

The Law of Unjust Enrichment in Kazakhstan is contained in the Civil Code Special Part Chapter 48 entitled "Obligations Due to Unsubstantiated Enrichment" (Articles 953–960 CC). Unjust enrichment is the residual category of personal obligations not encompassed within the fields of contractual and non-contractual obligations. The common thread of "unjust enrichment" is that the defendant has received money, property or other asset of quantifiable value that belongs to the plaintiff, or, alternatively, the defendant has benefited from the performance of some service provided by the plaintiff. The distinction between unjust enrichment and contract is that liability under unjust enrichment is not tethered to promise. The distinction between unjust enrichment and tort is that liability under unjust enrichment is not tethered to the commission of a civil wrong. The roots of unjust enrichment are based in quasi-contract and restitution. Kazakhstani unsubstantiated enrichment law follows these central characteristics.

The structure of the law of unjust enrichment in the RK is built around four main concepts: (1) definition, (2) obligation of return, (3) payment of losses (primary and incidental), and (4) exemptions from liability. In Kazakhstani terminology, the person who is unjustly enriched is deemed the "purchaser," and the person who ought to have received the benefit is deemed the "injured party." Subject to exceptions set forth in Article 960, unsubstantiated enrichment occurs when a purchaser acquires property (an asset) or retains control of property, contrary to law or contrary to the terms of a transaction at the expense and detriment of the injured party (Article 953 CC). The method by which the purchaser actually acquired the property is irrelevant, whether by conduct of the purchaser, the injured party, or third parties are matters of no consequence. In other words, scienter is not required. The primary obligation is the requirement that the purchaser return the property to the injured party. Provided the purchaser acquires or controls an asset contrary to the provisions of Article 953(1), the obligation to return is mandatory.

The scope of unsubstantiated enrichment extends to claims that satisfy the preconditions of Article 953 I: (1) in the event of an invalid transaction, the injured party has a claim to demand return of the property that was the object of performance; (2) in the event of unlawful possession of the property by another person, the injured party has a claim to demand return of the property; (3) in the event of transactions based on mutual obligation, the injured party has a claim to demand return of the property that was the object of performance; and (4) the injured party has a right to claim compensation for damages sustained as a result of the wrongful act of the purchaser (Article 954 CC).

The obligation to return is that of "in kind." The purchaser has an obligation to compensate the injured party for any deterioration or loss of value of the property during the duration of its unlawful possession or purported acquisition (Article 955 CC). If it is impossible to make a physical return of the property; then the purchaser must compensate the injured party as follows: (1) payment of the actual (market) value of the property/asset at the time of its wrongful disposition; and (2) payment for losses caused by a reduction in the value of the property/asset (Article 956 CC). In addition, any person who temporarily uses the property of another person, or receives the services of another without payment, has an obligation to compensate the injured party for the value of the benefits received by the unlawful use of property or non-payment of services rendered.

In addition to these general obligations, the Civil Code provides for specific compensation based on unreceived income. A purchaser must return to the injured party all income actually received by exercising unlawful acquisition or control over the property, or all income the purchaser should have received from the time he became or should have become aware of the unjust enrichment. If the property is money, then the purchaser must return to the injured party the principal sum plus accrued interest from the time the purchaser became or should have become aware of the unjust enrichment (Article 958 CC).

A purchaser has a right of set-off based on necessary expenses incurred from the time the purchaser is obliged to return the property to the injured party. Where the purchaser intentionally (scienter) acquired unlawful possession or control of the asset, the purchaser is not entitled to the remedy of set-off (Article 959 CC).

The Civil Code exempts certain transactions from the laws of unsubstantiated enrichment: (1) property transferred to the injured party prior to the time of execution unless the obligation stipulates otherwise; (2) property transferred to fulfill an obligation upon the expiration of the period of limitations; (3) the property subject to the claim of unsubstantiated enrichment was granted to the injured party, usually in the form of wages, benefits, scholarships, redress of injury, alimony, unless the property was obtained by the injured party in bad faith; and (4) monetary amounts or other property acquired or controlled by the purchaser as the result of a non-existent obligation, provided the purchaser proves that the injured party knew about the lack of obligation, or made the transfer for charitable purposes (Article 960 CC).

Selected Bibliography

Y. Basin, *Сделки* [*Transactions*] (VŠP Adilet, Almaty, 1999) [in Russian].

Y. Basin, *Ответственность за нарушение гражданско-правовых обязательств* [*Liability for the Violation of Civil Law Obligations*] (VŠP Adilet, Almaty, 1997) [in Russian].

O. Chensova, "Enforcement of Contracts in Kazakhstan," in M. Andenas & G. Sander (eds.), *Enforcing Contracts in Transition Economies* (EBRD, London, 2005), 153.

A. Dujsenova, "Die rechtliche Regelung des Leasingvertrages nach Gesetzgebung der Republik Kazachstan," in R. Knieper, L. Chanturia & H.-J. Schramm (eds.), *Probleme des Vertragsrechts und der Vertragssicherung in den Staaten des Kaukasus und Zentralasiens* (BWV, Berlin, 2008), 281.

M. Suleimenov (ed.), *Договор в гражданском праве: проблемы теории и практики* [*Civil Law Contracts: Problems of Theory and Practice*] (KazGYuA, Almaty, 2000) [in Russian].

M. Suleimenov (ed.), *Гражданское право в системе права* [*Civil Law in the System of Law*] (KazGYuU, Almaty, 2007) [in Russian].

M. Suleimenov, "Предпринимательский договор как комплексный институт гражданского права" (2008) 1 *Žurnal Rossiyskogo Prava* 10.

Chapter 9
Family and Inheritance Law

Zhenis Kembayev & Maria Baideldinova Dalpane

I. FAMILY LAW

A. Concept, Sources and Principles

Family Law is the branch of the Kazakhstani legal system that regulates the following matters: (a) conclusion of marriage; (b) invalidation of marriage; (c) termination of marriage; (d) civil rights and obligations of family members; and (f) adoption of children.

Its foundational source is the Constitution of RK, which stipulates that: (a) marriage and family, motherhood, fatherhood and childhood shall be under the protection of the state; (b) care of children and their upbringing shall be a natural right and responsibility of parents; and (c) able-bodied children of age must take care of their disabled parents (Article 27 CRK).

These constitutional rules find their detailed elaboration primarily in the Law of RK of December 17, 1998, No. 321-I, "On Marriage and Family" (LMF), which, reaffirming the constitutional provisions, provides the following fundamental principles of Family Law: (a) voluntary conjugal union between a man and a woman, (b) equality of the spouses' rights in the family, (c) prohibition of anyone's arbitrary interference into the family affairs, (d) resolving internal family problems by mutual consent, (e) priority of bringing the children up in a family, (f) ensuring the priority protection of the rights and of the interests of the

Zhenis Kembayev, *Introduction to the Law of Kazakhstan*, pp. 161–178.

minor and of the family members with disabilities, (g) need to ensure for all family members an opportunity to freely exercise their rights and the possibility to defend these rights in court, and (h) stimulation of a healthy lifestyle for all family members (Article 2 II LMF).

In addition, there are a number of international conventions and legislative acts that regulate specific family institutions or relations. Thus, children's rights are additionally regulated by the Convention on the Rights of the Child of 1989 and two Facultative Protocols to this Convention (relating to the Participation of Children in Armed Conflict and to the Sale of Children, Child Prostitution, and the Utilization of Children in Pornography), the CIS Convention "On Legal Aid and Legal Relations in Civil, Family and Criminal Cases" of January 22, 1993 as well as by Law of RK of August 8, 2002, No. 345-II, "On the Rights of the Child" and Law of RK of June 28, 2005, No. 63-III, "On State Allowances for Families with Children." The regulation of rights and guarantees of disabled family members can be found, for instance, in the Law of RK of June 11, 2002, No. 343-II, "On the Social and Medical-Pedagogical Corrective Support Of Children With Limited Abilities"; Law of RK of April 13, 2005, No. 39-III, "On the Social Protection of Invalids in the Republic of Kazakhstan." Rights of women are regulated by the Convention on the Political Rights of Women of 1953, the ILO Convention concerning Equal Remuneration for Men and Women of 1951 and Law of RK of December 8, 2009, No. 223-IV, "On State Guarantees of Equal Rights and Opportunities for Men and Women."

B. Marriage

1. Conclusion of Marriage

Marriage is defined as a free-will union between a man and a woman (Article 1 LMF). Furthermore, only a marriage registered with the authorized state body (which is the Office of Civil Registration under the Ministry of Justice) is recognized by the state and results in property[1] and non-property[2] consequences (Article 13 I LMF). Religious marriages of any confessions are not prohibited, but are inconsequential from a legal point of view. No same-sex marriages may be registered in Kazakhstan, and no cohabitation may be registered and/or recognized as valid marriage.

To enter into a marriage, the mutual voluntary consent of the marrying man and woman is necessary. Also, the marrying persons must meet several

1. Thus, the moment of the registration of the marriage is the starting point for the community property regime and the obligation of spouses to mutual maintenance, unless otherwise established by a marriage contract (see *infra*).
2. For example, the possibility to change the pre-marital surname and to have a common surname by either uniting the surnames of the spouses or by having one spouse assume the surname of the other.

requirements: (a) both of them must have reached the marriage age (which is the age of 18)[3] at the moment of the application for the registration of the marriage; (b) both must be sane; (c) neither of them may be married to another person; and (d) they may not be relatives in a direct line of descent, whole or half-siblings, or adoptive and adopted persons (Article 11 LMF).

The registration of the marriage is conducted upon the marrying persons' application, which must be submitted to the Office of Civil Registration (registry office) one month before the presumed registration date. This period may be either shortened or extended (but not for more than one additional month) upon the presentation of valid reasons. Under some exceptional circumstances (e.g., pregnancy, the birth of a child, a direct threat to the life of one of the parties), a marriage may be entered into on the date of submitting the application (Article 13 II LMF).

The application must be submitted personally. Moreover, legislation requires the personal presence of both marrying persons and does not allow representation. The registration of the marriage is done by an authorized officer. However, under exceptional circumstances whereby one of the marrying persons cannot come to the Office of Civil Registration (e.g., due to serious illness), the registration may be done in the location of this person (Article 13 I LMF).[4]

2. Invalidity of Marriage

A marriage may be deemed invalid if: (a) the requirements of its conclusion were violated (no mutual consent, violation of the marriage age, etc.); (b) it is fictitious (i.e., it is concluded without an intention to create a family); and (c) one of the persons entering into a marriage has concealed from the other person the existence of a disease which constitutes a threat to the family and the security of the person and the society (Article 24 LMF).

A marriage may be recognized as invalid only by the court, which, within three days from the date of the adoption of its decision, must notify the respective registry office. As a result, all legal property and non-property consequences that emerged after the registration of the marriage are annulled.[5] However, the *bona fide* spouse has the right to receive maintenance from the other spouse and to preserve the surname obtained upon entering into the marriage, to claim the compensation of material and moral damages caused to him and the application of the provisions related to the division of the spouses' common property (see *infra*).

3. However, under exceptional circumstances (e.g., pregnancy), the marriage age may be reduced by the Office of Civil Registration by a maximum of two years, i.e., to 16 years of age.
4. The registration of the marriage may be conducted in a solemn atmosphere (Art. 183 LMF). Traditionally, each of the marrying persons invites a witness, although this is not required by legislation.
5. Thus, the property which was acquired during the marriage is divided according to provisions of the Civil Code of RK on participatory share ownership. In case a marriage contract was concluded by the spouses, it will also be invalidated. However, interests of the children, who were born in such a marriage or during 270 days after the date of the invalidation of the marriage, may not be affected.

3. Termination of Marriage

Along with such grounds as the death of one of the spouses, or declaring one of the spouses dead or missing by court, marriage may be terminated because of its dissolution upon the application of one or both spouses (or the trustee of an incapable spouse).

Consensual divorce is possible at any time. The family legislation of RK does not require any argumentation of such a decision by the spouses (Article 20 I LMF). If there are neither minor children nor property claims between the spouses, the divorce can be done at the registry office upon the mutual application of the spouses. In certain cases, the office may register the dissolution of marriage even on the basis of a unilateral application, if the consent of the other spouse is difficult or impossible to obtain. This can due to such reasons as: (a) the other spouse is deemed to be missing; (b) the other spouse is deemed to lack dispositive legal capacity; (c) conviction of one of the spouses to deprivation of freedom for a term of not less than three years (Article 16 II LMF).

The dissolution of the marriage is done in the court if: (1) the spouses have common minor children; (2) the spouses have property claims to each other; (3) one of the spouses does not consent to dissolution of the marriage; and (4) one of the spouses, while raising no objections to it, avoids the dissolution of the marriage at the registry office (refuses to file an application, does not wish to attend the registering of the dissolution of the marriage, etc.). A marriage can be dissolved in court only if it has been established that the further life of the spouses together and the preservation of the family is impossible (Article 19 I LMF). When one of the spouses does not consent to the dissolution, the court may take measures for reconciling the spouses and is entitled to put off the proceedings by fixing for the spouses a three-month reconciliation term (Article 19 II LMF).

In cases where there is no respective agreement between the spouses, the court also resolves such issues as the custody of minor children after the dissolution of the marriage, the alimony payments for the maintenance of the children, and upon the demand of one of the spouses the division of the common property of the ex-spouses and/or the satisfaction of the claim for maintenance from the other spouse.

The court is obliged to notify the registry office at the place of the marriage's state registration of the dissolution of the marriage within three days of the court decision coming into legal force. The spouses may not enter into a new marriage until obtaining a certificate on the dissolution of the marriage from the registry office at their place of residence.

C. Property Relations of Spouses

1. Legal Property Regime

The matrimonial property regime that is applied by default according to the family legislation of Kazakhstan is the regime of limited community of property, specifically community of acquisitions. According to this regime, all pre-matrimonial property remains separate, while everything earned during marriage becomes the subject of the community regardless of the amount of money invested in it by each spouse and regardless of who is indicated as the owner on the registration documents (if any). The spouse who bears the burden of the household and takes care of the children[6] without bringing in any income has equal rights to the common property.

A spouse may possess, use and dispose of the common property and there is a presumption of another spouse's consent to do so. Written consent is required only in exceptional cases provided for by the law (e.g., regarding the disposal of immovable property). Family Law does not contain any regulation regarding the expenses that the spouses have to bear with respect to the common property. However, the legal regime of community of property allows the presumption that the spouses have an equal responsibility to sustain such expenses.[7]

The regime of community of property extends to objects and money received as a salary; pension; scholarship; income from business, whether separately or commonly owned; or from interest from investments (Article 32 II LMF). But it does not extend to each spouse's things of personal use (clothing, shoes, etc.) and property or money received during marriage by one of the spouses on a non-paid basis.[8] Jewelry is not included in the category of things of personal use and is the subject of the community together with other personal things of particular value.[9]

Separate property of one of the spouses can become common if during the marriage, the value of this property was increased at the common expense of both spouses or at the expense of the other spouse. Expenses can be carried out in the form of monetary or property investments as well as in the form of the work of the spouse or spouses. An increase in the price of the property due to investments of third parties or due to the circumstances that do not depend on either spouse (inflation, rising real estate prices, etc.) does not result in the transfer of the separate property into the community of the spouses.

6. According to the Labor Code of RK, a maternity leave is granted to one of the spouses upon the birth of a child (Art. 195 I LC). Thus, it is also possible for a man to take care of the children. In practice, however, such cases are very rare.
7. Debts of the spouses which derive from the ownership of the common property are also common, like the debts arising from education and care of common children (as it is a common duty of the spouses). However, debts that derive from the ownership of the separate property as well as individual debts of a spouse (e.g., connected to causation of damage to a third person by that spouses) are separate.
8. Property received during the marriage by one spouse *gratis* include, among others, gifts addressed personally only to one of the spouses, inheritance left to one spouse, lottery winnings of one spouse, compensation of health damage caused to one of the spouses, prizes etc. In cases where a gift was given to both spouses, or if the beneficiary was not defined by the donor, the gift becomes the common property of the spouses.
9. There are no legislatively determined criteria to define a thing as one of particular value, so the court considers each case separately depending in particular on the financial situation of the parties.

The common property of the spouses can be divided upon divorce or during the marriage. Such division can be done by mutual consent (by signing a marriage contract) or in the court. Upon division, the shares of the spouses usually are equal. In the marriage contract, however, the spouses can deviate from this rule, unless it puts one of them into a difficult financial situation. The court can also distribute shares differently from the common rule in the interests of minor children, who remain with one of the spouses upon divorce (Article 37 LMF).

2. Marriage Contract

The marriage contract is defined as "an agreement between the persons entering into a marriage, or an agreement between the spouses, defining the spouses' property rights and duties in marriage and/or in the case of its dissolution" (Article 38 LMF). As this definition indicates, the marriage contract can be either pre-nuptial or post-nuptial. If it is concluded before the marriage, it comes into force from the moment of the marriage's registration. If the agreement is signed during the marriage, it takes effect from the moment of signing. The termination of the marriage denotes the termination of the marriage contract (with the exception of those obligations which are envisaged by the marriage contract for the period after the termination of the marriage).

The marriage contract must be concluded in written form and is subject to notarial certification. In addition, those marriage contracts that change the legal regime of the spouses' immovable property must be registered according to the Civil Code (Article 118 I CC). It may be concluded only by a natural person possessing full dispositive legal capacity (i.e., persons who are sane and not less than 18 years old, with only exceptions being persons whose marriage age was reduced by the Office of Civil Registration or who were emancipated in the procedure established by law).[10]

The marriage contract can regulate only property relations (Article 40 LMF). It may concern the property of the spouses that they actually own or property that they may acquire in the future (Article 40 I LMF). Thus, it may change the legal regime of the matrimonial property, and the legislation sets no limitations on such changes. Accordingly, the spouses are free to establish any of the following regimes: (a) absolute community of property (i.e., a community of all the property of the spouses, regardless of which of the two acquired the property and when); (b) limited community of property (i.e., a limitation of community in time or in object);[11] (c) community of shares (when the spouses establish certain, not

10. On the issues of dispositive legal capacity of natural persons, see Chapter 6 "Law of Natural Persons," *supra*. Note that even though emancipated minors may conclude a marriage contract, they still do not posses marriage capacity.
11. For example, the spouses may agree that all property becomes common after five years of marriage or that only movable property becomes common).

necessarily equal, shares in the ownership of their property); and (d) absolute or limited separation of property (Article 40 I LMF).[12]

The spouses may define in the marriage contract their rights and duties involved in the mutual maintenance, in the ways of taking part in each other's incomes and in the way each of them bears family expenses. Also, they may delineate the property which is transferred to each of them in case of the dissolution of their marriage, and include any other provisions related to the spouses' property relations. A unilateral refusal to execute a marriage contract is not permitted.

However, the marriage contract may not restrict the spouses' legal capacity or dispositive legal capacity and their right to apply to a court for the defense of their rights. Also, the marriage contract may not regulate personal non-property relations between the spouses and their rights and obligations towards children; limit the right to maintenance of the incapable spouse in need; and contain other conditions that put one of the spouses into extremely unfavorable conditions or contradict the fundamental principles of family legislation (Article 40 III). The terms of the marriage contract violating these requirements are void.

The marriage contract may be amended or dissolved at any time by an agreement between the spouses.[13] Also, the marriage contract may be amended, terminated or invalidated by a court decision on the grounds and in conformity with the procedure established by the Civil Code of RK for the amendment, termination and invalidation of contracts.[14]

D. FAMILY

Family is defined as a group of people who are connected with each other through personal non-property and property rights and obligations that derive from marriage, kinship or adoption (Article 1 LMF).

Spouses' Personal Rights and Duties: Spouses have equal rights and bear equal obligations. Each of the spouses is free to choose the kind of occupation or trade, as well as the place of residence. All family issues must be resolved by the

12. The marriage contract may also regulate maintenance (in particular alimony) issues. However, in contrast to alimony agreements which serve to determine the amount and mode of payment of alimony, marriage contracts may change the very grounds for its payment. For example, the LMF indicates *that* an incapable spouse in need has the right to maintenance. Thus, according to the Law, a spouse must satisfy both requirements (viz. incapability and financial difficulties) in order to have the right to alimony. But a marriage contract may provide that the existence of only one of the grounds is sufficient for maintenance. However, spouses may only broaden, and not restrict, the grounds for the rights to alimony. Also, the LMF does not specify the meaning of the term "in need." But a marriage contract may establish the precise level of income that is necessary for the support of the other spouse. Furthermore, a marriage contract may broaden the application scope of maintenance, extending it not only to a spouse in need (as the law provides), but applying it also to cases of unilateral application for divorce.
13. Such agreement must be adopted in the same form as the marriage contract itself.
14. On the issues of amendment, termination and invalidation of contracts, see Chapter 8 "Law of Obligations," *supra*.

spouses jointly. They must build their relations in the family on the basis of mutual respect and mutual assistance, to facilitate the welfare and the consolidation of the family, and to take care of their children's well-being and development. When entering into a marriage, the spouses may choose a surname of one of them as a common surname. Alternatively, each spouse may retain his own pre-marriage surname or may add to his own surname that of the other spouse.[15]

Rights of Children: A child is a person who has not reached the age of 18 years. Every child has the right to live and to be brought up in a family by his parents, who must provide for his interests, his all-round development and the respect of his dignity.[16] Children born of unmarried persons have the same rights and duties with respect to the parents and to their relatives as the children, born of married persons. Furthermore, the legislation explicitly stipulates that a child has the right to communicate with his parents and other relatives; to the protection of his rights and legal interests; to express his opinion in resolving any issue in the family; to a first name, a patronymic and a surname; to indication of ethnic affiliation; and to receive maintenance from his parents and from other family members (Articles 53–59 LMF).

Parental Rights and Obligations emerge with the birth of the child and end when the child reaches the age of 18. Individuals have parental rights and obligations towards their child, regardless of whether the child was born inside or outside of the wedlock. According to the LMF, both parents have equal rights and bear equal obligations.[17] They have the right and at the same time bear the duty to raise their children. They must take care of the child's health and his physical, mental, spiritual and moral development. They must ensure the receiving of the secondary education by their children and create necessary conditions for achieving that purpose. Parents are the legal representatives of their children and are responsible for the protection of their rights and interests. However, the exercising of the parental rights may not be in contradiction with the children's interests. Ensuring the children's interests must be the major concern of parents.[18]

The parents (or one of them) may be deprived of their parental rights by the court, if they: (1) evade their parental duties (including the payment of the alimony); (2) abuse their parental rights; (3) treat the children cruelly (including physical or mental suppression, or infringe upon their sexual inviolability); (4) suffer from chronic alcoholism or drug addiction; or (5) have committed a premeditated crime against the life or the health of their children, or against the life or the health of their spouse (Article 67 LMF). Parental rights may also be restricted

15. The adding up surnames is not permitted, if the pre-marriage surname of one of the spouses is already a double one.
16. In the case of the absence of the parents (or deprivation of their parental rights), the right of the child to be brought up in a family must be ensured by the Trusteeship and Guardianship Agency.
17. Note, however, that in cases of divorce, when the court decides on the custody of children, the mother is preferred by default, unless there are extraordinary reasons.
18. Although the law does not oblige the spouses to have a common domicile; however, its absence, without a significant reason, may be regarded as a strong indication of the fictitiousness of the marriage.

by the court if residence of the child with his parents (or with one of them) is dangerous for him due to: (1) circumstances which do not depend on the parents (or one of them) (such as a mental derangement or another chronic disease, the incidence of grave circumstances, etc.); (2) the parent's behavior, even in the absence of sufficient grounds for depriving the parents (or one of them) of their parental rights.[19] The deprivation or restriction of parental rights does not result in the termination of parental obligations (Article 69 II LMF). Thus, a parent whose parental rights were terminated or restricted still has an obligation to pay alimony to his children, but has neither the right to receive allowances for the child nor financial support from the child in the future.

"Adoption of a child" is a priority form of placement of children who have remained without parental care. It is admitted only with respect to minor children and only in their interest. Adoption of brothers and sisters by different persons is not admitted, with the exception of the cases when such adoption is effected in the children's interest.

Adopters may generally be any adult persons. However, there are the following exceptions: (1) persons recognized incapable or partially capable by court; (2) spouses, one of whom is recognized as incapable or partially capable by court; (3) persons deprived of or restricted in their parental rights by court; (4) persons dismissed from the duties of a trustee (or a guardian) for improper fulfillment of their obligations; (5) former adopters, if the adoption has been cancelled by the court due to their fault; (6) persons who cannot perform parental duties due to their health.

Furthermore, there are also the following restrictive rules. Unmarried persons (e.g., cohabitants without legal registration) may not jointly adopt one and the same child. The age gap between an unmarried adopter and the adopted child may not be less than 16 years.[20] To adopt a child, it is necessary to obtain the consent of his parents.[21] If a child has reached the age of 10 years, his consent is also required.[22]

The adoption of children by foreign citizens or by stateless persons (who are not the children's relatives) may be admitted only in cases when it is impossible that these children are adopted by citizens of RK, who permanently reside on the territory of Kazakhstan, or by the children's relatives, regardless of their citizenship or the place of residence. Moreover, children may be adopted by foreign citizens or to stateless persons (who are not the children's relatives) only after the expiry of three months from the date of the registration of such children by the

19. If the parent's behavior remains unchanged after a six-month term, a Trusteeship and Guardianship Agency must file a case for cessation of parental rights (Art. 71 I LMF).
20. The age gap is not required, if the child is adopted by his stepfather (or stepmother). For reasons recognized by a court as valid, the age gap may also be reduced.
21. The parents' consent is not required if they are unknown; recognized missing or incapable by court; deprived of their parental rights; do not live with the child without valid reasons and avoid their parental duties for over six months.
22. If, prior to filing an application for his adoption, the child lived in the adopter's family and believes him to be his parent, the adoption, by way of an exception, may be effected without receiving the consent of the adopted child.

respective state body. Also, foreign citizens and of the stateless persons, wishing to adopt children in Kazakhstan, must be registered according to the procedure established by the Ministry of Foreign Affairs of RK.

The adoption is effected by the court upon the application of the persons (a person), wishing to adopt the child.[23] Within three days from the decision to adopt the child, the court must inform the local registry office for the purpose of the state registration of the adoption. The judge and the officials, who effected state registration, as well as other persons who learned about the adoption in any other way, must keep the fact of the child's adoption secret.

The adoption invokes the following legal consequences. First, the adopted children and their progeny are equalized in all personal and property rights and duties to the relatives of the adopters by kinship. Second, the adopted children lose their tangible and intangible rights and are relieved of their duties with respect to their parents (and their relatives).[24] However, the child retains the right to pension and allowances due to him in connection with his parents' death.

E. Protection of Children Left Without Parental Care

In the cases when parents are: (a) deceased; (b) deprived of or restricted in their parental rights; (c) recognized as incapable; (d) seriously ill or absent for a long time; (e) avoid raising and maintaining their children, the protection of the rights and interests of children is entrusted to Trusteeship and Guardianship Agencies (Article 100 I LMF).

Trusteeship and Guardianship Agencies identify children left without parental care, register such children and, proceeding from the specific circumstances of the loss of parental care, select the forms, suitable for the accommodation of such children, and also exert control over the conditions of their maintenance, raising and education.[25]

Officials of preschool educational establishments, general educational establishments, medical centers and other institutions and persons possessing information on the children left without parental care must report it to Trusteeship and Guardianship Agencies at the place of the child's actual stay.

The respective Trusteeship and Guardianship Agency must within three days from the date of receiving the information, carry out an inspection of the conditions of the child's life and, in the case of establishing the fact of the absence of parental care, must provide for protecting the child's rights and interests by placing him to a special educational (or medical) establishment. Furthermore, the Agency must

23. Adoption of such decisions requires the participation of representatives of the Trusteeship and Guardianship Agency.
24. If the child is adopted by one person, his tangible and intangible rights and duties may be retained at the discretion of the mother, if the adopter is a man, or at the discretion of the father, if the adopter is a woman.
25. No natural persons or legal entities may be involved in the accommodation of children left without parental care (Art. 100 II LMF).

within a month from the day of receipt of the information on the child ensure the transfer of the child to a family. Should that be impossible, the Agency must send the information about such child to the relevant local executive body (administering education affairs) for the purpose of his registration in the centralized database and facilitation of his accommodation.

There are the following forms of accommodation of children: (a) adoption; (b) trusteeship (guardianship); (c) placement into a foster family; and (if none of the above is possible) (d) placement into institutions for orphans (or children left without parental care). When accommodating the child, account may be taken of his ethnical origin, affiliation to a certain religion and culture, his native tongue and the possibility of ensuring continuity with respect to raising and education (Article 102 I LMF).

F. Alimony Obligations of Family Members

Alimony Obligations of Parents and of Children: The parents must maintain their minor children. They define the procedure and forms of maintenance of the minor children and may conclude an agreement on those issues (an alimony agreement).

If the parents do not provide maintenance to their minor children, the means for maintaining the children (the alimony) must be exacted from the parents through court. If, in the absence of the parents' agreement on the payment of alimony, no maintenance is provided for the children and no claim is filed with the court, the respective Trusteeship and Guardianship Agency may file a claim against their parents (or against one of them) to enforce the payment of alimony for the minor children.

In the absence of an agreement on the payment of alimony, the alimony for the minor children must be exacted by court in the amount of one-fourth of the parents' wages and/or other income for one child; one-third—for two children; and one-half—for three or more children (Article 125 I LMF). The amount of these shares may be reduced or increased by the court based upon the financial or family status of the parties and other circumstances.

Also, in the face of some emergency circumstances (a grave illness or a severe injury of a child, etc.) each of the parents may be obliged to bear extra expenses by the court, which also determines the method and the amount of these expenses. Moreover, the parents must maintain their disabled adult children in need of assistance. In the absence of an alimony agreement, the court may require the payment of alimony by parents.

In turn, the able-bodied adult children are required to maintain their disabled parents in need of assistance, and to take care of them. In the absence of an agreement on the payment of the alimony for disabled parents in need of assistance, the alimony is required from the able-bodied adult children by court. In the absence of the adult children's care of their disabled parents, and in the face of emergency circumstances (a serious illness or a grave injury of the parent, etc.), the adult children may be obliged to take part in bearing extra expenses by court.

Alimony Obligations of Spouses and of Ex-Spouses: The spouses are obliged to materially support each other. In case of refusal to render such support and in the absence of an alimony agreement, a needy disabled spouse (as well as a wife in the period of pregnancy and during three years after the birth of the common child and a needy spouse caring for the common minor invalid child) may claim for alimony from the other spouse by application to court (Article 133 LMF).

The right to claim alimony through court from the ex-spouse, who possesses the necessary means, belongs also: (a) the ex-wife in the period of pregnancy and in the course of three years after the birth of the child; (b) a needy ex-spouse, looking after the common minor disabled child; (c) a disabled needy ex-spouse, who has become disabled before the dissolution of the marriage or in the course of one year from the moment of the dissolution of the marriage; and (d) a needy ex-spouse who has reached pensionable age no later than five years since the dissolution of the marriage, if the spouses were married for a long time.

The amount of the alimony and the method of its payment to the ex-spouse after the dissolution of the marriage may be defined by an agreement between the ex-spouses. In the absence of such agreement, the amount of the alimony to be paid by the spouse (or the ex-spouse) is determined by court as a fixed monetary sum subject to the monthly payment, proceeding from the financial situation of the spouses (ex-spouses) and other circumstances.

The court may relieve the spouse of the duty to maintain the other disabled spouse in need of assistance, or restrict this duty by a definite term, both in the period of the marriage and after its dissolution, if: (a) the disability of the spouse arose as a result of the abuse of alcohol or drugs, or as a result of committing a premeditated crime; (b) the short term of the spouses' marriage; and (c) inappropriate behavior in the family of the spouse claiming alimony (Article 136 LMF).

Alimony Duties of Other Family Members: Minor brothers and sisters, who cannot be maintained by their parents, may receive through court alimony from their able-bodied adult brothers and sisters. The same right belongs also to disabled adult brothers and sisters, if they cannot be maintained by their able-bodied adult children or spouses (ex-spouses) or by their parents. Minor grandchildren, who cannot be maintained by their parents, may receive through court alimony from their grandfather and grandmother. The same right belongs also to disabled adult grandchildren, if they cannot be maintained by their spouses (ex-spouses) or by their parents. Furthermore, the disabled grandfather and grandmother, who cannot be maintained by their adult able-bodied children or by the spouse (the ex-spouse), may claim through court alimony from their able-bodied adult grandchildren. The disabled persons, who have raised and maintained minor children, may claim through the court a maintenance from their able-bodied wards, who have reached the age of majority, if they cannot get it from their able-bodied adult children or from their spouses (ex-spouses).[26] In such cases the amount and the method of

26. The court may relieve the wards of the duty to maintain those persons who have raised them, if they have maintained them less than five years and also if they have raised them in an improper way. The same rule applies to stepfathers and stepmothers with respect to their stepchildren.

payment of alimony may be defined by an agreement between the parties. In the absence of an alimony agreement, the amount of the alimony to be paid is established in each particular case by court.

Alimony Agreements: An agreement on the payment of alimony (on the amount, the terms and the method of payment of the alimony) is concluded between the person who is obliged to pay the alimony and its recipient. An alimony agreement is concluded in written form and is subject to the notarial certification. It may be amended or cancelled at any time by the mutual consent of the parties in the same form as the agreement on the payment of the alimony itself. A unilateral refusal to execute an agreement on the payment of alimony, or a unilateral amendment of its terms is not permitted (Article 145 III LMF). However, any of the parties may file a claim for modifying or terminating the alimony agreement with a court, in the case when an essential change takes place in the financial situation or in the family status of one of the parties (and if they fail to come to an understanding as concerns the amending or the canceling of the alimony agreement).

The amount of alimony paid under an alimony agreement must be defined by the parties to the agreement. However, the amount may not be less than the amount of alimony which they could have received if the alimony had been established by court. The alimony may be paid as a fixed monetary sum at regular intervals; by providing other valuables, and also in any other method (or combination of methods), on which an agreement is reached. Alimony obligations established by an alimony agreement cease with the death of one of the parties, the expiry of the term of the agreement, or on any other grounds stipulated by the agreement (Article 162 I LMF).

Payment of Alimony by a Court Decision: In the absence of an alimony agreement, the family members may file a claim with the court for determining the amount and the payment terms of alimony. The person, who has the right to receive alimony, may apply to court for an order requiring the payment of alimony, regardless of the term which has passed from the moment when the right to alimony arose. In general, alimony is determined from the moment of applying to court. However, if the court establishes that the measures aimed at obtaining the means for the maintenance were duly taken, but no alimony was received, because the person who was obliged to pay alimony avoided its payment, the court may order the payment of alimony in arrears for a three-year term since the first application to court was made.

The payment of the alimony exacted through the court ceases: (a) when the child reaches 18 or when the minor child acquires full legal capacity before reaching 18; (b) in case of adoption of the child for whose maintenance the alimony was ordered; (c) if a court recognizes that the work capacity of the alimony recipient has been restored or that he is no longer in need of assistance; (d) if the disabled ex-spouse in need of assistance who received the alimony enters into a new marriage; and (e) with the death of the person who received the alimony, or of the person obliged to pay the alimony (Article 162 II LMF).

II. INHERITANCE LAW

A. Concepts, Sources and Principles

Inheritance Law (or Law of Succession) regulates such questions as (a) what property can pass from a person who is deceased to his heirs; (b) who is entitled to inheritance by law; and (c) what can be written in a will and in which ways a will can change the legal order of succession.

The main specific source of Inheritance Law is the Special Part of the Civil Code of RK. There are, however, some laws and regulatory resolutions of the Supreme Court of RK that provide further explanations of some of legal issues related to inheritance (e.g., Resolution No. 5 of the Supreme Court of RK of June 29, 2009, "On Some Issues of Application by the Courts of the Legislation on Succession"). There are also a number of international treaties that regulate relations in the sphere of inheritance (e.g., the CIS Convention "On Legal Aid and Legal Relations in Civil, Family and Criminal Cases" of January 22, 1993).

Inheritance Law is based on the following principles: (a) freedom of testament; (b) freedom of heirs to accept or reject the inheritance; (c) non-discrimination between heirs on the basis of nationality, religion or language; (d) the necessity for both the testator and the heirs to freely exercise their rights and to reinstate these rights in cases of their violation and to protect them in court; and (e) universal succession, which means that the entire estate, including assets *and* liabilities, is immediately passed on to the heirs at the moment of testator's death.

B. General Provisions

Succession is the transmission of property of a deceased person (a testator) to another person (an heir) or other persons (heirs) (Article 1038 CC). In the case of succession, the deceased's estate (inheritance, assets of estate) passes to other persons by universal succession, i.e., in an unchanged, single form and at the same time, except as otherwise required by law. Succession may be by will and by operation of law; succession by operation of law takes place generally when a deceased person did not provide for succession by will.

An estate is opened on the death of a person (or announcement of his death by court). The deceased's estate incorporates the items and other property owned by the deceased as of the date of opening of the inheritance, in particular, rights *in rem* and liabilities.

Rights and liabilities inseparable from the personality of the deceased, in particular the right to membership in legal entities (if otherwise not provided by law or agreement); to damages for harm inflicted to the citizen's life or health; to alimony; to pension payments and allowances on the basis of Labor Law; and to personal incorporeal rights and other intangible wealth.

Persons who can be called upon to inherit include: (a) those left alive as of the date of opening of the inheritance; and (b) persons conceived during the lifetime of the deceased and born after the opening of the inheritance. In the case of succession by will, the state and the legal entities specified in the will and existing as of the date of opening of the inheritance can also be called upon to inherit (Article 1044 CC).

To acquire inheritance an heir must accept it. An inheritance can be accepted within six months after the date of opening of the inheritance. An accepted inheritance is recognized as owned by the heir from the date of opening of the inheritance, irrespective of the time of the actual acceptance and also irrespective of the time of state registration of the heir's rights to assets of estate where such a right is subject to state registration.

The Civil Code provides also a list of the so-called unworthy heirs. Thus, the following are not to be entitled to inherit either by operation of law or by will: (a) persons who deliberately attempted to or deprived a testator or any potential heir of life;[27] (b) persons who deliberately impeded the exercise of the last will of a testator for the purpose of increasing the value or share of their inheritance; (c) parents who were deprived of parental rights and whose rights were not re-established by the moment of opening inheritance may not inherit after their children; and (d) parents (adopters) and full age children (stepchildren) who evaded execution of duties entrusted to them by virtue of law with regard to taking care of a testator. An unworthy heir must return all property received without grounds from the estate.[28]

C. Succession by Will

A will is a unilateral transaction which creates rights and duties after the opening of the inheritance. It can be created by a person who had his full dispositive legal capacity as of the time when it was created. It must be created in person and thus cannot be created through a representative.

A testator is entitled to deprive one, several or all legal heirs of inheritance without indicating reasons for such a deprivation; to leave by will at his discretion property to any persons, to set heirs' shares in the estate in any way; to include other dispositions in the will in compliance with law; and to revoke or alter his created will. He is entitled to create a will containing dispositions relating to any property, in particular, a property that he might acquire in the future. However, a testator may

27. Persons, for whom a testator left a will after an attempt to take his life, are an exception.
28. These rules apply also: (a) to heirs who were entitled to a compulsory share in the estate; and (b) to the testamentary trust. If the subject matter of a testamentary trust was the performance of certain work for or the provision of a certain service to an unworthy beneficiary, the beneficiary must reimburse the heir who has discharged the trust for the value of the work or service performed for the unworthy beneficiary.

not require his heirs to distribute the property bequeathed by them in a certain manner in the case of their death.

A testator may also vest in one or several heirs a duty to perform an obligation for the benefit of one or several persons (beneficiaries), who acquire the right to claim performance of the duty (testamentary trust).

A will must be created in writing, signed by the testator's own hand and attested by a notary.[29] Failure to observe the written form and attestation of a will cause its invalidity. A witness can be in attendance when a will is drawn up and attested by a notary if the testator so wishes.[30] A notary, witnesses and other persons may not disclose information concerning the content of the will before the opening of the inheritance.

A will may be invalidated on the same grounds as all other transactions. However, slips of the pen and other insignificant breaches of the procedure for the creation, signing or attestation of a will may not serve as grounds for the invalidity of a will.

While interpreting a will the literal meaning of the words and expressions contained therein must be taken into account. If the literal meaning of a provision of a will is vague it is established by means of comparison with other provisions and the sense of the will as a whole.

Execution of a will is usually effected by heirs under the will. However, a testator may appoint a personal representative (executor) specified in the will to execute the will, irrespective of his being an heir or not.

D. Succession by Operation of Law

If no will is left, legal heirs are called upon to inherit in compliance with the priority ranking set out by law. The heirs of each next category may inherit if there are no heirs of the preceding categories. Heirs of one category inherit in equal shares, except for the heirs who inherit by right of representation.

First category heirs are the children (including those born after his death), spouse and parents of the testator. The testator's grandchildren and their descendents inherit by right of representation. The *second* priority of succession includes the whole- and half-siblings of the testator as well as maternal and paternal

29. The Civil Code provides also a number of wills qualifying as wills attested by a notary (e.g., wills of citizens undergoing medical treatment in in-patient institutions, hospitals, other stationary medical treatment institutions or residing in old-age and disabled nursing houses attested by their directors or chief physicians; will of citizens who are in prospecting, or other similar expeditions, attested by the chiefs of these expeditions; wills of military servicemen attested by the commanders of the military units) (Art. 1052 CC).
30. The following persons may not be such witnesses: a notary; a person being a beneficiary of the will or a testamentary trust, his spouse, children and parents; citizens without full dispositive capacity; citizens who do not understand the essence of the event in full; persons without a sufficient degree of command of the language in which the will is written.

grandparents. Children of whole- and half-siblings (i.e., nieces and nephews) inherit in accordance with their rights of representation. The *third* priority includes whole-blood aunts and uncles, while cousins inherit in accordance with their rights of representation (Articles 1061–1063 CC).

If, for any reason, the inheritance did not pass to any of the first three priorities of succession, other legal heirs are entitled to the estate. This group includes relatives of the testator of the fourth, fifth and sixth priorities of succession who are not recognized as heirs of the higher priorities. The fourth priority includes the great-grandparents of the testator. More distant relatives, like great-aunts, -uncles, -nieces and -nephews occupy the fifth priority. The most distant relatives recognized by law are part of the sixth priority, including the children of great-nieces and -nephews.

Stepbrothers and stepsisters, adopted sons and daughters, stepfathers and stepmothers of the testator are part of the seventh priority if they lived together with the testator as one family for not less than 10 years (Article 1064 III CC). If there are no legal heirs, disabled dependants of the testator may inherit independently as heirs of the eighth priority (Article 1068 II CC).

In addition, it should be noted that legal heirs who are not part of the abovementioned eight priorities and who, by the day of the commencement of the succession were disabled and for not less than one year prior to the death of the testator had been maintained by him and had resided with him, shall inherit together and equally with the heirs of whichever priority is called for succession (Article 1068 II CC). Certain categories of relatives have the right to an obligatory share, which means that even if the will left by the testator does not include these people in the group of heirs, they can claim their share in court. These relatives are: minors or incapable children, incapable spouses and parents. These relatives are entitled to not less than half of the share that would be due to each of them if no will existed (i.e., if succession followed the default legal process) (Article 1069 CC).

The right of inheritance that the surviving spouse of the testator has by will or by operation of law shall not diminish the spouse's right to the portion of property gained during the period of marriage with the testator and deemed their common property. However, pursuant to a court decision, a spouse may be excluded from the succession by law, provided it is proved that the marriage with the testator actually terminated prior to the opening of the inheritance and that the spouses lived separately for not less than five years prior to the opening of the inheritance.

If there are no legal heirs and heirs by will or if neither of the heirs has a right to inherit or all heirs have been deprived of their right of inheritance or neither of the heirs have accepted the inheritance or all the heirs refused their inheritance and neither of them has indicated that the inheritance is waived for the benefit of another heir, the decedent's estate is deemed escheat and passes into the ownership of the state.

Selected Bibliography

B. Aitzhan, *Семейное право* [*Family Law*] (Yurist, Almaty, 2007).

A. Didenko, "Толкование завещания" ["Interpretation of Testament"], in A. Didenko (ed.), *Гражданское законодательство* [*Civil Legislation*], vol. 25 (Yurist, Almaty, 2007).

M. Mukanova, *Брачный договор как способ регулирования отношений супругов* [*Marriage Contract as Means of Regulation of Relations between Spouses*] (KazGYuU, Almaty, 2003).

M. Sairbayev & D. Sairbayev, *Наследство* [*Succession*] (Yurist, Almaty, 2010).

M. Baideldinova, "Matrimonial Property and Its Contractual Regulation in Kazakhstan," in B. Atkin (ed.), *The International Survey of Family Law 2011* (Jordan Publishing Ltd, Bristol, 2011), 247.

Chapter 10

Labor Law

*Irina Mezhibovskaya**

I. INTRODUCTION

The RK proclaims itself to be, *inter alia*, a social state (Article 1 I CRK). According to the official interpretation of the Constitutional Council, this fundamental stipulation implies the commitment of the country to progressively develop towards the creation of a state based on the idea of social partnership, which pledges itself to alleviate social inequality, promote the development of all individuals and enable them to enjoy decent life conditions.[1]

In supporting its position, the Constitutional Council referred to numerous constitutional provisions ensuring the right of everyone to: (a) social protection against unemployment; (b) safe and hygienic working conditions; (c) just remuneration for labor without discrimination; (d) rest; (e) the length of working time, days-off and holidays, and paid annual leave established by law (Article 24 CRK); (f) a guaranteed minimum wage and pension; (g) guaranteed social security in old-age, in case of disease, disability or loss of a breadwinner and other legal grounds (Article 28 CRK); (h) protection of health; (i) free, guaranteed, extensive medical assistance established by law (Article 29 CRK); (j) a guaranteed free secondary education in state educational establishments; (k) higher education, on a competitive basis, in state higher educational establishments (Article 30 CRK); (l) state

* Translated by Zhenis Kembayev.

1. See Resolution of the Constitutional Council of RK of December 21, 2001, No. 18/2.

Zhenis Kembayev, *Introduction to the Law of Kazakhstan*, pp. 179–195.

protection of the environment favorable for the life and health of the person (Article 31 CRK); (m) state protection of marriage and family, motherhood, fatherhood and childhood (Article 27 CRK); and (n) the creation by the state of conditions such that each citizen can obtain housing (Article 25 CRK).

However, it should be noted that the current Constitution of RK does not guarantee the right to labor. It provides only the right of everyone to freedom of labor, which basically means the free choice of occupation and profession and the prohibition of involuntary labor (Article 24 I CRK),[2] a legal regime that is in obvious contrast to both the Constitution of KazSSR of 1978 and the first Constitution of RK of 1993.

Specifically, the Constitution of 1978 proclaimed "citizens of the KazSSR have the right to work (that is, to guaranteed employment and pay in accordance with the quantity and quality of their work, and not below the state-established minimum)" and that this right is "ensured by . . . free vocational and professional training, improvement of skills, training in new trades or professions, and development of the systems of vocational guidance and job placement" (Article 38). At the same time, however, labor was not only a right but also a "duty of, and matter of honor for, every able-bodied citizen of the KazSSR" and "evasion of socially useful work" was "incompatible with the principles of socialist society" (Article 58 of the Constitution of 1978).

The first Constitution of RK of 1993 was in full compliance with international standards and guaranteed the right both to labor and freedom of labor. In particular, it was provided that citizens of RK had the right to work either as independent producers or under labor agreement in accordance with their wishes, capabilities and professional training. At the same time, forced labor was explicitly prohibited (Article 19 of the Constitution of 1993).

Even though on November 28, 2005 Kazakhstan ratified the International Covenant on Economic, Social and Cultural Rights of 1966, which recognizes the right of everyone to labor, no amendments have been made so far to the Constitution of RK. Thus, the fundamental law of Kazakhstan still does not include one of the most essential rights of an individual, which is an obvious discrepancy with both the ideals of a democratic, rule-of-law and social state (set forth in Article 1 I CRK) and the international commitments of the country.

II. SOURCES OF LABOR LAW

Along with the Constitution of RK, sources of Labor Law include legislative and sub-law acts as well as international treaties.

For more than eight years after obtaining independence, labor relations in Kazakhstan were governed by the Labor Code of KazSSR of July 21, 1972. Despite numerous amendments made to that Code, it became obvious that the country,

2. Involuntary labor may be permitted only on the basis of a sentence of the court or in the conditions of a state of emergency or martial law.

which transformed itself from a socialist to a market economy, needs an absolutely new labor legislation. However, this need was realized only with the adoption of the Law of RK of December 10, 1999, No. 493-1, "On Labor in the Republic of Kazakhstan," which entered into force on January 1, 2000.

The fact that the Code was replaced not by another codified act (which has a higher status in the hierarchy of regulatory acts) but by an ordinary law is explained by the desire of the legislators of that time to reduce the number of Codes. However, that policy did not bring about the desired results with respect to Labor Law. In addition, the first labor legislation of independent Kazakhstan contained a number of inconsistencies and contradictions, both internal and with respect to other legislative acts. Therefore, on May 15, 2007 a new Labor Code of RK was adopted, an event that was preceded by long work and intensive debates involving public associations, trade unions, academic lawyers and practitioners. As a result, the Labor Code of RK, No. 251-III (LC) included a number of absolutely new progressive provisions based on international standards.

Along with the Labor Code, labor relations in Kazakhstan are also governed by a number of other legislative acts. In this regard, the Law of RK of April 9, 1993, No. 2107-XII, "On Trade Unions" provides rules with respect to the establishment, functioning and competences of employee associations. The Law of RK of April 9, 1993, No. 2107-XII, "On the Population's Employment" deals with issues related to employment assistance and placement. The Code of RK of September 18, 2009 "On People's Health and the System of Healthcare" regulates the order of conducting mandatory prophylactic medical examination of employees. The Law of RK of May 13, 2003, No. 415-II, "On Joint-Stock Companies" establishes peculiarities of the conclusion of employment contracts with the head and members of the executive body of a Joint-Stock Company. The Law of RK of April 25, 2003, No. 405-II, "On Compulsory Social Insurance" requires the employer to make payments to mandatory social insurance covering cases of pregnancy and childbirth (or adoption of a newborn child) as well as the loss of the ability to work by employees. The Law of RK of July 22, 2011, No. 477-IV, "On Migration" governs issues of migratory labor movements. There are also a number of other regulatory acts that regulate labor relations in certain spheres and of particular types of employees in compliance with the general provisions provided by the Labor Code.

Despite the continuing development of the Labor Law of Kazakhstan, in certain areas the reality often does not correspond to the formal stipulations.[3] Therefore, there is a strong need to monitor regulatory acts (both legislative and sub-law acts) governing labor relations with the purpose of updating and improving the norms of Labor Law and ensuring effective protection of the social and economic rights of people.

3. For example, the strike of thousands of oil workers in spring and fall of 2011 showed failure of the Kazakhstani legislation on Trade Unions and the absence of effective independent associations of employees. Another example includes the Law of RK of July 30, 1992 "On Social Protection of Citizens Who Suffered Due to Ecological Disaster in Aral Sea Area." This Law is still in force; however, most of its initial 24 articles were abolished on April 1, 1999.

A special place in the system of sources of Labor Law is taken by international treaties. In particular it should be mentioned that Kazakhstan has currently ratified 19 conventions elaborated by the International Labor Organization.[4] Also, Kazakhstan is a party to a number of international agreements adopted in the framework of the CIS and the EurAsEC.[5]

III. PRINCIPLES OF LABOR LAW

According to the Labor Code, the labor legislation of RK aims at creating the requisite legal conditions for achieving a balance of the interests of the parties to labor relations, economic growth, higher production efficiency and human welfare (Article 3 II LC).

This aim must be achieved on the basis of the principles of freedom of labor and prohibition of forced labor. Thus, everyone may freely agree to work without any discrimination or compulsion to do so and choose a profession and type of activity. Forced labor is only allowed if it is required of someone by virtue of: (a) mandatory military service; (b) civil duties of citizens (as established by legislation); (c) a court sentence that has come into legal effect (on the condition that the work is performed under the supervision and control of state authorities and that the person performing it is not yielded or handed over to any individuals and/or legal entities); and (d) under the conditions of an emergency or martial law.

In addition, Labor Law is based on the principles of inadmissibility of restrictions on human and civil rights and prohibition of discrimination. Accordingly, no one's rights may be restricted in the sphere of labor, apart from cases and in a manner envisaged by the legislation of RK. Moreover, everyone must have equal opportunities to exercise their rights and freedoms in the sphere of labor, and no one may be subjected to any discrimination. Persons who believe they have been subject to discrimination may enter a lawsuit in a court. At the same time, however, it is also explicitly provided that discrimination does not include differences,

4. Forced Labor Convention of 1930 (No. 29); Labor Inspection Convention of 1947; Convention on Freedom of Association and Protection of the Right to Organize of 1948; Employment Service Convention of 1948; Right to Organize and Collective Bargaining Convention of 1949; Equal Remuneration Convention of 1951; Abolition of Forced Labor Convention of 1957; Discrimination (Employment and Occupation) Convention of 1958; Employment Policy Convention of 1964; Labor Inspection (Agriculture) Convention of 1969; Representatives Convention of 1971; Minimum Age Convention of 1973; Tripartite Consultation (International Labor Standards) Convention of 1976; Working Environment (Air Pollution, Noise and Vibration) Convention of 1977; Occupational Safety and Health Convention of 1981; Asbestos Convention of 1986; Safety and Health in Construction Convention of 1988; Worst Forms of Child Labor Convention of 1999; and Seafarers' Identity Documents Convention (Revised) of 2003.
5. For example, the CIS Agreement of April 15, 1994 on Cooperation in the Field of Labor Migration and Social Protection of Migrants; the Decision of the EurAsEC Interstate Council of December 11, 2009 on the Conception of the Establishment of a Database on Labor Migrants who are Citizens of the EurAsEC Member States.

exceptions, preferences and restrictions determined by requirements inherent in the nature of the work or dictated by the state's concern for people in need of increased social and legal protection (Article 7 LC).

Another important principle of Labor Law is the principle of social partnership, which is defined as "a system of interrelations between employees (employees' representatives), employers (employers' representatives) and state authorities designed to ensure co-ordination of their interests on issues of regulation of labor relations."

Other principles of Labor Law include: prohibition of the worst forms of child labor; guaranteed right to working conditions meeting the safety and hygiene requirements; priority of the life and health of the employee over the results of production activities; guaranteed right to a fair remuneration for labor not below the minimum wage; guaranteed right to rest; equality of the rights and opportunities of employees; guaranteed right of association of employees and of employers for the purpose of protecting their rights and interests; state regulation of labor protection and labor safety; guaranteed right of employees' representatives to exercise public control over observance of the labor legislation of RK (Article 4 LC).

IV. LABOR CONTRACTS

A. Concept

An employment relationship arises on the basis of a labor contract between an employee (an individual directly performing work) and an employer (who may be either an individual or a legal entity). The Labor Code defines a labor contract as written agreement between the employee and the employer. In accordance with the agreement, the employee undertakes personally to perform specific work (labor function) and to observe labor regulations, while the employer undertakes to provide the employee with work involving the agreed labor function; to ensure the working conditions envisaged by legislation, the collective bargaining agreement and acts of the employer;[6] and to pay the employee wages in a timely manner and in full (Article 1 LC).

Labor contracts are to be differentiated from civil law contracts (and in particular from independent work contracts). The latter are fully based on the principle of the freedom of agreement and the provisions of the Labor Code regulating work and rest time, material and disciplinary liability, settlement of labor disputes, etc. are not applicable to them.

6. The employer may issue orders, directives, instructions, provisions and labor regulations, within the bounds of its terms of reference and in accordance with the legislation of RK, the labor contract and the collective bargaining agreement (Art. 11 LC).

B. Conclusion

Labor contracts may generally be concluded by citizens who have reached the age of 16 years. However, upon the written consent of one parent (guardian or adoptive parent), a labor contract may be concluded with: (1) citizens who have reached the age of 15 years, in cases when they have received a secondary education in a general educational institution; (2) pupils who have reached the age of 14 years for performance, during time free from study, of work that is not harmful to health and does not disrupt the study process; and (3) persons who have not reached the age of 14 years for participation in creating and/or performing works without detriment to health or moral development and in observance of the conditions as part of a theatrical or concert organization, circus or film shooting.[7]

A labor contract may establish a probationary period for the purpose of verifying that the employee's qualifications comply with the job allocated thereto. The probationary period is included in the employee's service record and may not exceed three months. Certain categories of employees may not be subject to probation: (1) persons hired on a competitive basis to take up a position; (2) persons completing a secondary or higher professional education and starting work for the first time in the specialty studied; and (3) the disabled.

A labor contract may be concluded: (1) for an indefinite period; (2) for a specific period of not less than one year; (3) for the time required to fulfill a specific job; (4) for the time required to replace an absent employee; and (5) for the time required to fulfill seasonal work (Article 29 LC).

If the labor contract does not specify its term of validity, it is deemed to have been concluded for an indefinite period. A contract will also be deemed to have been concluded for an indefinite period in the event of a new concluding of an employment contract with an employee that previously concluded a contract for a specific period of not less than one year (including in the event of prolongation of an employment contract). Furthermore, in the event that, on expiration of the employment contract, neither of the parties demands, within a period of one day, termination of the labor relations, it is deemed to have been concluded for an indefinite period.

C. Invalidation and Termination

A labor contract may be recognized as invalid by a court if it is concluded: (1) under the influence of deception, force or threat; (2) without the intent to create actual or legal consequences (a sham contract); (3) with a person declared legally incompetent; (4) with an underage person; and (5) with a person under the age of 16 years without the written consent of a parent (guardian or adoptive parent). Recognition of individual terms and conditions of an employment contract as null and void does not entail invalidity of the employment contract as a whole. Should a

7. In these cases, the labor contract must be signed by a parent (guardian or adoptive parent) alongside the minor.

labor contract be recognized as invalid at the fault of the employer, it may not entail loss by the former employee of his rights to payment for his labor and other payments and benefits (Article 39 LC).

The major grounds for termination of a labor contract are: (1) cancellation of the contract by agreement between the parties; (2) expiration of the term of validity of the contract; (3) cancellation of the contract on the initiative of the employer; and (4) cancellation of the contract on the initiative of the employee.

A party to a labor contract expressing the desire to cancel the contract by agreement between the parties must send a notification to that effect to the other party; and the party that receives this notification must, within a period of three working days, notify the other party in writing of its decision. On agreement with the employee, the employer may cancel the employment contract without observing this requirement but with payment of a severance fee in the amount of at least the average annual wage.

In general, a labor contract concluded for a specific period is terminated in connection with the expiration of its term of validity. The date of expiration of a contract concluded for a specific period is the final day on which the employee performs his job in accordance with the term stipulated by the contract. A contract concluded for the period of performance of specific work expires on the day on which the work is completed while a contract concluded to replace a temporarily absent employee ends on the day on which the employee whose job (position) has been maintained returns to work.

A labor contract may be cancelled on the initiative of the employer only in the cases provided by the Labor Code. In particular, these cases include: (a) liquidation of the enterprise and reduction in staff numbers or positions; (b) unfitness of employee for the work performed as a consequence of inadequate qualifications or as a consequence of health reasons;[8] (c) a negative result of work performed during a probationary period; (d) absence of the employee from work without good reason for a period of three or more hours in a row during a single working day; (e) presence of the employee at work under the influence of alcohol, narcotics or toxic substances (or their analogues); (f) violation by the employee of the rules for labor, fire or traffic safety entailing or capable of entailing serious consequences; (g) theft by the employee in the work place, or deliberate destruction or damage of other people's property, as established by a sentence of court that has come into legal effect; (h) an immoral act carried out by an employee fulfilling educational functions; (i) divulgence by the employee of information constituting secrets protected by law that he acquired in connection with the performance of his job duties; (j) repeated failure, without good reason, by the employee to duly fulfill his job duties, provided a disciplinary sanction has already been imposed thereon; (k) absence of the employee from work for over two months in a row as a consequence of

8. Cancellation of the contract as a consequence of inadequate qualifications must be based on a decision of an appraisal commission including an employees' representative while cancellation for health reasons must be confirmed by a medical examination in the manner established by legislation (Art. 56 III, VI LC).

temporary disability;[9] (l) a corruption-related crime committed by the employee and excluding, in accordance with a judicial act, the possibility of his continued work (Article 54 LC). The employer must serve at least one month's written notice on the employee of termination of the contract, unless the contract or collective bargaining agreement envisaged a longer notice period.

An employee may terminate the labor contract on his own initiative by giving the employer at least one month's written notice to this effect. In the case of non-performance by the employer of the terms and conditions of the employment contract, the employee may notify the employer in writing to this effect and after seven days (if non-performance continues) terminate the contract by serving at least three working days' written notice on the employer.

Moreover, a labor contract is subject to termination by virtue of the circumstances not dependent on the will of the parties and in the event of: (1) withdrawal by the employee from labor relations;[10] (2) transfer of the employee to an elected job (position) or his appointment to a position excluding the possibility of continuation of the labor relations, apart from cases envisaged by the laws of RK; (3) violation of the terms and conditions for the conclusion of the contract; and (4) grounds envisaged in the contract concluded with the head of the employer's executive body.

V. WORK TIME

According to the Labor Code, work time is the time during which the employee, in accordance with acts of the employer and the terms and conditions of the labor contract, fulfills his job duties (Article 1 LC). It also includes preparatory and concluding work, breaks necessitated by the production technology or organization, rules of labor safety, the employee's time of presence or waiting for work at the work place, etc.

Working time may be of normal duration, reduced duration or part-time. Normal duration working time may not exceed 40 hours a week (Article 77 I LC). Reduced duration working time is established for employees under the age of 18 years (from the age of 14 to 16, not more than 24 hours; from 16 to 18, not more than 36 hours a week);[11] for employees engaged in heavy work, work

9. With the exception of cases when the employee is on maternity leave or if the relevant disease is included on the list of illnesses for which a longer term of disability is established, approved by the Government of RK. For an employee disabled in connection with an industrial accident or occupational disease, his job (position) must be retained until his working capacity is restored or disability established (Art. 54 XVII).
10. For example, in such cases as refusal by the employee to transfer to another location together with the employer or to continue work in connection with a change in the working conditions (Art. 59 LC).
11. There are also special rules with respect to students of educational institutions combining study and work during the academic year. Those aged from 14 to 16 years may not work more than 2.5 hours a day and those aged from 16 to 18 years not more than 3.5 hours a day.

under harmful and/or hazardous working conditions (not more than 36 hours a week);[12] and for disabled employees of disability groups I and II (not more than 36 hours a week).

The normal working week is a five-day working week with two days-off. However, in organizations where the working conditions make a five-day working week unfeasible, a six-day working week may be established with one day-off. Under a five-day working week, the normal duration of the working day may not exceed eight hours while under a six-day working week it is limited to seven hours.

Overtime work is generally possible upon the written consent of the employee. It may not exceed two hours a day per employee or one hour of heavy work or work under harmful and/or hazardous working conditions. In addition, there is also a limitation that the aggregate duration of overtime work may not exceed 120 hours a year. Also, it is stipulated that overtime work is not permitted for: (1) pregnant women; and (2) employees under the age of 18 years. However, in exceptional cases overtime work may be permitted without the employee's consent. These cases include: (1) performance of work necessary for defense of the country, as well as for preventing emergencies, natural disasters or industrial accidents and for immediately eliminating their consequences;[13] (2) for eliminating other circumstances disrupting normal water, gas, heat and power supplies, and the functioning of other vital utilities; (3) for continuing work if a shift partner fails to turn up for work and if the work cannot be interrupted, provided that immediate measures are taken to find a replacement employee (Articles 88–90 LC).

Night work is deemed to be that performed between 22:00 hours and 06:00 hours. Pregnant women and women with young children may not undertake night work, and disabled persons may do so only with a medical certificate.

Part-time work may be agreed in individual cases between the employer and the employee, either when the worker is hired or later. It may take the form of a shortened working day or a shorter working week and may be established upon a written application from a pregnant woman, a woman with a child (children) under the age of three years, a father or adoptive parent bringing up children under the age of three years without a mother, as well as from an employee caring for a sick family member in accordance with a medical opinion (Articles 79, 80, 189 LC).

VI. REST TIME

There are the following types of rest time: (1) breaks during the working day (rest and meal breaks; shift and special breaks); (2) daily (inter-shift) rest; (3) days-off (weekly continuous rest); (4) official holidays; and (5) leave.

12. The list of heavy work or work under harmful and/or hazardous conditions is determined by the Ministry of Labor and Social Protection on agreement with the Ministry of Health.
13. In this case, the limit of 120 hours a year does not apply (Art. 89 III LC).

During the working day (work shift), an employee must be granted one rest and meal break of at least half an hour. The time of the rest and meal break is not included in working time.

For certain types of work, employees must be allowed shift breaks necessitated by the production technology and organization, which is included in working time. Also, employees working during a cold period in the open air or in enclosed, unheated premises, as well as those engaged in loading and unloading work, are allowed special warm-up and rest breaks, which are included in working time. In addition, working women with children up to the age of 18 months must be granted additional breaks for feeding the child.[14]

The duration of daily (inter-shift) rest of the employee between the end of work and its start on the next day (work shift) must be at least 12 hours. Also, employees are granted days-off every week. With a five-day working week, employees are granted two days-off per week, while with a six-day working week, one day-off. Sunday is a day-off common to both a five-day and a six-day working week. The second day off with a five-day working week is usually Saturday, unless otherwise established in the labor contract.[15]

According to the Law of RK of December 13, 2001, No. 267-2, "On Holidays," official holidays in Kazakhstan are January 1–2 (New Year); March 8 (International Women's Day); March 21–23 (Nauryz, traditional New Year); May 1 (People's Unity Day); May 9 (Victory Day); July 6 (Day of the Capital); August 30 (Day of the Constitution); and December 16–17 (Independence Day). The Labor Code of RK provides also that the first day of Kurban-ait (celebrated according to the Muslim calendar) and January 7 (the Orthodox Christmas) are also official non-working days.

Engagement to work on days-off and official holidays without the written consent of the employee is permitted only in the following cases: (1) for prevention of emergencies, natural disasters or industrial accidents or for rapid elimination of their consequences; (2) for prevention and investigation of accidents and destruction of or damage to property; (3) for fulfillment of urgent, unforeseen work required for continued normal operation of the organization as a whole or of its individual subdivisions. For work on days-off and official holidays, at the employee's discretion another rest day must be granted or additional payment made (Article 98 LC).

Furthermore, employees may be granted the following types of leave: (1) annual paid leave; and (2) social leave. The former is intended for the employee to rest, restore his working capacity, strengthen his health and fulfill other personal requirements and is granted for a specific number of calendar days with retention

---

14. Such women are granted additional breaks at least once every three working hours of the following duration: (1) with one child, each break must last at least 20 minutes; and (2) with two or more children at least one hour (Art. 188 LC).
15. For employees engaged in continuous production, where it is not possible to halt work on days-off, days-off are granted on different days of the week according to a shift timetable approved by acts of the employer issued on agreement with employees' representatives (Art. 96 V LC).

of the employee's job (position) and average wage; while the latter is understood as release of the employee from work for a specific period of time for the purpose of creating favorable conditions for maternity, childcare, education and other social purposes.

The duration of annual paid leave is 24 calendar days (not counting official holidays falling during the leave period), unless a greater number of days is envisaged by other regulatory acts, the labor contract, collective bargaining agreement or acts of the employer. Additional annual paid leave is granted to: (1) employees engaged in heavy work or work under harmful and/or hazardous working conditions (an addition of at least six calendar days); and (2) group I and II disabled workers (an addition of at least 15 calendar days).

Employees may also be granted the following types of social leave: (1) unpaid leave; (2) study leave; and (3) maternity leave and leave due to the adoption of a newborn. Upon application of the employee, he may be granted an unpaid leave, the duration of which is determined by agreement between the employee and the employer. Also, it is stipulated that the employer must provide unpaid leave of up to five calendar days for: (1) registration of marriage; (2) birth of a child; and (3) death of a close relative.

Moreover, employees studying at educational institutions must be granted study leave for preparing for and taking tests and examinations, preparing and defending diploma work (project). In addition, pregnant women, women who have given birth and women (men) who have adopted a newborn must be granted the following types of maternity leave: (a) ante-natal and post-natal leave;[16] (b) paid leave to employees adopting a newborn; and (c) unpaid childcare leave until the child reaches the age of three years.

VII. REMUNERATION

Payment for the labor of employees is made according to a time, piece-rate or other system of labor compensation. It may be made on the basis of individual and/or collective labor results.[17] To raise the employees' interest in greater production efficiency and better quality of the work performed, the employer may introduce bonus systems and other labor incentives. But the system of labor compensation must provide for the basic wage (or constant part of the wage) to constitute at least

---

16. Women are granted 70 calendar days ante-natal and 56 (or 70 in the event of a complicated birth or birth of two or more children) calendar days post-natal paid maternity leave (Art. 193 I LC).
17. The system of labor compensation may be formed on the basis of a rate, non-rate or mixed system. A rate system of labor compensation includes: a base rate (set wage), wage scale and rate coefficients. A non-rate system of labor compensation is based on proportional distribution of the funds intended for payment of labor, depending on criteria and principles for assessing the professional qualities of employees and their contribution to the final result. A mixed system of labor compensation may contain elements of both a rate and a non-rate system of labor compensation.

75% of the average monthly wage of employees, excluding one-time incentive payments.

The amount of the wage is set differentially depending on the qualifications of the employee, the complexity, amount and quality of work performed, as well as the working conditions. Also, the Labor Code provides for the following state guarantees in the sphere of labor compensation: (1) minimum monthly wage; (2) minimum hourly wage; (3) minimum standards for labor compensation; (3) payment for overtime work; (4) payment for work on public holidays and days-off; (5) payment for night work; (6) restrictions on withholdings from employee wages; and (7) the procedure and time schedule for payment of wages (Article 120 LC).

The monthly wage of an employee that has worked the full standard working time for the given period and has fulfilled the work-time standards (job duties) may not be lower than the minimum level established by the legislation.[18]

The terms and conditions of the labor contract, collective bargaining agreement and/or act of the employer may establish an hourly labor compensation for work actually performed during a shortened working day or less than fulltime, as well as for payment for work of a temporary or one-time nature. Hourly labor compensation may not be less than the minimum monthly wage divided by the average number of working hours in the month (the minimum hourly wage).

Also, the Labor Code of RK provides for the minimum standard labor compensation, which is determined on the basis of the minimum monthly wage established by the law of RK on the republican budget for the corresponding year, as well as branch multipliers determined by branch agreements and approved by the Government of RK.

Furthermore, there are special provisions with respect to payment for overtime work, for work on public holidays and days-off and for night work. The payment for overtime work must be at a rate of at least 150% in the event of time-based labor compensation and at least 50% of the wage rate established for the employee in the event of piece-rate labor compensation. Payment for work on public holidays and days-off must be at a rate of at least 200% proceeding from the daily (hourly) rate of the employee. Each hour of work during the night shall be paid at a rate of at least 150% proceeding from the daily (hourly) rate of the employee.

Withholdings from the wages of an employee may generally be made only by court. Withholdings for the purpose of redeeming the employees' debt towards his employer may be made on the basis of an act of the employer, but only upon the written consent of the employee. Also, the total amount of monthly withholdings may not exceed 50% of the wage due the employee.

Wages must be paid in monetary form in the national currency of RK at least once a month, no later than the 10th day of the following month. On payment of wages, the employer must notify each employee, every month, in writing, of the component parts of the wages due to him for the corresponding period, the amount of and grounds for withholdings made, including information about mandatory

18. The minimum monthly wage is established annually by the law of RK on the republican budget for the corresponding financial year. As of 2011, it was equal to KZT 15,999 (ca. USD 110).

pension contributions withheld and remitted, as well as about the aggregate monetary sum due for payment.

In the event of delayed payment, at the fault of the employer, of wages and other payments connected with termination of the employment contract with the employee, the employer must pay to the employee the debt and default interest.

VIII. LABOR DISCIPLINE

The Labor Code requires workers to comply with labor discipline (Article 22 II LC), which, in turn, is defined as "proper fulfillment by the employer and employees of their obligations established by regulatory acts of RK, as well as labor contracts, collective bargaining agreements, acts of the employer, and constituent documents of a legal entity" (Article 1 LC). Furthermore, the employer may establish internal labor regulations on agreement with employees' representatives. These regulations establish the working time and rest time of employees, the conditions for ensuring labor discipline and regulate other questions of labor relations. They are binding on both the employer and employees.

Labor discipline is ensured by the employer by creating adequate working conditions, promoting a conscientious attitude on the part of employees towards their work through persuasion and incentives, as well as applying disciplinary sanctions for disciplinary offenses committed by employees. For a disciplinary offense committed by an employee, the employer may apply the following types of disciplinary sanctions: (1) admonition; (2) reprimand; (3) strict reprimand; and (4) termination of the labor contract on the initiative of the employer. Application of any other disciplinary sanctions is prohibited.

There are the following rules for applying and appealing against disciplinary sanctions. *First*, disciplinary sanctions must be imposed by the employer by issuing an act of the employer. *Second*, the employer must demand a written explanation from the employee before applying the disciplinary sanction. *Third*, for each disciplinary offense, only a single disciplinary sanction may be imposed on the employee. *Fourth*, in determining the type of disciplinary sanction, the employer must take into account the content, nature and gravity of the disciplinary offense, the circumstances under which it was committed, the prior and subsequent conduct of the employee and his attitude towards his work. *Fifth*, an act of the employer imposing a disciplinary sanction on the employee may not be issued during a period of: (a) temporary disability of the employee; (b) release of the employee from work for fulfillment of state or public duties; (c) leave; or (d) a business trip. *Sixth*, an act imposing a disciplinary sanction must be announced to the employee subject to the disciplinary sanction within a period of three working days of its issue, with the requirement that the employee signs the notice of the sanction.

A disciplinary sanction must be imposed on the employee immediately for committing a disciplinary offense, but not later than one month from the date of its discovery. It may not be applied more than six months from the day on which the disciplinary offense was committed.[19] The term of validity of a disciplinary sanction may not exceed six months from the day on which it is applied. If, within this period, no new disciplinary sanction is imposed on the employee, he is deemed not to be subject to disciplinary sanction. Also, an employer that imposes a disciplinary sanction on an employee may lift it ahead of time either on its own initiative or at the request of the employee (his representative or immediate manager).

IX. MATERIAL LIABILITY

A party to a labor contract must recompense the other party for the damage (harm) inflicted provided that damage (harm) arises as a result of culpable, unlawful conduct (action or inaction) and there is a cause and effect link between the conduct and the damage (Article 161 I LC).

Thus, the employer bears material liability towards the employee: (1) for damage inflicted by unlawful deprival of the employee of the possibility of working at his work place; (2) for damage inflicted on property of the employee; and (3) for harm inflicted on the life and (or) health of the employee. At the same time, the employee bears material liability towards the employer: (1) for damage inflicted by loss of or damage to the property of the employer; and (2) for damage arising as a result of (in)actions on the part of the employee.

An employer causing any damage to the property, the life and/or health of an employee must reimburse the latter in full,[20] whereas an employee must make recompense only for direct and real damage inflicted on the employer. Liability of the employee for damage inflicted on the employer must be excluded if the damage arises as a result of force majeure or extreme necessity, necessary defense or failure by the employer to fulfill its obligations to provide the proper conditions for safekeeping of the property transferred to the employee. Moreover, it is not permitted to impose liability on the employee for damage that might be classed as normal production and business risk.

It should also be noted that the employee generally bears liability only within the limits of his average monthly wage. Full material liability may be imposed on the employee in particular with the following cases: (1) failure to ensure the safekeeping of property transferred to the employee on the basis of a written agreement on acceptance of full material liability; (2) infliction of damage under the influence of alcohol, narcotics or toxic substances (or their analogues); (3) short payments for or deliberate destruction of the employer's property; and (4) infliction of damage by means of unlawful actions on the part of the employee (Article 167 LC).

19. In case of a disciplinary offense due to audit of the financial and business activities of the employer (or other cases established by legislation) the term may be extended to one year (not including time occupied by criminal proceedings (Art. 74 II LC).
20. Harm inflicted on the life and/or health of the employee must be reimbursed in full provided the employee receives no insurance indemnity. If insurance indemnity is paid out, the employer reimburses the employee the difference between the insurance sum and the actual scale of the harm caused (Art. 164 II LC).

X. SOCIAL PARTNERSHIP

The establishment of a social partnership between employees, employers and the state is one of the major principles of Labor Law. It is designed to promote, *inter alia*: (1) social stability and consensus; (2) protection of employees' rights; (3) close contacts between the parties to the social partnership at all levels; (4) resolution of labor disputes; and (5) development of proposals for implementing state policy in the sphere of socio-labor relations.

In order to facilitate social partnership, there are special republican- (consisting of representatives of republican associations of employees and employers and the Government of RK), branch- and regional-level commissions. Meetings of commissions are held at least twice a year. However, it should be noted that due to the weakness of trade unions (associations of employees), the ideals of social partnership cannot be realized in full. Also, in many instances (especially in the view of the proliferation of national companies) the state is simultaneously the employer, which makes the position of employees even more unequal.

XI. COLLECTIVE BARGAINING AGREEMENTS

A collective bargaining agreement is defined as "a legal document in the form of a written agreement between a team of employees and the employer, regulating socio-labor relations in the organization" (Article 1 LC). Any party may initiate the preparation of such an agreement. A party that receives a notification from the other party proposing the commencement of negotiations on the conclusion of a collective bargaining agreement must, within a period of 20 days, consider it and start negotiations.

For holding negotiations and preparing a draft agreement, the parties set up a commission on a parity basis. The commission prepares the draft agreement, which must be discussed by the employees of the organization and then finalized by the commission in consideration of comments and proposals submitted. In the event of disagreements between the parties over individual provisions of the collective bargaining agreement, within a period of one month from the launch of the negotiations the parties sign a collective bargaining agreement on the terms and conditions agreed and, at the same time, draw up a disagreement report. The collective bargaining agreement must be submitted to the territorial subdivision of the state labor authority for monitoring purposes.

XII. LABOR DISPUTES

Individual labor disputes may be considered by courts and/or mediation commissions. The latter must be set up on parity principles, consisting of an equal number of representatives of the employer and of employees. The numerical strength of the mediation commission, the procedure by which it works and the term of the powers of the mediation commission is established by an agreement between the employer and employees at a general meeting (conference) of employees. The members of the mediation commission on the part of the employees are elected by a general meeting of employees. The members of the mediation commission on the part of the employer are appointed by an act of the employer. At their first meeting, members of the mediation commission elect a chairman and secretary from among them by a simple majority of votes. The mediation commission considers the labor dispute within seven days from the date on which the application is submitted. Consideration of the dispute in the absence of the employee (or his representative) who is a party to the dispute is permitted only on the basis of his written application. The commission may summon witnesses, invite experts to take part in its meeting and demand the employer to submit all required documents. At the demand of the applicant or one of the members of the commission, voting may be held in secret. The resolutions are adopted by a simple majority of the votes and must be fulfilled by the deadline set thereby.[21] In the event of non-fulfillment of a resolution of the commission, the employee or the employer may have the labor dispute resolution enforced through a court.

A collective labor dispute is deemed to have arisen from the day of written notification of the employer of the employees' collective claims, approved by resolution of the general meeting (conference) of employees. The employer (or association of employers) must consider claims entered by employees within seven calendar days from their receipt and take steps to settle them. If employee claims cannot be settled, they must be considered by mediation procedures; none of the parties may to refuse to participate in these procedures.

If agreement cannot be reached by the mediation commission, it must cease its deliberations, and resolution of the dispute must be referred to a labor tribunal. The tribunal consists of at least five members, including representatives of the republican, branch or regional commissions of social partnership. The Chairman of the tribunal is elected by the parties from among the members of the tribunal. The tribunal adopts its decision within seven calendar days from the day of its creation by a simple majority. At any stage in the consideration of a collective labor dispute, the parties may engage a conciliator. The conciliation procedure may run in parallel to the activities of the mediation commission or labor tribunal and is independent from them.

If disagreements between the parties to the collective labor dispute cannot be resolved by the mediation and the tribunal procedures, the employees' claims must be submitted to the owners (founder, shareholders) of the respective organizations.

If the employees still disagree, they may use all the other methods envisaged by law for protecting their interests, up to and including strikes.[22] A decision to call

21. In particular, the Commission may reinstate the employee in his previous job. In this case, the employee must be paid his average wage for the entire period of enforced absence (suspension from work) or the wage difference for time spent performing lower-paid work, but with a maximum of six months back pay (Art. 177 LC).
22. In the process of the settlement of a collective labor dispute, including during a strike, it is prohibited to enforce a lockout, that is, for labor contracts with employees to be cancelled on the initiative of the employer (Art. 305 LC).

a strike must be taken at a meeting (conference) of employees (their representatives) attended by at least half the total number of employees of the organization and is deemed to have been adopted if it is supported by at least a two-thirds vote by the participants in the meeting (conference). Participation in a strike must be voluntary. No one may be compelled to participate or to refuse to participate in a strike. Anyone forcing employees to participate in or refuse to participate in a strike may be held liable.

Strikes are declared illegal: (a) in periods of martial law or emergencies; (b) in military units and organizations in charge of firefighting, ensuring the country's defense, and preventing or eliminating emergencies; (c) in law-enforcement bodies; (d) at hazardous production facilities; (e) at first aid stations and in ambulance services; and (f) in railway transportation, civil aviation, organizations providing for domestic services to the population (public transportation, supply of water, electric power, heat and communications). A ruling recognizing a strike as illegal is issued by a court on the basis of an application submitted by the employer or the public procurator. If a strike is declared illegal, the employer may impose disciplinary liability on the employees participating in the strike.

Selected Bibliography

E. Nurgalieva, "Problems of Reforming Labor Legislation in the Republic of Kazakhstan" (1995) 21 *Review of Central and East European Law* 149.

E. Nurgaliyeva & G. Suragan, *Материальная ответственность сторон трудового договора* [*Material Liability of the Parties to Labor Contract*] (Baspa, Almaty, 2001).

E. Nurgaliyeva & S. Serikbekova, *Индивидуальные договоры о труде* [*Individual Labor Contracts*] (KazGYuU, Almaty, 2004).

A. Nurmagambetov, *Рынок труда: правовые проблемы и перспективы* [*Labor Market: Legal Problems and Perspectives*] (Baspa, Almaty, 1998).

V. Uvarov, *Трудовое право Республики Казахстан* [*Labor Law of RK*] (Raritet, Almaty, 2008).

B. Zhumagulov, *Правовое регулирование трудовых отношений государственных служащих в Республике Казахстан* [*Legal Regulation of Labor Relations of State Servants in RK*] (Gylym, Almaty, 2004).

Chapter 11
Private International Law*

Maidan Suleimenov

I. INTRODUCTION

The importance of Private International Law (PIL) has increased significantly in recent decades due to three factors: (a) the increased internationalization of commerce; (b) a significant rise in population movement; and (c) scientific and technological advances that have facilitated communication and transactions over great distances, and have created new modes of creating legal obligations, such as e-commerce and digital signatures.

In Kazakhstan, two additional factors required a rapid development of PIL rules. First, when Kazakhstan was a constituent part of the USSR, norms of PIL were rarely applied. International issues were decided in Moscow, and Kazakhstan implemented the decisions made by central governmental authorities. Second, after obtaining its independence, Kazakhstan was faced with a number of challenges such as building a market economy and attracting foreign investment that, in turn, necessitated establishing economic relations with many countries and developing a set of national conflict-of-law rules. In response, in the first years of independence Kazakhstan developed its own jurisprudence of PIL. On July 1, 1999 the Special Part of the Civil Code of RK, which contained a separate section

* Translated by Zhenis Kembayev. Editor's note: This chapter is restricted to the conflict of laws. Matters of jurisdiction and the recognition and enforcement of judgments are per se outside its ambit.

Zhenis Kembayev, *Introduction to the Law of Kazakhstan*, pp. 197–209.

on PIL (section VII), came into force. This legal document provides the basis for conflict-of-law rules.

As to the nature of PIL, the jurisprudence elaborates the three following viewpoints: (a) PIL is a part of international law in its broadest sense; (b) PIL is a part of domestic law; and (c) PIL incorporates both international and domestic norms. In this regard, Kazakhstani legal science has adhered to the view that PIL is a part of domestic law.

According to the Civil Code, private international law concerns general civil law relations with the participation of foreign natural persons or foreign legal entities or some other connection of a foreign element (Article 1084). Also, PIL governs relations connected with international family law, international labor law and international private procedural law (or law of alternative dispute-settlement) and, consequently, is a complex branch of law. However, international civil procedure is not considered a part of PIL since it is a branch of public law. As it is common in international practice, PIL employs two major methods of legal regulation: (a) the substantive method (implying direct regulation); and (b) the selective method (meaning the application of "renvoi").

II. SOURCES OF PIL

There are four main sources of PIL: (a) international treaties; (b) legislation; (c) customs; and (d) judicial precedents. Kazakhstan has become a party to numerous international treaties, so it is easier to mention those important agreements that the country has not joined yet: the United Nations Convention on Contracts for the International Sale of Goods (1980), the Convention Concerning International Carriage by Rail (COTIF) (1980), the Warsaw Convention for the *Unification* of Certain Rules Relating to International Carriage by Air (1929), many conventions adopted in the framework of International Labor Organization, etc.

The Constitution of RK of August 30, 1995 serves as the foundation of Kazakhstan's legislation and, therefore, as the primary source of PIL. It is followed by numerous legislative acts, with the most important of them being: the Civil Code of RK (General Part of 27 December 1994 and Special Part of July 1, 1999), Labor Code of RK of May 15, 2007, Law of RK of December 17, 1998 "On Marriage and Family" (in particular section VI "Application of Norms of the Marriage and Family Legislation to Foreign Citizens and Stateless Persons"), Law of RK of July 24, 2010 "On Subsoil and Subsoil Use," etc. It should be noted that (in contrast to the first years Kazakhstan's existence as an independent country) the number of laws specifically regulating relations only with respect to foreign elements is continuously decreasing (e.g., Law of RK of December 27, 1994 "On Foreign Investments" was superseded by Law of RK of January 8, 2003, No. 373-II, "On Investments" which does not distinguish between foreign and domestic investors). At present, there are only the following laws that govern relations exclusively with respect to foreign elements: Law of RK of June 19, 1995 "On the Legal Status of Foreigners in the Republic of Kazakhstan," Law of RK of December 28, 2003 "On International Commercial Arbitration," Law of RK of June 13, 2005 "On Currency Regulation and Currency Control" and (regarding labor relations) Law of the RK of December 13, 1997 "On Migration."

Furthermore, the Civil Code of RK stipulates that "civil relations may be regulated by customs, including customs of business relations, unless they are contrary to civil legislation prevailing on the territory of RK" (Article 3 III). Thus, customary rules (and especially INCOTERMS) are currently receiving increasingly widespread use.

Finally, judicial precedent is not a source of law in Kazakhstan (which, like the entire former USSR, is established in the civil law tradition). However, after the collapse of the USSR, discussions were held in many post-Soviet countries with respect to the legal nature of regulatory resolutions of the Supreme Court. In Kazakhstan, this matter was resolved by the Constitution of 1995, which provides that regulatory resolutions of the Supreme Court belong to the sources of law in Kazakhstan (Article 4 I).

III. CONFLICT-OF-LAW RULES

Conflict-of-law rules define which state's law will be applied in a civil law relation with a foreign element involved. The structure of such rules consists of two elements: (a) extent (*ob'yom*) and (b) connecting factor (*privyazka*). The extent indicates the kind of legal relationship with a foreign element that is involved while the connecting factor determines what law is to be applied with respect to this relationship.[1]

Depending on the type of connecting factor, conflict-of-law rules may be divided into: (a) unilateral rules that explicitly state the law of what country is to be applied (e.g., transactions involving immovable property listed in Kazakhstan's state register is governed by the law of RK (Article 1104 III CC)); and (b) bilateral rules that do not state the law of a particular country but formulate the principles for the choice of the law of one country or another (these principles are often referred to as "forms of attachment").

As in the conflict-of-law rules of other states (and in particular those related to the continental law system), in Kazakhstan there are the following main "forms of attachment":

(1) *Lex Personalis* (the personal law of a natural person) that, in turn, has two alternates: (a) *Lex nationalis* or *Lex Patriae* (national law or law of citizenship), the primary personal law of a natural person (Article 1094 I CC); and (b) *Lex domicilii* (law of the domicile), which is applicable both to stateless persons (Article 1094 II CC) and legal issues of inheritance (Article 1121 CC).

---

1. Editor's note: The concept of "extent" is the equivalent of "characterization" as used in British, EU and American jurisprudence.

(2) *Lex societatis* (the law of a legal entity) implies the application of the law of the state to which a legal entity belongs (nationality of a legal entity). In jurisprudence there are different doctrines to determine the nationality of a legal entity: (a) doctrine of settlement, i.e., law of the location of its administrative headquarters; (b) doctrine of the center of operations, i.e., law of the location of its core activities; and (c) doctrine of incorporation, i.e., law of the country where it was founded. The Kazakhstani legislation follows the third one and provides that "the law of a legal entity shall be deemed to be law of a country where that entity was established" (Article 1100 CC).

(3) *Lex rei sitae* (the law of the location of property) applies to rights *in rem* (Article 1107 CC) and inheritance of immovable property (Article 1123 CC).

(4) *Lex voluntaris* (law chosen by the parties to a particular civil law relation) may be found in the provision saying that "an agreement shall be regulated by the law of the country selected by agreement of the parties, unless it is otherwise stipulated in legislative acts of RK" (Article 1112 CC).

(5) *Lex loci actus* (law of the place where an act is performed) has many different expressions. (a) *Lex loci contractus* (law of the place where a contract is performed) may be applied with respect to the "dispositive legal capacity of a natural person regarding transactions or obligations that emerge in consequence to causing harm" (Article 1095 III CC). However, this law is rarely applied due to the fortuity of where international contracts are concluded, and difficulties in identifying the location of their conclusion. (b) *Lex loci solutionis* (law of the place where a contract is executed) may be taken into consideration with respect to the "formal acceptance of the execution of an agreement" (Article 1113 V CC) and to the "method and procedure of the execution as well as measures that must be taken in the case of an improper execution" (Article 1115 II CC). (c) *Lex loci celebrationis* (law of the place where a marriage is celebrated) applies to family relations (Article 200 LMF). (d) *Lex loci delicti commissi* (law of the place where the harm was caused) may be found in the provision stipulating that "the rights and obligations under obligations that emerge in consequence of causing harm shall be determined in accordance with the law of the country where the action has taken place" (Article 1117 CC). (e) *Locus regit formam actum* (the form of a transaction is subject to law of the place where it was performed) is stipulated in Article 1104 I of Civil Code.

(6) *Lex venditoris* (law of the country of a vendor) is applied in Contract Law when there is no agreement of the parties with regard to which law is applicable to their agreement (Article 1113 I CC).

(7) *Lex loci activitis* (law of the place where activities are carried out) is applied as a subsidiary connecting factor to legal capacity and

dispositive legal capacity of an individual entrepreneur (Article 1095 IV CC) and to contracts of joint ventures and construction (Article 1113 III CC).

(8) *Lex loci laboris* (law of the place where the labor takes place) is applied in international labor law.

(9) *Proper Law of Contract* (i.e., law that is most closely associated with a particular legal relation) is stipulated in the rule that "if it is impossible to determine the execution of a contract that has the principal significance to its contents the law of the country with which the contract is most closely associated shall apply" (Article 1113 V CC). Furthermore, in this regard we gave[2] a broader meaning to the Civil Code setting forth the rule that "if it is impossible to determine the law that is subject to application the law shall apply that is most closely associated with the civil and legal relations complicated by a foreign element" (Article 1084 II CC).

(10) *Lex fori* or *lex arbitri* (law of the place where a dispute is considered either by court or arbitral body) is applied quite extensively in the Civil Code, in particular with respect to recognition of legal capacity or dispositive legal capacity of a natural person (Article 1095 V CC), recognition of a natural person to be missing or deceased (Article 1096 CC) and protection of rights *in rem* (Article 1111 I CC).

The application of PIL (conflict-of-laws) rules is more complex than applying domestic law because different legal systems interact when PIL is applied. Therefore, the application of these laws involves the following two stages (which are regulated in detail by Civil Code):

(1) *Applying a conflict-of-law rule*: At this stage, it is necessary to find out whether a conflict-of-law rule is applicable, what rule is to be applied specifically and the law of what country it refers to. Consequently, many legal issues may arise in this regard (in particular related to reciprocity, retortion, legal qualification, circumvention of laws, renvoi and reference to the legal system of a third party).

(2) *Determining the law that a conflict-of-law refers to*: This stage commences after all legal issues of the first stage are clarified and involves the application of norms of substantive law (either domestic or foreign). Therefore, different legal issues arise (related to determining the foreign law's content, application of public law and imperative rules as well as application of the law of a country with multiple legal systems).

2. Editor's note: Professor Suleimenov was one of the most important drafters of the Civil Code of RK.

IV. SUBJECTS OF PIL

Subjects of PIL are natural persons (citizens, foreign citizens and stateless persons), legal entities as well as the state and other public law subjects.

Natural Persons: As a general rule, *Lex nationalis* (or *Lex Patriae*) applies to foreign citizens (Article 1094 I CC). However, it does not determine the legal capacity of foreigners. Foreign citizens who have a certain extent of their legal capacity in their home country are precluded from referring to the same extent of legal capacity during their stay on the territory of another country. During their stay in other countries, they possess the legal capacity defined by the legal order of that state and usually to the extent provided by applying national treatment to them. Thus, the Civil Code of RK provides that "foreign citizens and stateless persons shall enjoy civil legal capacity in RK on an equal basis with the citizens of RK, except for cases established by legislative acts or international treaties of RK" (Article 1095 I CC).[3]

The issues surrounding the conflict-of-laws occur mainly upon the application of provisions on the dispositive legal capacity of natural persons. Most often, it is connected with the age at which full dispositive legal capacity emerges, as this can differ between countries. In this regard, the Civil Code of RK stipulates that the dispositive legal capacity of a natural person is determined by his personal law (Article 1095 II CC).[4] However, there is an exclusion from this general rule: the dispositive legal capacity of a natural person in respect of transactions and obligations that emerge due to causing harm is determined by the law of the country where those transactions are performed (*lex loci actus*, *lex loci contractus*) or where the consequences resulting from the harm caused occur (*lex loci delicti commissi*).[5]

---

3. A similar approach is adopted in legislation of many other states (e.g., Armenia, Lithuania, Madagascar, Mongolia, France, the Czech Republic, Switzerland and Estonia). Meanwhile, a number of other countries (e.g., Austria, Hungary, Germany, Poland, Romania and Turkey) have adopted a different principle, whereby the legal capacity of foreigners is determined by their personal law. Both approaches are inefficient due to their one-sidedness: the first does not take into consideration the extent of legal capacity that is accorded to foreigners in their native countries while the second ignores the principle of national treatment that should be applicable to all foreigners. However, there is also a mixed approach that takes into account the legal capacity both in the country of citizenship and the country of stay. Thus, Civil Codes of Russia (Art. 1196), Belarus (Art. 1104) and Uzbekistan (Art. 1169) stipulate that the legal capacity of a natural person is determined by his personal law and that foreigners and stateless persons enjoy the same extent of the legal capacity as citizens of those countries except for cases specified by the legislation.
4. For example, in RK the age when full dispositive legal capability emerges is set at 18, whereas in Japan this age is 20. Therefore, a 19-year-old Japanese citizen in Kazakhstan will not possess the dispositive legal capacity, just as he would not in Japan, because his civil dispositive legal capacity is determined by Japanese law.
5. Consequently, if a 19-year-old Japanese citizen enters into a transaction in Japan, it can be rendered void as a result of his legal incapacity; however, if a transaction is performed in RK, the Japanese will be regarded as having the dispositive legal capacity to do so.

Legal Entities: As it was mentioned above, Kazakhstan applies the doctrine of incorporation with respect to legal entities (Article 1100 CC). Consequently, the legal capacity of a legal entity is generally defined by the law of the legal entity (Article 1101 I CC). However, there are certain exceptions from the doctrine of incorporation; in particular, a "foreign legal entity may not refer to the restriction of powers of its body or representatives with regard to carrying out a transaction that is not known to law of the country in which the body or the representative of the foreign legal entity carried out that transaction" (Article 1101 II CC).[6]

It should also be noted that the Civil Code provides a concept of a "legal entity with foreign participation," saying that agreements on its establishment are governed by "the law of the country where a legal entity is or was founded" (Article 1114 I CC). Furthermore, Law of RK of January 8, 2003, No. 373-II, "On Investments" provides that a "legal entity with foreign participation that is founded in an order set by the legislation of RK" is a legal entity of RK (Article 1 XI). At the same time, however, the legal concepts of "foreign enterprise" and "joint venture" (which existed according to the now obsolete Law of RK of December 27, 1994 "On Foreign Investments") were not retained.

State and Other Public Law Subjects: Apart from participating in public law relations, the RK can enter into property relations with foreign legal entities and natural persons governed by PIL. In this regard, the following two types of civil law relations are of the most importance: (a) contracts on concession of the subsoil to foreign investors; and (b) receipt of loans from foreign borrowers (by concluding simple or syndicated loan agreements or issuing Eurobonds).

An important feature of any state is its immunity, i.e., a state is not subject to the jurisdiction of another state. There are two theories of state immunity: (a) the theory of absolute immunity; and (b) a more modern and widespread theory of restricted (or functional) immunity.

Until recently Kazakhstan in principle had adhered to the former. However, on October 27, 2009 Kazakhstan ratified the UN Convention "On Jurisdictional Immunity of States and Their Property" of December 2, 1994, which is based on the doctrine of restricted immunity. Subsequently, on February 5, 2010 the Law of RK "On the Introduction of Amendments to Certain Legislative Acts of RK Concerning the Issues of Immunity of the State and its Property, Improvement

6. For example, the head of a legal entity of Greek nationality entered into a transaction in Kazakhstan, but the transaction was disputed because the head had breached a specific limitation of the powers of a legal entity provided under the Greek law. However, such limitations do not exist in Kazakhstan; therefore, the transaction is recognized as valid. Another example includes an arbitration case where a dispute emerged over which law is to be applied in deciding the issue of validity of a transaction. Mr. K. was the President of a company registered in Cyprus and a member of the Directors' Board of a subsidiary registered in Canada. He entered into a transaction in Kazakhstan. A question emerged as to what law should apply in determining the powers of K. acting as the body of two legal entities. Based on the Civil Code (Art. 1101 II), it can be inferred that, in this case, the laws of Cyprus and Canada would apply, whereas the law of Kazakhstan can be applied as an additional law. K. shall have powers in accordance with the laws of Cyprus and Canada; the law of Kazakhstan would apply only if the law of Canada (or Cyprus) specifies limitations not known to the law of Kazakhstan.

of the Activity of Arbitration Courts and International Commercial Arbitration" was adopted, which introduced amendments both to the Civil Procedure Code of RK and the Civil Code of RK. Currently both Codes have reintroduced the concept of absolute immunity. However, the principle of absolute immunity may be displaced by a respective international treaty.

V. RIGHTS *IN REM*

In Kazakhstan, rights *in rem* are subject to *lex rei sitae* (i.e., the law of the place where the property is located) with certain variations (Articles 1107–1111 CC). The main legal issues related to rights *in rem* within PIL deal with the legal regulation of nationalization, privatization and foreign investments.

Nationalization is defined by the Civil Code as the conversion of property owned by natural persons and legal entities to state ownership (Article 249 IV CC). The issues of nationalization (as well as privatization) are covered in detail by the Law of RK of March 1, 2011, No. 413-IV, "On State Property." This law provides a more comprehensive definition of nationalization specifying it as "compulsory and compensated alienation of property owned by natural persons and non-state legal entities to state ownership of the Republic of Kazakhstan" (Article 1 XII LSP). Also, it is stipulated that nationalization may apply not only to ownership rights but also to other property rights (in particular, to the right to book-entry shares (shares without a certificate), which are regarded not as ownership rights but as a right to claim). Furthermore, the LSP contains detailed regulations on the principles of the effectuation of nationalization, grounds for nationalization, procedure for compensation payments, competences of state bodies regarding nationalization and protection of the rights of the owner of the property subject to nationalization (Articles 54–60 LSP). However, the Law does not provide the detailed procedures of nationalization (that will be done by the Law of RK "On Nationalization," which has not yet been adopted).[7]

Privatization of state property was previously regulated by the Law of RK of December 23, 1995 "On Privatization" which defined privatization as any sale by the state of its property to natural persons or legal entities. However, the LSP, which superseded the Law "On Privatization," introduced a concept of "alienation of state property" and privatization is now regarded only as one type of alienation of state property. Thus, there are also other types of such alienation (e.g., transfer of property as a property contribution to the chartered capital of a limited liability partnership or as payment for the acquisition of shares of joint-stock companies; alienation of land plots; alienation of state property registered with the National Bank of RK; alienation of property that formed part of the state property for various reasons such as confiscation, contributions, escheat, etc.; and transfer of the state

7. This legal gap must certainly be filled as soon as possible as it leaves room for arbitrariness and the violation of an owner's rights during nationalization.

natural grant to private ownership). All provisions on privatization apply equally (without any exceptions) to foreign legal entities and natural persons.

Foreign investments, to which all types of property and titles thereto are related, are subjected to the regulation of the Law of RK of January 8, 2003 "On Investments." This Law establishes general provisions on investments and state guarantees that are provided by RK to foreign investors. It should also be noted that Kazakhstan acceded to many major international conventions in the area of investments (Seoul Convention establishing the Multilateral Investment Guarantee Agency of 1985, the Energy Charter Treaty of 1994, Washington Convention on the Settlement of Investment Disputes between States and Nationals of Other States of 1965) and concluded more than 40 bilateral agreements with other countries on promotion and mutual protection of investments.

VI. FOREIGN ECONOMIC CONTRACTS

A foreign economic contract is the same as a civil law contract, but the parties to it are located in different countries. The Civil Code does not contain any definition of a foreign economic contract, but it provides that such a contract must be concluded in written form if one of its participants is a Kazakhstani legal entity or a citizen (Article 1104 II CC) and that non-observance of this provision with respect to a foreign economic contract entails the contract's invalidity (Article 153 III CC).

The general connecting factor for this type of contract is *lex voluntaris* (Article 1112 CC). In the absence of *lex voluntaris*, *lex venditoris* is usually applied (Article 1113 I, IV CC). In addition, with respect to specific types of legal relations, the following connecting factors may apply: *lex rei sitae*, *lex loci activitis*, *lex loci actus*, *lex loci solutionis* and *proper law of contract*. Furthermore, *lex socieatatis* is applied regarding contracts that establish legal entities with foreign participation (Article 1114 CC). The latter rule met significant criticism by foreign investors (especially in cases involving legal entities exclusively made up of foreigners). Nevertheless, we kept[8] this norm and even strengthened it by applying it not only with respect to the establishment and termination of a legal entity, but also to the transfer of participation shares and other mutual relations between its participants (including those defined by subsequent agreements) (Article 1114 II CC).[9] These

8. See *supra* n. 2.
9. Presently, there is controversy surrounding the limits of applying Art. 1114 II CC. In particular, does this provision extend to the sale of the shares in a joint stock company if there is a transfer of a share of participation in a legal entity? For example, one of the shareholders of a joint-stock company that is registered as a joint venture in Kazakhstan sells its shares on the New York Stock Exchange. Does this mean that purchases and sales of shares, performed in New York, must be in compliance with the Kazakhstani law? The above article states that it applies to "the transfer of shares of participation and other relations between the participants of a legal entity related to their mutual rights and obligations." For example, when transferring a share of participation in a limited liability partnership, there are reciprocal rights and obligations between the party selling the share and other members of a partnership related to the implementation of the pre-emptive

provisions also apply in cases where other foundation documents establish the mutual rights and obligations of the participants in a legal entity with foreign participation (Article 1114 III CC).

Many international contracts (in particular related to transportation) are governed by international conventions and Kazakhstan is not an exception. Nevertheless, in this regard the following legislation should also be mentioned: Law of RK of January 17, 2002 "On Merchant Shipping," Law of RK of June 13, 2005 "On Currency Regulation and Currency Control," Law of RK of June 29, 1998 "On Payments and Money Transfers," Law of RK of April 28, 1997 "On Circulation of Bills in the Republic of Kazakhstan," Law of RK of December 15, 2000 "On Stamp Duty on Bills and Notes in the Republic of Kazakhstan," and Budget Code of RK of December 4, 2008 (in particular section XII "State and State-Guaranteed Borrowing and Debt as well as State Guarantee").

VII. INTELLECTUAL PROPERTY

Kazakhstan has acceded to almost every international conventions related to intellectual property. In addition, with regard to connecting factors, Kazakhstani legislation follows generally accepted international practice and applies *lex fori* (Article 1120 CC). As to domestic legislation, copyright and adjacent rights are regulated by the Civil Code of RK (Articles 971–983, 985–990) and the Law of RK of June 10, 1996 "On Copyright and Adjacent Rights."

Regarding copyright, there are the following three major provisions: (a) copyrights on the works of foreign authors first published on the territory of RK shall belong to those authors; (b) copyrights on works created by citizens of RK and published on the territory of the foreign state shall belong to those citizens; (c) copyrights on works first published on the territory of a foreign state shall belong to those foreigners in RK only upon the availability of an international treaty (Article 980 CC, Article 5 of the Copyright Law).

With respect to the sphere of effect of adjacent rights, the following rules are stipulated:

(1) The rights of the performer to a performance that has first taken place within the territory of RK shall be valid on the territory of Kazakhstan. In this case, the right shall be recognized as belonging to the performer and to

right to buy shares. But in selling shares of a joint-stock company, no mutual rights and obligations of the seller and the other shareholders arise. Other shareholders have no pre-emptive right to purchase shares. The purchaser of the stock shares takes the place of the seller and assumes the same rights and responsibilities as the former shareholder. One can draw an analogy with the re-registration of legal entities when its participant membership changes (a legal entity is subject to re-registration in cases of a change in participant membership in business partnerships (Art. 42 VI CC)). However, the change in membership of joint-stock companies do not require re-registration because the free sale of shares is the essence of the legal nature of a joint-stock company.

his heirs, as well as to other legal successors of the performer, irrespective of citizenship. The right of a Kazakhstani performer shall also be recognized as belonging to him in cases where the performance is first given within the territory of a foreign state, and equally to his legal successors.

(2) The rights of the creator of the recording of a performance shall be valid in the territory of Kazakhstan, if this recording was first publicly played back or its copies were publicly distributed in RK. The right of the producer of the recording shall be recognized as belonging to citizens of RK or legal entities that have their place of residence or place of location in the territory of Kazakhstan.

(3) The rights of an air or cable broadcasting organization shall be recognized as belonging to it in cases where the organization has its official location in the territory of RK and carries out the broadcasting with the help of transmitters located within the territory of RK.

(4) The rights of other foreign performers; producers of sound and performance recordings; and air and cable broadcasting organizations shall be protected on the territory of RK in accordance with international treaties of RK (Article 987 CC, Article 36 of the Copyright Law).

The main legislative acts with respect to industrial property are the Patent Law of RK of July 16, 1999 and the Law of RK of July 26, 1999 "On Trademarks, Service Marks and Appellations of Origin." Both acts (Article 38 of the Patent Law and Article 48 of the Law on Trademarks) extend national procedures to foreign citizens, foreign legal entities and stateless persons.

VIII. INTERNATIONAL LABOR LAW

In employment relations complicated by a foreign element, labor law applies either *lex loci laboris* (in most cases) or *lex voluntatis* as its connecting factor. The Labor Code of RK of May 15, 2007 stipulates that "the effects of this Code . . . shall apply to: (1) employees, including employees of organizations located on the territory of RK, owners of property, participants or shareholders that are foreign individuals or legal entities; (2) employers, including organizations located on the territory of RK, owners of property, participants or shareholders that are foreign individuals or legal entities" (Article 9 II). Thus, it is evident that Kazakhstan generally applies the principle of *lex loci laboris*.

The procedure for attracting foreign workers to Kazakhstan is determined by a number of laws and regulations, including the Law of RK of January 23, 2001 "On Employment"; the Law of RK of December 13, 1997 "On Migration"; the Regulations "On Determining Quotas as well as Conditions and Procedure for Issuing Permits to Employers for Attracting Foreign Labor to RK" approved by the Resolution of the Government of RK of June 19, 2001, No. 836; and the annual Resolutions of the Government of RK establishing quotas for attraction of foreign labor for the upcoming year. In order to attract foreign workers, an employer must obtain permission from the local governmental executive body in particular and afterwards enter into an individual employment contract with the foreign worker.

IX. INTERNATIONAL FAMILY LAW

There are two major legislative acts in this area: the Law of the RK of December 17, 1998 "On Marriage and Family" and the Law of RK of August 8, 2002 "On Rights of a Child." The main connecting factor to the conclusion of marriage (as well as to its termination or invalidation) is *lex loci celebrations*, although the conditions of the conclusion of marriage may also be determined by *lex nationalis* or *lex patriae* (Articles 200–204 LMF).

Of great significance are also legal issues related to adoption (Article 209 LMF). The procedure for the adoption of children who are citizens of RK by foreigners has a number of conditions. Adoption is permitted only in those cases where it is not possible to transfer these children to the care of citizens of RK or the child's relatives, regardless of their citizenship and place of residence. The foreigners applying to adopt a child are required to personally choose a child; to have direct contact with him for at least two weeks; to submit a written statement testifying to their will to adopt the child to the relevant Trusteeship and Guardianship Agency; and to present information to the Agency verifying their financial solvency, marital status, health status and moral qualities (confirmed by agencies licensed to provide such services) (Article 76 LMF).

X. PRIVATE PROCEDURAL LAW

Though many disagree,[10] international civil procedure, as it is public in nature, should not be considered a part of PIL.[11] Instead of international civil procedure, PIL should include as its fundamental component international law of alternative dispute-settlement or, in other words, private international procedural law. Private international procedural law should consist of three major institutions: (a) negotiation; (b) mediation; and (c) arbitration.

Negotiation as a means of dispute resolution is still rarely applied in Kazakhstan, although it is increasingly common in relations with foreign partners. In contrast, mediation has achieved some progress. On January 28, 2011 the Law of RK "On Mediation" was adopted; it defines mediation as a procedure for

10. Those views are reflected in the fact that many PIL textbooks include a chapter on international civil procedure.
11. Thus, we will not consider issues related to international civil procedure in this chapter and will only note that the Civil Procedure Code of RK of July 13, 1999 contains section V called "International Procedure" (which, in turn, includes Chapter 45 "Proceedings in Cases with the Participation of Foreign Persons"; Chapter 45-1 "Proceedings in Cases of Appealing Arbitration Decisions"; and Chapter 46 "Jurisdictional Immunity of a Foreign State and Its Property").

resolving disputes (conflicts) between parties through the assistance of a mediator (mediators) with the aim of achieving a mutually acceptable solution that will be implemented by the voluntary agreement of the parties (Article 2). However, the most considerable development was enjoyed by another type of dispute resolution, international commercial arbitration (ICA). ICA is conducted on the basis of the Law of RK of December 28, 2004, No. 23, "On International Commercial Arbitration."[12] On the whole, this law meets the standards of international practice and, in particular, the provisions of the UNCITRAL Model Law on International Commercial Arbitration of June 21, 1985. In addition, it should be noted that RK is a signatory to the New York Convention on the Recognition and Enforcement of Foreign Arbitral Awards of June 10, 1958. That Convention requires Kazakhstan to enforce final arbitral awards (unless an Article V exception applies) and the courts of RK are prohibited from reviewing the final award on its merits.[13]

Selected Bibliography

M. Sarsembayev, *Международное частное право* [*Private International Law*] (Daneker, Almaty, 1998) [in Russian].

M. Suleimenov (ed.), *Право и внешнеэкономическая деятельность в Республике Казахстан* [*Law and External Economic Activity in the Republic of Kazakhstan*] (KazGYuA, Almaty, 2001) [in Russian].

M. Suleymenov, "Private International Law as Part of the Legal System of the Republic of Kazakhstan" (2001) 8 *The Journal of East European Law* 35.

M. Suleimenov, "Международное частное право в системе права" ["Private International Law in the System of Law"], in M. Suleimenov (ed.), *Гражданское право в системе права* [*Civil Law in the System of Law*] (KazGYuU, Almaty, 2007) [in Russian].

M. Suleimenov, *Актуальные проблемы международного частного права* [*Modern Problems of Private International Law*] (KOU, Almaty, 2011) [in Russian].

---

12. It should be noted that simultaneously the Law of RK of December 28, 2004, No. 22-3, "On Arbitral Tribunals" was adopted. The difference between international commercial arbitration and arbitral tribunals consists in the issue whether disputing parties are residents of Kazakhstan. All disputes between the residents of RK are considered by an arbitral tribunal, whereas the disputes involving non-residents are considered by the international commercial arbitration (Art. 6 IV of the Law on International Commercial Arbitration).
13. Editor's note: For more information see also Chapter 12 "Civil Procedure."

Chapter 12
Civil Procedure

Roman Nurpeissov

I. INTRODUCTION

A. Sources, Purposes and Principles of Civil Procedure

The rules of civil procedure are primarily contained in the Civil Procedure Code of RK of July 13, 1999, No. 441-I (CPC), which is based on the Constitution and generally accepted principles and norms of international law (Article 2 I CPC).[1] The CPC must also be in compliance with constitutional laws of RK (Article 3 II).[2] In addition, international treaties and other obligations of RK and regulatory resolutions of the Constitutional Council and the Supreme Court of RK may also be recognized as components of civil procedure (Article 2 II).

The Code defines three major purposes of civil litigation: (1) to protect infringed or contested rights, freedoms and lawful interests of citizens, the state and organizations; (2) to strengthen law and order; and (3) to prevent civil violations (Article 5). To achieve the above purposes, the CPC sets forth the following

1. Hereinafter all references are to the CPC unless explicitly indicated otherwise.
2. Editor's Note: An example includes the Constitutional Law of RK of December 25, 2000, No. 132-II, "On the Judicial System and the Status of Judges." See also *infra* n. 6.

Zhenis Kembayev, *Introduction to the Law of Kazakhstan*, pp. 211–229.

principles of civil litigation, the violation of which may result in reversal of judicial decisions or orders (Article 23):

Principle of Legality: This principle means that courts should follow the Constitution, the Code and other laws during hearings; judicial orders and decisions violating the law will be reversed. Should a court believe that a given law infringes upon constitutionally guaranteed rights and freedoms, it must suspend the case and raise the issue with the Constitutional Council (Article 78 CRK). The court may proceed with the case only after receiving the Constitutional Council's decision. If there is no provision in the law that governs the specific dispute at issue, the court applies the law that governs similar situations. Should that be impossible, the court must solve the dispute based on the general principles of law (Article 6).

Administration of Justice Only by Courts and Obligatoriness of Judicial Decisions: The misappropriation of the power and authority of the court by anyone will entail judicial liability (Article 7 I).[3] Also, the establishment of special and extraordinary courts under any name shall not be allowed (Article 75 IV CRK). Furthermore, if a given court heard a case in violation of its jurisdiction, its decision shall be illegal and subject to reversal. Likewise, only specifically authorized courts may hear appeals.

Kazakhstani courts do not render advisory opinions. Judicial acts that have entered in force are mandatory for all state organs, local self-government bodies, legal entities and individuals and must be unconditionally followed throughout the territory of RK. Failure to comply with judicial acts entails administrative and/or criminal liability (Article 21).

Protection of Rights, Freedoms and Lawful Interests of Persons: This principle includes many essential provisions, which are stipulated both in the Constitution of RK and the CPC. *First*, everyone has the right to protect his rights and freedoms with all means not contradicting the law (Article 13 I CRK). *Second*, everyone has the right to inviolability of private life, personal or family secrets, protection of honor and dignity (Article 18 I CRK). In particular, everyone has the right to maintain the secrecy of his personal savings and investments, letter exchanges, telephone conversations, posts, telegraphs and other communications. *Third*, no one is obliged to testify against oneself, one's spouse or one's close relatives. An imam (priest, etc.) is not obliged to testify against someone who confided in them during the confession (Article 77 III CRK). Furthermore, everyone has the right to qualified legal representation (Article 13 III CRK).

Also, the Constitution of RK guarantees everyone the right to use his native language and to freely choose the language of communication (Article 19 II CRK). Although civil litigation is conducted in either Kazakh or Russian,[4] individuals

3. This principle, however, does not prohibit arbitration. The parties may agree to arbitrate and the resulting arbitral awards are enforceable in Kazakhstan (see section on enforcement of arbitral awards *infra*).
4. The language of the proceeding is set by the court's order based on the language of the filed complaint. Once set, the language of the proceeding of a given matter cannot be altered.

participating in a hearing who do not speak the language in which the hearing is conducted can receive explanations in their language as to their procedural rights (e.g., how to make statements, provide testimony and evidence, file petitions and complaints, review the case materials and use free translator services). In addition, the CPC also provides that court documents must be issued to the parties together with a translation into their native language or into another language of which they have command (Article 14).

Equality of Everyone before the Law and the Court and the Adversarial Nature of Litigation: During court proceedings no person may be treated preferentially or discriminated against on the basis of their origin, social or official status, sex, race, ethnicity, language, faith, beliefs, residence or any other criteria. Likewise, legal entities may not be treated preferentially or discriminated against on the basis of their residence, organizational or ownership form or any other criteria (Article 13). Accordingly, the parties to a civil dispute enjoy equal rights and bear equal obligations. They may independently choose their positions and the means of supporting them.[5] The court must be impartial and treat the parties with equal respect (Article 15).

Independence of Judges: When administering justice, a judge must be independent and subordinate only to the law. Cases must be settled under conditions that exclude any outside influence on judges. Any interference with the activity of the court is prohibited and entails judicial liability in accordance with the law (Article 12). Also, a judge must assess evidence on the basis of his intrinsic conviction (inner belief) based on an impartial, comprehensive and fully-considered review of the evidence available for the case in its entirety. A judge must be guided only by the law and his conscience; and no evidence has a predetermined force for the court (Article 16).

Transparency: As a general rule, judicial proceedings at all levels of courts are open to the public (except for individuals younger than 16 years old unless they are parties or witnesses). Closed hearings are conducted only on the basis of a judge's order to that effect in cases involving state secrets or certain sensitive matters (e.g., matters of intimate character).

In an open hearing personal written communications, photographs, audio and video recordings and any other messages generated via any technical means may be disclosed only upon the consent of the individuals involved. Parties to a dispute and individuals present at an open court hearing may make written or audio recordings of the hearing while video recording, radio or TV transmission are allowed only with court's permission (Article 19).

Since open hearings may attract many people, the CPC also contains a provision saying that court hearings must take place in conditions that ensure the court's normal operation and the security of the parties. In order to ensure safety, a judge may order a screening of the individuals wishing to watch the

5. The court is free from the burden of collecting evidence, i.e., it does not act as a fact-finder. A party, however, may motion the court to assist it in obtaining the requisite evidence (e.g., if the other party has blocked access to it).

hearing, which may include an identity check, a pat-down and/or an inspection of the items they are carrying (Article 20).

Freedom to Appeal Judicial Decisions and Orders during the Court Proceedings: Judicial decisions and orders may be appealed to a higher court (Article 22).

B. Jurisdiction

Subject-matter jurisdiction: Trial courts may hear any cases, including those ensuing from civil (including corporate disputes), family, labor, housing, administrative, financial, business, land, environmental and other legal relations (Article 24 II). The courts also adjudicate cases involving foreign citizens and legal entities and international organizations, unless an international treaty of RK, the legislation or an agreement of the parties stipulates otherwise (Article 24 VI).[6]

The CPC also regulates the subordination of civil cases to specialized courts. Thus, specialized inter-district economic courts hear property and non-property-related disputes in which the parties are individual entrepreneurs and legal entities (including corporate disputes) (Article 30 I). Specialized district administrative courts consider cases challenging the resolutions of the state organs or officials that are authorized to handle administrative violation cases (Article 30 I-I). Military courts hear cases involving military personnel (Article 30 I-II). Specialized inter-district juvenile courts hear cases on adoption, guardianship, determination of a child's place of residence, abolishment/limitation or reinstatement of parent's rights, etc. (Article 30 I-III).

Personal jurisdiction: The general rule is that the plaintiff files his complaint with the court closest to the defendant's dwelling. If the defendant is a legal entity, the claim is filed with the closest court to the legal entity's location (Article 31). If more than one court has personal jurisdiction to hear the case, then it is up to the plaintiff where to file, except for the cases of exclusive jurisdiction addressed below (Article 32 XI).

Exclusive jurisdiction: Complaints involving rights to land, buildings and other immovable property or those requesting a release of seized property are filed in the district where such immovable or seized property is located. Complaints by a testator's creditors—if they are filed before the heirs acquire the concerned property—are heard by courts located in the district where the property or its main part is located. Complaints against carriers of passengers, cargo or luggage are filed in the district where the carrier's permanent place of business is located (Article 33).

6. However, the courts cannot hear certain cases under the Constitutional Law of RK of September 28, 1995, No. 2464, "On Elections in the Republic of Kazakhstan" and the Constitutional Law of RK of November 2, 1995, No. 2592, "On the Republican Referendum" (e.g., the courts cannot decide on a refusal of the Central Elections Commission to register an individual as a candidate for the post of the President of RK) (Art. 27). Instead, those cases fall under the jurisdiction of the Supreme Court of RK.

Contractual jurisdiction: The parties may, upon their agreement, change the territorial jurisdiction of their future potential dispute. The parties, however, cannot contractually change the exclusive jurisdiction described above (Article 34).

C. Composition of the Court

Civil cases in trial and appellate courts are heard by a single judge (Article 37 I). Cassation and supervisory panels (at the Supreme Court) must have an odd number of judges, with three being the minimum (Article 37 II). Usually, there are three judges on a cassation panel and five judges on a supervisory panel. A panel is headed by a Chairman; however, all judges have equal rights (Article 38 I). All judges vote on the issues under consideration (with the chairman always voting last) and the majority's opinion prevails. None of the judges may abstain from voting.

A judge who disagrees with the majority's decision should nevertheless sign the panel's resolution but may write a dissent, called a "special opinion" (Article 38 III). The special opinion is attached to the case materials in a sealed envelope and only the supervisory panel's judges may read it. In other words, the special opinion is not announced in court and the parties to the case are unaware of its existence.

D. Court Recusals

A judge may not participate in the adjudication of a case and must be subject to recusal if: (1) he participated in the preceding adjudication of a given case (as a witness, expert, specialist, translator, counsel, secretary of the court session, court enforcement officer or bailiff); (2) he is a relative of one of the persons participating in the case or their representatives; (3) he is personally directly or indirectly interested in the outcome of the case; or (4) there are other circumstances that cause reasonable doubt with regard to his impartiality (Article 40 I).

A party may challenge a judge (or any other state participants of the case including the procurator) at the beginning of the litigation, before the judge starts hearing the parties' arguments. Later challenges and self-recusals are allowed if the challenging party became aware of the disqualifying grounds after the judge started hearing the case on the merits. In the event of a recusal (or self-recusal) of the judge adjudicating a case in a trial court, that case is adjudicated in the same court by another judge. If the replacement of a judge becomes impossible, a case may be transferred to a different court by a higher court (Article 43 I).

E. Participants of a Civil Case and Their Representatives

Participants of civil litigation include: (a) the parties to a dispute; (b) third parties claiming their rights to the disputed subject-matter; (c) third parties claiming no rights to the disputed subject-matter;[7] (d) the procurator; (e) authorized state organs; and other participants.

All of them enjoy broad rights that they must exercise in good faith. These rights include, but are not limited to: (a) familiarizing themselves with the case materials and making copies of them; (b) making motions and challenges; (c) producing and reviewing evidence and making motions to obtain additional evidence; (d) making verbal and written statements to the court; (e) making arguments as to all issues arising during the hearings; (f) voicing objections to the motions and arguments of other participants; (g) familiarizing themselves with the record of proceedings and making written notices to the court with respect to its accuracy; and (h) appealing judicial decisions and orders (Article 47 I).

Parties to a Dispute: The parties to a civil dispute are the plaintiff (party that filed a civil complaint or on whose behalf the complaint was filed) and the defendant (the party against whom the complaint was filed) (Article 48 I).[8] Parties may be individuals, legal entities (including branches and representative offices) or the state (Article 48 II). They enjoy equal procedural rights and bear equal procedural obligations (Article 48 V).

Before a trial court issues its decision, the plaintiff may change the grounds of his complaint, increase or decrease his amount of claims or withdraw his complaint by filing a written statement with the specific demand (Article 49 I). At any time during the hearing, the defendant may acknowledge the complaint in writing, i.e., admit to its allegations. The parties may also settle their dispute by signing a settlement, which the court then approves. The court, however, will not accept a plaintiff's withdrawal of his complaint or a defendant's admission of the complaint and will not approve a settlement if the withdrawal, admission or settlement violates someone's rights, freedoms or lawful interests (Article 49 II).

Procurator: The procurator's participation is necessary in the following cases: (1) when the state's interests are affected and the procurator was the party that initiated the case; (2) in certain labor disputes (e.g., involving non-payment of labor compensation and maternity allowances); (3) in eviction cases; and (4) in tort claims for damage caused to individual's life or health (Article 55 II). Also, a procurator may enter into the process upon his initiative for the protection of the rights, freedoms and legitimate interests of citizens, as well as the rights and legitimate interests of organizations or public or state interests.

Parties' Representatives: Individuals may handle their cases in the court personally or through representatives (Article 58 I). Legal entities may be represented by their management and/or directors or other employees authorized by their charters or by outside professional counsel (Article 58 II). Representatives must have a duly authenticated (usually notarized) power of attorney to represent a party

7. These are the participants whose rights or obligations toward one of the parties to a dispute may be affected by the outcome of the case.
8. Cases involving multiple plaintiffs or defendants are possible. The parties may authorize one plaintiff or one defendant to represent the others on their behalf in a given dispute (Art. 50).

in court unless their authorities are based on a legal entity's charter or a legislative, judicial or administrative act.

The CPC does not generally allow judges, state investigators, procurators or deputies of the Parliament or "Maslikhats" (local representative bodies) to be representatives in court except when they represent the interests of their respective state organs or act in private capacity. A person cannot act as a party's representative if he formerly rendered or is rendering legal assistance to such party's adversary; participated in the same case as a judge, procurator, expert, specialist, interpreter or witness; or if he is a relative of an official participating in the consideration of the case (Article 60).

F. Costs of Litigation and Procedural Terms

Litigation costs include the state filing duty and costs associated with conducting the hearings. The state filing duty depends on the type of complaint filed and may either be calculated as a percentage of the complaint's amount or set in the so-called MCIs (Article 101).[9] Certain categories of plaintiffs are relieved from paying the state filing duty (Article 104).

The losing party must cover the prevailing party's expenses; including attorney's fees. If the court partially satisfies the complaint, the litigation costs shall be distributed between plaintiff and defendant in proportion to their respective prevailing claims (Article 110 I).

Procedural deadlines are set by the law; if the law does not specify a term within which the parties must perform their procedural acts, the court sets the deadline (Article 123). The term begins on the day that follows the calendar date of the event that initiated the term; any procedural act must be performed by 12:00 AM (24:00) of the last day of the set term (Article 125 II). Missing the deadline entails unfavorable consequences. If, for instance, a party files its appeal after the deadline, the court will not accept it, unless the party simultaneously motions the court to disregard the fact that the deadline has expired (Article 126 I). The court will grant the motion and accept the party's appeal only if it finds the moving party's excuse for missing the deadline acceptable (Article 128 II).

G. Stages of Civil Procedure

The CPC provides the following stages of civil procedure. The *first* stage is institution of a civil case by way of filing a complaint in the courts of first instance (trial courts)[10] (see section II *infra*). *Second*, a trial court's decision can be appealed with

9. In this regard, the Tax Code of RK lists the rates of various types of state duty collected in courts (Art. 535 TC). See "List of Abbreviations" for an explanation of the concept of MCI.
10. Courts of first instance (trial courts) are district and various "specialized" courts (e.g., specialized inter-district economic courts, specialized district administrative courts, specialized inter-district juvenile courts and the Specialized Financial Court of Almaty).

the respective appellate court (see section III *infra*). *Third*, the appellate court's resolution can be further appealed to the pertinent cassation panel (see section IV *infra*). *Fourth*, an aggrieved party may file its petition with the Supreme Court of RK, requesting it to reconsider the case in the supervisory manner (see section V A *infra*). *Fifth*, in very rare instances, the ruling of the Supreme Court's supervisory panel can further be appealed to the plenary session of the Supreme Court (see section V B *infra*). *Finally*, there may be also the stage of resumption of the proceedings on account of the newly revealed circumstances (see section VI *infra*).

II. PROCEEDINGS AT THE TRIAL COURT

A. Filing the Complaint

The plaintiff's written complaint may be filed either in paper or electronic form.[11] It must also include a number of attachments, important information and the plaintiff's motions, if any. Within five days of the complaint's filing, a judge must rule on the issue of rejecting,[12] returning,[13] suspending[14] or accepting the complaint. If the judge accepts the complaint, he issues a ruling on initiating the civil case (Article 152).

B. Preparation of the Case to the Hearing and Defendant's Answer

Within seven days of filing the complaint, the judge prepares the matter for the hearing (Article 167)[15] and performs various procedural acts (including sending a subpoena together with a copy of the complaint to defendant). After receiving the

11. Any complaint must state, *inter alia*, the following: (1) the gist of the violation or threat to the plaintiff's rights, freedoms or lawful interests and the relief sought; (2) arguments on which the plaintiff's claims are based and evidence supporting these arguments; and (3) value of the complaint if it is subject to valuation (Art. 150 II).
12. The complaint is rejected if: (1) it cannot be considered and solved via civil litigation; or (2) it was already considered by another court (which issued a decision regarding the same dispute or ruled to cease the proceedings). Refusal to accept an application prevents a repeated petition of the applicant to the court against the same defendant, on the same subject matter and bases. The ruling on rejecting the complaint may be appealed to a higher court (Art. 153).
13. The complaint is returned if, e.g.: (1) the plaintiff did not follow the mandatory procedure of pre-trial settlement of the dispute and the possibility of such settlement still exists; or (2) the court does not have jurisdiction to hear the case. In this event, the judge passes a motivated ruling indicating what court the applicant must petition or how to eliminate the circumstances which impede the institution of a case. The ruling may be appealed to the higher court (Art. 154).
14. The complaint is suspended if it does not satisfy one of the requirements listed in footnotes 14 and 15. A judge may set a deadline for the plaintiff to correct the deficiencies. The ruling may be appealed to the higher court (Art. 155).
15. In exceptional cases, the term of preparation may be extended to one month (e.g., exacting alimonies) (Art. 167).

summons with a copy of the plaintiff's complaint, the defendant should file his signed (by him or his representative) answer. The defendant's failure to file his answer does not prevent the court from proceeding to hearing the case on the merits (Article 169 II). At any time before the court issues its decision, the defendant may also file a counter-claim to be reviewed jointly with the plaintiff's complaint (Article 156).[16]

C. Summons

Participants of a civil dispute and their representatives, as well as witnesses, experts and interpreters (if any) must be notified of the time and place of the judicial hearing or other procedural events (Article 129). Judicial subpoenas must be sent in advance, so that the sought party has ample time to prepare for the case and appear in court. Subpoenas are served on the defendant together with a copy of the plaintiff's complaint and any other documents that were attached to the complaint (Article 130 II). Subpoenas served on the plaintiff must contain a copy of the defendant's answer and any other documents attached thereto.

Subpoenas must be served personally on a party and, if a party is a legal entity, then on its representative or appropriate person who performs managerial functions (Article 132 I). If the intended addressee is absent from his place of residence or employment then the serving party may leave the subpoena with adults living together with the missing individual upon their consent, or with the respective local administration (the housing maintenance organization, body of local self-government or the executive body). The person who accepted a subpoena must, at the nearest opportunity, hand it to the addressee without delay. A party's refusal to accept the subpoena does not prevent the court from considering the case or commissioning procedural acts (Article 133 II).

D. Injunctive Relief

Upon a party's motion, the court may take measures to "secure the claim" via injunctions (Article 158). Injunctions are allowed at any stage of the case where omission of such measures may impede or make impossible the implementation of the court decision. They may provide for the following types of restrictions: (1) seizure of the defendant's property and/or money; (2) ban on defendant's certain activity; (3) ban on the transfer of property to the defendant or the performing of

16. The defendant's counter-claim is accepted and reviewed if: (1) it is aimed at offset of the initial claim; (2) its satisfaction excludes in full or in part the satisfaction of the initial lawsuit; and (3) there is a mutual connection between the counter-claim and the initial lawsuit and their joint consideration will facilitate the proceedings (Art. 157).

other obligations with respect to the defendant by other parties;[17] (4) suspension of the ongoing sale of property if the complainant asks to lift the lien on certain property; (5) suspension of a given disputed act of a state body, organization or official; (6) suspension of collection measures under the disputed document; and other restraining measures (Article 159 I).

The motion for injunctive relief is reviewed within a day of it being filed without notifying the defendant or other participants of the case (Article 160). Having reviewed the motion, the judge may issue an order granting or denying it. The ordered injunction must be commensurate to the plaintiff's claims (Article 159 III). The order granting the motion is effective immediately and is enforced in the same way as judicial decisions (Article 161). The aggrieved party may appeal the order with the appellate court (Article 164 I); however, the injunction's effect will not be suspended during the appeal period (Article 164 III). In addition, the court may require the plaintiff to post security for the defendant's potential loss as a result of the sought injunction (Article 165).

E. EVIDENCE

Evidence is the legally acquired factual data that the court uses to determine the presence or absence of circumstances supporting the parties' claims and counterclaims as well as other conditions that bear on the case's correct resolution (Article 64 I). These factual data are determined through the testimony of the parties, third parties and witnesses; items; expert conclusions; records of procedural actions; and judicial hearings and other documents (Article 64 II).

Each party is responsible for proving the circumstances it refers to as the basis for its claims or counterclaims (Article 65). When it is problematic to produce certain evidence, the concerned party may motion the court to assist it in acquiring the sought evidence (Article 66 IV). Should the court believe the sought evidence is needed, it issues a demand that obliges the evidence holder to present the evidence to the court. If the evidence holder refuses to present the evidence, he may be arraigned either to administrative or (in the case of malicious non-execution) to criminal liability. Also, if a party to the case refuses to produce evidence that the court demanded, it is assumed that the data the evidence contains are against such party's interests, and the party is deemed as having admitted those (Article 66 X).

Any offered evidence must be relevant (i.e., be comprised of factual data that prove, disprove, weaken or strengthen the arguments related to circumstances that have a bearing on the case), admissible (i.e., acquired by lawful means)[18] and

17. Disobeying injunctions (2) and (3) entails administrative liability. Moreover, the plaintiff may claim damages stemming from such violations (Art. 159 II).
18. Examples of inadmissible evidence include (but are not limited to) those acquired through violence, assault, deceit, substantial violation of procedural rights, those acquired from an unknown or unidentifiable source or those acquired via the application of methods that contradict the current state of modern scientific knowledge (Art. 69 I).

trustworthy (i.e., consistent with the reality). Each piece of evidence must be evaluated by court from the point of view of relevance, admissibility and reliability and all collected evidence together must be sufficient for the settlement of the civil case (Article 77).

F. Judicial Orders without a Hearing

In the following instances, courts may issue orders without holding a formal hearing: when a claim is based on, *inter alia*, (1) a notarized transaction; (2) a transaction in writing that is recognized by the defendant; (3) exacting alimony for juvenile children, if the case is not associated with the establishment of fatherhood or the need to engage third parties; (4) exacting arrears in respect to taxes or other obligatory payments; (5) exacting wages and other payments accrued but not paid to the employee; and (6) imposing a demand upon a pledged item (when a claim is filed by a pawn-shop against a debtor-pledger) (Article 140).

After the order is issued, its copy is immediately forwarded to the defendant (Article 147 I). Within 10 days of receiving the order, the debtor (or a third party affected by the order) may file his objections to the order with the court. If the debtor or a third party does not file his objections within 10 days of receiving the order, the court mails an authenticated copy of the order to the creditor for the latter to enforce it (Article 149 I). Alternatively, the creditor may ask the court to enforce the order (Article 149 II). If the debtor or a third party contests the order, the court cancels it (Article 148 I). Within three days, the court notifies the parties that the order is cancelled and that the creditor may file his formal complaint to be heard as part of the regular trial process.

G. The Hearing

As a rule, civil cases must be considered and settled within a period up to two months from the date of completing the preparation of the case for the court trial. The case is heard by a single judge in all trial courts (Article 37 I). The judge performs the duties of the chairman during the hearing, and his orders are mandatory for all other participants (Article 176).

Opening the hearing: The judge opens the hearing and announces what civil dispute is to be considered. He then establishes the identity of those who are present and reviews the authority of the official persons and the representatives. Subsequently, the judge announces the membership of the court; communicates who is participating as the procurator, expert, specialist, secretary of the court session and bailiff; explains to the participating persons their procedural rights; and asks whether the parties are willing to make any motions.

The adjudication of a case begins with the clarification by the judge of the issues, of whether the plaintiff sustains his claims and whether the defendant recognizes the claims of the plaintiff and of whether the parties wish to settle the case by a reconciliation agreement or to pass the case to a third-party tribunal for consideration (Article 192). If the plaintiff withdraws his complaint in full, the defendant admits the plaintiff's complaint in full, or the parties have reached a settlement agreement or have decided to arbitrate, the court explains to the parties the legal consequences of their acts. If the plaintiff confirms his complaint (or withdraws only some of his claims) and if the defendant does not admit the plaintiff's claims (or admits only some of them) and the parties do not wish to settle or arbitrate, the court continues to hear the case (Article 193).

Opening statements of the parties: The court first hears the plaintiff's (or his representative's) explanations with respect to the case. Then the defendant (or his representative) states his position. The court may interrupt the speakers and ask questions. The parties may also ask questions of each other during and after their respective presentations (following the court's call to ask questions). Having listened to the parties explanations, the judge invites witnesses and experts (if any) to testify and reviews any other produced evidence (Article 195).

Witness testimony: Before a witness testifies, the judge warns him of criminal liability for his refusal to testify or for a false testimony (Article 196 I).[19] Then the judge clarifies the attitude of the witness to the persons who participate in the case and requests the witness to communicate to the court all that he personally knows about the case (Article 197 II). The judge may ask questions of the witness at any time. A questioned witness must remain in the court session room until the end of the trial of the case, unless the court allows him to retire earlier. Where needed, the court may ask two or more witnesses to testify simultaneously, in order to clarify contradictions in their testimonies.[20]

Investigation of Documents: Any documents or items produced during the hearing must be provided to all participants for their review and comments (Articles 201, 203). However, the contents of any written correspondence, telegraph message or audio or video recording may be revealed in court only upon the consent of the individuals involved in such correspondence or messaging or depicted in the recordings. Without that consent, the contents of these communications and recordings may be revealed only during a closed hearing (Article 202). After examining all evidence the judge asks the participants and their representatives whether they want to add anything to the materials of the case. If there are no such statements, he announces that the trial of the case is over, and the court proceeds to oral arguments.

Oral arguments and rebuttals: During the oral arguments, the plaintiff or his representative speaks first (Article 211 II). In his argument, the plaintiff essentially reiterates his position as stated during his prior opening statement, but also adds anything that he deems pertinent in light of defendant's opening statement, their

19. A witness must also take an oath and sign a statement that the court explained to him his obligations and liability (the statement is attached to the record of the court proceedings).
20. Essentially the same rules apply to experts' testimony (Art. 206).

subsequent exchange of questions and answers, the expert or witness testimonies and other evidence that has been offered during the hearing. The defendant or his representative states his argument after the plaintiff. In their oral arguments, the parties may not make reference to circumstances that were not ascertained by the court or to evidence that was not examined during the court session, unless they mentioned those circumstances and evidence in their statements prior to the adjudication of the case (Article 214 I).

After the oral arguments are over, the parties are allowed to rebut each other's arguments (Article 212). The right of last rebuttal belongs to the defendant. If a procurator participates in a dispute but is not a party to it, he must give his evaluation of the case (as to whom, in his opinion, the court should rule for) after the oral arguments, and rebuttals are over (Article 213).

Announcement of the court's decision: After the rebuttals and the procurator's evaluation, the judge leaves the courtroom to rule on the matter (Article 215). The judge lets the participants know the date and time at which he will announce his decision. On the agreed date, the judge signs the decision and announces it to the parties. He must also inform the parties on when they or their representatives may get a copy of the decision, let them know of their right to appeal the decision and explain to them the proper order of filing their appeals. Finally, the judge announces that the trial is thus over.

H. Court's Decision and Its Enforcement

The court's decision must be well-grounded and be based only on evidence reviewed during the trial (Article 218). The decision consists of four parts: introductory, descriptive, declaratory and operative (Article 221 II). The introductory part contains basic information about the case (e.g., the date of the decision) and the disputed issue. The descriptive part includes the plaintiff's claims, the defendant's counterarguments and any explanations of third parties participating in the case. The declaratory part deals with the circumstances of the case the court established; evidence on which the court bases its opinion; the court's arguments as to why it rejects certain evidence; and the law that the court applied. Finally, the operative part provides the court's opinion as to satisfying the complaint's claims or denying them fully or partially; the distribution of judicial expenses; the period and procedure for appealing the decision; and any other pertinent statements.

A party may appeal the court's decision within 15 calendar days after the decision was handed to the party (Article 334 III). If the party does not appeal the decision within this term, the decision becomes enforceable and may only be appealed in supervisory manner with the Supreme Court within one year of the date of its announcement (Article 388 I). After the decision enters in force, the judge fills in the enforcement paper and hands it either to the prevailing party or to the respective state enforcement agency (Article 236 II). The state enforcement agency must notify the court within 10 days after the enforcement of the court's decision or let the court know the reasons for its failure to enforce the decision (Article 236 VI).[21]

At the plaintiff's request, the court may enforce its decision immediately where any delay may lead to either the impossibility of the decision's implementation or to material losses for the exactor (Article 238 I). The order on immediate enforcement of the decision may be appealed with a higher court. Therefore, the court may ask the plaintiff to provide some collateral as a security in case the court's decision is later reversed (Article 238 II). Pursuant to a petition of the court enforcement officer or an application of parties, the court may postpone or provide an installment plan for the implementation of the court resolution.

Should an individual or legal entity refuse to comply with the court's decision, such failure entails administrative[22] or criminal liability[23]. Imposition of administrative or criminal liability does not relieve them from their obligation to comply with the court's decision.[24]

III. PROCEEDINGS AT THE APPELLATE COURT

If a party is dissatisfied with the decision of the trial court, it may appeal it with the appellate court within 15 calendar days from the date of receiving the trial court's decision (Article 334 III). A party may appeal the trial court's decision if it believes that the trial court: (1) incorrectly defined the circle of circumstances having a bearing on the case; (2) failed to substantiate its conclusions with proper evidence; (3) made wrong conclusions that do not correspond to the circumstances of the case; or (4) violated or incorrectly applied substantive[25] or procedural law[26] (Article 364 I).

The appeal together with any attachments is usually filed with the trial court (Article 334 I), which then transfers the case to the appellate court (Article 338 I). Having received the appeal, the appellate judge must, within 10 calendar days, schedule the case for an appellate hearing (Article 348 I). As a rule, the appellant

21. The following decisions are subject to immediate implementation: (1) those awarding alimony; (2) those awarding a maximum of three months' wages to an employee; (3) those demanding restoration of an individual's employment; (4) those awarding compensation for harm caused by injury or any other harm to health as well as for the loss of the breadwinner, but only for a maximum of three months' worth of compensation; (5) those recognizing a strike as unlawful; and (6) those restructuring financial legal entities (Art. 237).
22. Code of RK of January 30, 2001, No. 155-II, "On Administrative Violations" (Art. 524).
23. Criminal Code of RK of July 16, 1997, No. 167-I (Art. 362).
24. Law of RK of April 2, 2010, No. 261-IV, "On the Enforcement Process and Status of Judicial Enforcers" (Art. 125).
25. The rules of the substantial law are violated or incorrectly applied if the court: (1) did not apply the law that is to be applied; (2) applied a law which is not subject to be applied; (3) incorrectly interpreted the law; or (4) incorrectly applied analogy of law or analogy of right (Art. 365).
26. Procedural law is violated if, e.g., the case was considered by a judge who has no right to consider that case or the case was considered by a court in the absence of one of participants who was not notified of the time and place of court session (Art. 366).

may not submit new evidence. If, however, he demonstrates that he had no opportunity to present additional facts during the trial, the appellate court may examine new evidence (Articles 345, 355). The appellee has the right to file written objections to appellate complaints (or protests) and attach documents that confirm those objections. The court then notifies the parties of the date of appellate hearing (Article 348 II).

The appellate judge must consider the case and issue his decision within one month from the date when the appellate court received the appeal (Article 349). The appellate hearing in many respects mirrors the trial court's hearing in that the appellate court hears the parties' opening statements, witnesses (if any), oral arguments and rebuttals (Articles 351–356).

Having heard the parties' arguments, the appellate court issues its resolution in which it may: (1) uphold the trial court's decision (thereby dismissing the appeal); (2) amend the trial court's decision; (3) abolish the trial court's decision and pass a new decision; (4) abolish the trial court's decision and send a case for a new adjudication to the trial court in the case of establishing violations of the rules of the material or procedural law; or (5) abolish the trial court's decision fully or partially and terminate proceedings with respect to this case (Article 358).

IV. PROCEEDINGS AT THE CASSATION PANEL

If a party is dissatisfied with the resolution of the appellate court, it may appeal it further to the cassation panel (*kassatsionnaya instantsiya*) within 15 calendar days from the date of receiving the appellate court's resolution (Article 383-4 I). The cassation appeal, along with its attachments, must be filed with the cassation panel, which then calls up the case from the appellate court (Article 383-3). The cassation panel consists of at least three judges (Article 383-2). It hears the cassation appeal and passes its resolution within one month from the date when the panel received the appeal (Article 383-14). The other party may file his objections to the cassation appeal (Article 383-9 I). The cassation panel then informs the parties about the date and time of the upcoming cassation hearing (Article 383-7). The panel's Chairman opens the cassation hearing (Article 383-15 I), and then one of the judges on the panel responsible for previewing the case summarizes the case to the other judges (Article 383-17). Afterwards, the panel hears the parties' arguments (Article 383-18).

Having heard the parties' arguments, the cassation panel issues its resolution in which it may: (1) uphold the appellate court's resolution (thereby dismissing the cassation appeal); (2) abolish the appellate court's resolution fully or partially and remand the case for a new hearing at the trial or appellate court (but in front of a different judge) if the mistakes that the appellate court made cannot be rectified at the cassation panel's level; (3) reverse the appellate court's resolution fully or partially and cease any court proceedings with respect to this case; (4) reverse the appellate court's resolution, upholding the trial court's decision; or (5) amend the resolution, or issue a new one thereby reversing either one of the lower courts' decisions without remanding the case for a new hearing if the case does not require any new gathering or examining of evidence, and the circumstances of the case have been fully and correctly established, however, a mistake in applying substantive law was made (Article 383-20). The resolution of the cassation panel becomes enforceable from the moment it is announced (Article 383-23).

V. PROCEEDINGS AT THE SUPREME COURT

A. Supervisory Panel

If a party is dissatisfied with the cassation panel's decision, it may file a petition with the Supreme Court of RK within one year from the date the cassation panel's decision became enforceable (Article 388 I). The Supreme Court's review is *discretionary*: it does not immediately convene the supervisory panel, but assigns one judge to examine (preview) the matter. This preview process must be completed within one month (if the case files must also be examined, then the preview takes place within one month from the date the files were transferred from the lower court to the Supreme Court) (Article 393 II).

Upon the end of the preview period, a preliminary hearing is held during which three judges of the Supreme Court decide on whether to initiate the supervisory proceedings or not (Articles 393, 394). The petitioner and a procurator are notified of the date and time of the preliminary hearing, and they may participate in it (the petitioner's opposing party does not participate in the preliminary hearing). Their absence, however, does not prevent the Supreme Court from holding the preliminary hearing. During the preliminary hearing, the petitioner briefly states his argument, and then the procurator expresses his opinion on the case. If the three judges decide not to initiate the supervisory proceedings, the case is terminated, and the cassation panel's decision remains in force.

If during the preliminary hearing the Supreme Court decides to initiate supervisory proceedings, the supervisory panel is formed (consisting of at least five judges) to hear the case on the merits. Usually, at the time the Supreme Court hears the matter, the respective judicial decisions have already been enforced. If, however, the decisions are still in the process of enforcement, the Chairman of the Supreme Court or the General Procurator may suspend their enforcement for a period of up to three months (Article 396). The supervisory panel must consider the case within one month from the date the panel was formed (Article 395 II).

The presiding judge opens the hearing, introduces the other panelists and asks if the parties have any challenges (Article 398 I). The supervisory panel may hear the case even in the absence of parties to the dispute that the court had duly notified of the hearing. The procurator's participation, however, is mandatory. After ruling on the parties' challenges (if any) the panel proceeds to hear the case and requests the petitioner to state his arguments as to why the lower courts' decisions are unlawful and must be reversed (Article 398 III). The petitioner's opposing party next states his counterarguments. The procurator's speech follows in which the procurator gives his view as to whether the lower courts' decisions should be upheld or not.

The supervisory panel then issues its resolution in which it may: (1) uphold the decision of the trial, appellate or cassation court; (2) reverse the decision of the trial, appellate or cassation court fully or partially and remand the case for a new hearing at the trial, appellate or cassation court level (but before a different judge or panel); (3) reverse the trial, appellate or cassation court's decision fully or partially and cease any court proceedings with respect to the case; (4) uphold only one of the lower courts' several decisions; or, if the decision mistakenly applies to the substantive law, (5) amend the decision of the trial, appellate or cassation court, or issue a new resolution, thereby reversing the lower courts' decisions without remanding the case for a new hearing (Article 398 IV). The supervisory panel's decision enters in force as of the moment it is adopted (Article 400).

B. Plenary Session

In very rare instances, the decision of the supervisory panel of the Supreme Court can be reviewed by the plenary session of the Supreme Court. The plenary session consists of at least two-thirds of the judges of the Supreme Court (Article 403-2 I). It hears only those cases that threaten to lead to "irreversible effects on the life and health of people or the economy and national security of the Republic of Kazakhstan" (Article 384 III).

The plenary session may be convened by the Chairman of the Supreme Court or the General Procurator (Article 403-1). In this event, the official who convened the plenary session must explain to the judges the need for reconsideration of the case (Article 403-2 II). Should the majority of the judges of the Supreme Court believe that there are no grounds for rehearing the case, the plenary session adopts a resolution denying the motion to reconsider the case (Article 403-2 III). If the majority of judges believes that the given decision poses a threat to the life and health of the population, economic stability or national security, the plenary session adopts a resolution on appointing a hearing for the case. The hearing of the plenary session takes place on the basis of the same rules as the proceedings in the supervisory panel (Article 403-2 IV).

VI. PROCEEDINGS ON ACCOUNT OF NEWLY REVEALED CIRCUMSTANCES

All judicial decisions, rulings and resolutions that have been entered into legal force may be revised on the basis of newly revealed circumstances. The legislation indicates the following instances of such situations: (1) circumstances material for the case, which were not and could not have been known to the applicant; (2) deliberately false testimony of a witness established by a court sentence to that effect that has been entered into legal force, deliberately false report of an expert, deliberately false translation, counterfeit of documents or material evidence that entailed the decreeing of an illegal or unreasonable decision; (3) criminal acts of parties or other persons participating in the case or their representatives or criminal acts of the parties (established by a court sentence to that effect that has entered into legal force) committed while the case was being considered; (4) abolition of a decision, sentence, ruling or resolution of the court or resolution of any other body that served as the basis for the passing of a given decision, ruling or resolution; (5) the recognition by the Constitutional Council of RK of the law or other regulatory legal act that was applied by the court when passing the judicial act as contradicting the Constitution (Article 404).

Applications to revise decisions, rulings or resolutions on the basis of newly opened circumstances are filed by the persons who participated in the case (within three months from the date of the establishment of the circumstances, that serve as the basis for the revision) or by the procurator to the court that passed the decision, ruling or resolution. Accordingly, a first instance court decision that has entered into legal force is revised by the trial court that passed that decision; while rulings, decisions or resolutions of appellate, cassation or supervisory instances that change the decision of the first instance court or pass a new decision are revised by the court that changed the first instance court's decision or passed a new decision (Article 405).

VII. FOREIGN COURTS' DECISIONS AND ARBITRAL AWARDS

The decisions of foreign courts and arbitration tribunals are recognized and implemented by the RK on the principle of reciprocity as provided for by the legislation and international treaties of RK (Article 425 I). At present, Kazakhstan has ratified the CIS Treaty "On the Order of Solution of Disputes Related to Business Activities" of March 20, 1992 (entered in force on April 20, 1994). Along with Kazakhstan, the Treaty was also ratified by Armenia, Belarus, Kyrgyzstan, Russia, Tajikistan, Turkmenistan, Ukraine and Uzbekistan. These countries thus agreed to recognize and enforce each other's judicial decisions on business-related disputes (Article 7 of the CIS Treaty). Also, Kazakhstan joined the New York Convention "On the Recognition and Enforcement of Foreign Arbitral Awards" of June 10, 1958 and accordingly pledged itself to recognize and enforce foreign arbitral awards.[27]

According to the CPC, a decision of a foreign court or arbitration tribunal may be enforced in Kazakhstan within three years from the moment of its entry into legal force. A missed deadline may be restored by the court of RK if it finds that the party had a sufficient excuse for missing the deadline (Article 425 III).

27. Editor's note: see section X "Private Procedural Law," in Chapter 11 "Private International Law."

Selected Bibliography

Z. Abdullina, *Гражданское процессуальное право Республики Казахстан* [*Civil Procedure Law of the Republic of Kazakhstan*] (Kazak Universiteti, Almaty, 2001) [in Russian].

Z. Abdullina, *Производство гражданских дел в суде первой инстанции* [*Civil Proceedings in the Court of the First Instance*] (Daneker, Almaty, 2005) [in Russian].

Z. Baimoldina, *Гражданское процессуальное право Республики Казахстан* [*Civil Procedure Law of the Republic of Kazakhstan*] (KazGYuA, Almaty, 2001) [in Russian].

A. Daulbaev, "Reform der zivilprozessrechtlichen Gesetzgebung in der Republik Kasachstan" (2004) *Reform des Zivil- und Wirtschaftsprozessrechts in den Mitgliedstaaten der GUS* 77.

M. Suleimenov, *Арбитражные (третейские) суды в Казахстане: прошлое, настоящее, будущее* [*Arbitral Tribunals in Kazakhstan: Their Past, Present and Future*] (KMA, Almaty, 2007) [in Russian].

Chapter 13
Criminal Law*

Igor Rogov

I. INTRODUCTION

A. Concept, Methods and System of Criminal Law

Criminal Law of RK, as one of the major branches of the Kazakhstani legal system, is a body of legal norms that defines the concept and attributes of crime, the grounds and limits of criminal liability for the commission of a crime as well as the conditions necessary for an exemption from criminal liability and punishment. It regulates relations between the state, represented by courts and law-enforcement organs, on the one hand, and a person who committed an offense dangerous to the public (a crime), on the other hand (thus carrying out its regulatory function). Along with the regulatory function, Criminal Law performs also the protective function, defending natural persons, the society and the state from criminal encroachments. This function is realized both by statements of legal prohibition of particular actions and by applications of legal punishment to individuals found guilty in the commission of publicly dangerous acts.

The primary method employed by Criminal Law to regulate and protect public relations is coercion, which consists of the application (or threat of the application) of enforcement actions provided by criminal legislation, viz. bringing a guilty person to criminal liability. In addition, Criminal Law applies the incentive

* Translated by Zhenis Kembayev.

Zhenis Kembayev, *Introduction to the Law of Kazakhstan*, pp. 231–250.

method, which defines particular conditions under which a person who is in conflict with Criminal Law has the opportunity to bring the conflict to an end. Should such a person choose a law-abiding way of life, the state commits itself to consider the person's lawful behavior and either (completely or partially) release him from criminal liability or mitigate his criminal punishment. Accordingly, the state adopts norms establishing the basis for exemption from criminal liability and punishment, as well as conditions that mitigate criminal liability and punishment.

The system of Criminal Law is characterized by a hierarchical structure that includes a General and a Special Part. The General Part contains norms that define the purposes and principles of the criminal legislation of RK; the basis for criminal liability; the limits of the application of criminal legislation; the concepts of crime, guilt, criminal sanity and insanity, stages of the commission of a crime, complicity and punishment; the types of punishments, the order of their appointment and the bases for exemption from criminal liability and punishment; etc. The Special Part contains norms elaborating the amount and content of criminal liability regarding each legally defined crime, i.e., it lists all specific actions recognized as crimes and defines their characteristics.

B. The Criminal Code as the Source of Criminal Law

The only source of Criminal Law is the Criminal Code of RK (CrC) (Article 1 I CrC). It was adopted on July 16, 1997 and entered into force on January 1, 1998; from this date on, the Criminal Code of KazSSR of July 22, 1959 ceased to be effective.

The new Criminal Code completely changed the criminal legislation of Kazakhstan. In contrast to the Criminal Code of KazSSR, the Criminal Code of RK stipulates that "the criminal legislation of the RK shall consist exclusively of the present Code" and "other laws that stipulate criminal liability shall only be subject to application after their inclusion in the present Code" (Article 1 I CrC). Moreover, it is stipulated that the Criminal Code of RK "shall be based on the Constitution of the RK and generally accepted principles and norms of international law" (Article 1 II CrC). Thus, the legislation recognizes the Constitution and norms of international law as material sources of Criminal Law, which is fully in line with the constitutional provisions concerning the direct application of the Constitution and the attribution of international treaties of RK to the functioning law of Kazakhstan (Article 4 CRK).

The Constitution of RK recognizes an individual and his rights and freedoms as the highest values of state (Article 1 I). In full conformity with the Constitution, the Criminal Code indicates as its first objective "the protection of the rights, freedoms and legitimate interests of individuals and of citizens." Further objectives of the Criminal Code aim at the protection of: (a) the property, rights and legitimate interests of organizations; (c) public order and safety; (d) the environment; (e) the constitutional system and the territorial integrity of RK; (f) the peace and safety of mankind; and (g) the prevention of crime (Article 2 CrC). For the implementation of these objectives, the Criminal Code establishes the bases for criminal liability. Consequently, it defines which acts are dangerous for a person, society or the state are recognized as crimes and establishes punishments and other measures of criminal-legal retribution for their commission.

C. PRINCIPLES OF THE CRIMINAL LAW OF KAZAKHSTAN

Although in contrast to some other CIS countries there is no separate article on the principles in the Criminal Code, it is possible to formulate the following set of principles of Criminal Law based on the Constitution of RK and provisions of the criminal legislation.

The first and foremost principle is the *principle of lawfulness (or legality)*, which implies that the criminality and punishability of any action must be determined only by the Criminal Code. Thus, application of criminal legislation by analogy is prohibited by the Constitution (Article 77 III-10) and the Criminal Code (Article 9 CrC).

Another major principle of Criminal Law is the *principle of equality* of all persons. In this regard, the Constitution provides in particular that "everyone shall be equal before the law and court" and that "no one shall be subject to any discrimination for reasons of origin, social status, property status, occupation, sex, race, nationality, language, attitude towards religion, convictions, place of residence or any other circumstances" (Article 14 CrC).

Furthermore, Criminal Law is also based on such principles as: the principle of guilt-based liability; the principle of personal liability; the principle of justice; the principle of humanism; the principle of retrenchment of criminal repressions and the principle of inevitability of criminal liability and punishment.

The *principle of guilt-based liability* for commission of a crime implies that a person may be subject to criminal liability only for those publicly dangerous acts (or failures to act), and those publicly dangerous consequences that have emerged, with regard to which his guilt (i.e., his negligence or intent to cause harm) was established by court. Strict liability (*naqty eriksiz beru, ob'ektivnoe vmenenie*), i.e., criminal liability without negligence or intent to cause to harm, is not allowed.

The *principle of personal liability* is directly connected with the above principle and means the following: first, only a natural person may be subject to criminal liability (Article 14 CrC) and second, a person may be liable only for the actions he himself committed. The effect of this principle is strongly expressed in the norms regulating the liability of accessories in a crime (Articles 29 I, 30 CrC).

The *principle of justice* is expressed in the provision of the Criminal Code requiring the courts to appoint a just punishment to a person who was recognized as guilty in the commission of a crime. In doing so, the courts must take into consideration the character and degree of public danger of a given crime, the personality of the convict, including his behavior prior to and after the crime, circumstances that aggravate or mitigate liability and punishment and the influence of the established punishment upon the correction of a given convict and upon the conditions of life of his family or persons dependent on him (Article 52 I, III CrC). To be mentioned also is the constitutional provision that no one may be subject twice to criminal prosecution for one and the same offense (i.e., double jeopardy) (Article 77 III-2 CRK).

The *principle of humanism* also finds its reflection both in constitutional provisions and in the Criminal Code. Thus, according to the Constitution, "no one must be subject to torture, violence or other treatment and punishment that is cruel or humiliating to human dignity" (Article 17 II CRK), while the Criminal Code provides that "punishment shall not have as its purpose the infliction of physical sufferings or humiliation upon human dignity" (Article 38 II CrC). Another principle, which is associated with the principle of humanism but is not wholly covered by it, is the *principle of retrenchment of criminal repressions.* In this regard, the Criminal Code provides that a person who committed a crime must be sentenced with a punishment necessary and sufficient for his correction and the prevention of new crimes. Moreover, a stricter type of punishment from those stipulated for a given crime is to be appointed only in case a lesser punishment cannot provide for the achievement of the goals of punishment (Article 52 II CrC).

Last but not the least, the *principle of inevitability* of criminal liability and punishment implies that every individual convicted in the commission of a crime is subject to criminal liability and punishment or other measures provided by the criminal legislation.

D. Effect of Criminal Law in Time and in Space

Effect of Criminal Law in Time: The criminality and punishability of an act is defined by the law that was in effect during the time of the commission of that crime (irrespective of the time of the emergence of consequences) (Article 4 CrC). Criminal Law may be applied retroactively when it eliminates the criminality or punishability of a criminal act; mitigates liability or punishment for it; or otherwise improves the status of a person who committed it. If a new criminal law mitigates the punishability of a given act for which a person is serving a term, then the appointed punishment is subject to reduction as provided by that newly adopted criminal law. Simultaneously, the Criminal Code explicitly prohibits the retroactivity of laws that establish the criminality or punishability of an act; increase liability or punishment; or otherwise deteriorate the status of a person who committed that act (Article 5 CrC).

Effect of Criminal Law in Space: A person who committed a crime on the territory of RK (and within its continental shelf and the exclusive economic zone) bears liability in accordance with the Criminal Code of RK. Also, all criminal acts which were begun, continued or ended on the territory of RK are recognized as a crimes committed on the territory of RK. The only exemption is made with respect to diplomatic representatives of foreign states and other citizens who enjoy immunity in accordance with the norms of international law.

Furthermore, the Criminal Code stipulates that citizens of RK who committed a crime outside of the boundaries of RK are subject to criminal liability in accordance with Kazakhstani criminal legislation if a given criminal act is recognized as a crime on the territory of a state where it was committed, and if the offenders were not convicted in that other state. In the event of the conviction of said persons, punishment may not exceed the upper limit of the sanction that is stipulated by law of the state on whose territory a given crime was committed.

In addition, it is provided that foreigners who committed crimes outside of the boundaries of RK are subject to criminal liability in accordance with the Criminal Code of RK in cases in which a given crime was directed against the interests of Kazakhstan if those foreigners were not convicted in that other state (Article 6 CrC).

E. Extradition of Persons who Committed a Crime

According to the Constitution of RK, "a citizen of the RK may not be extradited to a foreign state unless otherwise stipulated by international treaties of the Republic" (Article 11 I). This provision is fully reflected in the Criminal Code, which stipulates that "citizens of RK who committed a crime on the territory of another state are not subject to extradition to that other state, unless it is otherwise established by international treaties (Article 8 I CrC).

Foreigners and stateless persons who committed a crime outside of the boundaries of RK and are currently on the territory of Kazakhstan may be extradited to another state in accordance with an international treaty of RK (examples of such treaties constitute two Conventions on Legal Assistance Regarding Civil, Family and Criminal Cases concluded between the CIS states in Minsk on January 22, 1993 and in Kishinev on October 7, 2002). In cases where there are no international treaties, the issue of the extradition may be resolved by diplomatic channels (often on the basis of the principle of reciprocity).

It should also be noted that persons who have received political asylum in Kazakhstan are not subject to extradition (according to Article 44 CRK, issues of political asylum are resolved by the President of RK).

II. CRIME

A. Concept of Crime and Its Basic Attributes

The Criminal Code defines a crime as "a committed publicly dangerous act (or failure to act) for which someone is found guilty, and which is prohibited by the present Code, under the threat of legal punishment" (Article 9 CrC). Accordingly, the following set of the attributes of a crime may be distinguished: (1) danger to society; (2) illegality; (3) culpability (guilt); and (4) punishability. Only if all these attributes are available can an act be recognized as a crime.

The first attribute, danger to society, is an objective feature of an act (or failure to act) to cause (or threaten to cause) a substantial harm to public relations that are under the protection of Criminal Law. In this regard it should also be noted that the Criminal Code provides that "those acts or failures to act that, though formally containing the elements of an act stipulated by the Special Part of the present Code, but by virtue of their insignificance do not present a public danger, that is, which did not cause any harm, and did not create a threat of causing harm to a person, society, or the state, shall not be considered crimes" (Article 9 II CrC).

The second (in the order of consideration, but not in significance) attribute of crime is criminal illegality, i.e., the prohibition of an action by criminal legislation. As the formal attribute of a crime, illegality is closely connected with two additional characteristics of a crime: culpability and punishability.

Defining culpability as an attribute of crime by the legislation is a striking illustration of the significance given to the existence of guilt in the act (or failure to act) of a person. According to the Criminal Code, objective incrimination, that is, criminal liability for the non-guilty causation of damage is not allowed. Furthermore, only a person who committed a given act deliberately or by negligence may be recognized as guilty in a given crime (Article 19 II, III CrC).

Finally, another attribute of a crime, punishability, implies the legal establishment of a coercive measure for the commission of a crime. Punishability means the existence of the threat of legal punishment, but not necessarily the real execution of punishment. In certain cases, a person found guilty in the commission of crime does not incur a punishment (due to the expiration of a limitation period, amnesty, etc.), but his action will still be considered a crime.

B. Categories of Crime

Depending on the character and degree of public danger involved, all crimes are divided into the following categories: (a) crimes of lesser gravity; (b) crimes of medium gravity; (c) grave crimes; and (d) especially grave crimes.

Crimes of lesser gravity are deliberate acts, for the commission of which the maximum punishment stipulated by the Criminal Code does not exceed two years of deprivation of freedom as well as negligent acts for which the maximum punishment does not exceed five years of imprisonment.

Crimes of medium gravity are deliberate acts for which the maximum punishment does not exceed five years of deprivations of freedom as well as negligent acts for which punishment is stipulated in the form of imprisonment for a period of more than five years.

Only deliberate acts may be recognized as grave and especially grave crimes. The former are those whose maximum punishment does not exceed 12 years of imprisonment; the commission of the latter results in imprisonment for a period of more than 12 years or capital punishment.

The division of crimes into the above-mentioned categories allows a differentiated approach to persons who have committed a crime while making decisions about arraigning them to criminal liability, the qualification of the crime, the establishment of punishment or their release from criminal liability and punishment.

C. The Basis for Criminal Liability

According to the Criminal Code, the only basis for criminal liability is the commission of a crime, that is, an act which has all of the attributes of a "legally defined crime" (*qylmys qüramy, sostav prestupleniya*).

The concept of a "legally defined crime," as a body of objective and subjective attributes established by the Criminal Code and defining a particular publicly dangerous act as a crime, is indispensable for the proper qualification of the respective crime. Moreover, it is a juridical basis of criminal liability while the commission of a crime is its factual basis. These two bases are interconnected and, in fact, constitute one entire whole.

Attributes of a "legally defined crime" are contained both in the General and the Special Parts of the Criminal Code. The General Part provides attributes that are common for all crimes (e.g., rules with respect to the form of guilt, the starting age for criminal liability, uncompleted criminal activity, complicity, etc.). The Special Parts stipulates specific attributes of each "legally defined crime."

D. Elements and Kinds of a "Legally Defined Crime"

In juridical literature, it is widely recognized that each "legally defined crime" has four mandatory elements: (a) object; (b) objective element; (c) subject and (d) subjective element. Should committed actions lack even one of them, it means that there is no "legally defined crime," and therefore no basis for criminal liability.

The object of a crime is understood to be those social values which are harmed by the crime. These social values are recognized by the domestic criminal science as the public relations protected by Criminal Law. A set of attributes, characterizing an external action by the criminal (called *actus reus* in common law systems) constitutes the *objective element of a crime.* Those attributes include both publicly dangerous acts (active behavior; e.g., robbery) and failures to act (passive behavior; e.g., failure to perform a necessary service). In addition, the objective element of many "legally defined crimes" may also include consequences of the crime; the causal relationship between a criminal act (or failure to act) and its criminal consequences; circumstances; time; place; methods; as well as tools and means of the commission of crime. A *subject of a crime* is an individual who committed a crime and possesses attributes specified by the Criminal Code: sanity, achievement of certain age and, in some cases, special characteristics (such as official capacity, profession, etc.). The *subjective element of a crime* comprises attributes characterizing the internal (psychic) element of the criminal's behavior such as negligence or intent to harm, as well as the motives and goals of the crime (*menus reus* in common law).

For the practical application of the above theoretical provisions, it is important to know the classification of "legally defined crimes." First of all, it is to be noted that depending on the degree of public danger, the "legally defined crimes" are divided into: (a) main; (b) qualified (with aggravating attributes); (c) especially qualified (with especially aggravating attributes); and (d) privileged (with mitigating attributes).

A *main* "legally defined crime" contains a set of basic, constant attributes of a particular criminal act and does not foresee any additional attributes mitigating or aggravating the degree of public danger of that act (e.g., Article 175 I CrC provides that "theft, that is the furtive stealing of someone else's property, shall be punished by . . . imprisonment for a period of up to three years"). Should a "legally defined crime" include aggravating or especially aggravating attributes, it may be classified as either *qualified* (e.g., as represented by Article 175 II CrC, which provides that "theft committed . . . by a group of persons upon a preliminary collusion . . . shall be punished by imprisonment for a period . . . up to six years with forfeiture of property, or without it") or *especially qualified* (e.g., Article 175 III CrC says that "theft committed . . . by an organized group . . . shall be punished by imprisonment for a period . . . up to 10 years with forfeiture of property"). However, a *privileged* "legally defined crime" means that it has mitigating attributes (e.g., Article 100 CrC limits the sentence for a murder committed in the process of detaining an individual who has committed crime if that murder was in excess of the necessary measures to effect the detention).

Depending on their structure, "legally defined crimes" may be further differentiated into: (a) simple; (b) complicated; and (c) alternative. In contrast to *simple* "legally defined crimes," *complicated* ones have a compound structure of their elements (e.g., a brigandage encroaches upon two objects of crime, property and a person, while rape may include a number of objective elements such as application of emotional or physical violence, or the use of the helpless state of a victim and sexual intercourse). A separate kind of a complicated "legally defined crime" is an *alternative* one, which may contain a number of options of criminal behavior, each serving as a basis for criminal liability (e.g., creating impediments to legal entrepreneurial activity (Article 189 CrC); illegal entrepreneurship (Article 190); and output or sale of goods, performance of work or the rendering of services that do not comply with the rules for the safety of consumers' life and health (Article 269 CrC)).

Of great importance is also the classification of "legally defined crimes" depending on the construction of their objective element. Differentiated under this criterion are: (a) material; (b) formal; and (c) truncated "legally defined crimes." Material crimes require the existence of publicly dangerous consequences to be recognized as consummated (e.g., a murder) while formal crimes may be recognized as consummated without publicly dangerous consequences (e.g., espionage). In some cases crimes may be truncated, meaning that the moment of their consummation is connected with one of the stages of preliminary criminal activity, i.e., preparation or attempt (e.g., the creation of a stable, armed gang).

E. Stages of the Commission of Crime

In Criminal Law theory, the stages of the commission of crime are understood to be phases of the development of a deliberate crime. At present, Criminal Law differentiates three independent stages of the commission of crime: (a) preparation for a crime; (b) attempt; and (c) consummation of a crime (Articles 24, 25 CrC).

Preparation for a crime is recognized as the search for, crafting or adjustment of means or instruments of a crime, carried out with direct intent; the search for partners; the collusion to commit a crime; or any other deliberate creation of conditions for the commission of a crime if the crime was not consummated due to circumstances that did not depend on the will of a given person. Criminal liability emerges only for preparation for a grave or especially grave crime.

An attempted crime is constituted by acts (or their omission) that are carried out with direct intent and that are aimed directly at the commission of a crime if the crime was not consummated due to circumstances that did not depend upon the will of a given person. In the case of an attempted crime, criminal liability exists with respect to medium gravity, grave or especially grave crime.

The last stage, the consummation of crime, is considered to be done if an act contains all the elements of a legally defined crime stipulated by the Criminal Code. When examining the phases of a given crime, it is important to know whether that crime is classified as material, formal or truncated.

F. Multiple Crimes

Repeatedly committed crimes are highly dangerous for society. That is why Criminal Law specifically addresses the issue of multiple crimes, meaning the commission of two or more crimes by one and the same person.

However, a crime may not be recognized as multiple if a given person was released from criminal liability for a previously committed crime through the procedure established by law, a former conviction was cancelled or exculpated or the limitation period expired for holding the convicted liable for such a crime. Also, a continuous crime, a crime that consists of a chain of the same criminal act, united by a single design and purpose and forming one crime, may not be considered a repeated one (e.g., malicious evasion from repayment of accounts payable). Furthermore, multiple crimes must also be differentiated from single "complicated" and "alternative" crimes. Thus, Article 202 CrC regarding the "violation of the procedure for the emission of securities" provides that this crime consists in the "approval of a securities prospectus that contains deliberately false information as well as the approval of a deliberately inaccurate report on the securities issue"; regardless whether a person committed one or both of these actions, this crime may not be considered as multiple. In addition, administrative and disciplinary offenses, civil law delicts and acts (and failures to act) under Article 9 II CrC (see *supra*) may not be considered in the context of multiple crimes.

The current legislation defines the following kinds of multiple crimes: (a) repetition of a crime; (b) cumulative crimes; and (c) criminal recidivism.

"Repetition of a crime" means the commission of two or more actions stipulated by one and the same article or part of the Special Part of the Criminal Code (Article 11 I CrC). Actions are recognized as repeated irrespective of whether they were fully consummated or not, or whether the guilty person acted alone or in complicity.

The above rule has two major juridical meanings: (a) repetition may be considered by a court as a circumstance aggravating criminal liability and punishment when establishing punishment (Article 54 I-(a) CrC); and (b) "in cases in which the repetition of a crime is stipulated as a circumstance that entails a stricter punishment, crimes committed by a given person shall be qualified in accordance with the relevant part of a given article" (Article 11 V CrC).

A "cumulative crime" may be recognized either as the commission of two or more actions stipulated by different articles or parts of a given article of the Criminal Code, for neither of which a person was convicted or released from criminal liability. In certain cases, a cumulative crime may even be constituted by one action that contains elements of crimes stipulated by two or more articles of the Criminal Code (the so-called ideal cumulative crime).

In cumulative crime cases, a person bears criminal liability for each committed crime under the relevant article of the Criminal Code, unless the indications of the committed acts are covered by the provision of one article, which provides for a stricter punishment (Article 12 CrC).

"Criminal recidivism" implies the commission of a deliberate act by a person who has a previous conviction for a past deliberate crime. It indicates that a criminal presents a high level of public danger because his punishment for the previous crime did not achieve its purposes. The particularly hazardous forms of recidivism are specifically dealt with by the Criminal Code, which distinguishes "dangerous"[1] and "especially dangerous"[2] forms of criminal recidivism.

Further, the Criminal Code provides that the term and amount of punishment may not be less than: (a) in case of criminal recidivism, one-third the maximum term and amount of the strictest type of punishment stipulated for a given crime; (b) in cases of dangerous criminal recidivism, not less than one-half; and (c) in case of especially dangerous criminal recidivism, not less than two-thirds (Article 59 II CrC).

To be mentioned also is that convictions of crimes committed by a person under the age of 18 may not be taken into account in the determination of criminal

1. Thus, criminal recidivism is considered dangerous if a person commits: (a) a deliberate crime for which he is to be imprisoned if earlier that person was convicted twice to imprisonment for a deliberate crime; or (b) a grave crime if earlier he was convicted of a grave crime (Art. 13 II CrC).
2. Criminal recidivism is recognized as especially dangerous if a person commits: (a) a deliberate crime for which he is convicted and sentenced to imprisonment if earlier that person was convicted and sentenced to imprisonment not less than three times for past grave crimes, or deliberate crimes of medium gravity; (b) a grave crime for which he is convicted and sentenced to imprisonment if earlier that person was sentenced to imprisonment for the commission of a grave crime or was convicted of an especially grave crime; or (c) an especially grave crime, if he was previously convicted of a grave or especially grave crime (Art. 13 III CrC).

recidivism, nor sentences served or exculpated through the procedure established by the present Code.

G. Criminal Complicity

1. Concept and Forms of Complicity

Deliberate, joint participation by two or more persons in the commission of a deliberate crime is recognized as criminal complicity (Article 27 CrC). This definition gives grounds to distinguish the following attributes of criminal complicity: (a) participation in the commission of crime of two or more persons complying with the requirements put to subjects of crime; (b) acting of accessories in concert; and (c) presence of intentional guilt, which presupposes mutual awareness, consciousness and desire of participants to achieve a common criminal goal.

Depending on the character and degree of interrelations between partners in the commission of crime, four forms of criminal complicity may be distinguished: (a) a group of persons; (b) a group of persons under preliminary collusion; (c) an organized group; and (d) a criminal association (criminal organization).

The Criminal Code defines a group of persons as "two or more performers who jointly participate in the commission of crime without preliminary collusion" (e.g., when the collusion emerges while, or immediately before, a crime is already in progress). A group of persons under preliminary collusion is constituted by persons who have earlier agreed on the joint commission of crime. An organized group is defined as "a stable group of persons who earlier united for the commission of one or several crimes"; and the most dangerous form of criminal complicity, a criminal association, is "a united organized group (organization) that is created for the commission of grave or especially grave crimes, or an association of organized groups created for the same purposes" (Article 31 CrC).

A person who created an organized group or a criminal association, or who guided them, is subject to criminal liability not only for all crimes committed by the organized group or criminal association (if those crimes were covered by his criminal intent) but also for their organization and guidance (in cases stipulated by the relevant articles of the Criminal Code). Other participants of an organized group or a criminal association bear criminal liability for participation in them (in cases stipulated by the relevant articles of the Criminal Code), as well as for crimes that they participated in the preparation or commission of.

2. Types of Accessories in a Crime

The criminal legislation of RK distinguishes four types of accessories in a crime: (a) a performer; (b) an organizer; (c) an abettor; and (d) an accomplice (Article 28 CrC). The criteria of the division are the degree and character of participation of each of them in the commission of crime.

A performer is defined as a person who directly committed a given crime, or who directly participated in its commission, together with other persons (co-performers). There are two types of performers: (a) "direct" performers, i.e., those who commit the crime personally; and (b) "indirect" performers, i.e., those who reach their criminal purpose by using other persons who are not subject to criminal liability due to their age, insanity, or other circumstances, or by using persons who committed a given act by negligence.

An organizer is a person who organized the commission of a given crime or who guided its execution; or a person who created an organized criminal group or criminal association or who managed such a group. The actions of an organizer usually consist of planning a crime, finding and training accessories, managing the execution of the criminal plan, etc. An organizer is the most dangerous among all other types of accessories; consequently, he usually bears the strictest punishment.

An abettor is a person who made another person more inclined to commit a given crime. Actions of an abettor may be directed either at motivating another person to participate in the crime or reinforcing that person's intent. The methods of an abettor may include persuasion, subornation, threats or other such means (e. g., blackmail, bribery, etc.).

An accomplice is a person who co-operated in the commission of a crime by giving advice or instructions, granting information, providing instruments or means, or eliminating impediments for the commission of a crime. A person who promised in advance to conceal a criminal; the instruments or other means of a given crime; the traces of a crime; or any objects acquired by criminal means (as well as a person who earlier promised to acquire or to purchase such objects) is also recognized as an accomplice.

H. Circumstances Excluding the Criminality and Punishability of an Act

The major method used by Criminal Law to implement its objectives (outlined above) is the prohibition of violations of the social relations protected by criminal legislation. At the same time, Criminal Law also applies the method of permission, when the protection of social relations is realized by the authorization of citizens to commit certain actions, even though those actions may lead to physical, property, moral or other kind of harm. Although those acts may formally contain all the attributes of a crime, they are not recognized as such because they lack one of the major attributes of a crime, namely danger for society.

For the general designation of these cases, the theory of Criminal Law uses the concept of "circumstances excluding the criminality and punishability of an act." Presently, the Criminal Code contains the following seven such circumstances.

Necessary Self-Defense or Defense of Another: According to the Constitution of RK, everyone has the right to recognition of his legal capacity and can protect his rights and freedoms by all legal methods including necessary self-defense

(Article 13 I CRK). This constitutional provision is fully reflected in the Criminal Code, which provides that the causation of damage to an assaulting person in one's own defense is not considered a crime. Self-defense implies cases of the protection by a defending person of his rights and property, as well as rights of other persons and the interests of the society or the state protected by law from publicly dangerous assault. All persons have the right to necessary self-defense in equal measure, regardless of their professional or other special training or official position. This right belongs to a person regardless of whether it is possible to avoid a publicly dangerous assault or to appeal for help to other persons or state bodies.

However, an obvious discrepancy between measures taken in self-defense and the character and degree of public danger of an assault, as a result of which a given attacker was caused obviously excessive damage, a consequence not justified by the situation, may be recognized as being in excess of the limits of necessary self-defense and, as such, entail criminal liability in cases of deliberate causation of harm. At the same time, causation of harm to a person who attempts to kill a person, or when deterring another violation associated with the use or an attempt to use arms, may not be recognized as in excess of the limits of necessary defense (Article 32 CrC).

Extreme Necessity: Damage inflicted in a situation of extreme necessity, that is, in order to eliminate a danger that directly threatens the life, health, rights or legitimate interests of a given person or of other persons, as well as the interests of society, is not considered a crime. Thus, extreme necessity covers cases when the existing real danger to the interests of a person, society or the state is eliminated by means of causing lesser harm to other social relations (e.g., the use of somebody's car without permission of the owner for transporting a seriously ill person to hospital).

However, there are two major conditions necessary to legitimate extreme necessity: (a) the danger could not have been eliminated by other means; and (b) the limits of extreme necessity were not exceeded. The deliberate infliction of damage in excess of extreme necessity entails criminal liability (Article 34 CrC).

Justifiable Risk: The causation of damage is not considered a crime in case of a justifiable risk for the achievement of a publicly useful goal. Risk is recognized as justifiable in the following instances: (a) if a said goal could not have been achieved by actions (or inactions) not associated with the risk, and if a person who admitted the risk undertook sufficient measures for the prevention of damage; and (b) if it was directly associated with a threat to people's life or health, of ecological catastrophe, social disaster or other serious consequences (Article 35 CrC).

Physical or Psychic Coercion: The causation of damage as a result of physical coercion is not considered a crime if, as a consequence of such coercion, a person could not control his actions (or inactions). Should a given person have retained the possibility to guide his actions, the issue of his criminal liability is resolved subject to provisions related to extreme necessity (Article 36 CrC).

Execution of an Order or an Instruction: The causation of damage by a person who acted in pursuance of an order or instruction obligatory for him is not considered a crime. In the case of an illegal order or instruction, criminal liability for the causation of damage is borne by a person who issued that order or instruction. To be noted also is that non-execution of a deliberately illegal order or instruction excludes criminal liability, while a person who commits a deliberate crime in pursuance of an order or instruction that he knows to be illegal bears criminal liability on general bases (Article 37 CrC).

The causation of damage to a person who had committed a crime, when detaining him in order to deliver him to the relevant state bodies, and to stop the possibility of the commission by him of new violations, is not considered a crime if it was not possible to detain that person by other means, and if the measures necessary for that purpose were not exceeded (Article 33 CrC).

Finally, an act committed in the course of *the performance of operative investigative measures* (*operativno-rozysknykh*) in accordance with the law by a member of the authorized state body's staff is not recognized as a crime, provided that the act was committed for the purpose of prevention, detection or investigation of crimes committed by a group of persons on the basis of a preliminary collusion or by an organized group or criminal association, and if the crimes' prevention, exposure or investigation could not be carried out in any other manner (Article 34-1 CrC). However, the above provisions do not apply to acts related to threats to the lives or health of persons or related to ecological disaster, public calamity or other grave consequences.

III. PUNISHMENT

A. Concept and Purposes of Punishment

In contrast to the criminal legislation of the Kazakh SSR, the Criminal Code of RK contains a norm that precisely defines the concept of punishment, determined as "a measure of state coercion appointed pursuant to a court's sentence." Further, it is stipulated that "punishment shall apply to a person who was found guilty in the commission of a crime, and it shall consist of imprisonment or the restriction of the rights and freedoms of that person" (Article 38 I CrC).

The purposes of punishment are defined as: (a) the restoration of social justice; (b) the correction of a given convict; (c) the prevention of the commission of new crimes both by that convict; and (d) by other persons. It is also emphasized that punishment may not have as its purpose the infliction of physical sufferings or humiliation upon human dignity. In contrast to socialist times, re-education of convicts (which was supposed to be done strictly in the light of communist ideology) was excluded from the purposes of punishment.

B. Types of Punishment

Persons who were found guilty in the commission of a crime may be subject to the following principal types of punishment: (a) fines; (b) deprivation of the right to hold a certain office or to engage in certain activities; (c) engagement in public works; (d) correctional labor; (e) restriction in military service; (f) military detention; (g) restriction of freedom; (h) deprivation of freedom; and (i) capital punishment. Aside from principal types of punishment, convicts may be subjected to the following additional types of punishment: (a) deprivation of a special, military or honorary rank; class rank, diplomatic rank or qualification class; or state award; and (b) confiscation of property.

It should also be noted that the following three types of punishment may be applied either as principal or additional types of punishment: (a) fines; (b) deprivation of the right to hold a certain position or to engage in a certain type of activity; and (c) engagement in public works.

Fines may be appointed within the limits of 25 to 20,000 MCIs,[3] or in the amount of wages or income of a given convict for a period from two weeks to one year. The amount of a fine is determined by a court subject to the gravity of a given crime committed and property status of a given convict.

Deprivation of the right to hold a certain position or to engage in a certain type of activity consists in a ban on holding certain positions in national or local government bodies, or on engaging in certain professional or other activities. This prohibition may be established for a period of one to five years as a principal type of punishment or for a period of six months to three years as an additional type of punishment.

Deprivation of special, military or honorary rank; class rank, diplomatic rank or qualification class; or state award may be appointed for the commission of a grave or especially grave crime. In case a convicted person has awards or ranks awarded by the President of RK, a court, when passing a sentence, must decide on the issue of the expediency of the submission to the President of the RK of a recommendation to deprive the convicted of those awards and ranks.

Forfeiture of property means the forcible transfer of all or part of the property that is in the ownership of a given convict to the ownership of the state, without compensation. Forfeiture may be established for mercenary crimes.

Engagement in public works consists of the performance, without compensation, of publicly useful works by a convict in his time free from work or studies. The type of work is defined by local executive bodies or local self-government bodies. The engagement is established for a period of between 62 to 240 hours, and is performed for not longer than four hours per week.

Correctional labor is appointed for a period of two months to two years, and is served in the place of work of a given convict. Under this regime, withholdings of 5% to 25% of the convict's salary are made to the state budget.

3. See "List of Abbreviations" for an explanation of the concept of monthly calculation index.

Restriction in military service and *military detention* are imposed on convicted military servicemen. Restriction in military service is designated for a period from three months to up to two years for the commission of crimes against military service. In this case, withholdings of up to 20% are made from the convict's monetary allowance. While serving this punishment, a convict may not be promoted to a higher office or military rank, and a period of punishment is not counted as part of the length of service needed for the conferment of the next military rank (Article 44 CrC). Military detention consists of the strict isolation of a convict from society for a period of one to six months (Article 46 CrC).

Restriction of freedom consists of the imposition on a convict of certain duties that restrict his freedom (e.g., not to change the permanent place of residence or not to depart for other areas without a permit from the specialized authority; also other duties may be imposed such as to undergo a course of medical treatment for alcoholism). This restriction (which does not involve isolation from society) is endured in his place of residence under the supervision of a specialized body for a period of one to five years (Article 45 CrC).

Deprivation of freedom consists of isolation of a given convict from society by way of sending him to a settled colony or placing him in a jail or a penitentiary settlement of a general, strict or special regime. Generally, the deprivation is established for a period of six months up to a maximum of 15 years, and for especially grave crimes up to 20 years or for a lifetime (when establishing punishments for a cumulative crime, the maximum term of deprivation of freedom may not exceed 25 years, 30 years in cases of accumulative sentencing). For crimes of negligence, a term of deprivation of freedom may not exceed 10 years.

Lifetime deprivation of freedom may be established only for the commission of especially grave crimes and as an alternative to capital punishment. This punishment is not sentenced upon women, persons who committed the crime while under the age of 18 or men who have reached the age of 65 by the moment of the passing of a given sentence.

The criminal legislation of RK still foresees the application of "capital punishment" as an exceptional form of punishment. Nevertheless, at the time of the adoption of the Criminal Code of RK, the number of articles providing for capital punishment was significantly reduced in comparison to the Criminal Code of KazSSR (from 34 to 17). Moreover, as noted above, several categories of people must be sentenced with life imprisonment in place of capital punishment.

Further, on September 20, 2002, the "Conception of Legal Policy of RK" was adopted, which proclaimed the necessity of a gradual reduction of the areas of application of the death penalty and announced the possibility of suspending the punishment. On December 17, 2003 a Decree of the President of RK, "On the Introduction of a Moratorium on the Death Penalty in RK," No. 1251, prohibited the use of the capital punishment beginning January 1, 2004.

The next modification was made during the constitutional reforms of May 15, 2007. Following these amendments, the Constitution stipulates that "capital punishment shall be established by law as an exceptional form of punishment for terrorist crimes that cause the death of people, as well as especially grave crimes committed in war time, with granting the convict the right to petition for pardon" (Article 15 CrC). This constitutional provision was reiterated in the Criminal Code.

C. Exemption from Criminal Liability and Punishment

The major principle of criminal law is inevitability of criminal liability and punishment. At the same time, however, the principles of humanism and of retrenchment of criminal repressions allow, under certain conditions, a refusal to criminally prosecute a person who committed a crime, or to mitigate his liability or punishment. The state may extend its mercy even if an individual committed a crime and exhibited guilty behavior, assuming that the Criminal Law conflict will be resolved in the interest of all concerned parties: a criminal, his victim, society and the state. In this regard, section V of the Criminal Code titled "Exemption from Criminal Liability and Punishment" contains a number of bases for the termination of measures of state coercion on a person who committed a crime.

The bases of exemption from criminal liability may be classified in the following manner: (a) due to active repentance (Article 65 CrC); (b) in cases of exceeding the limits of necessary self-defense (Article 66 CrC); (c) due to reconciliation with the victim of a crime (Article 67 CrC); (d) in relation to a change in a given situation (Article 68 CrC); (e) in relation to the expiration of a statutory limitation period (Article 69 CrC); and (f) on the basis of an act of amnesty or pardon (Article 76 CrC).

At the same time, grounds of exemption from punishment include: (a) conditional release ahead of time from serving punishment (Article 70 CrC); (b) substitution of an unserved term of punishment for a more lenient type of punishment (Article 71 CrC); (c) postponement of endurance of punishment for pregnant women and women who have small children (Article 72 CrC); (d) release from punishment due to an illness (Article 73 CrC); (e) release from punishment or postponement of the serving of punishment due to extraordinary circumstances (Article 74 CrC); (f) release from endurance of punishment due to the expiration of the limitation period for the effect of an incriminating judgment (Article 75 CrC); and (g) exemption from criminal liability and punishment on the basis of an act of amnesty or pardon (Article 76 CrC).

As shown above, the Criminal Code foresees, along with traditional grounds (such as expiration of a statutory limitation period, conditional release ahead of time from serving punishment, etc.) a number of new grounds for exemption from criminal liability and punishment. First to be mentioned is the rule that a person who exceeded the limits of necessary self-defense as a consequence of fear, fright or confusion caused by an impingement dangerous to society may be exempted by a court from criminal liability subject to the circumstances of a given case (Article 66 CrC). This rule does not exist in other CIS countries and was borrowed from the criminal legislation of Germany.

Also, exemption from criminal liability due to reconciliation with the victim of a crime is stipulated (Article 66 CrC). This means that a person who committed a crime of lesser gravity, or who committed a medium-gravity crime for the first time, that is not related to the causation of death or grievous harm to an individual's health is subject to release from criminal liability if that person has reconciled himself with the victim and made good for the harm caused. Moreover, a person who committed a medium-gravity crime may be conditionally released from criminal liability if he reconciled himself with the victim and made good for the harm caused to the victim. Thus, reconciliation significantly reduces the scope of public criminal prosecution, essentially, the issue of the arraigning to criminal liability of individuals who committed a crime of a lesser or medium gravity for the first time is left to the discretion of victims.

The principle of humanism, which underlies the new criminal legislation of RK, is apparent also in the rule that a court may postpone the endurance of punishment for convicted pregnant women and women who have a child under 14 years of age for a period of up to one year, or until the child reaches 14 years, respectively (women convicted and sentenced to deprivation of freedom for a period of more than five years for grave and especially grave crimes against a person are not eligible for postponement) (Article 72 I CrC).

Another humane rule is that a person who suffers from a serious illness that impedes his serving of the punishment may be exempted by a court from serving it, or the penalty may be substituted for a more lenient type of punishment. In this respect, the gravity of a committed crime must be taken into consideration, as well as the personality of the convict, the character of his illness and other circumstances (Article 73 II CrC).

Further, the Criminal Code provides for the possibility of the release from punishment or the postponement of the serving of punishment due to extraordinary circumstances. Thus, a person convicted of a crime of lesser or medium gravity may be released by a court from punishment if enduring it may entail especially grave consequences for a given convict or his family due to a fire or natural disaster, a serious illness or the death of the only family member capable of work, as well as due to other extraordinary circumstances. Under such circumstances, a court may postpone the endurance of punishment for a period of up to three months for a person sentenced to deprivation of freedom for a grave or especially grave crime (Article 74 CrC).

To be mentioned also is that the new criminal legislation contains detailed rules with respect to acts of amnesty and pardons. In this regard, it is provided that acts of amnesty are issued by the Parliament of RK with regard to a category of persons who are not individually defined while acts of pardon are issued by the President of RK concerning individually defined persons, with regard to whom an incriminating judgment came into legal force. Acts of amnesty and pardons may either exempt an individual from punishment, reduce his sentence or substitute a more lenient penalty. Both types of acts may remove a conviction from a person having served his punishment (Article 76 CrC).

IV. STRUCTURE OF THE SPECIAL PART OF THE CRIMINAL CODE

The Special Part of the Criminal Code determines specifically that publicly dangerous acts are crimes and establishes legal punishments for their commission. It constitutes an organized and scientifically grounded system that facilitates the proper understanding, interpretation and application of the criminal legislation. At present it consists of the following 16 Chapters differentiated by the generic object of the crime:

(1) Crimes against an Individual (Articles 96–130 CrC);
(2) Crimes against the Family and Juveniles (Articles 131–140 CrC);
(3) Crimes against the Constitutional and Other Rights and Freedoms of Individuals (Articles 141–155 CrC);
(4) Crimes against the Peace and Safety of Mankind (Articles 156–164 CrC);
(5) Crimes against the Basics of the Constitutional Order and the Safety of the State (Articles 165–174 CrC);
(6) Crimes against Property (Articles 175–188 CrC);
(7) Crimes in the Sphere of Economic Activity (Articles 189–227-1 CrC);
(8) Crimes against the Interests of Commercial and Other Organizations (committed by employees of said organizations) (Articles 228–232 CrC);
(9) Crimes against Public Safety and Public Order (Articles 233–258 CrC);
(10) Crimes against the Health of the Population and Morality (Articles 259–276 CrC);
(11) Ecological Crimes (Articles 277–294 CrC);
(12) Transportation Crimes (Articles 295–306 CrC);
(13) Corruption and Other Crimes against the Interests of the State Service and State Administration (Articles 307–316 CrC);
(14) Crimes against the Governmental Order (Articles 317–338 CrC);
(15) Crimes against Justice and the Order for Carrying Out Punishment (Articles 339–365 CrC);
(16) Military Crimes (Articles 366–393 CrC).

In contrast to the Criminal Code of the Kazakh SSR of July 22, 1959, which reflected the old system of values and therefore began with crimes against the state, the contemporary Criminal Code of RK (fully in compliance with the Constitution of RK) emphasizes the priority of individuals' rights and freedoms. Another major difference is that there is no separate chapter on crimes against state property, which generally provided for more severe sanctions than the respective provisions of the chapter dealing with citizens' rights. Since the Constitution of RK declared the equality of state-owned and private property (Article 6-I), the Criminal Code of RK contains only one single chapter on crimes against property (without its differentiation into state- or private-owned and providing for the same sanctions with respect to crimes against them). The transition to a market economy is also reflected by Chapter 7 "Crimes in the Sphere of Economic Activity" and Chapter 8 "Crimes against the Interests of Commercial and Other Organizations," the provisions of which obviously demonstrate the change of the state's role in economic relations (from dictation to co-ordination and equal participation), the recognition and protection of private property and the freedom of entrepreneurship.

Selected Bibliography

A. Agybayev, *Қылмыстық құқық* [*Criminal Law of RK*] *General Part* (Žeti Žargi, Almaty, 1998); *Special Part* (Žeti Žargi, Almaty, 2000) [in Kazakh].

A. Agybayev & G. Baimurzin (eds.), *Уголовное право Республики Казахстан* [*Criminal Law of RK*] (Kazakh Universiteti, Almaty, 2003) [in Russian].

I. Borčašvili, *Уголовное право Республики Казахстан* [*Criminal Law of RK*] (Žeti Žargi, Almaty, 2006) [in Russian].

I. Borčašvili, *Комментарий к уголовному кодексу Республики Казахстан* [*Commentary to the Criminal Code of RK*] (Žeti Žargi, Almaty, 2007) [in Russian].

U. Jekebayev, *Основные принципы уголовного права Республики Казахстан* [*Main Principles of Criminal Law of the Republic of Kazakhstan*] (Žeti Žargi, Almaty, 2001) [in Russian].

G. Polenov, *Уголовное право Республики Казахстан* [*Criminal Law of RK*] (VŠP Adilet, Almaty, 1997) [in Russian].

I. Rogov & S. Rakhmetov (eds.), *Комментарий к уголовному кодексу Республики Казахстан* [*Commentary to the Criminal Code of RK*] (Baspa, Almaty, 1999) [in Russian].

Chapter 14
Criminal Procedure

*Daniyar Kanafin**

I. INTRODUCTION

A. Generally

The main regulatory act that governs criminal trials in Kazakhstan is the Criminal Procedure Code (CrPC) of RK of December 13, 1997. It is based on the Constitution of RK and generally recognized principles and norms of international law (Article 1I CrPC).[1]

Criminal proceedings on the territory of RK are carried out in accordance with the CrPC, irrespective of where and by whom (citizen of RK, foreign citizen or state person) the crime was committed (Articles 4-I, 6-I). The only exception is provided with respect to persons enjoying diplomatic immunity (Articles 6-II, 496–504). Application of the Criminal Procedure Law of a foreign state is allowed only if it is provided for by an international treaty ratified by RK. As a rule, criminal proceedings are carried out in accordance with the law that is in force at the moment of the performance of the procedural action or the adoption of the procedural decision. At the same time, it is emphasized that a law that imposes new duties or abolishes or reduces the rights of the participants of a criminal proceeding may not be retroactive (Article 5).

* Translated by Zhenis Kembayev.

1. Hereinafter all references are to the CrPC unless explicitly indicated otherwise.

Zhenis Kembayev, *Introduction to the Law of Kazakhstan*, pp. 251–273.

B. Objectives and Principles of Criminal Proceedings

Objectives of criminal proceedings include: (a) the quick and full revelation of crimes; (b) the arraigning to criminal responsibility of persons who committed them; and (c) the fair proceeding and correct application of Criminal Law. Also, it is stipulated that criminal proceedings must provide protection from unreasonable accusation and conviction as well as from illegal restrictions of the rights and freedoms of individuals. In the case of an unlawful prosecution or the conviction of an innocent person, immediate and full rehabilitation must be provided. Furthermore, criminal proceedings must contribute to the promotion of the rule-of-law, the prevention of crimes and the formation of a respectful attitude towards law (Article 8).

Criminal proceedings must be carried out in compliance with a number of principles (Articles 10–31), the violation of which may result in recognition of the proceedings to be invalid, in the abolition of decisions passed in the course of such proceedings or in the recognition of the materials collected in this case as having no force of evidence (Article 9). These principles may be divided into the following groups: (1) the principle of legality; (2) principles ensuring the protection of human rights during the criminal proceedings; and (3) principles determining the course of the criminal proceedings.

The *principle of legality* implies that the court, procurator, investigator, inquiry agency and inquiry officer are obliged to precisely comply with the requirements of the Constitution of RK, the CrPC and other regulatory legal acts when handling criminal cases.

The principles ensuring the protection of human rights during criminal proceedings include the following fundamental rules and assumptions:

- *Equality of all persons before law and court*, meaning that in the course of proceedings, no one may be subjected to any discrimination on the basis of origin, social or property status, sex, race, ethnicity, language, religion, views, place of residence or any other circumstances.
- *Inviolability of the individual*, implying that arrest and imprisonment is allowed only in the cases provided for by the CrPC and only with the sanction of the court; without the sanction of the court, an individual may be detained for a period not longer than 72 hours.
- *Judicial protection of rights and freedoms*, indicating that everyone has the right to judicial protection of his rights and freedoms. In particular *everyone has the right to be heard in court*. Also, it is specifically stated that the state must provide the victim access to justice and compensation of harm caused to him.
- *Ensuring the right to qualified legal assistance*, meaning that everyone has the right to receive qualified legal assistance in the course of criminal proceedings; this right may be exercised either personally or with the assistance of a defender or legitimate representative in accordance with the procedure established by the CrPC. It is also emphasized that a suspect or accused has the right to a defense.

- *Respect of the individual's honor and dignity*, denoting that it is prohibited to make decisions or execute actions that humiliate the dignity or diminish the honor of persons who are participating in a criminal proceeding.
- *Inviolability of property, housing, private life, personal and family secrets* as well as *confidentiality of personal deposits and savings; correspondence; telephone conversations; and post, telegraph and other messages.*
- The principle of *presumption of innocence*, meaning that everyone is deemed to be innocent until his guilt in a commission of a crime is proven in accordance with the procedure established by the CrPC and is determined by a court sentence that enters into legal force; furthermore, no one is obliged to prove his innocence and any doubts with regard to the guilt of an accused person must be interpreted for his benefit.
- The principle of *protection of the rights and freedoms of citizens who participate in the criminal procedure*, indicating that the harm caused to a citizen as a result of violation of his rights and freedoms in the course of a given criminal case is subject to compensation; and that if there is a sufficient evidence that a victim, witness or any other persons who participated in a criminal procedure, or the family members or other close relatives of these participants, are threatened with the application of violence, destruction or harm to their property or any other dangerous illegal acts, the body that leads the criminal procedure must, within the bounds of its authority, take measures to protect the rights and freedoms of those persons.
- The principle of *release from the duty to issue witness testimony against oneself, one's spouse or one's close relatives*; also, clergymen are not be obliged to witness against those who confided in them through confession.

The principles determining the course of criminal proceedings embrace the following fundamental provisions:

- *Administration of justice solely by the court*, denoting that no one may be recognized as guilty in the commission of a crime and subjected to criminal prosecution except pursuant to a court sentence and in accordance with the law; this principle also contemplates that a defendant may not be deprived of the right to have his criminal case heard by a judge in a court having jurisdiction over that case.
- *Independence of judges*, meaning that judges must be independent and subordinated only to the Constitution of RK and the law when administering justice.[2]

2. At this point it should, however, be noted that the issue of independence of courts is problematic in Kazakhstan since judges in practice get their power from the executive branch (see section VII "Judicial Power in Kazakhstan" of Chapter 3 "Constitutional Law" *supra*), which is not conducive to their true independence. Moreover, there is another factor that significantly restricts the independence of judges: the evaluation of their activities on the basis of how many of their decision have been reversed. These statistics have a major impact on the career development of judges and, thus, area disguised form of control of the judges' actions. The judges are afraid to make decisions unwanted by higher instances as each reversal is perceived as improper

- The principle of *prohibition of a repeated conviction and criminal prosecution*, implying that no one may be subjected repeatedly to criminal liability for the same crime.
- The principle of *competitiveness of the parties*, indicating in particular that: (a) proceedings are carried out in accordance with adversarial principles; (b) prosecution, defense and adjudication are separated from each other and are exercised by different bodies and officials; (c) the burden of proving the accusation rests with the procurator; (d) the defendant may use all the remedies and methods for protection provided for by law.
- *Comprehensive, full and objective examination of the circumstances of cases*, meaning that the court, procurator, investigator and inquiry officer are obliged to take all measures provided for by law for a comprehensive, complete and objective examination of the circumstances that are necessary and sufficient for a correct settlement of the case.
- *Evaluation of Evidence on the Basis of Internal Convictions* by the judge, procurator, detectives and investigators, who must be guided in this respect only by law and their conscience. In doing so, no evidence may have a predetermined force for them.
- *Evidence obtained by illegal means has no juridical force*, and *no person may be sentenced on the basis of his own admission of guilt.*
- *The laws establishing or intensifying liability, imposing new responsibilities on citizens or deteriorating their conditions may have no retroactive force.*
- The principle of *publicity of criminal proceedings*, stipulating that the restriction of publicity is allowed only for the purposes of: (a) protecting state secrets; (b) preventing information concerning the intimate parts of the lives of persons participating in a case (crimes of minors, sexual crimes, etc.); and (c) protecting the safety of the victim, a witness or any other participants in a case as well as their family members and close relatives.
- The proceedings are carried out in Kazakh or, where appropriate, in Russian or any other language; participants in proceedings who have a poor or no command of the language in which the proceedings are conducted have the right to use their native tongue, or another language of which they have a good command, and to make use, free of charge, of interpreter's services.
- The principle of *freedom to challenge procedural acts and decision*, meaning that acts and decisions of court and prosecution agencies may be challenged and each convicted person has the right to have his sentence revised by the upper court and to ask for a pardon or mitigation of punishment.

---

performance and may lead to negative conclusions about the professional suitability of judges. See A. Kishkembayev, "Легко ли вынести оправдательный приговор?" ["Is It Easy to Issue an Acquittal"], *Yuridicheskaya Gazeta* (Almaty March 16, 2006) <http://base.zakon.kz/result.asp?uid=44FE6DE1-EB74-4C79-A1F15AAAF2D8304F&fromclass =eng> (October 9, 2011).

The above-mentioned principles are the ideals that must serve as guidance for the activities of all participants in criminal proceedings. In actual practice, however, the degree of compliance with them leaves much to be desired.[3]

C. Stages of Criminal Proceedings

Criminal proceedings are carried out in the course of a number of stages, which proceed in a consecutive order and are differentiated from each other by particular procedural actions and rules and by their range of participants. Typically, each stage is separated from the previous one by a final procedural decision. At present, the following stages may clearly be distinguished (a detailed account of these stages is offered in subsequent sections):

- (1) Pre-Trial Stage:
  - (i) Initiation of Criminal Case;
  - (ii) Preliminary Investigation;
- (2) Judicial Stage:
  - (a) Proceedings in the Court of First Instance;
    - (i) Assignment and Preparation of the Main Trial;
    - (ii) Main Trial;
  - (b) Revision of the Court's Judgments That Have Not Yet Come into Force:
    - (i) Appellate Proceedings;
    - (ii) Cassational Proceedings;
    - (iii) Execution of Judgments;
  - (c) Revision of the Court's Judgments That Have Entered into Force:
    - (i) Proceedings in the Supervisory Authority;
    - (ii) Resumption of the Proceedings on Account of Newly Revealed Circumstances.

II. LEGAL STATUS OF PARTICIPANTS OF CRIMINAL PROCEEDINGS

Participants of criminal proceedings may be differentiated into the following categories: (a) the court; (b) state bodies and officials that exercise the function

---

3. Unfortunately, it must be noted that criminal proceedings continue to be unduly oppressive, human rights and freedoms are unreasonably restricted by law enforcement agencies and courts are not always objective and impartial when resolving criminal cases on merits. Despite the large number of liberal norms outline above, the number of acquittals does not exceed 2% of the total number of cases before the courts. See, e.g., "Результаты мониторинга судебных разбирательств в Республике Казахстан 2005–2006" ["Results of the Monitoring of Judicial Handlings in the Republic of Kazakhstan 2005–2006"] <http://www.osce.org/ru/astana/24154> (October 9, 2011).

of criminal prosecution; (c) participants who defend either their own or represented rights and interests; and (d) other persons that participate in criminal proceedings.

A. Court

According to the CrPC, justice in criminal cases in Kazakhstan is exercised by: (a) the Supreme Court of RK; (b) regional (and equivalent) courts; (c) district (and equivalent) courts; (d) specialized inter-district criminal courts; (e) specialized inter-district military criminal courts; (f) specialized inter-district juvenile courts; and (g) military courts of garrisons (Article 57).

A court has the sole power: (1) to find a person guilty of a crime and impose punishment on him; (2) to order involuntary medical treatment of a person or apply informal correctional measures to a person; (3) to reverse or alter a decision made by a lower court; (4) to approve a pre-trial restraint in the form of incarceration or house arrest (as decided by the investigator or inquiry agency) as well as to extend a term of pre-trial detention; (5) to review previous judicial acts upon the discovery of new facts; and (6) to commit a suspect or accused who is not in custody to a medical institution for forensic medical examination (Article 59).

B. State Bodies and Officials Exercising the Function of Criminal Prosecution

Participants in criminal proceedings on the prosecution side include: (a) the procurator; (b) the head of the investigation department; (c) the investigator; and (d) the inquiry agency.

A procurator (*prokuror*) is an official authorized, within the limits of his powers, to exercise supervisory control over the legality of the investigatory activity, the simplified pre-trial proceedings, the inquiry, the operational investigations and adjudication, as well as the criminal prosecution at all stages of criminal proceedings. He represents the interests of the state and is the state procurator. Also, he may bring a suit advocating the interests of victims who are notable to independently exercise their right to make a claim by virtue of their helpless condition, dependence on the defendant or due to other reasons (Article 62). In the course of criminal prosecution, and when supervising the legality of criminal investigations, the procurator is, *inter alia*, authorized to: (1) initiate criminal cases or to deny the initiation of such cases; (2) sanction actions by officials performing the preliminary investigation, in the cases provided for by law; (3) participate in the performance of certain investigative acts; and (4) arraign an accused to the court, presenting to the court the criminal case received from the bodies of preliminary investigation (Article 197). The procurator represents the interests of the state by leading the prosecution: he presents evidence and participates in examining it, expresses his opinion to the court on the essence of the charges and on other issues that arise during the court trial and makes proposals to the court as to the application of the law and the establishment of the punishment for the defendant (Article 317 IV). He may also have other authorities as established by the legislation.

The head of the investigation department (and his deputies) may exercise the following authorities: (1) to entrust the performance of the investigation to an investigator; (2) to ensure the timeliness of investigative acts; (3) to recuse an investigator from specific proceedings in cases provided for by law; (4) to send finished criminal cases to the procurator, etc. He may also initiate criminal cases, accept criminal cases for his processing and personally carry out the preliminary investigation, enjoying in this last case the powers of an investigator.

An investigator (*tergeushi*, *sledovatel'*) is an official authorized to carry out preliminary investigations with regard to criminal cases within the bounds of his authorities. There are the four types of investigators: (1) special procurators; (2) investigators part of bodies of internal affairs; (3) investigators part of the bodies of national security; and (4) investigators part of the bodies of the financial police. An investigator may initiate criminal cases and perform preliminary investigations and all other investigative acts. He must take every measure for a comprehensive, full and objective examination of the circumstances of the case in question, and, once sufficient evidence has been gathered to indicate that an individual committed the crime, carry out the criminal prosecution of said individual by holding him as the defendant, compiling and presenting the accusation and electing a method of suppression. Any decisions concerning the direction of the investigation and the performance of investigative acts are adopted by the investigators independently, except for cases provided by law that require the sanctions from the procurator or decisions by the court. Unlawful interference with his activities entails criminal liability (Article 64).

An inquiry agency is either a body of internal affairs or of national security (Article 65).[4] It consists of agency heads and inquiry officers. The head of an inquiry agency is responsible to organize the adoption of appropriate procedural and investigative measures for the purposes of preventing and eliminating of crime and, when a crime has been committed, finding those who committed it. Pursuant to the requirements of the body conducting the criminal proceedings, or pursuant to his own initiative, he organizes the facts found as a result of investigative activity that are necessary for the accurate solution of the criminal case.

An inquiry officer (*anyqtaushy*, *doznavatel'*) is an official person authorized to perform pre-trial activities associated with criminal cases within the bounds of

4. Agencies that have jurisdiction for specific types of cases include: (1) bodies of justice (for crimes connected with the procedure for the executing criminal punishments); (2) bodies of the financial police; (3) customs bodies (for cases of contraband and evasion of customs payments); (4) the bodies of military police (for crimes committed by military servicemen) or, if there is no military police, commanders of military units; (5) commanders of frontier units (for cases involving the violation of laws concerning the state borders of RK, as well as crimes committed on the continental shelf of RK); (6) heads of diplomatic and consular representations of RK (for cases of crimes committed by their employees in the country of their stay); and (7) the bodies of state fire-prevention service (for crimes associated with fires) (Art. 65).

his authority. He may make decisions on the commencement and performance of such actions in the forms defined by the CrPC and independently perform investigative and other procedural acts, except for in cases where the law demands the approval of the head of the inquiry agency, the sanctioning of the procurator or the consent of the court. He must comply with the instructions of the court, procurator, body of preliminary investigation and the body of interrogation with regard to ensuring the security of the persons who are participating in the criminal procedure (Article 67).

C. Participants Who Defend Their Own or Represented Rights and Interests

Participants who defend either their own or represented rights and interests may be differentiated into: (a) those on the prosecution side and (b) those on the defense side. Participants on the prosecution side are: (1) victims; (2) private prosecutors; and (3) civil plaintiffs; while participants on the defense side include: (1) suspects; (2) accused persons; (3) civil respondents; and (4) defenders.

A victim (*zhäbirlenushi*, *poterpevshiy*) is a person who is believed to have received moral, physical or property harm (Article 75). He has, *inter alia*, the following rights: (1) to provide testimony; (2) to submit evidence; (3) to file petitions and recusals; (4) to participate in judicial discovery concerning the case in the first instance court; (5) to participate in court debates; (6) to bring an accusation, in particular in cases when the state procurator refuses to bring one; (7) to file complaints regarding acts of the body leading the criminal procedure; and (8) to challenge court resolutions and the sentence. At the same time, a victim is obliged: (1) to arrive when summoned by the body leading the criminal procedure; (2) to truthfully communicate all circumstances he knows on the case and to answer questions asked of him; (3) to not disclose information on circumstances known to him with regard to the case; and (4) to comply with the established procedure when investigative acts are performed and during the court session.

A private prosecutor is a person who has filed a complaint with and brought an accusation to the court with regard to a case of private prosecution. Additionally, in cases of public and public-private prosecution, a private prosecutor may be a victim who independently maintains an accusation in court after the procurator refuses to continue the charge (Article 76). A private prosecutor has all the rights and bears all the obligations of a victim and also all the rights necessary to maintain the accusation in the court.

A civil plaintiff may be a natural person or legal entity who, with sufficient reasons to do so, files a claim stating that a crime directly caused property harm to him and requesting compensation for that harm. He may also file a lawsuit for property compensation for moral harm.

A suspect (*sezikti*, *podozrevaemyi*) is the person against whom a criminal case is initiated, due to the suspicion that he committed a crime. He may be notified of the suspicion by an investigator or inquiry officer, or he may be detained or otherwise restrained prior to his notification. A suspect has the following rights: (1) to know what he is suspected of; (2) to have the assistance of a defender; (3) to have a one-on-one meeting with the defender, in a confidential setting, before the suspect is questioned for the first time; (4) to refuse to give explanations or testimony; (5) to present evidence; (6) to file petitions and recusals; (7) to file complaints concerning acts or decisions of the court, procurator, investigator, or inquiry officer; and (8) to defend himself through the use of any other means that are not prohibited by law (Article 68 VII).

An accused person (*ayiptalushy*, *obvinyaemyi*) is a person who is the subject of an accusation or a criminal case through private prosecution; his accusation is compiled and approved by the head of the inquiry agency. An accused person has the following rights: (1) to protect his rights and legitimate interests by any means that does not contradict the law; (2) to have sufficient time to prepare his defense; (3) to know what he is accused of; (4) to receive an immediate explanation of his rights from the criminal prosecution body; (5) to be notified of the adoption of procedural decisions that concern his rights and interests by the body that leads the criminal procedure; (6) to provide explanations and testimony about the accusation(s) presented to him; (7) to abstain from giving testimonies; (8) to present evidence; (9) to file petitions and recusals; (10) to have a defender and to have meetings with him alone and in a confidential setting starting before his first interrogation; (11) to set questions before experts and to examine expert evaluations; (12) to examine any materials upon completion of investigation on the case; (13) to file complaints concerning acts and decisions by the court, procurator, investigator or inquiry officers; (14) to demand a public court session, etc. (Article 69).[5]

A civil respondent is a natural person or legal entity who is accused by of causing property harm to the civil plaintiff in the complaint of a civil action (Article 78).

A defender (*korgaushy, začšitnik*) is a person who defends the rights and interests of suspects and accused persons and who renders legal assistance to them. As a rule, the defense is represented by an attorney (*advokat*). Along with an attorney, the defense may be exercised by spouses, close relatives and legitimate representatives. Foreign attorneys are allowed to participate in cases as defenders where so provided by international treaties of RK. The defense is allowed to participate in a given case from the moment the accusation is presented or the person is recognized as a suspect, or from any other moment of the criminal proceedings. The participation of a defender is obligatory when: (1) suspected or accused persons petition for it; (2) they have not reached the age of majority; (3) they may not independently exercise their right to defense by virtue of physical or mental shortcomings; (4) they have no command of the language in which court

5. The most important difference in the legal status of a suspect and an accused person is that the restrictions of the rights of the latter have a more severe character (e.g., the former may be detained for not more than 10 days while the latter up to one year).

proceedings are carried out; (5) a person is accused of commission of a crime for which the sentence may result in the deprivation of freedom for over 10 years or in capital punishment; (6) a procurator participates in the consideration of the case in court; and (7) in other specific cases (Article 70).

When, in the event of the above-mentioned circumstances, a defender is not invited by the suspect or accused themselves (or their legitimate representatives), the body that leads the criminal procedure is obliged to provide for the participation of a defender at the appropriate stage of the procedure. In this case, the body passes a resolution that is obligatory for the professional organization of attorneys. From the moment he begins participating in the case, the defender is entitled to: (1) have meetings with the accused or suspect alone and confidentially without restrictions to their number or length; (2) collect and present documents and information, that are required for rendering legal assistance; (3) be present when the accusation is presented and participate in the interrogation of the suspect or accused and in other investigative acts; (4) to file recusals; (5) to examine all documents of the proceedings and to copy from it any information in any volume; (6) file petitions; (7) participate in legal proceedings in every stage of the case; (8) to exercise any other means and methods of defense, that do not contradict law.[6] At the same time, a defender may not commit any acts against the interests of the defendant nor impede the exercise of his rights. In particular, he may not recognize the guilt of the defendant or disclose information that became known to him in connection with the application for or exercise of legal assistance.

D. Other Persons That Participate in Criminal Proceedings

Other persons that participate in criminal proceedings include: (1) persons maintaining the process of proof (such as witnesses, experts, specialists, translators, hired witnesses and mediators); and (2) persons maintaining the due order of procedural acts (such as the secretary of the court session and the bailiff).

A witness (*kuä*, *svidetel*) is any person who may know certain circumstances that are material to a case (Article 82), though certain people may be exempted from testifying (e.g., clergymen regarding facts they discovered through confession).Witnesses reserve several rights, including the right to refuse to provide testimony that may entail for himself, his spouse or close relatives prosecution for the commission of a criminally punishable act or administrative violation, among other rights. A witness may also provide testimony in the presence of

6. However, it must be noted that the declared rights of a defenders are often not respected and are violated by law-enforcement agencies. For example, there are cases where confidential meetings of a defender with a suspect or an accused were wiretapped in detention centers and other facilities or offices of law enforcement agencies. There are problems with timely access to a client; as a rule, a lawyer is not allowed to enter the facilities of offices of the law enforcement agencies without being invited by a law enforcement staff. Also, in criminal cases involving state secrets, only those defenders are allowed to participate who are selected by the national security agencies (i.e., a body of investigation) on the basis of their internal regulations.

his attorney. At the same time, a witness is obliged as follows: (1) to arrive when summoned by the inquiry officer, detective, procurator or court; (2) to truthfully communicate all he knows about the case and to answer any questions asked of him; (3) not to disclose information with regard to the case if he was warned against this by the inquiry officer, investigator or procurator; (4) to comply with the procedure established for the performance of investigative acts and during the court trial.

An expert is a person who has special scientific expertise, while a specialist is a person who has special knowledge that is required in the collection, examination and evaluation of evidence as well as the application of technical facilities. When some participants in a legal proceeding do not have mastery of the language of the proceeding, a translator translates for them. A hired witness is a person engaged by the body of criminal prosecution to certify facts of the performance of investigative acts, their course and results; he may be only a person who is not dependant on the bodies of criminal prosecution, is of full age and capable of a full and accurate understanding of the acts that took place in his presence.[7] Experts, specialists, translators and hired witnesses must be persons who are not interested in the case (Articles 83–86). Another participant in criminal proceedings maintaining the process of proof may be a mediator, an independent natural person brought in by the parties for the purposes of mediation (Article 88-1).

III. EVIDENCE AND PROOF

Evidence is legitimately obtained factual data on the basis of which, in accordance with the procedure defined by the CrPC, the inquiry officer, detective, procurator or court establishes the existence or non-existence of an act provided by the Criminal Code of RK, the commission or non-commission of a given act by the indicted person and/or the guilt or non-guilt of the defendant, as well as other circumstances that are material for the correct resolution of the case. These data are established by: (a) the testimony of a suspect, defendant, victim or witness; (b) expert reports; (c) material evidence; and (d) the record of procedural acts and other documents.

Evidence must be recognized as inadmissible if it is received due to a deprivation or restriction of the rights of one or more participants of the procedure or by a violation of other rules of criminal procedure in the course of the investigation or court trial. The forms of inadmissible evidence include data received: (1) through the use of torture, violence, threats, deceit or other equally illegal acts; (2) by providing misinformation to a participant in the criminal procedure regarding his rights and obligations, or if the evidence was found after a failure to properly explain his rights and obligations to him; (3) in connection with the performance of procedural acts by a person who has no right to perform those acts in the context of the concerned criminal case; (4) through a material violation of the procedure for

7. The CrPC requires that not less than two hired witnesses must participate in investigative acts.

the performance of procedural acts; (5) from an unknown source or from a source that is not allowed to be established during the court trial; (6) by the use of methods that contradict contemporary scientific knowledge (Article 116).

The legislation obliges the following circumstances to be subject to proof in all criminal cases: (1) the event and features delineated by Criminal Law of the composition of a crime (time, place, method and other circumstances of the crime's commission); (2) the individual(s) who committed an act prohibited by the criminal law; (3) the guilt of a person of committing a crime, the form of his guilt (i.e., through negligence or intent), the motive of the act committed; (4) circumstances that affect the degree and nature of the liability of the defendant; (5) the background of the defendant; (6) the consequences of crime commissioned; (7) the nature and amount of harm caused by the crime; (8) circumstances that exclude the criminality of a given act (e.g., self-defense); and (9) circumstances that entail a release from criminal responsibility and punishment.

The burden of proof consists of collecting, researching, evaluating and using evidence for the purposes of establishing the circumstances that are material for a legitimate, substantial and fair settlement of a given case (Article 124). The collection of evidence includes its discovery, registration and seizure. It is carried out in the course of pre-trial proceedings and throughout the trial by performing investigative and judicial acts provided for by the CrPC.

Evidence collected for a case is subject to comprehensive and objective examination. The examination comprises an analysis of obtained evidence and a comparison of each part with the other evidence, the collection of additional evidence and a review of the sources from which the evidence was obtained. Each piece of evidence is subject to an evaluation of its relevance, admissibility, veracity, and all the evidence in their entirety is judged as to its sufficiency for the resolution of a given criminal case. The judge, the procurator, the investigator and the inquiry officer evaluate evidence on the basis of their internal conviction based on a comprehensive, full and objective consideration of evidence in its entirety, guided by law and their conscience.

IV. MEASURES OF PROCEDURAL COMPULSION

According to the CrPC, measures of coercion include: (a) detention and (b) measures of suppression.

Detention (*üstau, zaderzhanie*) of a person suspected to have committed a crime is a measure of coercion applied for the purposes of discovering his complicity in the crime or in order to decide whether he should be charged (and thus held for a more substantial period of time). In this regard, the Constitution of RK provides that "without the sanction of a court, a person may be detained for a period no more than 72 hours" (Article 16 II). An individual can only be detained in the following cases: (1) a given person is caught in the commission of a crime or directly after its commission; (2) an eye-witnesses in particular a victim, directly implicates a given person in the commission of a crime; (3) the obvious traces of a crime are found on a given person's clothes or body, or in his house; (4) there are reliable data, based on material obtained in accordance with the laws of investigative activities, demonstrating that a given person was involved in the commission of a crime or in the preparation of a grave or especially grave crime (Article 132).

Within three hours of the moment of actual detention, the investigator or inquiry officer must compile a record of the detention, in which they indicate the reasons, motives, place and time of the detention; the results of the personal search of the detained; and the time when the official record was compiled. The record must be read to the detainee and his rights as a suspect must be explained to him, after which the compiler and detainee both sign the record. The inquiry officer (or the investigator) is obliged to notify the procurator in writing of the detention within 12 hours of the compilation of the record.

A person detained must be interrogated in full compliance with the CrPC. In particular, he must be ensured the right to meet, in person and confidentially, prior to the first interrogation with his defender (Article 134). The inquiry officer or the investigator is obligated to notify an adult member of the family of the detained person or, if no such person is available, other relatives or close friends of his detention and his current location, or to provide the suspect or accused person an opportunity to make such a notification himself. If the detained person is a foreign citizen, his embassy, consulate or another representative of his state must be notified within the period established by law (Article 138).[8]

Measures of suppression (*bültarpau shara*, *mera presecheniya*) are methods of coercion that are applied when there are sufficient reasons to believe that a given defendant will elude interrogation, preliminary investigation or orders of the courts; impede an objective investigation and trial of the case in court; or continue to engage in criminal activities, and also for ensuring the implementation of a sentence. Such measures include (*inter alia*): (1) an oath to not leave a certain location and to maintain appropriate behavior; (2) a personal pledge; (3) bail; (4) house arrest; and (5) arrest (Article 140). When deciding which measure, if any, of suppression is necessary, the following circumstances must be taken into account: the gravity of presented charges, the personality of the defendant, his age, the condition of his health, his family status, his occupation, his property status, the availability of a permanent place of residence, etc. A defendant (or suspect) may not be subject to more than one measure of suppression. Once the decision is made, a resolution is passed by the body leading the criminal procedure on the application of measures of suppression, which contains an indication of the crime for which the person is suspected or charged and the reasons for the application of a given

---

8. However, it should be noted that there are views that the court's role with respect to the authorization of detentions is often reduced to being pro forma. See, e.g., "Судебное санкционирование ареста в Республике Казахстан" ["Judicial Authorization of Arrest in the Republic of Kazakhstan"], The OSCE Office for Democratic Institutions and Human Rights, <http://www.zakon.kz/analytics/214163-sudebnoe-sankcionirovanie-aresta-v.html> (October 9, 2011).

measure of suppression. A copy of the resolution is handed to the subject individual, and he is notified of the procedure for challenging decisions on the application of the measure of suppression.

An oath to not leave a certain location and to maintain appropriate behavior consists of the subject signing a written obligation, drafted by the body leading the criminal procedure, not to leave his permanent or temporary place of residence without a permit from the inquiry officer, detective or court; not to impede the investigation and trial of the case; and to answer the summons of the body leading the criminal procedure (Article 144).

Personal pledges consist of an assumption by trustworthy persons of a written obligation that a given suspect or defendant will maintain appropriate behavior and come when summoned by the body leading the criminal procedure; at least two persons must make such a pledge on behalf of a single suspect or accused (Article 145).

Bail is a deposit to the court to ensure the compliance of a suspect or defendant with summonses by the bodies of interrogation, investigation or the court; it may be paid by the suspect or defendant himself or by any other physical person or legal entity. The amount of the bail is determined by the authority that selected this measure of suppression, subject to the gravity of the charges, personality of the suspect/defendant and the property status of the pledger (Article 148).

House arrest applies to suspects and defendants with the sanctions of the procurator or upon a court decision, when the full isolation of the person is not necessary or is not expedient due to, e.g., the suspect or defendant's age, health condition or family status. A person so detained may be prohibited from communicating with certain individuals; receiving or sending correspondence; conducting negotiations with the use of any communication facilities; as well as restrictions may be established in respect of leaving the housing. The place of house arrest may be guarded and the subject's behavior may be subject to monitoring (Article 149).

Arrest as a measure of suppression only applies with the approval of the procurator or upon a decision by the court, and generally is only applied to persons suspected or accused of committing a deliberate crime that entails punishment in the form of deprivation of freedom for more than five years; in exceptional cases this measure may be applied to persons suspected/accused of lesser crimes. The period of arrest during the pre-trial stage associated may not exceed two months, but, in the event that it is impossible to complete an investigation within this period and when there are no reasons for the ending the arrest, this period may be extended up to 12 months.

V. PRE-TRIAL PROCEEDINGS ASSOCIATED WITH CRIMINAL CASES

A. Initiation of a Criminal Case

Initiation of a criminal case is an early stage of criminal proceedings that consists of receiving, registering and verifying information about the crime and, subsequently, deciding whether to conduct a preliminary investigation.[9] The basis for the initiation of a criminal case is the availability of sufficient evidence indicating that a crime has been committed, assuming there are no circumstances that exclude proceeding with a given criminal case. Grounds for initiating a criminal case include: (1) the application of a citizen; (2) a confession; (3) a report by a state official or a manager at an organization; (4) reporting in the mass media; (5) the direct discovery of evidence of crime by officials or agencies authorized to initiate criminal cases (Article 177). A decision pursuant to an application or report on a crime must be made within 72 hours of the moment of its receipt (Article 184).[10] If there are sufficient grounds to initiate the case, the inquiry officer, the body of interrogation, the head of the investigation department, the investigator or the procurator must pass a resolution to that effect, thereby beginning the preliminary investigation; this decision must be communicated to the applicant, the person subject to the investigation and the procurator (Article 187).

B. Preliminary Investigation

Preliminary investigation is a stage of criminal proceedings that consists of the efforts of the inquiry agency, investigator and procurator to prove the circumstances of the criminal case, promptly and fully disclose the crime, reveal the person(s) who committed it and facilitate judicial adjudication on the merits. There are three main forms of the preliminary investigation: (a) investigation; (b) inquiry; and (c) simplified pre-trial proceedings.

Investigation is the main form of pre-trial proceedings in all grave and especially grave crimes, as well as in certain crimes of lesser and medium gravity. Essentially, it is a basic standard procedure for establishing the circumstances of the crime and preparing materials of the case for further consideration by the court. It includes such activities as interrogation; confrontation; inspection; search and seizure; expert examinations; seizing and analyzing postal correspondence; eavesdropping and the recording of conversations; reviewing and clarifying testimony; and investigative experiments. Upon completing all necessary investigative acts and collecting sufficient evidence, the investigator compiles an accusatory conclusion and sends the case to the procurator, who decides to either arraign the accused or dismiss the criminal case.

Inquiry is a shortened form of preliminary investigation conducted by bodies of interrogation in crimes of lesser and medium gravity; while an investigation is not limited to time, an inquiry can only last one month.

Simplified pre-trial proceedings are exercised with respect to crimes of lesser and medium gravity only when the collected evidence establishes the existence of the crime and the person(s) who committed it admits his guilt and does not contest the collected evidence or the character and extent of harm caused. This type of

9. This stage does not exist when applying the simplified pre-trial proceedings (see below).
10. If necessary, this period may be extended for a period of up to two months.

proceedings must be completed within 10 days from the date of the registration of the application or report on the crime and before the case is transferred to the procurator.

VI. PROCEEDINGS IN THE COURT OF FIRST INSTANCE

Proceedings in the court of first instance consist of two stages: (a) stage of assignment and preparation of the main trial; and (b) main trial.

The first stage starts from the moment of the receipt of the criminal case by the court and consists of verifying the compliance of the pre-trial stages of criminal proceedings with the law and established procedures, as well as deciding whether a main trail is necessary and, if so, preparing for it. According to the legislation, when a criminal case is received by a court, the Chairman of the court (or another judge pursuant to his instructions) decides whether to accept the case for processing by the court. In doing so, he may either: (1) appoint the main trial court; (2) return the case for additional investigation; (3) suspend proceedings on the case; (4) forward the case to a court that holds jurisdiction; (5) terminate the case; or (6) merge the case with another criminal action. A decision must be taken not later than five days from the moment of the case receipt by the court. If necessary, the judge may also decide to hold the preliminary hearing of the case with the participation of the parties. The preliminary hearing of a case is carried out by the judge individually in a closed court session with the mandatory participation of the procurator, the defendant and his defense for the purposes of the due examination of the case and the adoption of one of the above-mentioned decisions.

The main trial is the pivotal stage of the criminal proceedings, during which the hearing on the merits takes place, the essence of the case is established, the final legal assessment of the investigated facts is done and a fair judgment is made. The main trial consists of the following sub-stages:

Preparation of the Main Trial: At this stage, the judge opens up the hearing and announces what criminal case will be considered and whether the proceedings will be open or closed. Furthermore, the judge establishes the identity of the defendant, declares the court's composition, introduces the participants of the process and explains their rights and responsibilities. Also, the judge may hear any petitions from the concerned parties and may dismiss the case if grounds exist to do so.

Court Investigation: The trial begins with a procurator's presentation of the essence of the accusation to the defendant. Subsequently, the evidence submitted by the parties is explored, interviews of witnesses and victims are conducted, expert examination may be assigned, and reports of investigative acts may be announced in full or in part. If needed, additional investigative activities may be conducted.

Judicial Pleadings and Final Statement of the Defendant: Judicial pleadings consist of speeches of the procurator, the victim(s) or his representative, the civil plaintiff and civil defendant or their representatives, the defendant and his defense.

The sequence of the speeches is established by the court based on the proposals of the participants of the pleadings, but in all cases, the first word is given to the procurator. After finishing judicial pleadings the chairman gives the last word to the defendant. Upon hearing this statement the court retires into the conference room for a compilation of the sentence, which the Chairman announces to those present in the court session room.

Statement of a Sentence: Sentences are resolved on behalf of the Republic of Kazakhstan. They must be legitimate and motivated, i.e., resolved in compliance with all the requirements of the law and on the basis of a comprehensive and impartial research of the evidence presented to the court at the court session. The sentence is resolved in the conference room under conditions that exclude the possibility of rendering any influence on the court. After the signing of the sentence, the court returns to the court session room, and the Chairman (or another judge) reads the sentence. The court also explains to the convicted person the procedure and period for challenging the sentence and other rights provided by law.

VII. REVISION OF JUDGMENTS THAT HAVE NOT ENTERED INTO FORCE

A. Appellate Proceedings

Court sentences that have not entered into legal force, except for the sentences of the Supreme Court of RK, may be challenged and protested through the appellate procedures. The right to challenge the sentence rests with the defense and his representatives (whether convicted or acquitted) and the victim and his representatives. Moreover, the civil plaintiff, civil defendant or their representatives have the right to challenge those portions of the sentence that pertain to a civil claim.

Appellate complaints and protests against the sentences of district (or equivalent-level) courts that have not entered into force are considered by the panel for criminal cases of regional courts and courts equated to them. Complaints against the sentences of regional courts are considered by the panel for criminal cases of the Supreme Court of RK (Article 397).

Pursuant to appellate complaints (or protests), the appellate instance court reviews the accuracy of the established circumstances of the case and the application of Criminal Law, whether the proceedings complied with accepted criminal procedure and the legality of and motivation for the sentence or resolution of the first instance court based on the materials available in the case file or presented separately.

A case must be considered through the appellate procedure not later than one month from the date of its receipt.[11] As a result of considering a case through the appellate procedure, the court may adopt one of the following decisions: (1) leave

11. If there are sufficient reasons, that period may be extended pursuant to the resolution of the appellate instance court which is processing the case.

the sentence (or resolution) without change; (2) alter it; (3) abolish it and terminate the case; or (4) abolish it and submit the case to the first instance court for a new consideration or for additional investigation.

B. Cassational Proceedings

The sentences (resolutions) not yet having legal force of courts that are authorized to consider grave and especially grave crimes (specialized inter-district criminal courts and specialized inter-district military criminal courts), courts with the participation of jurymen or appellate courts may be reviewed through cassational proceedings.

A court of cassation verifies whether a judgment or any other court decision is lawful, well-founded and fair. In other words, a court of cassation examines only the observance of the legal side of the criminal case. After considering a case through the cassational procedure, the court may adopt one of the following decisions: (1) leave the sentence (or resolution) without change; (2) alter it; (3) abolish it and terminate the case; or (4) abolish it and submit the case to the first instance court for a new consideration or for additional investigation.

VIII. REVISION OF JUDGMENTS THAT HAVE ENTERED INTO LEGAL FORCE

A. Supervisory Proceedings

Court sentences and resolutions that have entered into legal force may be revised through the supervisory procedure; sentences and resolutions of the court of first instance, appellate courts and cassational instance courts may be challenged in this way. Resolutions of the Collegium of the Supreme Court of RK are final. Only in exceptional circumstances may a resolution of the Supreme Court be revised in connection with the establishment of information that the decision may lead to grave and irreversible consequences for the life, health or security of the people of RK or for the Kazakhstani economy.

Revising an accusatory sentence due to the need to apply the punishment of a less grave crime, the severity of punishment or other reasons that entail an improvement in the status of the convict is not limited by deadlines. However, challenges that would result in the deterioration of the convict's position, as well as challenges to a resolution that terminated a case, are only allowed within six months of the contested resolution's coming into force.

A supervisory complaint (or protest) is filed in writing to the Supreme Court of RK, which is authorized to exercise this revision. It must be indicated in the complaint (protest) what violations were made during the case's proceedings, how those violations resulted in the erroneous judicial decision in question and what grounds exist for the revision of the judicial act. The preliminary consideration of a supervisory complaint is carried out pursuant to the instructions of the Chairman of the Supreme Court of RK (or the Chairman of the Collegium of the Supreme Court) by a panel consisting of three judges within one month from the day of its receipt. Depending on the results of the preliminary consideration of a supervisory complaint, it is decided to either initiate the supervisory procedure or deny the initiation of the supervisory procedure and return the complaint.

Following the decision on the initiation of the supervisory procedure, the supervisory instance notifies the parties about the time and place of the consideration of the case through the supervisory procedure. A case in the supervisory instance must be considered within one month from the date of the initiation of the supervisory procedure. As a result of considering the case through the supervisory procedure, the court may leave the complaint (protest) without satisfaction; alter the sentence (resolution) of the appellate and cassational instances; or even abolish the sentence and terminate the case or direct it to a new court consideration.

B. Resumption of Proceedings in View of Newly Discovered Circumstances

A court sentence (or resolution) that has entered into legal force may be abolished, and proceedings on the case may be resumed in view of newly discovered circumstances related to: (1) a premeditated falsehood in the testimony of a victim or witness or expert; a falsehood in the material evidence, records of investigative, judicial acts or other documents; or a premeditated false translation that resulted in an illegitimate or unreasonable sentence or resolution that has already entered into force; (2) criminal acts by the inquiry officer, investigator or procurator that resulted in an illegitimate or unreasonable sentence that has already entered into force; (3) criminal acts by a judge or judges, committed while considering the concerned case; (4) other circumstances unknown to the court when passing the sentence, which, by themselves or together with the circumstances that were established previously, confirm that the convict is innocent or committed a crime of a lesser gravity, or alternatively, confirm the guilt of an acquitted person or a person whose case has been terminated; (5) a petition by a convict whose case has been considered without his participation; and (6) the recognition by the Constitutional Council of RK that a law applied in the sentence is unconstitutional.

Revision of a sentence in view of newly discovered circumstances in favor of the convict is not restricted by any deadlines, while revisions detrimental to the convict must be brought within one year of the day of the discovery of the new evidence.

The right to institute proceedings in view of newly discovered circumstances rests with the procurator, who may do so upon applications of citizens and due to additional information received in the course of the investigation and consideration of other criminal cases.

Upon the completion of the review or investigation of the newly discovered circumstances, if there are reasons for reinstituting case proceedings, the procurator sends his conclusion and materials of investigation to the appropriate court. If there are no reasons for the resumption of proceedings, the procurator terminates the proceedings initiated by him. The resolution terminating the proceedings is communicated to the interested parties, with a notification of their right to appeal the termination to court, which will decide the question of resuming the proceedings of a given case in light of newly discovered circumstances.

Upon considering the conclusion of the procurator regarding resuming the proceedings due to newly discovered circumstances, the court passes one of the following resolutions: (1) abolition of the court sentence or resolution and transfer of the case for the performance of new investigation or new court investigation; (2) abolition of the court sentence or resolution and termination of the case (if new investigation is not required to adopt the final decision of the case); or (3) rejection of the conclusion of the procurator.

IX. PROCEEDINGS ON JUVENILE CRIME CASES

The peculiarities of juvenile crime cases include the following major issues. *First*, additional circumstances must be established in cases of juveniles, such as the degree of his intellectual and mental development. *Second*, the right of a juvenile suspect/accused to confidentiality must be observed at all stages of the criminal court procedure. *Third*, the case of a juvenile who participated in the commission of a crime together with adults is separated from the adults' proceedings at the preliminary investigation stage. *Fourth*, the interrogation of a juvenile suspect/accused is carried out in the presence of a defense lawyer, a legitimate representative and, where appropriate, a psychiatrist and/or teacher. The interrogation must be carried out during the day and may not continue for more than two hours without a break, with a four hour maximum per day; if the juvenile is obviously fatigued, the interrogation must be interrupted. *Fifth*, the participation of a defense lawyer and the parents (or legitimate representatives) in cases of juveniles is obligatory. *Sixth*, it is also obligatory to perform psychological and psychiatric expert evaluations to decide whether the juvenile suspect/accused has a mental illness or deviation in his development and whether he has the capacity to realize the meaning of his actions and to control them in specific situations. *Seventh*, arrest and detention may only be applied to a juvenile in exceptional cases involving the commission of a grave or especially grave crime. *Eighth*, if, in the case of a crime of lesser or medium gravity, it is recognized that the juvenile may be reformed without the application of criminal punishment measures, the court may release the juvenile defendant from punishment, instead imposing mandatory educational measures on him.

X. PROCEEDINGS WITH THE PARTICIPATION OF JURYMEN

Proceedings with the participation of jurymen (i.e., a court consisting of a judge and 10 jurymen[12]) were introduced in Kazakhstan on January 1, 2007. Despite its short existence, this type of proceedings is now an integral part of Kazakhstani Criminal Procedure.

The proceedings may take place only in cases of especially grave crime. They may be authorized by the court at the petition of the accused during the preliminary hearing before the appointment of the main trial. After a date for the trial is set, the court reporter, at the direction of the presiding judge, randomly selects a pool of prospective jurors from the regular and alternate annual lists kept at the court. However, the same person may not take part in more than one trial per year. Once the members of the jury pool have been selected, a tentative list of prospective jurors is drawn up and signed by the court reporter. No later than seven days prior to the commencement of the trial, the prospective jurors on the list are served with notices indicating the time and date they are to appear in court.

In the preparatory phase of the trial, the presiding judge makes a brief opening statement to the prospective jurors in which he, *inter alia*, introduces the parties, states what criminal case is to be tried and advises the jurors of the tasks facing them. Each of the prospective jurors appearing in the trial is entitled to point out any reason that would interfere with his serving as a juror and to request to be excused. If the number of the prospective jurors exceeds 17, the presiding judge draws lots to reduce the number of remaining jurors to 17. Following this, the defendant and/or his defense counsel may peremptorily challenge three jurors while the procurator may object to inclusion of two jurors. Afterwards, the presiding judge draws lots again and the first 10 jurors drawn are considered to be the main jurymen, while the last two are alternates. The jurymen then take an oath.

Proceedings with the participation of jurymen have some special features. Information about the defendant's character may be presented in the presence of the jury only to the extent that it is essential for the determination of particular elements of the crime. Information about prior convictions, the defendant's status as a chronic alcoholic or drug addict or other information that may prejudice the jury against the defendant may not be considered. Following the completion of the trial, the court proceeds to closing arguments. The closing arguments consist of two parts. The first part is composed of arguments with respect to proof of the guilt of the defendant; the second part deals with qualifications of the defendant's actions (the latter is conducted without jurors).

Upon the completion of the closing arguments, the presiding judge drafts questions in writing to be decided by the jury, reads them aloud and gives them to

12. In contrast to the common law model, where the jury may decide on the merits of the case in the deliberation room by themselves, in Kazakhstan jurymen may only pass a sentence together with the judge, the chairman of the court.

the parties. The parties have the right to make comments regarding the content and wording of the questions and to submit proposals for additional questions. During the discussion and formulation of questions, the jurors are sent out of the courtroom. After taking the parties' comments and proposals into account, the judge prepares and signs a list of questions to be decided by the jury in the deliberation room. This list is read aloud in the presence of the jury and the parties.

Before the judge and the jury retire to the deliberation room to return a verdict, the presiding judge addresses the jury with final instructions summarizing the content of the charge and explaining the principal rules for evaluating the evidence. After hearing the final instructions by the presiding judge and reviewing the questions submitted to them, the jurors have the right to seek additional explanations from the presiding judge while the parties have the right to raise objections regarding the contents of the final instructions of the presiding judge based on violations by him of the principles of objectivity and impartiality.

After receiving the final instructions from the presiding judge, the judge and the jury retire to the deliberation room to consider their verdict. The jury's deliberations are supervised by the judge, who places before the jury the questions to be decided in the order they are listed on the question list, takes votes on the answers and counts the votes. Generally, three basic questions are asked about each of the acts the defendant is charged with committing: (1) whether it was proved that the act took place; (2) whether it was proved that the act was committed by the defendant; and (3) whether the defendant is guilty of committing the act (i.e., he acted with intent or is responsible due to his negligence). The answers to questions submitted to the jury must be in the affirmative or negative and are required to be accompanied by a clarifying word or phrase explaining or clarifying the meaning of the answer (e.g., "Yes, guilty," "No, not guilty," etc.). The jury may seek additional explanations from the presiding judge regarding the questions submitted to them.

A guilty verdict is deemed to have been decided when a majority of the jurors vote in the affirmative on each of the three above questions (the judge and every individual juror each have one vote and may not abstain from voting). A not guilty verdict is deemed to have been decided when no less than six jurors vote in the negative on any one of the three basic questions on the question list. A punishment in the form of the deprivation of freedom for more than 15 years may be appointed only when no less than eight jurors vote in the affirmative and capital punishment only when the judge and jurors unanimously vote in the affirmative.

Pursuant to the decision of the jury, the presiding judge makes one of the following decisions: (1) an order dismissing the criminal case; (2) a judgment of acquittal in those situations when the jury votes for a not guilty verdict or when the presiding judge finds that the act does not constitute a crime; or (3) a judgment of conviction imposing a sentence. The sentence of a court with participation of jurymen may be appealed only to the cassational and supervisory instances.

Selected Bibliography

N. Abdikanov, *Организация главного судебного разбирательства по уголовным делам в РК* [*Organization of the Main Trial in Criminal Casesin RK*] (Baspa, Almaty, 2001) [in Russian].

D. Kanafin, *Гарантии прав личности в уголовном судопроизводстве* [*Guarantees of an Individual's Rights in Criminal Proceedings*] (KazGYuU, Almaty, 2005) [in Russian].

D. Kanafin, "Criminal Justice Reform in Kazakhstan and OSCE Commitments" (2009) 20 *Security and Human Rights* 56.

M. Kogamov, *Комментарий к уголовно-процессуальному кодексу Республики Казахстан* [*Commentary on the Criminal Procedure Code of the Republic of Kazakhstan*] (Žeti Žargi, Almaty, 2008) [in Russian].

M. Narikbayev, *Актуальные вопросы применения нового уголовного и уголовно-процессуального законодательства РК* [*Actual Issues of the Application of New Criminal and Criminal Procedure Legislation of RK*] (Däuir, Astana, 2005) [in Russian].

B. Toleubekova, *Уголовно-процессуальное право Республики Казахстан* [*Criminal Procedure Law of the Republic of Kazakhstan*] (Žeti Žargi, Almaty, 2005) [in Russian].

Chapter 15

Investment and Energy Law

Gani Bitenov

Investment Law and Energy Law are two new but rapidly developing components of the Kazakhstani legal system. In light of the country's abundant natural (and in particular energy) resources,[1] both Investment and Energy Law have evolved incrementally over time, dynamically reacting to perceived needs of the country's transitional economy. At present, they may certainly be viewed as special complex areas with an inter-disciplinary character representing a mix of public administrative law and private civil law and, as such, depending on the question under review, are subject to legal principles established in those fields of law.

I. HISTORICAL BACKGROUND

Private investment and subsurface use were present in Kazakhstan before the Soviet era. At the dawn of the twentieth century, a number of concessions were granted in colonial Kazakhstan by the Russian Tsar to develop subsoil resources and expand the area's infrastructure (concessions included the construction of the

1. The country's proven reserves of coal stand at 31.3 billion tons (3.8% of the world), oil at 39.8 billion barrels (3% of the world), and natural gas at 1.82 trillion cubic meters (1% of the world). BP Statistical Review of World Energy June 2010 <www.bp.com/statisticalreview> (June 15, 2011). Kazakhstan possesses 12.1% of world uranium reserves and is the top producer of uranium in the world (accounted for 34% of the world uranium production in 2010). Nuclear Energy Agency, 2010 Annual Report <http://www.oecd-nea.org/pub/webpubs> (June 15, 2011).

Zhenis Kembayev, *Introduction to the Law of Kazakhstan*, pp. 275–301.

Siberian and Orenburg-Tashkent railroads). However, after the October Revolution these investments were expropriated by the Soviet government, and state ownership was established over almost all economic assets

Following its declaration of sovereignty (October 25, 1990) Kazakhstan started to undertake efforts to transform the socialist centrally planned system into an open market economy. Investment (especially in the energy sector) became a vital factor for the country's development. Hence, the establishment of an appropriate investment climate (in particular to attract investment from abroad) became a corner stone of the nascent government's economic policy. As a result, a number of important laws had already been enacted by Kazakhstan by the time it officially obtained full state independence (December 16, 1991), including such Laws as "On Free Economic Zones" of November 30, 1990, "On Foreign Investment" of December 7, 1990, "On Basic Principles of Foreign Economic Activity" of December 15, 1990, "On Concessions" of December 23, 1991, "On Freedom of Economic Activity and the Development of Entrepreneurship" of January 15, 1991, and "On Enterprises" of April 1, 1991. This basic legal framework was instrumental for attracting an initial injection of foreign investment into the transitional economy.

By the mid-1990s Kazakhstan had managed to establish its core business legislation, including the Civil and Tax Codes and financial regulations. While this legislation was developing, the earlier adopted investment laws had to be made consistent within the wider framework of business regulations. Moreover, amendments were necessary to rectify provisions found inefficient in the course of their application to business reality. Thus, new legislative acts on foreign investment were adopted: the Law of RK of December 27, 1994, No. 266-XIII, "On Foreign Investment" and later the Law of RK of February 28, 1997, No. 75-1, "On State Support of Direct Investment." At the same time, the Law of RK of June 28, 1995, No. 2350, "On Petroleum" and the Law of RK of January 27, 1996, No. 2828, "On Subsurface and Subsurface Use" were adopted; two Laws concluded during relatively low petroleum prices and a strong need by the state for foreign investment thereby containing a constellation of investment stability guarantees. Viewed as a whole, the legal acts enforced in the mid-1990s established a favorable investment climate in Kazakhstan, which may have been unique in the world in terms of its scope and variety of guarantees offered to investors (in order to attract technology, expertise and capital, especially for the development of the country's energy infrastructure).[2]

Its abundance of natural resources and favorable legislative framework triggered dynamically increasing foreign investment inflows into Kazakhstan, and the country became the largest foreign direct investment recipient *per capita* in the CIS.[3] Furthermore, starting from the early 2000s, world prices for oil started to rise

2. P Cameron *International Energy Investment Law: the Pursuit of Stability* (Oxford University Press 2010) 320–321.
3. R. Ahrend & W. Tompson, "Realizing the Oil Supply Potential of the CIS: The Impact of Institutions and Policies" (Organisation for Economic Cooperation and Development (OECD) Working Paper No. 484 2006) <www.oecd.org/dataoecd/11/43/37003365.pdf> (July 1, 2011) 29.

dramatically. Higher oil prices strengthened the Government's political standing at both the national and international levels, advanced the domestic economy and developed a local business elite that now was able to invest into the capital intensive energy industry. Due to its stronger bargaining position, the Government proceeded to increase state stakeholding in the upstream industry and enhance health, safety and environment regulations to protect the interests of the people of Kazakhstan.[4]

In the light of these developments, Kazakhstan began to revise both its investment and subsoil use policy. As a result, the Law of RK of January 8, 2003, No. 373-II, "On Investments" (LI) was adopted, repealing both the Law on Foreign Investment of 1994 and the Law on State Support of Direct Investment of 1997. The most critical novelty of the new Law on Investment was the elimination of certain guarantees that had been available to investors such as: (a) the political risk guarantee that protected them from changes in domestic legislation and international treaties of Kazakhstan; and (b) the guarantee of recourse to international arbitration in the absence of an arbitration agreement.[5] Moreover, the LI did not include provisions providing special status to foreign investors, who were now formally equalized with domestic investors.[6]

Significant changes took place also in the energy legislation of RK. Specifically, Kazakhstan adopted the Law of RK of June 24, 2010, No. 291-IV, "On Subsoil and Subsoil Use" (SUL), which replaced the former Law on the Subsurface and Subsurface Use of January 27, 1996 and the Petroleum Law of June 28, 1995.[7] Furthermore, on March 1, 2011 the LSP was adopted, which lays down,

---

4. However, the following opinion is of interest in this regard: "Unreasonable intervention of officials in the economic activities of enterprises is increasing and the number of the laws that foresee licensing, certification, approvals and other permission procedures is growing. All these measures are introduced under the pretext of... protecting state interests and the interests of the people. But quite frequently it's not state interests behind all of this but the ministerial or corporate interests of some officials who try to receive privileges and advantages for themselves." See M. Suleimenov & Y. Osipov "Review of the Legislative Base for Investments in Oil and Gas Sector of RK" (2010) IIED Report <http://pubs. iied.org/pdfs/G02764. pdf?> (June 15, 2011).
5. For analysis of the changes brought by the LI, see I Bantekas "The 2003 Investment Law Its Impact and Compatibility with International Foreign Investment Law" in I Bantekas J Paterson and M Suleimenov (eds) *Oil and Gas Law in Kazakhstan: National and International Perspectives* (Kluwer Law International 2004).
6. One may assert that the LI is a success of the Calvo doctrine implying that a foreigner is entitled only to a national standard of treatment. See M Sornarajah *International Law on Foreign Investment*, 3rd ed. (Cambridge University Press 2010) 37. However, at least from Kazakhstan's perspectives, full equality of treatment for foreign and domestic investors cannot be practically achieved, as domestic investors naturally enjoy certain privileges that are not available either in law or in fact to foreign investors, while foreign investors may apply provisions of bilateral investment treaties and the general rules of international investment law, which are not available for domestic investors.
7. For analysis of the principal changes brought by the SUL in comparison to the previous subsurface legislation, see S. Akhmetova, S. Daumov & T. Yuldabayev, "Review of the Draft Law of RK on Subsurface and Subsurface Use" (2010) Oil, Gas & Energy Law Intelligence <www.ogel. org> (June 15, 2011).

inter alia, rules for requisition and nationalization, as well as imposing limitations on the rights of private persons respecting strategic objects.

II. INVESTMENT LAW

This section provides an overview of the current legislation of Kazakhstan governing investment activity. It is organized in three parts: (1) an overview of the main provisions of Investment Law, (2) a description of the legal regime for concessions (other than subsurface use contracts) and, (3) a summary of the regulations regarding special economic zones.

A. Main Provisions of Investment Law

The Law of RK of January 8, 2003, No. 373-II, "On Investments" stipulates that it governs the relations "associated with investments in RK" and guarantees protection of investor's rights "when they make investments in RK" (Preamble LI); thus, it deals only with inward (and not outward) investment.[8] Also, the law neither encompasses investments made out of state budget funds nor is applicable to investing capital into non-commercial organizations, including for educational, scientific, charity or religious purposes (Article 2 II LI).

According to the LI, the term "investments" is defined as "all types of property (other than goods intended for personal use), including items of financial leasing from the moment a lease agreement is executed, as well as rights to such property, that are invested into the charter capital of a legal entity or that increase fixed assets used for entrepreneurial activities" (Article 1 LI). At first glance, this definition seems broad enough to embrace all types of rights and assets associated with investment. Its interpretation is further enhanced by defining the term "investment activities" as "activities of individuals and legal entities related to participation in the charter capital of commercial organizations or related to the creation or increase of fixed assets used for entrepreneurial activities" (Article 1 LI).

However, it is not clear if liens, debts and contractual obligations not related to fixed assets or the capital of business entities constitute investments under the law. Most Bilateral Investment Treaties (BITs) signed by RK[9] have a broader or, at

8. There is no special legal act governing outward investments of Kazakhstani residents. However, applicable provisions can be found in a number of legal acts primarily governing taxation, currency, anti-money laundering and other issues. Moreover, an export credit agency, JSC "KazExportGarant," provides credit and insurance services to promote exports by Kazakhstani residents. The agency was established by the Resolution of the Government of RK of May 12, 2003, No. 442, and is owned by the state through the JSC Sovereign Wealth Fund Samruk-Kazyna.
9. Currently Kazakhstan has BITs with over 40 countries, and this investment treaty network is continuously expanding. Also, Kazakhstan is a party to the Convention Establishing the

least, more detailed definition of the term.[10] Thus, given the general rule of Kazakhstani law on the prevailing power of provisions set in international treaties ratified by the state over its national legislation (Article 4 CRK), a foreign investor may enjoy higher protection if its country has an effective BIT with RK.[11]

The LI provides a number of guarantees to investors. *First*, investors enjoy legal protection of rights and interests within the territory of Kazakhstan (Article 4 LI). Such protection is provided on a full and unconditional basis as ensured by the Constitution of RK, which states that: "No one may be deprived of his property unless otherwise stipulated by a court decision. Forcible alienation of property for state needs in extraordinary cases stipulated by law may be exercised on the condition of its equivalent compensation" (Article 26 III). *Second*, investors are guaranteed stability of the terms of contracts concluded between them and state bodies of Kazakhstan, except for: (a) changes made to investment contracts by mutual agreement of the parties; (b) changes in the legislation and/or enactment of (or amendments to) the international treaties of RK that alter the procedure for and the terms of importation, production and sale of excisable goods;[12] and (c) changes that are introduced to the legislation of RK in order to ensure national and environmental security, public health and morality (Article 4 III LI). *Third*, the law guarantees the rights of investors to use income gained from their activities at their discretion after payment of taxes and other obligatory payments to the budget, and

---

Multilateral Investment Guarantee Agency, the International Convention on Settlement of Investment Disputes between States and Nationals of Other States, the Energy Charter Treaty and also the CIS Convention on Protection of Investor's Rights.

10. For example, the US-RK BIT defines investment as: "every kind of investment in the territory of one Party owned or controlled directly or indirectly by nationals or companies of the other Party, such as equity, debt, and service and investment contracts; and includes: (i) tangible and intangible property, including movable and immovable property, as well as rights, such as mortgages, liens and pledges; (ii) a company or shares of stock or other interests in a company or interests in the assets thereof; (iii) a claim to money or a claim to performance having economic value, and associated with an investment; (iv) intellectual property which includes, *inter alia*, rights relating to: literary and artistic works, including sound recordings, inventions in all fields of human endeavor, industrial designs, semiconductor mask works, trade secrets, know-how, and confidential business information, and trademarks, service marks, and trade names; and (v) any right conferred by law or contract, and any licenses and permits pursuant to law." See Treaty between the USA and RK Concerning the Encouragement and Reciprocal Protection of Investment of May 19, 1992 (Art. 1 I).
11. Treaty-based protection is crucial for foreign investors in Kazakhstan, due to its clearer rules and better protection mechanism in the case of disputes. In fact, in a number of cases foreign investors successfully applied BIT-based protection. See, e.g., *AIG Capital Partners, Inc. and CJSC Tema Real Estate Company v. Republic of Kazakhstan*, ICSID Case No. ARB/01/6.
12. In this regard, the following provision of the Civil Code should be noted: "If, after the conclusion of a contract, legislation establishes for the parties rules that are different from those that were effective when the contact was concluded, the terms of the concluded agreement shall retain force, except for instances when it is established by legislation that its operation extends to relations that arose from contracts previously concluded" (Art. 383 II CC). On the conflict between the norms of the LI and the CC, see A Didenko "The Law on Foreign Investments in Kazakhstan' in K Hendley (ed) *Remarking the Role of Law: Commercial Law in Russia and the CIS* (Juris Publishing Huntington, NY 2007) 278.

to open bank accounts within Kazakhstan in national and/or foreign currency in accordance with banking and currency legislation (Article 5 LI). *Fourth*, an investor has the right to be reimbursed for damages arising out of the issuance by a state body of acts conflicting with legislative acts of RK or as result of illegal (in)actions of state officials. Such compensation must be made pursuant to the civil legislation of RK. *Fifth*, the LI ensures transparency in the activities of state bodies with respect to investors and guarantees investor's access to information pertaining to investment activities. Thus, all official declarations of state bodies and all regulatory acts that affect the interests of investors must be published. Also, investors are entitled to freely receive all information related to entrepreneurial activities, unless such information contains commercial secrets or other secrets protected by law.

Furthermore, nationalization and requisitioning of an investor's property is permitted only in exceptional cases provided for by the laws of RK (Article 8 I LI). In the case of nationalization, the investor must be fully reimbursed by RK for any losses caused as a result of the issuance of legislative acts on nationalization. It must be noted that this provision is unqualified, quite general and unconditional. Therefore, in the event of nationalization, reimbursable losses should include unrealized revenue or lost profit. In the case of requisitioning, the investor must be reimbursed by way of payment of the full market value of the seized property. The market value is estimated in accordance with the laws of RK, and such estimation is contestable in the court. Should the investor's requisitioned property cease to exist, the investor may demand that the remaining property be returned to him. If the property is so returned, the investor must return the amount of compensation it received, taking into account losses resulting from the reduction in the value of the property (Article 8 LI). Issues of requisitioning and nationalization are also governed by the Law of RK of March 1, 2011, No. 413-IV, "On State Property," which establishes very detailed procedural regulations, including those related to appraising property and documenting the acts, terms of reimbursement, payments and responsibilities of state bodies.

In addition, the LI contains provisions on the resolution of investment disputes. The term "investment dispute" is defined as "a dispute arising from contractual obligations between investors and state bodies in connection with the investment activities of the investor." Investment disputes may be resolved through negotiation, including through expert mediation, or in accordance with a dispute resolution procedure previously agreed to by the parties. If an investment dispute cannot be so settled, it must be resolved in accordance with international treaties and legislative acts of RK either by national courts or by international arbitration, as determined by an agreement of the parties. In fact, in the absence of an arbitration agreement, foreign investors from states that have signed a BIT with Kazakhstan or are parties to the International Centre for Settlement of Investment Disputes (ICSID) Convention or the Energy Charter Treaty may submit the dispute to international commercial arbitration, provided all the conditions set in the respective treaty are met (Article 9 LI).

B. State Support of Investments

State support of investments is purported to create a favorable investment climate to help develop the economy, establish new production facilities and modernize existing ones, acquire modern technologies and increase the professional expertise of local personnel. As Kazakhstan is highly dependent on its mining industry, the state is attempting to diversify its economy. Consequently, the state may grant investment preferences in priority sectors of economy, the list of which is approved by the Government. This list encompasses a wide range of economic spheres, including agriculture, consumer goods manufacturing, the chemical and metallurgy industries, transportation and telecommunication, construction, etc.[13] To ensure the smooth diversification of economy and to avoid disbalances in investment flows, the Government may limit the maximum amount of investment eligible for state support in each type of economic activity (Article 14 II LI).

The principal state body implementing state policy to support investment on behalf of the Government is the Investment Committee of the Ministry of Industry and New Technologies. It has wide powers and discretionary authority to grant investment benefits and to exercise control over investors' compliance with their obligations. In particular, the Investment Committee is charged with negotiating and signing investment contracts with investors. As a state authority and as a party to investment contracts, the Investment Committee may temporarily waive certain contractual obligations imposed on investors in the view of an unfavorable economic climate.[14]

Currently, state support of investments under the law is provided in two major forms of investment benefits: (a) exemption from customs duties; and (b) state in-kind grants.[15] Under the former, equipment and its component parts imported for the purposes of implementation of an investment project may be exempt from customs duties for a period of up to five years after the date of contract registration (IL Article 17). As to state in-kind grants, they may be transferred in the form of land plots, buildings and other immovable facilities, machinery and equipment, transport vehicles (except for motor cars) and production and household inventories. The in-kind grants are provided by the Investment Committee upon consultation with the relevant government authorities responsible for the management of state property and/or land resources as well as, when applicable, with local

---

13. See the Resolution of the Government of RK of May 8, 2003, No. 436.
14. The 2008 world economic downturn affected many investors in Kazakhstan. In the author's own experience, the Investment Committee was willing to accommodate investors' needs and reasonably flexible in approving their requests for waivers when investors faced unforeseen difficulties.
15. Formerly, the support measures included a number of tax incentives. Corporate income taxes could be exempted for five to eight years and investors were allowed to fully deduct for corporate income tax purposes the cost of the objects of investment and the cost associated with their reconstruction and modernization. Moreover, investors enjoyed tax holidays for land and property taxes for five years from the date of signing of an investment contract. However, these tax incentives were eliminated starting from January 1, 2009.

executive bodies (Article 18). The assets may be provided for temporary free of charge use, with the possibility of their subsequent free of charge transfer into ownership (or, in the case of land plots, long-term land use) if the investment obligations under contract are fulfilled.[16] In order to apply for the investment benefits, a foreign investor must establish a separate legal entity in Kazakhstan or acquire interest in an existing local company.

Once granted, investment benefits may be terminated unilaterally by the Investment Committee upon provision of a three-month advance notice to the investor if: (a) the information provided by the investor in its application was untrue, incomplete or misleading to the point that it influenced the decision of granting the investment benefits; (b) the investor has failed to comply with its obligations according to the contract providing investment benefits; or (c) the investor has provided untrue, incomplete or misleading information in its reports submitted pursuant to the investment monitoring requirements set in the law (Article 22 LI). While in the first case the law sets an effect test, i.e., the deficiency of information has to be material to affect the decision of the Investment Committee, the other two failures are not specifically qualified. Even the first case, the effect test, provides little safety to investors as it is dependent on the Investment Committee's discretion. Thus, in each of the three cases, there is a room for abuse by the Investment Committee of its authority in the event of investors' minor failures.[17]

These provisions are mandated by their inclusion in the state's model contract, which must be the basis for all contracts involving investment benefits (Sec. 18). Furthermore, the model contract unambiguously sets the law of RK as the only applicable law with regard to investment contracts (Sec. 14) and encourages the parties to settle any dispute amicably (Sec. 12). If the issue is not settled amicably within two months of a respective notice from the initiating party, the parties may theoretically submit the dispute to the courts of RK or international arbitration according to the agreement of the parties. However, the model contract has no specific arbitration clause; thus, if the parties fail to agree on arbitration, the dispute will have to be considered by a national court (unless the foreign investor's country has a BIT with RK or is a party to the ICSID Convention).

C. Concessions

Unlike the first Law on Concessions (LoC) of December 23, 1991, the Law of RK of July 7, 2006, No. 167-III, "On Concessions" does not limit its application only to foreign investors. However, it does not extend to the issues of subsurface use,

16. It should be noted that the maximum value of in-kind grants cannot be in excess of 30% of the total value of investment made in the fixed assets of a legal entity of Kazakhstan.
17. If the contract providing investment benefits is terminated early, unilaterally or by mutual agreement, the investor must return all assets received in the form of in-kind grants (or their initial monetary value) and pay retroactively all taxes and customs duties that were not paid due to the investment preferences together with penalty fees accrued from their respective due dates.

which are currently regulated by the SUL. Thus, all state-owned assets (except for subsurface) can generally be transferred by concession, but certain strategic assets (as determined by the President of RK) are prohibited from concessionary transfer.[18]

The law defines a concession agreement as a written agreement between a concessor (*kontsedent*), the Government of RK or government bodies authorized by it, and concessionaire, a legal entity, except for state enterprises and government institutions, determining rights, liabilities and responsibilities of the parties and the concession implementation conditions. Concession itself is determined as a "transfer under a concession agreement of state property objects for temporary ownership and use for the purpose of their improvement and efficient running, and rights to construct new objects at the expense of the concessionaire providing the latter the right of ownership, use and management or without this right, subject to mandatory financing of the construction by the concessionaire and further transfer of the facilities constructed to the government" (Article 1 LoC).

Concession-related activity is based on the following core principles: (a) that the concessor's and concessionaire's activities be public and transparent; (b) that the interests and risks of concessors and concessionaire are balanced; and (c) that the rights and legal interests of consumers of the goods (works, services) provided by a concessionaire under a concession agreement be protected (Article 3 LoC).

The transfer of objects by concession is implemented in three phases: (a) compiling a list of objects to be transferred; (b) conducting a concession competition; and (c) determining a concessionaire and entering into a concession agreement.

The list of objects to be transferred by concession is compiled by the Ministry of Economic Development and Trade on the basis of proposals formulated by central government bodies in the respective sectors and regional government bodies (which, in turn, must take into consideration proposals made by individuals and legal entities on their private initiative). Finally, the list must be approved by the Government of RK.[19]

The selection of the concessionaire is implemented through open competition. Information on the competitive bidding process must be published in periodical prints distributed across Kazakhstan and must include data on the concession objects, a list of the necessary documents to be submitted to the competition organizer, and the requirements for potential participants. Generally, a legal entity applying for a concession has to meet a number of qualification requirements,

18. The list of strategic assets is approved by the Decree of the President of RK of March 5, 2007, No. 294, and includes land and water resources as primary objects of concessions (as opposed to land and water resources supplementary to other primary assets which do not belong to the list), wild flora and fauna, natural parks, assets used for military and national security purposes, main-line railways, assets of historical and cultural value, etc.
19. This is usually done once every three years. Thus, the list of assets offered for 2011–2013 was approved by the Resolution of the Government of RK of October 31, 2010, No. 1506.

including possessing the financial resources necessary to fulfill the liabilities.[20] Concession projects are selected by a commission established by either the Government of RK or regional executive bodies. The commission's working body (competition organizer) engages independent experts determined by the Government of RK to carry out an evaluation of the concession projects contained in the competition applications submitted. The competition participant whose concession project has been acknowledged as the best may enter into negotiations with the commission to conclude a concession agreement.

While the parties are preparing for negotiations, the commission may send its remarks and proposals on the relevant concession project to the participant. If the participant agrees to include those remarks and proposals from the negotiations,[21] the commission declares him the competition winner and enters into a concession agreement with him within 30 calendar days from the date of stating the competition results (Article 20 LoC).[22] The maximum term of a concession agreement is 30 years; however, it may be prolonged by the agreement of the parties if the concessionaire has been duly fulfilling its obligations (Article 23 LoC).

The agreement may stipulate the right of the concessor to alter or terminate the concession unilaterally if needed to protect the interests of the state or society (in particular related to national and environmental safety or the health or morality of population). The state must reimburse to the concessionaire all losses incurred with respect to a cancellation or related to a change of agreement conditions, as the case may be (Article 21 IV, V LoC).[23]

All disputes arising out of or in connection with a concession agreement are to be resolved through negotiations in accordance with the legislation of RK and the disputes resolution procedures agreed upon in the concession agreement. If a dispute related to the implementation or termination of a concession agreement cannot be resolved through negotiations, the parties must resolve the dispute in line with the legislation of RK in court, or through appealing to international arbitration in accordance with the Law of RK of December 28, 2004, No. 23-3, "On International Commercial Arbitration" (Article 27 LoC).

In this regard, recent developments include the adoption of the Program of Development of Public-Private Partnership in RK for the period of 2011–2015

20. The other two requirements usually are that: (1) it must be financially solvent; its property must not be under arrest; and its financial and economic activities must not be suspended in accordance with the legislation of RK; and (2) it must not have been indicted for non-fulfillment or inappropriate fulfillment of liabilities under a concession agreement entered into in the previous three years, with a court resolution still in force.
21. If not, the next best concession project must be selected again out of the competition applications submitted.
22. A concession agreement is drafted on the basis of the respective model contract approved by the Government. See the Resolution of the Government of December 29, 2006, No. 1326.
23. Unlike investment contracts under the LI, no explicit rights of the state to terminate concession agreements were provided. Also, the model concession contract, unlike the model investment contract reviewed above, allows parties to conclude the contract in Kazakh and any other language acceptable to the parties and sets parity of languages for the purposes of interpreting the contract.

(adopted by the Resolution of the Government of RK of June 29, 2011, No. 731). It is expected that public-private partnerships will be employed in financing the construction of highways, water, heating and gas supply infrastructure, real estate development and waste recycling, as well as maintaining private prisons and educational, healthcare and scientific institutions.[24]

D. Special Economic Zones

To facilitate regional development and to ensure efficient use of competitive advantages bestowed in particular geographic areas, a government may localize specific favorable investment climates according to the needs of the national economy. In Kazakhstan this policy is primarily implemented through the creation of Special Economic Zones (SEZ), the status of which is currently governed by the Law of RK of July 21, 2011, No. 469-IV, "On Special Economic Zones in the Republic of Kazakhstan" (LSEZ).

An SEZ may be established by the President of RK on the proposal of the Government of RK (Article 7 VIII LSEZ). It may be created for a period of up to 25 years (LSEZ Article 8) and is operated by a managing company, which is formed as a joint-stock company under Kazakhstani law.[25] If an SEZ is established on the proposal of a state body, then over 50% of the managing company's shares must be in state ownership, unless otherwise is provided in the respective Decree of the President of RK. If the establishment of an SEZ is initiated by a private company, then state ownership must comprise at least 26% of the shares (Article 8 LSEZ). Foreign companies may also initiate the establishment of an SEZ and, in such a case, they may effectively hold up to 74% of the respective managing company's voting stocks.

At present there are six SEZs operating in Kazakhstan.[26] The status of each SEZ is precisely defined by a respective presidential decree. Participation in an SEZ is open to local and foreign legal entities, except for: (a) subsurface users (legal entities holding subsurface use contracts); (b) entities manufacturing excisable goods; (c) entities already enjoying tax preferences provided by the Tax Code; and (d) gambling businesses (LSEZ Article 9). In order to participate in an SEZ,

---

24. As a result of the program, the Government plans to attract around KZT 900 billion (ca. USD 6 billion) of investments by 2015.
25. Except for SEZ "Astana – New City" in the capital city of Kazakhstan, which is administered by a state enterprise of the municipal administration of Astana (Art. 17 II LSEZ).
26. (1) SEZ "Burabay" founded to promote regional eco- and cultural tourism, located in Akmola Province; (2) SEZ "Information Technologies Park" established to develop IT-industry, located near Almaty; (3) SEZ "Ontustik" established to promote the national textile industry, located in South Kazakhstan Province; (4) SEZ "Astana – New City" organized to advance the urban and industrial development of the capital of Kazakhstan; (5) SEZ "National Industrial Petrochemical Technology Park" established to expand the petrochemical industry, located in Atyrau Province; and (6) SEZ "Seaport Aktau" founded to expand maritime transport services and the Aktau seaport. Since one of the purposes of the LSEZ was to expand the activities of SEZs, it is expected that the number of SEZs will be increased in the future.

legal entities must conclude an agreement with the managing company (LSEZ Article 18). This agreement entitles them to economic benefits provided within the SEZ (such as tax privileges and exemption from customs duties).[27] Also, SEZ participants enjoy a simplified procedure for getting work permits for foreign personnel (Article 28 LSEZ).[28] Moreover, to eliminate bureaucratic barriers, a single state agency is set in each SEZ to provide one-stop shop services (Article 8 VI LSEZ). These additional advantages were not previously provided to SEZs before the enactment of the LSEZ. To be effectively implemented, these new provisions need to be elaborated in sub-laws acts, a step that is expected in the near future.

III. ENERGY LAW

This section consists of three parts. The first part introduces the government institutions involved in the regulation of the energy market and industry. The second part deals with the regulatory framework for subsurface energy resources' exploration and production, i.e., the upstream petroleum sector,[29] coal and uranium. The last part provides an overview of legal provisions for mid- and downstream operations, with further specifics for each type of these energy resources.

A. Government Institutions Regulating the Energy Market and Industry

The main body responsible for regulating the energy market and industry is the Government of RK, which exercises the general management and control of the exploration, production and distribution of energy resources, the generation of electricity, environmental pollution, industrial safety, etc.

The Government's structure currently includes the Ministry of Oil and Gas (MOG) and the Ministry of Industry and New Technology (MINT) (the former is responsible for the regulation of the oil and gas industry, while the latter is vested with regulatory functions in the sphere of electrical energy, nuclear power and natural resources other than oil and gas). In addition to these ministries, a significant role in regulating the energy market and industry is also played by: the Ministry of Labor and Social Protection (overseeing compliance with labor safety

27. In order to be eligible for tax privileges, an SEZ participant must derive more than 90% of its income from sale of its goods, works and services related its SEZ activity (Art. 150 TC). In addition, an eligible participant is exempted from land, property and corporate income tax (Art. 151 TC).
28. This procedure means that SEZ participants need not prove the lack of local specialists for a respective vacancy.
29. Throughout this chapter the term "petroleum" signifies both crude oil and natural gas, a common international practice (see, e.g., Malaysian Petroleum Development Act of 1974, Nigerian Petroleum Act of 1969 and Norwegian Petroleum Activities Act of 1996).

and work permit requirements), the Ministry of the Environment (controlling the environmental impact of subsurface users and energy producers), the Ministry of Agriculture (exercising control over the production of biofuels) and the Agency Regulating Natural Monopolies (responsible for pricing policies of suppliers of energy goods and services).

It should also be noted that a significant role in energy sector is currently played by national holdings and national companies and in particular by the National Managing Holding "National Welfare Fund Samruk-Kazyna" (hereafter simply referred to as Samruk-Kazyna) and its subsidiaries.[30] Even though national holdings and national companies do not perform explicit regulatory functions in the energy sector,[31] they are important policy tools of the Government that procure effective state participation in both the industry and the market. At present, all energy-related national companies in Kazakhstan are subsidiaries of Samruk-Kazyna, which was established to facilitate the modernization and diversification of the national economy, promote the sustainable development of the country and enhance the efficiency of state companies. It is vested with special priority powers to acquire, on behalf of the Government, strategic entities and assets when such priority acquisition rights are stipulated in the laws of Kazakhstan. In addition to priority rights over strategic entities and/or assets, Samruk-Kazyna (and its subsidiary national companies) has priority rights to acquire, on behalf of the Government, alienable subsurface use rights (or a part thereof) and/or assets related to subsurface use rights (Article 6 of the Law on the National Welfare Fund). The concept of the state's priority rights is elaborated in further sections of this work;

30. It is not clear why national companies in Kazakhstan have been organized in the form of JSCs rather than, e.g., state enterprises. At present a national company is defined as a JSC with a state-owned controlling block of shares. In turn, the term "controlling block of shares" refers to a block of shares that entitles the holder to determine decisions of the JSC (see the Law of RK of May 13, 2003, No. 415-II, "On Joint-Stock Companies"). Thus, it can be presumed that more than 50% of the national companies' shares may be in private hands of multiple minorities as long as the state's stake allows the Government to exercise control over the company. The arising problem is that the national companies participate in public policy and are delegated with certain privileges and special rights previously owned by the state. At the same time, however, there may be also a minority private shareholder who may benefit from those special rights and privileges that were delegated to the national company.

31. A judgment on whether a national company acts as a regulator in the industry or not depends on the degree of regulatory authority vested in the national company by the state. Kazakhstan's national companies have a number of special rights and privileges that are not available to private companies. Being a policy tool of the Government, national companies collect economic data for the Government, participate in the development of state industrial policy and, on the instruction of the Government, intervene in the energy market through supply/demand instruments (and thus influence behavior of private companies). Yet they are not vested with explicit regulatory powers with respect to the private actors as, e.g., Malaysian Petronas, which has "the entire ownership in, and the exclusive rights, powers, liberties and privileges of exploring, exploiting, winning and obtaining petroleum" in Malaysia (see Malaysian Petroleum Development Act of 1974, section 2 I) and is responsible for regulation of all activities in the upstream petroleum industry (see World Trade Organization (WTO) Secretariat "Trade Policy Review: Malaysia' WTO Doc WT/TPR/S/156 December 2005 83).

however, at this point it is worth noting that the delegation of priority rights by the state to national companies or any other state-owned enterprises has been sharply criticized in legal scholarship.[32]

The main arms of Samruk-Kazyna in the energy sector are JSC National Company "Kazmunaigaz," JSC National Atomic Company "Kazatomprom," JSC Kazakhstan Electricity Grid Operating Company (KEGOC), and JSC Samruk-Energo.[33] Kazmunaigaz manages state petroleum assets including those related to state participation in companies and joint ventures operating oil and gas fields, refineries and pipelines. Kazatomprom explores and produces uranium and manages state interests in uranium producing companies. KEGOC and Samruk-Energo are very important players in the electricity market. The former owns and operates the national network of electricity grids whereas the latter owns and operates (or manages the state shareholding of) many hydro-power and coal-fired power plants.

B. Regulatory Framework Concerning the Upstream Energy Industry

1. The Subsurface Use Right

The subsurface use right is defined as the right to possess and to use the subsurface acquired by the holder in accordance with the laws of Kazakhstan. The subsurface use right is granted to local and foreign, natural and legal persons, individually or jointly. The right is granted for conducting the following operations: (a) state geological surveys of the subsurface; (b) exploration; (c) production; (d) combined exploration and production; and (e) construction and/or operation of underground facilities unrelated to exploration or production (Article 28 SUL).

The subsurface use right is granted on the basis of a subsurface use contract, which is preceded by either a tender or direct negotiations. Any individual or legal entity may participate in a tender, while direct negotiations for subsurface use rights are restricted to cases provided for by law.[34] After the tender or direct

32. Note the following opinion: "The realization of priority rights means the implementation of the state's public functions and that must be done by the Government on behalf of the state (Art. 193-1 CC)... The fact that a national company acts on behalf of the state contradicts the Constitution, which stipulates that only authorized state bodies within the limits of their authorities may act on behalf of the state (Art. 3 III)." See M. Suleimenov & Y. Osipov, "Review of the Legislative Base for Investments in Oil and Gas Sector of RK" (2010) IIED Report <http://pubs. iied.org/pdfs/G02764.pdf?> (June 15, 2011).

33. Besides these state companies, in 2009 the Government established a new JSC National Mining Company "Tau-Ken Samruk," which is established to operate with solid minerals. Presumably, this national company will serve state interests in the coal mining industry, which has so far been dominated by private companies. Also, in May 2011 the Government announced its intention to establish a new national geological survey company.

34. In particular, direct negotiations are conducted with: (a) a person having the exclusive right to the production of minerals discovered on the basis of an exploration contract granted to that

negotiations, one of the following types of subsurface use contracts is concluded with the winner of the tender or with the direct negotiator: (a) an exploration contract; (b) a production contract; (c) a contract for combined exploration and production;[35] (d) a contract for the construction and/or operation of underground facilities unrelated to exploration or production; (e) a contract on the state geological survey of subsurface.[36]

Some Kazakhstani scholars classify these types of transactions as civil law contracts,[37] which gives grounds to two important consequences: (a) the application of the principles of Civil Law (such as equality of persons, inviolability of property, freedom of agreement, restitution of violated rights, etc.), which effectively undermines the power of the state to dominate subsurface users in contractual relations (e.g., it eliminates the right to amend or terminate a subsurface contract unilaterally); (b) the compliance with the legal regime set by Civil Law for each type of contract (which may imply the mandatory application of either imperative or default rules in absence of an express agreement to the contrary).

However, there is another school of lawyers who advocate a dual nature of subsurface use contracts. This group argues that, although such contracts are similar to private law agreements, they bear important constituents from the domain of public law. Thus, the state may adjust the contract to preserve the interests of its population, whether by making amendments to contract or by adopting new legislation. Although the concept of administrative contracts is not applied in the legislation of Kazakhstan, the arguments of the dualists are close to French legal doctrine justifying the concept of *contrat administratif*. In short, according to the dualists, the Government, by entering into the subsurface use contracts, administers public rather than its own welfare; therefore, the fundamental principle of equality of parties, presumed in civil law contracts, may be sacrificed in subsurface use contracts to preserve the public interest.[38]

Despite this legal debate, it is clear that the legal regime of subsurface use contracts is departing from its civil law origins. Thus, the SUL states that the

---

person; (b) an applicant who participated in a tender that was declared twice as not having been held because only that applicant participated in it; and (c) a person intending to perform exploration and/or production operations jointly with the national company provided that, in the case of offshore petroleum deposits, the participation of the national company is not less than 50% (Art. 93 III SUL).

35. This type of contract can be concluded by the decision of the Government only with respect to mineral deposits having strategic value and/or a complex geological structure (Art. 61 IV SUL).
36. The SUL does not mention production-sharing agreements, which had been popular in the petroleum industry until the enactment of the new Tax Code on January 1, 2009 (which cancelled the Law on Production-Sharing Agreements). However, production-sharing agreements signed before enactment of the Tax Code remain in force (e.g., Kashagan, the largest oil field of Kazakhstan, is operated through a production-sharing agreement).
37. See, e.g., Y. Bassin et al., "Контракты на недропользование: проблемы юридической квалификаЦии и систематизаЦии" ["Contracts on Subsoil Use: Problems of Juridical Qualification and Systematization"] (2007) 2 *Energeticheskoe Pravo* 2-3.
38. See S Zimanov *Государство и контракты в сфере нефтяных операЦий* [*State and Contracts in the Sphere of Oil Operations*] (Almaty 2007).

conclusion, execution, amendment and termination of a subsurface use contract are conducted in accordance with the SUL, i.e., the Civil Code provisions governing contracts can be applied only to the aspects not governed by the SUL (Article 61). The Law contains detailed provisions on subsurface use contract formation as well as the terms and conditions thereof. Moreover, the contract must be drafted on the basis of the Model Contract approved by the Government and contain all compulsory provisions prescribed in the Law. The laws of other states cannot be applied to subsurface use contracts in RK. The signed subsurface use contract and the grant of the subsurface use right contemplated under the contract become effective after registration of the contract with the competent body.[39]

Contracts for exploration are concluded for a term not exceeding six years. With respect to offshore petroleum exploration, this term may be extended for a two-year period if the contractor applies for an extension no later than six months prior to the contract's expiration. In the event of discovery of natural resources, the contract may be extended for a term necessary to assess the commercial discovery. Production contracts are concluded for a term not exceeding the term specified in the production work program, which, in turn, may not exceed 25 years for mineral deposits and 45 years for mineral deposits with large reserves or extraordinary features.

It should also be noted that subsurface use contracts may be invalidated on the following grounds: (a) the tender for granting the subsurface use right is recognized as void; (b) the contract lacks the compulsory terms prescribed by the Subsurface Law; (c) the subsurface user submitted misleading information to the competent authority, which influenced the decision to conclude the contract with that party; and (d) on other grounds stipulated by law.

2. The Right of the State to Amend and Terminate a Contract Unilaterally

The SUL guarantees the protection of the rights of subsurface users and provides, in particular, that "any amendments or additions to the legislation that deteriorate the results of the entrepreneurial activities of a subsurface user under contract shall not apply to the contracts concluded prior to the introduction of such amendments and additions ... [except for] changes of the legislation of RK in the area of ensuring national security and defense capacity and the areas of environmental protection, healthcare, taxation and customs regulation" (Article 30 SUL).

The Law contains provisions entitling the state to amend or terminate the subsurface use contract on the grounds set in the law.[40] In particular, it states

39. Except for limited cases (set in Art. 37 X SUL), the subsurface use right cannot be alienated within two years from the date of its granting. Also, all agreements contemplating alienation of, creation of security interest over or establishing servitude rights with respect to subsurface use rights and/or related objects are subject to state registration.
40. These provisions were introduced to the preceding law in October 2007 and attracted strong criticism from lawyers and investors because, despite stabilization clauses contained in the

that "if the actions of a subsurface user in the course of subsurface use operations in relation to subsurface areas (deposits) that have strategic value lead to a change in the economic interests of RK, thereby posing a threat to national security, the competent body may demand an amendment to be made to the contract, including an earlier concluded contract, in order to restore the economic interests of RK" (Article 71 III SUL).[41] Within two months after the receipt of a notice of a forthcoming amendment to the contract from the competent body, the subsurface user must consent in writing to negotiations to amend the contract terms; within four months of this written consent, the parties must agree on the amendments; and within six months of the date of this consensus with respect to the restoration of the economic interests of RK (i.e., to the amendment), the parties shall sign the amendments. If any of these terms and/or conditions is not satisfied, the competent body is entitled to terminate the subsurface contract unilaterally.

Moreover, the competent body may terminate the contract if: (a) the subsurface user fails to cure more than two breaches of the obligations set in the subsurface use contract or related project documents within the period set by the competent body in the default notice; (b) the subsurface user alienates its subsurface use right and/or related objects, or (c) its controlling (parent) entity undergoes an initial public offering of voting stocks, depository receipts or other notes or certificates convertible to shares without the consent of the competent body. Finally, by a decision of the Government, the competent authority may unilaterally terminate a contract when subsurface use operations with regard to areas (deposits) of strategic value affect the economic interest of RK and threaten its national security. In the event of unilateral termination of a contract, the competent authority must notify the subsurface user no later than two months prior to the termination.

3. Pre-emptive and Priority Rights of the State

Subsurface users may own mineral raw materials (i.e., minerals extracted from subsurface),[42] unless otherwise provided by law or contract, and conclude any civil law transactions in respect of them (Article 10 SUL).[43] However, the state has a pre-emptive right to acquire subsurface user's minerals for a cost not exceeding

contracts signed before 2007, the unilateral right provisions were given retroactive effect. See, e.g., J. Hines, A. Shyngyssov & K. Nurgazieva "Kazakhstan Further Stiffens its Mineral Development Regime: New Controls for Strategic Fields and Pipelines" (2008) 1(2) *Journal of World Energy Law & Business* 180; Z. Yelyubayev. "Role of Investment Law in Regulating Relations in the Sphere of Subsoil Use in the Republic of Kazakhstan" (2010) Oil, Gas & Energy Law Intelligence <www.ogel.org> (June 15, 2011).

41. The current list of subsurface areas (deposits) having strategic value was approved by the Resolution of the Government of August 13, 2009, No. 1213.
42. It should be noted that associated gas flowing out of wells during oil production is owned by the state unless otherwise stipulated in the subsurface use contract (Art. 86 III SUL).
43. If there is no information on the prices of minerals applied by the subsurface user in the conclusion of transactions, the prices that do not exceed those prevailing in the world markets must apply.

regular prices set by the subsurface user with respect to the relevant minerals, less transportation and sales costs (Article 12 SUL).[44]

Moreover, the SUL establishes the priority right of the state to acquire the subsurface use right (or a part thereof) and/or items related to subsurface use rights that are to be alienated by the right-holder. The term "objects related to subsurface use rights" refers to shares, holdings or stocks (including notes, certificates and depository receipts convertible to shares) of a legal entity that is the subsurface user or the entity that controls the subsurface user if the main business of that controlling entity is linked to Kazakhstan. The term "control" is not defined nor are guidelines provided to identify such control. It is not clear whether control is limited to shareholding or also embraces contractual and other types of control between entities. Similar uncertainty exists with respect to determining the linkage of a business with its controlling entity and the term "main business."[45]

Unlike the pre-emptive right to acquire minerals, the procedure for the exercise of the priority right by the state to acquire subsurface use rights and related objects is set in the law. The SUL stipulates that a subsurface user willing to alienate its subsurface use right or related objects has to submit application for permission for the alienation to the competent body (Article 13). The competent body forwards the application, along with any relevant information, to the Interdepartmental Commission for the Exercise of the Priority Right of the State, which recommends to the competent body whether to exercise the priority right or refrain from it. If the national managing holding company or any national company expresses its intention to acquire the alienable assets to the Interdepartmental Commission, the Commission recommends that company to the competent body. In absence of such an intention, if there is a positive recommendation from the Interdepartmental Commission, the Government shall appoint a state body that will acquire the alienable assets. On the basis of the recommendation, the competent body decides whether to exercise the state priority right or refrain from it. If the right is to be exercised, the national managing holding company or the national company or a state body appointed by the Government negotiates with the subsurface user the terms and conditions of the acquisition of the subsurface use right or related objects. The acquisition by the state must be under terms that are no worse than those offered by other applicants. If the subsurface user is intending to

44. The rules for state pre-emptive acquisition of minerals are stipulated by the Resolution of the Government of RK of January 28, 2011, No. 38.

45. As non-compliance with the priority right provision may lead to a cancellation of the subsurface use right, subsurface users in Kazakhstan strictly comply with the law requirements and, to be on the safer side, tend to comply excessively if there is any doubt as to the requirements of the law. An example from the author's own experience: after the enactment of the SUL, a subsurface user, half-owned by one of the national companies of Kazakhstan, applied for permission for sale of shares in its second parent company headquartered abroad, even though that parent company's major business activity was spread in a number of foreign countries with relatively minor fraction of activity in Kazakhstan. After surpassing all formalities and procedures the subsurface user was granted permission for a sale of shares in the parent company.

alienate the assets free of charge or through a contribution to the charter capital of another legal entity, such assets are acquired by the state at market value.

However, if the state refrains from the exercise of its priority right, it may still prohibit the alienation of the subsurface use rights or related objects, i.e., dismiss the application for permission for the alienation.[46] Also, the alienation may be prohibited on the following grounds: (a) the acquirer of the subsurface use rights or related objects does not comply with the requirements established for subsurface users and persons seeking to obtain a subsurface use right; (b) the subsurface user failed to provide the required documents or comply with other requirements set for the application procedure; (c) the alienation of subsurface use rights or related objects would entail a violation of the requirements of the legislation of RK (including the requirements for ensuring national security, concentration of rights within the contract and/or concentration of rights in subsurface use operations) or international agreements concluded by RK.[47]

4. Procurement of Goods, Services and Works by Subsurface Users

Procurement of goods, services and works (GSW) by state-owned companies, natural monopolies and subsurface users is highly regulated in Kazakhstan. Procurement regulations are issued with respect to each type of purchaser, with some common rules established on the methodology for calculating domestic content in the course of procurement. The overall trend in procurement law reflects efforts by the Government to diversify the national economy and decrease its dependency on the export of minerals, as well as to increase transparency in procurement transactions.

Procurement of GSW by subsurface users and their contractors is carried out by using one of the following methods: (a) an open tender; (b) a single source; (c) price proposals; (d) a system of electronic procurement; and (e) a commodity exchange (Article 77 SUL). Unless a subsurface user makes procurement on an organized commodity exchange or through a system of electronic procurement, the general rule prescribes making procurement through an open tender. Procurement from a single source is allowed in certain cases, e.g., there is an absence of a

---

46. Pursuant to the procedure established by law, the competent body, after getting recommendations from the Interdepartmental Committee, forwards all materials related to the subsurface user's application to a special expert commission. After review of the materials, the expert commission directs its proposal to the competent body on granting permission or banning alienation. On the basis of the proposal, the competent body makes its final decision.
47. The law defines the term "concentration of rights in subsurface use operations" as the holding by one person or a group of persons from one country of such interest in contracts in the territory of RK or such participating interest in the charter capitals (number of shares) of legal entities that are subsurface users in RK as is capable (or in the process) of creating a threat to the economic interests of RK. The term "concentration of rights within a contract" means the size of the interest of one of the joint holders of the subsurface use right in a contract entered into with RK is such that a single participant can determine the activities of the subsurface user in accordance with the contract.

quorum of bids. Price proposals may be accepted for homogeneous GSW on a small-scale basis.[48]

The SUL requires subsurface users and their contractors to conditionally consider the price of bids submitted by Kazakhstani producers to be 20% lower than the actual bid (Article 78). The term "Kazakhstani producer" implies citizens of RK and/or legal entities established in accordance with the laws of RK that are located on the territory of RK and with a workforce of 95% Kazakhstani. Failure to comply with local content requirements may result in the termination of the subsurface use contract or administrative fines.

VI. REGULATORY FRAMEWORK CONCERNING MID- AND DOWNSTREAM ENERGY INDUSTRY

A. Common Provisions

To ensure the safety of operations in mid- and downstream energy sectors, Kazakhstan established an extensive licensing regime, reflected in the Law of RK of January 11, 2007, No. 214-III, "On Licensing" and various derivative legal acts. This Law sets a complete list of activities that are subject to licensing in Kazakhstan.[49] A license may be granted to any national or foreign entity or individual that satisfies the requirements for that specific license, after approval by the Government.[50] A license can be general (i.e., for an unlimited period of time) or one-off (to perform a one-time operation). Licenses are non-transferable, and conducting activity without a proper license may result in civil, administrative or criminal liability (including fines, forfeiture of revenue derived from misconduct and forced liquidation of the legal entity).

Also, as operations in mid- and downstream energy involve higher risks for the health of population and the environment, they are subject to more frequent inspection sessions from various state bodies on the basis of Law of RK of January 6, 2011, No. 314-IV, "On State Control and Supervision in RK," Environmental Code of RK of January 9, 2007, No. 212-III, Labor Code of RK of May 15, 2007, No. 251-III, etc. Furthermore, the energy sector is subject to a special monitoring regime based on the Law of RK of October 4, 2003, No. 490-II, "On State Monitoring of Assets in the Fields of Economy That Have Strategic Significance."

Additionally, most of the operations in the mid- and downstream energy sector, including the production and distribution of electricity, transportation and the

48. If the value of an allotment of such homogeneous GSW within a single purchase does not exceed 14,000 MCI.

49. Fields requiring extensive licensing include: the exploitation of petrochemicals, petroleum storage, transportation and processing facilities, production and distribution of electricity, the exploitation of power stations and distributional electricity grids and the performance of activities related to nuclear power facilities.

50. Except for requirements for licenses in the field of financial services, which are approved by the National Bank.

refining and distribution of petroleum are subject to regulation by anti-monopoly acts (and in particular the Law of RK of July 9, 1998, No. 272-I, "On Natural Monopolies and Regulated Markets"). Accordingly, a number of consequences arise: (a) a natural monopoly may not engage in "non-core economic activity" unless such activity is necessary to perform their "main business" or immaterial in terms of revenue derived; (b) it must get approval for any increase in prices for its goods or services from the Agency Regulating Natural Monopolies; (c) it may not own shares or participatory interests in other legal entities; (d) it must conclude agreements with customers of regulated goods and services on the basis of respective model contracts approved by the Government; and (e) it must conduct procurement of GSW in accordance with special rules approved by the Government (which are similar to those prescribed for subsurface users).

A number of laws were amended in 2007 to tighten state control over transactions with assets of critical importance for the national security and economy of Kazakhstan.[51] The key concept introduced by these amendments is the concept of "strategic objects," which was introduced to the Civil Code.[52] On June 30, 2008 the Government adopted Resolution No. 651 "On the List of Strategic Objects," which includes, *inter alia*, all main-line petroleum pipelines within the borders of Kazakhstan, the national electricity grid and all hydro-power plants as well as shareholding and/or participatory interests in the legal entities owning them.

Alienation of strategic objects and creation of security interests over them is permitted only with the approval of the Government.[53] The state has a priority right to acquire strategic objects that are to be alienated. If the Government decides to execute the state priority right, the strategic object must be acquired at market value. The acquired strategic object is transferred to the share capital of a new state-owned company, or of a national managing holding company, a national holding company or a national company. Transactions involving the alienation of strategic objects or creation of security interest over them concluded without the permission of the Government may be declared invalid by court.[54]

---

51. For analysis of these amendments see J. Hines, A. Shyngyssov & K. Nurgazieva "Kazakhstan Further Stiffens Its Mineral Development Regime: New Controls for Strategic Fields and Pipelines" (2008) 1(2) *Journal of World Energy Law & Business* 180.
52. See in Chapter 7 "Property Law" and Chapter 8 "Law of Obligations" *supra* for further details.
53. The procedures for applying for governmental permission for transactions with strategic objects as well as for the execution of the state's priority rights is stipulated in the Law on State Property. They are similar to procedures established for transactions with subsurface use rights (discussed *supra*), except for which authorities are involved in the process. The owners of strategic objects have to submit the application to the state planning authority, which is the Ministry of Economic Development and Trade of RK. The state planning authority prepares a draft of the government resolution and forwards it, along with the application and corresponding documents, to the republican budget committee. The latter, after consideration of the documents, directs its recommendations to the Government, which makes the final decision on the realization of the state priority right, the permission for alienation or encumbrance or the prohibition of the transaction.
54. It should be noted that the right of a government to block the alienation of a strategic object on national security grounds is not a novelty. Note, for example, the intervention of the US

B. PETROLEUM

Main-line Petroleum Pipelines. Besides provisions regulating activities of subsurface users in the upstream sector, the SUL contains provisions governing the use of main-line petroleum pipelines and the construction of offshore pipelines, i.e., the mid-stream sector. The usage of main-line pipelines must be conducted in compliance with technical regulations approved by the Government. Main-line petroleum pipelines can be either in state or private property. However, the decision on their construction can only be made by the Government. Regardless of the identity of the owner, the operator of a main-line pipeline must allow third-party access to it, provided that the pipeline has the necessary flow capacity. Transportation services are provided in accordance with a delivery schedule agreed in the relevant contract between the consumer and the pipeline operator.[55]

Refining and Distribution. There are only three oil refineries in Kazakhstan.[56] Hence, to maintain a stable supply of oil products to the domestic market, the Government extensively controls refining activity on the basis of the Law of RK of July 20, 2011, No. 463-IV, "On State Regulation of Certain Types of Petroleum Products." According to this Law, the refineries must observe requirements of the MOG on technical standards and monthly established minimal processing volumes of oil products. Both the refineries and distributors of oil products must also regularly submit information to the MOG on produced and distributed oil products. In addition, they must give priority to agricultural businesses during sowing and harvesting campaigns (from March 1 to May 31 and from August 1 to October 31 of each year) and to heating energy producers during the heating season (from October 31 to March 1).

Even though the wholesale prices as well as prices for crude oil and gas condensate are not regulated, the MOG, jointly with the Agency Regulating Natural Monopolies, may set the maximum retail prices for regulated oil products. Moreover, the Government may ban the export or import of oil products from time to time.[57] Furthermore, there is a custom duty on the export of oil

---

Congress into the takeover of Unocal by the Chinese national oil company or its block of the alienation of the British company Peninsula and Oriental to Dubai Ports World in 2006, or the Spanish Government's prohibition of Endesa's purchase by a German company. See UNCTAD "The Protection of National Security Interests in IIAs" (UNCTAD/DIAE/IA/2008/5 Geneva 2008) 11.

55. For further information on Kazakhstan's main-line pipelines see R. Gaissin, "Regulation of Oil and Gas Transportation by Pipelines in Kazakhstan," in I. Bantekas J. Paterson & M. Suleimenov (eds.), *Oil and Gas Law in Kazakhstan: National and International Perspectives* (Kluwer Law International, 2004), 311–336 and Y. Osipov, "Regulation of Transportation and Processing of Oil and Petroleum Products," in the same book at 337–342.

56. The state, through the National Company Kazmunaigaz and its subsidiaries, owns around 99% of shares of Atyrau refinery, and around 50% in the other two refineries located in Pavlodar and Shymkent.

57. For example, the Resolution of the Government of June 30, 2011, No. 740 prohibited the export of light oil products for period of six months effective from July 1, 2011.

products that is regularly adjusted by the Government in response to domestic market conditions.[58]

Gas and Gas Distribution. As has been observed above, natural gas is included in the definition of petroleum of the Subsurface Use Law and, therefore, that law's provisions on petroleum and main-line pipelines are applicable to natural gas. However, with the growing production of natural gas and a tightening of state control of flaring of associated gas, a separate legal regime for gas has taken a long time to come into existence.[59] In May 2011, the Government announced the preparation of a draft of a new Law on Gas and Gas Supply. It is expected that the new law will provide comprehensive guidance for the mid- and downstream gas industry and, in particular, contain such novelties as (a) regulations on processing natural gas, including the processing of associated gas, (b) the establishment of a national operator for the domestic gas supply that would be entitled to have pre-emptive rights for purchasing gas, (c) state control over the domestic market through the setting of wholesale prices, (d) measures stimulating the production of liquefied natural gas (LNG), and (e) rules for selling liquefied-petroleum gas (LPG) through commodity exchanges and other markets.

Meanwhile, the mid- and downstream sectors of the gas industry are regulated by the Resolution of the Government of June 11, 2003, No. 568, which established "Regulations on the Supply, Transportation and Marketing of Natural Gas" and "Regulations on the Supply, Transportation and Use of LPG." These rules cover each stage of gas flow from main-line pipelines, through the distributional network and finally to households and other final consumers.[60] Like those of oil products, producers, transporters and distributors of gas are required to keep and report inventory to the competent body on a regular basis. The regulations set a detailed list of rights and responsibilities of the producers, transporters, distributors and consumers of gas as well as technical, safety and other requirements for its transportation. They also establish the priority of gas consumers that must be observed by distributors: (1) households; (2) public establishments (health, sports and educational facilities, etc.); (3) businesses using gas as primary input of their production; (4) power plants; and (5) all other consumers. Furthermore, operators of gas transportation and storage facilities must comply with the rules of equal access to regulated services established by the Agency Regulating Natural Monopolies. The equal access rules obligate the monopolies to provide their services on a

---

58. For example, by the Resolution of the Government of September 5, 2011, No. 1012, the custom duty was established for light oil products at the level of USD 143.54 per ton, and for heavy oil products at USD 95.69 per ton.
59. There are four gas processing plants located in the regions of Atyrau, Aktobe and Mangystau. Another one (in Zhambyl) is expected to be completed by the end of 2011, and the construction of two more plants is planned.
60. It has to be noted that these Regulations have not been adjusted with adoption of the Subsurface Use Law. Some provisions of the Rules relating to the use of main-line gas pipelines contain more excessive regulatory regime than that established in the SUL. We avoid further elaborations on this point as it is expected that the draft Law on Gas and Gas Supply will rectify these provisions and also cancel the Rules.

transparent, non-discriminatory basis to all customers at unified fees. In the case of limited transportation and/or storage capacities, the equal access rules transpose the aforementioned priority regime for the entities supplying gas and regulated services to the gas distributors.

C. Nuclear Power and Coal

Since the early days of independence, Kazakhstan has adhered to the principle of non-proliferation of nuclear weapons and has destroyed all Soviet nuclear weapon facilities left on its territory. This fact, combined with their status as the top uranium exporter in the world, means that Kazakhstani nuclear power legislation (and in particular Law of RK of April 14, 1997, No. 93-I, "On the Use of Nuclear Energy") deals primarily with control over of uranium exporting[61] and emphasizes the prohibition of the development, creation, production, testing or storage of nuclear weapons in Kazakhstan. The Law also bans any disposal of radioactive waste from other states on the territory of RK (Article 3). Currently, there are no active nuclear power stations in the country. However, Kazakhstan's leadership announced plans that construction of several such plants will begin in near future, a development that will certainly facilitate the further development of nuclear power legislation.

There are no specific regulations laid down in the mid- and downstream sectors of the coal industry, except for detailed safety and technical standards established by competent bodies.[62] At present, no national company is specifically established to deal with coal production and marketing in Kazakhstan. Nevertheless, given the overall trend of increasing state control in the energy sector, it may be expected that legislation will develop in this regard as well.

D. Electricity

The electricity market of Kazakhstan is regulated by the Law of RK of July 9, 2004, No. 588-II, "On Electric Energy" and the Law of RK of December 25, 1997, No. 210-I, "On Energy Saving," as well as a large number of sub-law acts.

Despite the debate on the legal nature of electricity (i.e., whether it should be treated as a commodity, a service or something else) in legal scholarship, the legislation treats electrical (heating) energy as a commodity (Article 14 II of the Law on Electric Energy). The electricity market is divided by the law into

61. State control over the export and import of nuclear materials is regulated in detail by the Resolution of the Government of March 9, 1993, No. 183, which is in line with the regulations of the International Atomic Energy Agency (in particular related to safety and security of radioactive sources and their import and export).

62. See the Orders of the Minister of Energy, Industry and Trade of September 25, 2000, No. 327, and the Chairman of the Emergency Agency of October 13, 2000, No. 235.

wholesale and retail sectors. The wholesale market participants are power generating stations, national and regional power transmitting organizations, distribution organizations, the system operator (JSC KEGOC) and the operator of centralized trade (JSC KOREM), as well as consumers of electricity. These participants, except for the system operator and the operator of centralized trade, may also be involved in the retail market.

The state controls the market through price ceilings for electricity and transmission services. Moreover, power producing organizations must sign an agreement with the competent body setting obligations on the producer to make investments that will maintain and upgrade their generation capacities. Also, agreements on the supply of electricity in the retail market must be concluded on the basis of a model agreement approved by the Government (*inter alia* setting forth quality standards of electricity and consumer protection rules). Likewise, the Government imposes standards for the relationship between the distributors and consumers of electricity. In addition, all legal entities in Kazakhstan are obliged to report periodically the volume of energy they consumed to the Agency of Statistics.

The Energy Saving Law sets rules on energy efficiency certification for all energy consuming goods manufactured in or imported to Kazakhstan. Moreover, it requires conducting state expert energy saving evaluations for all projects that contemplate the construction of an asset (building, facility, etc.) that will consume 500 or more of tons of oil equivalent annually. Legal entities with the same level of total annual energy consumption are also subject to such evaluations at least once in a three-year period. In the course of the evaluation, a normative energy consumption volume is prescribed for each asset, which is reflected in the energy certificate of those assets.

E. Renewable Energy

Although endowed with a large base of conventional energy resources, Kazakhstan is making efforts to develop its renewable energy potential. The Energy Saving Law of 1997 declared the commitment of RK to expand its usage of renewable energy. However, it took almost 12 years before the Law of RK of July 4, 2009, No. 165-IV, "On Support of the Use of Renewable Energy Resources" was adopted. This Law establishes a number of privileges for renewable energy producers. First, operators of regional transmission networks are obliged to purchase electricity produced by renewable energy producers to cover up to 50% of their transmission losses, while the remaining portion of the electricity must be purchased by the system operator. Second, such a purchase must be conducted on the basis of a long-term contract, the term of which may not be shorter than the cost-recovery period of the project implementing the renewable energy development. Third, the operators of regional transmission networks must connect the renewable energy producers at the nearest point of connection to their networks in order to suffer less transmission losses and lower the cost of connection for producers. Fourth, transmission services must be provided to renewable energy producers free of charge, but the costs of transmission are accounted when evaluating the tariffs of the relevant transmission companies. Finally, in cases of limited transmission and dispatch capacities, the regional transmission companies and the system operator must give priority to renewable energy producers over all other producers.

Also, it should be noted that recent legislative developments in Kazakhstan include the adoption of the Law of RK of November 15, 2010, No. 351-IV, "On State Regulation of Biofuels."[63] Unlike the Renewable Energy Support Law, the Biofuels Law does not provide explicit privileges to biofuel producers, but instead establishes a clear regulatory framework for their activity. Thus, the construction of biofuel producing plants must be authorized by the Ministry of Agriculture. The Law details the procedure for such applications and authorizations and clearly defines the grounds for denying an application. A number of constraints on the activity of biofuels producers is provided in the Law (e.g., prohibition of selling biofuel products to persons other than those licensed for blending oil products; prohibition of the use of durum wheat for the production of biofuels; prohibition of use of feedstock in excess of quotas set by the Government).

Selected Bibliography

I. Bantekas, J. Paterson & M. Suleimenov (eds.), *Oil and Gas Law in Kazakhstan: National and International Perspectives* (Kluwer Law International, The Hague, London, New York, 2004).

A. Didenko, "The Law on Foreign Investments in Kazakhstan," in K. Hendley (ed.), *Commercial Law in Russia and the CIS* (Juris Publishing, New York, 2007).

E. Dosmukhamedov, *Foreign Direct Investment in Kazakhstan: Politico-Legal Aspects of Post-Communist Transition* (Palgrave Macmillan, London, 2002).

G. Eliot, "Kazakhstan, Nazarbayev, Foreign Investment & Oil" (1993) 53 *Louisiana L Rev* 1243.

W.G. Frenkel, *Foreign Investment in Kazakhstan: Legal Regulation and Practice* (Transnational Juris Publications, Irvington, NY, 1994).

K. Maulenov, *Государственное управление и правовое регулирование в сфере иностранных инвестиций в Республике Казахстан* [*State Management and Legal Regulation in the Sphere of Foreign Investments in the Republic of Kazakhstan*] (Zhety Zhargy, Almaty, 2000) [in Russian].

S. Moroz, *Инвестиционное право* [*Investment Law*] (Yurist, Almaty, 2007) [in Russian].

P. Nichols, "The Viability of Transplanted Law: Kazakhstani Reception of a Transplanted Foreign Investment Code" (1997) 18 *U Pa J Int'l Econ L* 1235.

63. Although biofuels are not always considered as renewable sources of energy, the legal framework for biofuels is reviewed in this section.

A.E. Peck, *Economic Development in Kazakhstan: The Role of Large Enterprises and Foreign Investment* (RoutledgeCurzon, New York, 2004).

M. Suleimenov (ed.), *Право и иностранные инвестиЦии в Республике Казахстан* [*Law and Foreign Investment in the Republic of Kazakhstan*] (Zhety Zhargy, Almaty, 1997) [in Russian].

M. Suleimenov & W. Holland, "The Energy Charter Treaty and the Development of Kazakhstan Legislation," in T Wälde (ed.), *The Energy Charter Treaty an East-West Gateway for Investment and Trade* (Kluwer Law International, The Hague, London, New York, 1996).

S. Zimanov, *Государство и контракты в сфере нефтяных операций* [*State and Contracts in the Sphere of Oil Operations*] (Almaty, 2007) [in Russian with some English translation].

Chapter 16
Tax Law

Yevgeniy Porokhov

I. INTRODUCTION

The formation of Kazakhstani Tax Law can be traced to 1991, when Kazakhstan was granted independence from the Soviet Union. The subsequent transition to a market economy and the large-scale privatization of state property necessitated the adoption of new tax legislation, the development of which can be divided into three stages: (1) the formation of the Tax Law of Kazakhstan (1991–1995); (2) the consolidation of the Tax Law (1995–2002); and (3) the codification of the Tax Law (2002-present).

The first stage commenced with the adoption of both the Law of RK of December 25, 1991, No. 1072-XII, "On the Tax System in RK" and over 40 specific laws on different kinds of taxes. The second stage, the goal of which was to consolidate all existing legislative acts on taxation, commenced with the enactment of the Decree of the President of RK having the force of law of April 24, 1995, No. 2235, "On Taxes and Other Obligatory Payments into the Budget" (effective from July 1, 1995 until January 1, 2002). Subsequently, the third stage started when Kazakhstan began to codify its Tax Law to arrange its tax norms into an organized system. This process resulted in the adoption of the Tax Code of RK of June 12, 2001, No. 209-II, (effective from January 1, 2002), later superseded by the Tax Code of RK of December 10, 2008, No. 99-IV (TC) (in force since January 1, 2009).

Zhenis Kembayev, *Introduction to the Law of Kazakhstan*, pp. 303–314.

The subject matter of Tax Law is constituted by relations arising between the state, on the one hand, and taxpayers, on the other hand, regarding the establishment, levying and administration of taxes and other compulsory payments to the budget, as well as the protection of taxpayers' rights. In principle, Tax Law is mainly imperative, but in certain cases it may also be dispositive (e.g., the TC allows for the signing of contracts for the provision of tax benefits in exchange for investments).

Tax Law is based on a number of principles stipulating that taxation must be clearly defined and fair; consist of a single tax system; and be transparent. These principles reflect constitutional values of the state; if Tax Law regulations contradict these principles, then such regulations may be invalidated. Noteworthy is also the fact that Kazakhstan has adopted the principle of universal taxation.

Tax Law consists of a general and a special part. The *general part* includes regulations related to principles, sources and subjects of Tax Law; tax policy; tax procedure; tax obligations; etc. The *special part* includes provisions on legal regulation of specific tax obligations.

Fundamental source of Tax Law is the Constitution of RK embodying legal principles regarding payment of taxes as well as legal values underlying taxation. In particular, the Constitution provides that "human rights and freedoms shall . . . define the contents and implementation of laws and other regulatory legal acts" (Article 12 II). This constitutional provision determines tax norms. However, Tax Law is an important factor in realizing constitutional provisions (in particular those related to the formation and maintenance of the social state).

The Tax Code of RK of December 10, 2008 is the keystone of Kazakhstan's tax system. The Code is supplemented by numerous ordinary laws that have been adopted with the aim of establishing certain elements of taxation (e.g., tax rates), to approve the forms of legal documents (e.g., forms of tax authorities' notifications) or to establish the procedure of performing certain actions (e.g., the procedure of Value Added Tax (VAT) registration and deregistration).

Furthermore, the Code empowers the Government of RK and the Tax Committee under the Ministry of Finance of RK (a specialized tax body) to issue regulatory acts on taxation within the limits of their competences. Other executive bodies are entitled to adopt regulatory acts on taxation only in exceptional cases provided by the TC (e.g., according to Article 552 II TC, the Ministry of Foreign Affairs of RK may establish consular fee rates within the limits established by the Government). Regulatory acts on taxation may also be issued by "Maslikhats" (local representative bodies) with respect to establishing rates for certain taxes and other mandatory payments.

Regulatory acts on taxation are subject to official publication as they are related to the rights and freedoms of citizens and impose obligations upon them (as provided by Article 4 IV CRK). Official publication of regulatory acts concerning rights, freedoms and obligations of citizens is a mandatory condition for their application. Furthermore, regulatory acts of the Tax Committee and Maslikhats are subject to state registration at the Ministry of Justice or its regional territorial departments, which is mandatory for them to come into force.

In addition, sources of Tax Law may also include regulatory resolutions of the Constitutional Council and the Supreme Court, as well as international treaties of RK.

II. TAX POLICY, ADMINISTRATION AND PROCEDURE

A. Tax Policy

The President of RK formulates the tax policy of RK since he is authorized to determine the objectives of the tax and budget policies of the state (Article 40 I CRK) and to define both short- and long-term priorities for the development of the state and the society.[1] The Government of RK also has an important role, elaborating the main guidelines of the social and economic policy of the state and organizing their implementation (Article 66 I CRK). The Parliament of RK also influences the formulation of tax policies, since it approves the republican budget (Article 54 I CRK) and has exclusive powers to establish and terminate taxes and fees (Article 54 II CRK).[2]

B. Tax Administration and Procedure

Tax administration in Kazakhstan is exercised by the Tax Committee under the Ministry of Finance of RK and its territorial departments which carry out the following activities: (1) registration of taxpayers and other indebted persons; (2) registration of taxable objects; (3) control and enforcement of tax obligations; and (4) tax collection in case of non-fulfillment or improper fulfillment of tax obligations. These actions must be implemented fully in compliance with regulatory acts and the decisions of the superior tax authorities.

Acts and failures to act of tax authorities and officials may be appealed by taxpayers both by applying to the court (thus initiating administrative, civil or even criminal procedure) or submitting a complaint to a superior tax authority. A letter of complaint to a superior tax authority is to be submitted within 30 working days from the notification date (Article 667 I TC).

1. Thus, the Conception of Legal Policy of the Republic of Kazakhstan for the period from 2010 to 2020 was confirmed by the Decree of the President of RK of August 24, 2009, No. 858.
2. In addition, tax policy may often be influenced by non-governmental organizations, public and business associations, etc. Currently, due to the growth of this influence, a draft law "On Lobbying" is being discussed. Note in this regard the following opinion: "The viewpoint of any specific class is inevitably narrowed and reflects specific interests. [Thus,] representation of the position of one class or another should not be politically overemphasized." M. Baimakhanov "О научном статусе политологии" ["On the Scientific Status of Political Science"], in M. Baimakhanov *Избранные труды по теории государства и права* [*Selected Works on Theory of State and Law*] (VŠP Adilet, Almaty, 2003), 168.

III. LAW OF TAX OBLIGATION (GENERAL PROVISIONS)

A tax obligation is defined as "an obligation of a taxpayer to the state arising in accordance with tax legislation, by virtue of which a taxpayer is required to register with a tax authority, identify objects of taxation and objects related to taxation, calculate taxes and other mandatory payments to the budget . . . prepare tax reports, and file them . . . within the established deadlines" (Article 26 TC). "Objects of taxation and objects related to taxation" are understood to be property and actions, whose existence means that a taxpayer incurs a tax obligation (Article 27 TC).

A tax obligation refers to a periodic obligation arising within a specified period. At the end of a "tax period" the tax base is determined, and the amount of taxes and other mandatory payments payable to the budget is calculated (Article 30 TC). The concept of "tax period" serves to fulfill tax obligations by the establishment of a time frame during which a taxpayer determines the objects of taxation and the amount of taxes to be paid. A tax is calculated by means of the application of a "tax rate," which is the amount of tax assessed per unit of measure of the tax base. The tax rate is established as a percentage or as an absolute amount per unit of measure of the tax base (Article 29 TC).

Also, there are optional elements of taxation which are established at the discretion of the state (e.g., tax privileges established by the state with regard to some categories of taxpayers). However, presently in RK it is legally prohibited to grant any individual concessions (Article 7 II TC).

Furthermore, the Tax Law of RK is based on the notion that the execution of a tax obligation is carried out under the *presumption of honesty* of fulfillment of a tax obligation by a taxpayer. It is assumed that taxpayers independently (on their own behalf, by their efforts and at their own expense), voluntarily and in a timely and proper fashion fulfill all tax obligations before the state. Tax obligations are to be fulfilled within a certain time period. In case of non-fulfillment or improper fulfillment of tax obligations, the state is entitled to enforce payment of taxes.

IV. SPECIFIC TAX RULES

A. Corporate Income Tax

The Corporate Income Tax (CIT) is applied to the income of legal entities registered in Kazakhstan as well as to foreign legal entities earning income from Kazakhstani sources or doing business in Kazakhstan through a permanent establishment.[3]

Since 2009, the CIT rate is 20% (Article 147 I TC). The CIT is calculated using the accrual method, and generally the tax base for the CIT is the aggregate annual income. In certain cases, it is paid monthly in advance installments, and the

3. In addition to the generally applied CIT, the latter category of taxpayers is also subject to the net income tax at the rate of 15% (Art. 147 V TC).

final calculations and payment of the remaining amount (if any) are due after the end of the fiscal year. The CIT is reported quarterly (the calculation of advance installments) and annually (the CIT return).

Taxable income and deductions. The CIT is levied on all income earned by a legal entity worldwide based on the gross annual income tax basis. Expenses can be deducted, and adjustments are available for calculation of taxable income. There are special rules for particular types of income and deductions that are highlighted below.

Dividends received by a Kazakhstani legal entity are exempt from taxation (Article 99 I 1 TC). At the same time, the dividends paid out to foreign legal entities are subject to the CIT at the source of payment (Article 193 I, Article 192 I 9 TC). Properly documented expenses related to profit-generating activities are deductible (Article 100 TC). The law limits the amount of certain deductible expenses, e.g., interest on loans, business representation expenses or expenses arising from social programs. The maximum deductible interest is calculated using a formula that factors in such variables as the taxpayer's equity and the amount of interest payable to affiliated parties and to residents of low-tax jurisdictions. The formula is structured to promote the development of domestic capital markets while restricting the export of capital as payments of interests on loans to affiliated parties and residents of tax havens. Other limits are set in a proportion to certain results of a legal entity.

The cost of fixed assets is deductible by calculating depreciation amounts at fixed rates. Depending on the asset category, the depreciation rates vary from 10% (buildings/structures) to 40% (computers) (Article 120 TC). In certain cases, subsoil users may apply during one-year double declining balance depreciation rates to assets operating within territory of RK. The depreciation is calculated at the end of the fiscal year.

Research and development and high-tech operation expenses are fully deductible. Banking organizations may deduct expenses on certain debts. Subsoil users can deduct their contributions to waste disposal sites, expenses related to the training of Kazakhstani personnel and to the development of local social infrastructure, geological survey and exploration costs and pre-production costs. Foreign currency losses and gains related to assets and liabilities accounted in foreign currency are considered in determining taxable income and calculating the respective deductions.

Small business enterprises whose income and number of employees are not over a certain threshold may opt for the special tax regime that allows payment of CIT at the rate of 3% of the total income (Articles 433–438 TC). This special tax regime, which allows payment of a single land tax instead of the CIT, is also available for farmers (Chapter 62 TC). The special regime for agricultural enterprises provides for 70% reduction in the amount of taxes to be paid (Chapter 63 TC).

Organizations doing business in special economic zones, where at least 90% of their income is earned from the sales of certain goods (and services) produced; non-profit organizations; and organizations operating in the social services sector (e.g., hospitals or libraries) are CIT-exempt (Article 134, 135, 150–152 TC).

Capital gains taxes: Capital gains are included in taxable income of CIT payers. This type of income is generated from such assets as land plots, securities, participation interests, objects under construction and assets contributed to the charter capital (Article 87 TC). Proceedings from a sale of depreciable fixed assets are treated similarly (Article 92 TC). Subject to certain conditions, income from capital gains from (a) the sale of shares or participation interests in a legal entity or consortium organized under the laws of RK and (b) from the public sale of securities through a stock exchange operating in RK where such securities are officially listed are excluded from taxable income.

Losses/carry-forward of losses: Losses resulting from deductions in excess of total annual income and losses from disposal of buildings and structures can be carried forward for a full 10 years to be repaid from taxable income in respective tax periods (Article 136, 137 TC). The following losses can be carried forward for a full 10 years: (a) losses from the sale of land plots, assets under construction and uninstalled equipment are compensated from capital gains from the sale of the same categories of assets; (b) losses from the sale of securities are repaid from capital gains income from the sale of other securities; and (c) losses transferred in connection with a restructuring by a division or spin-off are allocated in proportion to the successors' participation interests in the restructured taxpayer and are carried forward in a standard manner. No carry-back of losses from the current accounting period to the preceding accounting periods is allowed.

Position of resident legal entities: For tax purposes, the Tax Code defines residents as legal entities organized under the laws of RK and/or other legal entities whose place of effective management (actual location of the management body) is in RK (Article 189 V TC). Taxable income of a resident legal entity is comprised of income receivable (received) by such an entity both in and outside Kazakhstan. Income tax credits are also allowed within the limits set forth by the Tax Code or a relevant double tax treaty.

Consolidated taxation: The Tax Code does not recognize the concept of consolidated taxation, except if a resident of RK holds 10% or more of the charter capital of a non-resident legal entity domiciled in that resident's tax jurisdiction, in which case a resident of RK must include in his taxable income a portion of the legal entity's income (Article 224 I TC).

B. Indirect Taxes

VAT rates and exemptions: The VAT rate is 12% and applies to the amount of taxable turnover and taxable import. A zero rate applies to turnover from export of goods from Kazakhstan and turnover from sale of self-produced goods by persons if their subsoil use contract with the government provides accordingly. In determining the amount of tax payable to the budget, offset is allowed for input VAT payable for goods, works and services used in VAT taxable turnover subject to a number of other conditions. VAT exemptions apply to turnover from sale of such goods, works and services as residential real estate, financial services (including financial leasing), insurance services, research and development and educational services, health care services and international transportation. Import VAT exemptions apply to such products as pharmaceuticals and medical equipment as per the list approved by the government (section 8 TC).

Other indirect taxes: Kazakhstan applies excise taxes to all types of spirits, alcohol products, tobacco products, petrol, diesel fuel, cars, crude oil and gas condensate (section 9 TC).

C. Personal Taxes

Personal income tax (PIT) is applied to income received in monetary form, as benefits or in kind. Income in kind is received when a person, for instance, receives property for free or when a third party pays for goods, work or services received by such a person. Income in the form of benefits is received when, for instance, an employer reimburses an employee's expenses that are not related to the employer's activities or pays insurance premiums for an employee's insurance.

Certain types of income are not taxable, including a number of compensation payments (compensation for harm to health, pecuniary loss or per diems; Article 155 TC) and capital gains from sale of residential property, land plots and motor vehicles owned for one year or longer. Other types of income such as interest on bank deposits and debt securities are excluded from taxable personal income (Article 156 TC).

Personal income of residents, except for dividends, is taxed at the rate of 10%. Dividends received by residents are subject to tax at the rate of 5% (Article 158 TC). Personal income of non-residents is subject to tax at the rate of 5%, 15% or 20%, depending on the type of income (Article 194 TC). Generally, the PIT is calculated, withheld and paid at the source of payment by tax agents. Tax agents include private entrepreneurs, notaries, attorneys and legal entities, including non-resident legal entities. Regarding salary, the tax base is reduced by the minimum monthly salary and any contributions for obligatory or voluntary pension insurance, as well as by a certain amount of mortgage interest and a limited amount of medical expenses. No other deductions (e.g., for children) are available.

Other types of income, such as property income (rent income and capital gains), income of private entrepreneurs, income of notaries and attorneys and income from sources outside Kazakhstan are personally subject to PIT (the taxpayer himself should calculate, pay and report the tax on such kinds of income).

In certain cases, dividends or capital gains received by individuals are exempt from taxes. Such exemptions include, for instance, dividends and capital gains on securities officially listed on the Kazakhstan stock exchange. Another example is dividends received from a resident legal entity if the recipient of such dividends has owned the shares or participation interest for over three years and if 50% or more of the assets of the payer of the dividends are not shares of subsoil users. Capital gains fulfilling similar criteria (except for the three-year limit) are also tax exempted.

Domicile and residency requirements: An individual is deemed a tax resident of RK if the taxpayer stays in Kazakhstan for at least 183 calendar days (including the arrival and departure dates) within any consecutive 12-month period that ends within the current tax period. Persons whose center of vital interests is located in Kazakhstan are also deemed residents of RK, subject to the following requirements: (1) they are citizens of RK or have a Kazakhstani residence permit; (2) their families or close relatives reside in Kazakhstan; and (3) they have real estate in RK that is owned either by themselves and/or their family members and that is at any time available for residence to such persons and/or their family members. Personal income of individuals who are not tax residents of RK is taxable in RK only if such income is derived from a Kazakhstan source.

D. Social Tax and Pension Fund Contributions

In Kazakhstan, employers' tax expenses (including Kazakhstani entities and representative offices and branches of foreign legal entities) are comprised of the following taxes and compulsory payments. First, the *social tax* applies to employers' expenses on payments to resident and non-resident employees under employment agreements (contracts) and to income of foreign personnel provided by a non-resident; the tax rate is 11% (Article 358 I TC). Taxpayers using special tax regimes (e.g., private entrepreneurs, notaries and attorneys) are subject to a different tax rate. The social tax is reduced by the amount of social security contributions (Article 359 III TC). Second, under *social security contributions*, employers make monthly payments to the State Social Security Fund in the amount of 5% of the income payable to employees for performed work and provided services. Third, *compulsory pension fund contributions* are monthly payments withheld and directed by employers to pension funds at the rate of 10% of the employee's monthly income that are not to exceed 10% of 75 minimum wages.[4]

E. Taxes on Capital and Property

There is no special tax on capital in Kazakhstan. The transfer of rights to immovable property is not subject to tax; however, the registration of rights to and transactions with such property as well as registration of encumbrances and claims on immovable property are subject to a registration stamp duty ranging from zero to 25 MCIs (one MCI is KZT 1,512, about USD 1),[5] depending on the type of property and nature of the transactions to be registered.

A "land tax" is paid by the persons who hold the land plot on the basis of ownership, permanent land use or primary temporary free land use. Land tax rates

4. See section VII "Remuneration" of the Chapter 10 "Labor Law," *supra*.
5. See the "List of Abbreviations" (*supra*) for an explanation of the concept of MCI.

vary depending on the designation, category and location of the lands and are determined in monetary terms per unit area of the land plot.

A "property tax for legal entities and individual entrepreneurs" applies to buildings and structures located in Kazakhstan and shown in the books of accounts of legal entities, including facilities under concession as well as buildings and structures owned by individuals. The tax base is the annual average book value of the taxable property, which is determined based on the accounting data or, if there is no accounting, the assessed market price. Depending on the type of property and category of the taxpayer, property tax is assessed at rates ranging from 0.1% to 1.5%.

A "property tax for individuals" applies to the living premises and other permanent structures (which are subject to state registration); the rate is determined based on the value of the taxable property as of January 1 of each year by an authorized government body using formulas taking into account such variables as location, floor space, depreciation/wear ratio, etc.

A "transportation tax" is applied to individuals and legal entities who own transportation vehicles registered in their name. Tax rates are determined based on, *inter alia*, vehicle type, category, engine capacity, time in operation, etc.

F. Subsoil Use Taxes

In addition to taxes paid under the general tax regime, individuals and legal entities having the right to carry out subsoil use operations, including petroleum exploration and extraction, are also subject to special charges and taxes, including special charges for the use of subsoil, the minerals extraction tax, the excess profit tax and the export customs duties.[6]

Special charges for the use of subsoil include: (a) *signature bonus*, a one-time fixed payment for the acquisition of the right of subsoil use within the contract territory that is determined individually for each contract using respective established formulas depending on the type of the contract (i.e., exploration or production), kind of the natural resources, etc.; (b) *commercial discovery bonus*, which is paid at the rate of 0.1% of the tax base (i.e., the value of the volume of recoverable reserves) for each commercial discovery of natural resources within the contract territory; and (c) *historical costs recovery charge*, a fixed charge, determined by a competent government authority, paid by the subsoil user to recover the total costs incurred by the government on geological surveys and exploration of the contract territory.

The "minerals extraction tax" is paid in monetary form and is charged with regard to the value of the volume of the minerals extracted by the subsoil user for the

6. It is worth noting that several dozen production sharing agreements (PSAs) providing specific tax regimes for particular subsoil users are still in effect in Kazakhstan. However, the general policy is to no longer conclude them, so the Tax Code does not stipulate any specific provisions in this regard (except to recognize the existing PSAs).

tax accounting period (i.e., crude oil, gas condensate, natural gas, minerals, etc.), which is determined using formulas set forth in the Tax Code. For crude oil, including gas condensate, the rate depends on the planned production volumes for the current tax period and may range from 7% (for volumes of up to 250,000 tons per year) to 18% (for volumes exceeding 10,000,000 tons per year). The rate for natural gas is 10% if sold abroad, and varies from 0.5% to 1.5% if sold in the domestic market. Rates for minerals that have been under primary processing (enrichment) and coal vary from 0% (for coal) to 22% (for uranium). Rates for widespread mineral resources vary from 2.5% (non-metal raw materials for metallurgy, sand, limestone) to 10.6% (underground water, curative mud) (Chapter 45 TC).

"Excess profit tax" applies to the portion of net profit of the subsoil user separately for each subsoil use contract for the tax accounting period that exceeds 25% of the amount of the subsoil user's deductions using a sliding scale of rates varying from 10% to 60% (Article 351 TC). Exporters of petroleum, gas condensate and coal are subject to an *export rent tax*. The rates for crude oil and gas condensate depend on the world price of oil and vary from 0% to 32% of the value of the exported oil at the world price; the rate for coal is fixed at 2.1% of the actual value of the exported coal (Article 303 TC). In addition, *export customs duties* are applied on a temporary basis in accordance with resolutions of the Government of RK.

G. International Taxation Issues

The TC contains specific section on international taxation (section 7 TC). It stipulates that non-residents (both legal entities and individuals) should pay income tax on their income from sources in RK. Such sources include selling goods and rendering services within the territory of RK, capital gains on the selling of property registered in RK or shares of legal entities residing in RK, property income received in RK, income from labor or civil law contract with Kazakhstani residents, dividends, royalties and interest from Kazakhstani sources etc. The rates depend on the type of income and may be 5% (international transportation, reinsurance contributions), 15% (capital gains, dividends, interest, royalty, insurance contributions) or 20% (other types of income), and they may be applied to both legal entities and individuals (Article 194 TC). The tax base is the total amount of the income; deductions are generally not available for non-residents.

Note that in certain cases, dividends received by non-residents are exempt from both corporate and personal income tax (Article 193 V-5 TC). Such exemptions include, for instance, dividends on securities officially listed on the Kazakhstani stock exchange and dividends received from a resident legal entity if the recipient of such dividends has owned the shares or participation interest for over three years and if 50% or more of the assets of the payer of the dividends are not shares of subsoil users.

Withholding income tax applies to the income of a non-resident from capital gains from sale of: (a) property located in Kazakhstan, where rights to or transactions with such property are subject to state registration (real estate, securities, motor vehicles, etc.); (b) securities issued by a Kazakhstani resident and participation interests in the charter capital of a resident or consortium located in Kazakhstan; and (c) shares issued by a non-resident and participation interests in the charter capital of a non-resident legal entity or consortium if 50% or more of the value of such shares, participation interest or assets of the non-resident legal entity is comprised of property located in RK. No tax is applied to income from capital gains from the public sale of officially listed securities on a Kazakhstani stock exchange or a foreign stock exchange (Article 193 V-7 TC).

However, the situation differs if the foreign legal entity has a permanent establishment in RK. The TC recognizes such establishment as the locating of a constant place of business activity (except some auxiliary activities for less than three years, such as marketing research) or possession of a construction site (irrespective of duration) within the territory of RK or the hiring of personnel for more than 183 days during 12 consecutive months to perform services in RK; there are also some other cases (TC, Article 191). Legal entities with a PE are taxed as if they were Kazakhstani legal entities; in addition, CIT on net income at a rate of 15% is charged (Articles 198, 199 TC).

Special rules apply to Kazakhstani controlled foreign companies. If a resident of RK owns, directly or indirectly, 10% or more of the charter capital of a non-resident legal entity that is located and/or incorporated in a low-tax jurisdiction or if the resident holds, directly or indirectly, 10% or more of the voting shares of such a non-resident legal entity, then a portion of the profits of the non-resident legal entity, determined based on the resident's share in the charter capital of the concerned non-resident legal entity, is included in the resident's taxable income in RK. These rules also apply to a resident's participation in other unincorporated legal forms of entrepreneurial activities where its participation interest makes up, directly or indirectly, 10% or more (Article 224 TC). The total amount of profit of the non-resident legal entity partially owned or controlled by a resident of RK and located and/or incorporated in a low-tax jurisdiction must be shown in the non-resident's financial statements.

A foreign state is recognized as a low-tax jurisdiction if it fulfills one of the following criteria: (a) income tax in the jurisdiction does not exceed 10%; or (b) the jurisdiction has laws on the confidentiality of financial information or laws permitting the actual owners of property or income or actual owners, founders and shareholders of companies to be confidential.[7] In addition, the treatment of particular international issues may also be different under bilateral double tax treaties.[8]

7. The list of low-tax jurisdictions is determined by the Government of RK and, as of the current date, includes 45 countries or their regions. See the Resolution of the Government of RK of July 28, 2005, No. 784.
8. As of the present, Kazakhstan has ratified 44 double-tax treaties, most of which follow the OECD Model Convention.

Selected Bibliography

S. Alibekov, *Налоговое право Республики Казахстан* [*Tax Law of the Republic of Kazakhstan*] (JurLit Almaty, 2008) [in Russian].

A. Khudyakov, *Налоговая система Казахстана* [*Tax System of Kazakhstan*] (Baspa, Almaty, 1997) [in Russian].

A. Khudyakov, *Налоговое право Республики Казахстан* [*Tax Law of the Republic of Kazakhstan*] *General Part* (Žeti Žargi, Almaty, 1997); *Special Part* (Žeti Žargi, Almaty, 2006) [in Russian].

A. Khudyakov, *Избранные труды по финансовому праву* [*Selected Works in Financial Law*] (JurCenter Press, St. Petersburg, 2010) [in Russian].

Index

A

M

www.ingramcontent.com/pod-product-compliance
Lightning Source LLC
Chambersburg PA
CBHW071238230926
51849CB00001B/152
9789041138927